CENTRAL EUROPE

Central Europe

Enemies, Neighbors, Friends

Second Edition

LONNIE R. JOHNSON

❄

New York   Oxford

OXFORD UNIVERSITY PRESS

2002

Oxford University Press

Oxford   New York

Athens   Auckland   Bangkok   Bogotá   Buenos Aires   Cape Town
Chennai   Dar es Salaam   Delhi   Florence   Hong Kong   Istanbul   Karachi
Kolkata   Kuala Lumpur   Madrid   Melbourne   Mexico City   Mumbai   Nairobi
Paris   São Paulo   Shanghai   Singapore   Taipei   Tokyo   Toronto   Warsaw

and associated companies in
Berlin   Ibadan

Copyright © 2002 by Oxford University Press

Published by Oxford University Press, Inc.
198 Madison Avenue, New York, New York 10016

Library of Congress Cataloging-in-Publication Data
Johnson, Lonnie, 1952–
Central Europe : enemies, neighbors, friends / Lonnie R. Johnson.—2nd ed.
p. cm.
Includes bibliographical references and index.
ISBN-13 978-0-19-514825-1 (pbk.)
ISBN 0-19-514826-6 — ISBN 0-19-514825-8 (pbk.)
1. Europe, Central—History.   I. Title.
DAW1038.J64   2001
943—dc21   2001021342

5 7 9 8 6 4

Printed in the United States of America
on acid-free paper

CONTENTS

PREFACE

This book is a historical survey of Central Europe, a region that encompasses contemporary Germany, Poland, the Czech Republic, Slovakia, Austria, Hungary, Slovenia, and Croatia. The historical frontiers of Central Europe extend somewhat farther to the east and the southeast than the current borders of these states. Therefore, on occasion this book also will deal peripherally with the Baltic states, western Belarus, and western Ukraine, because they were parts of Poland between the fourteenth and eighteenth centuries, as well as with Transylvania in Romania, parts of Serbia, and Bosnia-Herzegovina because they were territories of the kingdom of Hungary in the Middle Ages, the Habsburg Empire thereafter, or the Dual Monarchy of Austria-Hungary after 1867.

Unlike a considerable amount of the previous literature on the region, this book does not cover the eastern part of Central Europe—Poland, the former Czechoslovak Republic, and Hungary—as one region belonging distinctly to "the East" and the western part of Central Europe—Germany and Austria—as another that is part of "the West," nor does it venture out onto the Balkan Peninsula or into Russia, as many surveys of the post-1945 Communist version of "Eastern Europe" have done in the past. The religious, cultural, economic, and political criteria used to define Central Europe as one region instead of two, on the one hand, and to distinguish it from Eastern and Southeastern Europe, on the other, are outlined in the Introduction.

As a survey, this book covers literally a lot of ground; from the fall of the Roman Empire in the fifth century to the fall of the Soviet empire at the end of the twentieth century. It is designed to introduce readers to the histories of Central Europe's kaleidoscope of peoples. One of the guiding ideas behind this book is to look at historical patterns of conflict, cohabitation, and cooperation in Central Europe—hence its subtitle: *Enemies, Neighbors, Friends*. In particular, it tries to acquaint readers with the central events in the histories of the smaller peoples in the region.

Each chapter is thematically organized around a few key issues or events important to understanding the period addressed. The complexity of Central Europe that stems from its delightful, astonishing, and sometimes puzzling diversity is something all students of the region discover, and the brevity of a survey conceived for nonspecialized readers demands a relatively high level of generalization and also some omissions. It has not been my intention to make the region appear less complex than it really is but to reduce the difficulty to a point of comprehensibility.

Owing to the scope and the format of this book, I have limited the use of notes to a minimum. They document the major works on which I have relied and serve as recommendations for readers interested in further pursuing specific topics. Translations, unless noted otherwise, have been by me. I would like to thank Paul Robert Magocsi, professor of history and political science at the University of Toronto and director of the Multicultural History Society of Ontario, for kindly granting permission to base the maps in this book on his *Historical Atlas of East Central Europe* (Seattle: University of Washington Press, 1993), an indispensable reference work for students of the region. Hans-Michael Putz, a Viennese cartographer, drafted the maps for this book.

Central Europe: Enemies, Neighbors, Friends has been written by a non–Central European; therefore, it should have avoided some of the traditional biases that creep in when Central Europeans write about themselves or one another. I have attempted to describe dispassionately the premises and motives for conflicting national interpretations of the same phenomena and to point out which assumptions and clichés still are operative for specific nations today.

Although I am not a native of the region, I have lived, studied, traveled, and worked there for more than twenty years. Born and raised in Minneapolis and a graduate of St. John's University in Collegeville, Minnesota, I went to Vienna to study for one year in 1973 and then stayed on a bit longer and enrolled at the University of Vienna, where I studied political philosophy and history. In the process of completing my doctorate, I met, fell in love with, and married a Viennese woman.

While working at the Institute of European Studies (IES) in Vienna, the oldest study-abroad program for American undergraduates in Austria, I had opportunities between 1979 and 1991 to travel regularly in the East Central Europe under the auspices of cooperative agreements that the IES had with the Jagiellonian University in Kraków, the Karl Marx University in Budapest (now the Budapest University of Economics), and the Bruno Leuschner University of Economics in East Berlin (closed by the German authorities after German unification). I also had the good fortune to get to know faculty affiliated with these institutions, who regularly "came out" of the East bloc to teach American students in Vienna. From 1991 until 1994, I worked at the Institute for Human Sciences in Vienna, a center of advanced study founded in 1982 that has a particular interest in East Central Europe and since 1989 has established a number of programs to analyze the post-Communist transition in the region.

Working at these institutions brought me into contact with scores of people who directly or indirectly contributed to this book, which has been a product of travel and friendship as much as teaching and research. I would like to take this opportunity to thank the following people for their contributions to this project by reading portions of the manuscript, providing criticism and information, and, in some cases, just being Central Europeans themselves: György Borsányi, the biographer of Bela Kun; Géza Kállay, a comparativist from Etvös Loránd University, Budapest; Attila Pók, a historian from the Hungarian Academy of Sciences and the Europa Institut, Budapest; and János Mátyás Kovács, an economist and permanent fellow at the Institute for Human Sciences, Vienna, for helping me develop an appreciation of the fundamental differences between Hungarian and Austrian perceptions of the Habsburgs and the fact that Budapest is just as important as Vienna; Peter Demetz, Sterling Professor Emeritus of German language and literature, Yale University, and Ladislav Matejka, professor emeritus of Slavic languages and literature, University of Michigan, Ann Arbor, and founder and editor of *Cross Currents: A Yearbook of Central European Culture*, both natives of Prague, for providing exceptionally valuable advice on all things Bohemian; Andrzej Bryk, a political scientist and constitutional historian, as well as Janus Mucha and Jan Jerschina, both sociologists, from the Jagiellonian University, Kraków, for initiating me into the mysteries of Polish perceptions; and Drago Roksandić, a Serbian historian from Croatia who taught at the University of Belgrade and now is on the faculty of the University of Zagreb, for his insights into the complexity of the shifting frontiers between Central and Southeastern Europe. Michael Benedikt, professor of philosophy at the University of Vienna, introduced me to the peculiarities of Central European intellectual history and philosophy, especially "postponed enlightenment." Otto Kallscheuer, an essayist and philosopher from West Berlin, and Ingo Klein and Hans-Peter Krüger, political economists from East Berlin, contributed to my understanding of German histories, and Dan Chirot, professor of international studies and sociology at the University of Washington, warned me at one critical point about the pitfalls of what he called "Central European metaphysics." Herbert Czermak, Inge Lehne, Harry E. Bergold Jr., faculty members at IES Vienna, and James and Linda Miller, a historian and a psychologist from the University of Arkansas at Little Rock, provided encouragement and helpful comments on an early version of the manuscript, as did Mary Kirk and, in particular, Mark Lazar from the Institute of International Education's Regional Office for East Central Europe in Budapest, on a latter version.

I am especially indebted to István Deák, Seth Low Professor of history at Columbia University, and Gloria, his wife, who spent the 1993/1994 academic year at the Institute of Human Sciences in Vienna and both read and commented on the manuscript as it approached completion and were delightful company, too. I am grateful to William B. Goodman for the faith he had in this project all along, and Nancy Lane and the editorial staff at Oxford University Press, who have shepherded this book to completion. Every step of the way, I have relied on my gracious and understanding wife, Monika, and this book is dedicated to her.

Note to Second Edition

The publication of a second edition of this book has allowed me to make a series of minor revisions in the body of the text and to substantially update the Epilogue to take into account key events that have transpired between 1995 and 2000. The prospects of Central Europe for the future continue to change dramatically with the events of its recent past, and the uncertainties of the region undoubtedly will persist until the processes of redefining Europe come to a new, if tentative closure.

CENTRAL EUROPE

Introduction

Where Is Central Europe?

Historical memory, the presence of a past that is so remote that it bears little or no resemblance to the so-called realities of the contemporary world, is an important Central European attribute. History in this part of the world is epic and tragic; small nations frequently have struggled against larger ones and have lost regularly. The past consists of inexcusable transgressions and missed opportunities; the present is filled with unfinished business from the past; and the future is a chance finally to rectify a historical record that has been inauspicious at best and unjust at worst. Developing a sense for what could be called the subjective dimensions of Central Europe—the (usually pretty good) stories that Central European peoples tell about themselves and the (usually pretty bad) ones they tell about their neighbors—is important to understanding the region. Some of the problems Central Europeans have with themselves and with one another are related to the fact that their history haunts them.

Several different criteria are used in the following chapters to define Central Europe as a region distinct from Western, Eastern, and Southeastern Europe. The first is the relationship between religion and cultural orientation. Central Europeans consider themselves long-standing historical representatives of Western European culture because the various nations in the region were converted to Roman Catholicism, the Western form of Christianity, at the turn of the millennium. If one is willing to accept the Mediterranean world as the proverbial "cradle of Western civilization," then Central Europe was drawn into the sphere of Western civilization relatively late. The Romans colonized only small portions of Central Europe west of the Rhine and south of the Danube, and the missionary work of the Christian churches in the early Middle Ages beyond the former frontiers of the Roman Empire proceeded from two different poles: Rome and Byzantium. The pagans of Central Europe were converted to Roman Catholicism, whereas the pagans of Southeastern and Eastern Europe were brought into the fold of the Eastern Orthodox Church. The differences between Roman Catholic and Eastern Orthodox ideas of "Christian dominion" led to fundamentally different societies and institutions in Central Europe than in Southeastern and Eastern Europe,[1] and Central Europe never really abandoned "the West" as a primary point of cultural orientation, although the formative impulses from Western Europe changed throughout the ages.

The frontiers of medieval empires and kingdoms provide a second criterion for defining Central Europe, and they correspond to a great extent to the religious frontiers between the Roman Catholic West and the Orthodox East. The "maximum" historical borders of this region date back to around 1500 and correspond to the western frontier of the Holy Roman Empire of the German Nation, the southern and eastern frontiers of the Kingdom of Hungary, and the eastern frontier of Poland-Lithuania. Central Europe is a dynamic historical concept, not a static spatial one;[2] therefore its frontiers have shifted throughout the ages. For example, Lithuania, a fair share of Belarus, and western Ukraine are in Eastern Europe today, but they were in Central Europe 250 years ago because they then were parts of Poland.

Multinational empires are a third characteristic of this region. Hungary and Poland, small and medium-size states today, were empires in their own right early in their histories. The historical kingdom of Hungary reached its territorial peak at the end of the fifteenth century, and until 1918 it was three times larger than Hungary is now. Poland was the largest state in Europe in the sixteenth century, but it virtually disappeared from the map of Europe at the end of the eighteenth century. Both these kingdoms housed a wide variety of different peoples, and the Habsburg and Russian empires that eventually swallowed them were equally multinational, too. The experience of multiethnicity—a patchwork of peoples with different languages, cultures, and traditions living closely together—and imperial subjugation—smaller nations being conquered and ruled by larger ones—are essential parts of the Central European historical experience.

Western Christendom's centuries-long confrontation with the Oriental and Islamic empire of the Ottoman Turks also helped define Central Europe as a cultural and historical region. The fact that much of the Balkan Peninsula became part of the Ottoman Empire during the fourteenth and fifteenth centuries and stayed under Ottoman rule until the nineteenth century enhanced the differences between Central Europe as a "Western European" region and Southeastern Europe, which not only was religiously Eastern Orthodox but also became part of an "Oriental" empire. (The Central European use of the term "oriental" can be confusing. It does not refer to the Far or the Middle East, but to the Near East and the Ottoman Empire that was established on the Balkan Peninsula. The nineteenth-century Austrian statesman Clemens von Metternich once pointed out that the Orient started southeast of the city walls of Vienna.)

Peculiar patterns of Central European development provide a fifth criterion for defining the region. After the Middle Ages, Western European polities, societies, and economies began to modernize at much more rapid rates than did Central European ones, and the gap between the levels of development in these regions increased steadily as time passed. Indeed, retarded development or "backwardness" became one of the structural characteristics of Central Europe. As a region it undoubtedly stayed ahead of Islamic Southeastern and Orthodox Eastern Europe (or Russia), but it lagged behind the West.[3] It will have to suffice at this point to state that the impact of Western European economic revolutions—from agriculture in the early Middle Ages to industry in the nineteenth century—and political revolutions—in seventeenth century England and in late-eighteenth century France—decreased in Central Europe in an almost proportionate relationship to the region's distance from these epicenters. Why did ultimately more prosperous and more democratic societies develop in Western Europe than in Central Europe? How did Central Europe fall behind and stay there?

One of the purposes of this text is to acquaint readers with the different national stories, histories, and historiographical traditions of Central Europe. Each nation in the region has its own story to tell. Consequently there is no one definitive Central European story but, rather, a number of conflicting national accounts colored by moral indignation, historical speculation, and nostalgic transfiguration. Central Europeans also have in their heads a number of different historical maps and milestones that are not particularly well known outside the region or necessarily respected by their neighbors, and they still regularly use them as points of orientation.

Furthermore, historians always have devoted more attention to the larger states and nations in European history, the "big players." Who knows much about the venerable traditions of Central European kingdoms like Poland-Lithuania, Bohemia, and Hungary and their valiant struggles for freedom? What does 1102 mean to Croats, 1389 to Serbs, 1526 to Hungarians, 1620 to Czechs, or 1772 to Poles? These are dates of world historical importance for these smaller peoples because they mark tragedies or defeats that led to the loss of national independence. Central Europeans sometimes expect other inhabitants of the so-called civilized world to know much more about their histories than they do. Many Poles, for example, assume that average Americans know something about the great American revolutionary figure Tadeusz Kościuszko. (Kościuszko was a "Polish Lafayette" who fought in the Continental Army against the British during the Revolutionary War. He finished the war as a brigadier general and an American citizen but migrated back to Poland, where he played a major role in a revolutionary uprising against Russia in 1792.)

Central Europeans also always seem to be able to find some remote historical precedent for an explanation of the present. They flash back from the present into the past—not in years or decades, but in centuries—and they flash forward with great facility from the past to the present. If you ask a Hungarian about the date of the most important *recent* event in Hungarian history, the chances of getting 1918 instead of 1989 are pretty good, and

1526 would not be out of the question in light of the fact that Hungarians look back on a continuous historical tradition that started in 896. Readers occasionally will be confronted with these kinds of jumps in the following chapters, too. Such leaps may violate the rules of chronological historical narrative, but they are important because they show to what extent Central Europeans think in historical terms, which points of reference they rely on, and how they deal with their own histories.

Moreover, Central Europe is a mode of self-perception. This voluntaristic definition may not be methodologically very sophisticated, but some people in this part of the world refer to themselves as Central Europeans, and others do not. Although Central Europeans may quibble among themselves about Central Europe, they generally agree on which peoples are to be excluded from this club: for example, Serbs, Bulgarians, Romanians, and Russians.

Central Europe also may be defined by invitation. In April 1994 Czech President Václav Havel asked Central European heads of state attend a summit to discuss the region's future. At this occasion, Thomas Klestil from Austria and Richard von Weizsäcker from Germany posed for a picture in an Baroque palace in Litomysl in front of a life-size portrait of the Habsburg empress Maria Theresia with their Czech host and Lech Wałęsa from Poland, Michal Kovác from Slovakia, Arpád Göncz from Hungary, and Milan Kučan from Slovenia.[4]

Many histories of Eastern or East Central Europe focus primarily on Poland, the former Czechoslovakia, and Hungary. This history of Central Europe has a somewhat broader focus and brings "West Central Europe"[5] into the picture by treating Germany and Austria as integral parts of the region. Slovenia and Croatia, small nations and newly independent states, appear primarily in their historical capacities as parts of Austria and Hungary before 1918 or Yugoslavia between 1918 and 1991.

Despite the preceding criteria that justify treating Central Europe as one region, the concept of Central Europe can be confusing because it may refer to different things for different people. Its meaning changes in different national and historical contexts, or as Jacques Rupnik, a Czech-born political scientist from Paris, observed: "Tell me where Central Europe is, and I can tell who you are." For example, when Germans start talking about Central Europe, *Mitteleuropa*, or their historical relations with "the East," everyone starts getting nervous because this inevitably conjures up negative historical associations starting with the conquests of the Teutonic Knights in the Middle Ages and ending with German imperialism in the nineteenth century, World War I, the Third Reich, Nazi imperialism, World War II, and the Holocaust.

The Germans have not played an exclusively negative role in the region, however. The most important Western European impulses for East Central Europe, ranging from Christianity in the tenth century to industrialization in the nineteenth century, passed through the filter of the German-speaking world. The edifying, classical, nineteenth-century concept of enlightened German science and humanistic culture, *deutsche Wissenschaft und Kultur,* embraced all humanity and was the culture that most Central European Jews embraced during their assimilation in the nineteenth century. Cosmopolitan German-speaking Jews transcended the narrow confines of nationalism and became representatives of what many people would consider to be Central European culture at its best: liberal, innovative, critical, humane. Martin Buber, Sigmund Freud, Theodor Herzl, Franz Kafka, Gustav Mahler, and Ludwig Wittgenstein, just to mention a few, were assimilated Central European Jews from turn-of-the-century Vienna, Budapest, and Prague. However, between 1933 and 1945 the Nazi versions of *deutsche Kultur* and *Mitteleuropa* destroyed this kind of Central European culture. It ended in emigration for a fortunate few and Auschwitz for millions of ill-fated others.

Not only did the Third Reich drive out or destroy some of the most important carriers of Central European cultural traditions, but the defeat of Nazi Germany led to the establishment of the Soviet version of Eastern Europe, which divided Central Europe between East and West. Furthermore, Allied policy sanctioned the expulsion of well over 10 million Germans from their homes throughout East Central Europe. If the Jews and the Germans had been catalysts of Central European culture, they were, for the most part, gone after World War II, and the Soviet Union, an Eastern superpower, imposed its version of Marxism, a Western European ideology, on East Central Europe. These events changed the entire cultural complexion of the region forever.

Some western Slavic versions of the concept of Central Europe also exclude the Germans from being Central European because they postulate smallness as the essential criterion for qualifying as a Central European nation. This version of Central Europe consists of a cluster of small, freedom- and peace-loving nations that have had the historical misfortune of living between two big, nasty ones, the Germans and the Russians. The histories of these smaller nations consequently have been chronicles of their heroic but futile attempts to defend their freedom against German (and sometimes German-Austrian) and Russian imperial transgressions. David versus Goliath is a recurrent metaphor in Polish history, and similar although less combative comparisons can be found in Czech national traditions as well.

There also is an Austro-Hungarian or Habsburg variation of this "small nations" version of Central Europe that lets the Austrians be good Central Europeans, too. According to this version of the story, the Habsburgs were benevolent or at least benign emperors compared with the German Hohenzollerns and the Russian Romanovs. The Habsburgs created and maintained a relatively progressive, tolerant, multiethnic, and religiously heterodox empire; indeed, the empire's historical mission was to protect smaller peoples from German and Russian dominion. Given the course of events in the region after 1918, Emperor Francis Joseph and imperial Vienna were retrospectively much more pleasant points of orientation than Hitler and Berlin or Stalin and Moscow.

A relatively modern version of this Habsburg or Austro-Hungarian version of Central Europe reappeared in the 1970s. The Austrian federal chancellor, Bruno Kreisky (1970–1983), incorporated Austria's glorious imperial history into Austria's judicious foreign policy as a neutral state. Austria had a unique position in Cold War Europe after its proclamation of neutrality in 1955. Although Austria jutted like a peninsula into the Communist East, it was a Western democracy. However, its neutrality demanded at that time that it refrain from military and economic alliances; and so Austria was neither East nor West in this respect. Austrian neutrality plus its grand old "imperial history" allowed it to cultivate good relations with those Eastern European Communist states that had been part of the Habsburgs' multinational empire before 1918, especially Hungary, and Austrian–Hungarian relations developed in such an auspicious manner during the 1970s that they became a paragon of East–West cooperation.

The stretch of the Iron Curtain between Austria and Hungary became increasingly permeable, and some people viewed Austrian–Hungarian cooperation as a model for the evolution of future relations between Eastern and Western European states. Austria was a small, neutral, social democratic, welfare state in the West, and Hungary, in terms of its human rights record and economic policies, was an increasingly liberal Communist state in the East. Since neutral Austria was not a military threat to the East, it helped create an environment of trust which, in turn, promoted democratic reform in Hungary.

Extrapolated to European politics, this fortuitous type of bilateral relationship implied that if Western Europe were to become neutral, then Eastern Europe could become more democratic. In the long run, the two different ideological systems might structurally "converge" on the middle ground of neutral, social democratic welfare states. Neutral Austria and Sweden served as models for the denouement of the East–West conflict, and there were fears that the Soviet Union might succeed in neutralizing or "Finlandizing"[6] Western Europe. From this perspective, the withdrawal of the Federal Republic of Germany from the North Atlantic Treaty Organization (NATO) and West German neutrality were the prerequisites for German unification.

This was the type of Central European scenario that the post-1968 Western European Left loved—the Green–environmentalist–peace movement that emerged in the West Germany during the 1980s, in particular—and that the Soviet Union actively promoted: "Struggling for Peace." The idea of Central Europe as a neutral, nuclear-free, and demilitarized zone was based on anti-Americanism and a faith in the reform potential of Marxism. NATO and "American imperialism" were the big problems. If the "American threat" receded, peace-loving Communist states would not only reform; they would also start exhibiting all those traits that made socialism organizationally and morally superior to capitalism.

This was a leftist Western European vision for Central Europe, but the vision that Eastern European dissidents and intellectuals had for Central Europe was fundamentally different and ultimately more important. They also were responsible for bringing the term "Central Europe" back into circulation and popularizing it.[7] When the term "Central Europe" started to gain or regain currency at the beginning of the 1980s, it referred to a controversial and speculative cluster of ideas, not a European region. The bipolar order that was created in Europe after World War II—democracy versus Communism, the North Atlantic Treaty Organization (NATO) versus the Warsaw Pact, the European Economic Community versus the Council for Mutual Economic Assistance (COMECON)—hardly allowed us to think of Europe in terms other than East and West, and these mutually exclusive and convenient concepts were more than sufficient for describing the division of Europe. Barbed wire, minefields, watchtowers, and border guards with orders to shoot clearly marked the junction of East and West in the center of Europe. The Iron Curtain and the Berlin Wall were symbols of not only a bipolar European order but also a global one.

Communism was a monolithic ideology and a global threat. Colors were more important than national borders on political maps. The Eastern bloc and the Soviet Union were one, big, uniform, red mass. Much to the consternation of those Eastern Europeans who believed in Western freedoms, most people in the West had accepted the division of Europe as a matter of fact and were convinced that sustaining the political and ideological status quo in Europe was essential to maintaining European and global peace. Eastern Europe and Western Europe had coexisted relatively well for more than two generations, and there was no reason to assume that they would not do so for a third and a fourth. Communism was here to stay. The Berlin Wall, as some Germans commented after it came down in 1989, was in our heads, too.

Under these conditions, the term "Central Europe" implied that there was something in between East and West at a time when the old East–West conflict entered a new phase of escalation. The Soviet Union invaded Afghanistan in 1979. Ronald Reagan began the first of his two presidential terms in 1980 by referring to the Soviet Union as "an evil empire." General Wojciech Jaruzelski squelched the Solidarity movement in Poland by declaring martial law in December 1981. American defense spending spiraled, and work began on the Strategic Defense Initiative, or "Star Wars," program. The Cold War, the East, and the West seemed to be here to stay.

Central Europe was by no means a new concept, but it did provide an alternative to looking at Europe in exclusively bipolar terms. Judging by the standards of the professional policymaking communities in East and West, the initial proponents of the idea of Central Europe were a rather marginal and motley crew: poets, essayists, and dissidents in Eastern Europe, Eastern European émigrés in the West, and Western intellectuals and academics with East European backgrounds dating as far back as the 1930s but including representatives from every generational wave of Communist oppression in Eastern Europe since then: the initial period of postwar Stalinization, 1956, 1968, and 1981. However, there also were a few stray "real Westerners" who, for some odd reason, had specialized in the study of those small countries between Germany and the Soviet Union—and usually had a spouse from the region to enhance their insights (and partiality) and to prove how heartfelt their interest was. "Central Europe" was a biographical or at least a marital affair, and Central Europe was an Eastern European idea.

Hardened by four decades of confrontation, most professionals and experts in East–West relations dismissed the idea of Central Europe. For them it was merely a manifestation of the psychological problems that sentimental, artsy, and emigrant–immigrant eggheads have: an idea for those who lived in the past and could not let history go or preferred fantasies to the tough realities of the contemporary world. And given the realities of East and West, Central Europe was admittedly a fantastic idea. Its advocates appealed to the past to show that the division of Europe was illegitimate, and in so doing, they animated the present and provided a utopian vision for the future. The proponents of the idea of Central Europe were not realists, and they initially refrained from defining Central Europe in real terms. They did not propose concrete policy options, and they avoided circumscribing it as a specific European region. Instead, Central Europe was an area somewhere between France and the Soviet Union, and the people who wrote and spoke about Central Europe did so in German or English or French. Central Europe was above all a memory, on the one hand, and "a kingdom of the spirit,"[8] on the other.

These initial advocates of the idea of Central Europe dismissed the legitimacy of the post–World War II division of Europe—or "Yalta Europe"[9]—by insisting that the nations that inhabited the Eastern bloc had neither historically nor culturally ever been part of the East but had been abandoned by the West to the new, expanded Russian-Soviet version of the East after World War II.[10] If these Eastern Europeans were not Eastern Europeans in the Russian or Soviet sense of the word—and also not Western Europeans—they were Central Europeans: They lived in the long shadow of the East, historically had looked to and identified themselves with the West, but had ended up in the Soviet East after World War II. The idea of Central Europe at least gave people a choice. It was a means of questioning the legitimacy of the Soviet domination of the Eastern bloc, and the adherents to this idea legitimized their version of the region by appealing to culture, to history, and to Truth.[11]

When Mikhail Gorbachev came to power in the mid-1980s, he was greeted with a combination of skepticism and hope. There were basically two schools of Sovietologists in the West: the hard-liners or hawks, who believed that the system could not be reformed, and the soft liberals or doves, who believed that it could. There were two analogous schools of thought among Communists in the East: the hard-liners or representatives of the old Brezhnev era, who wanted to keep things just as they were, and the disciples of Gorbachev, who wanted to change them. Most of the Eastern Europeans, who believed in the idea of Central Europe because they were anti-Communists, sympathized with the predictions of the hard-liners in the West, not because they did not want more freedom, but simply because they had seen so many previous attempts to reform Communism fail. They said that Gorbachev would fail, too, and he did. But he failed at a much later date and under much more auspicious circumstances than anyone would have dared to imagine in the mid-1980s.

Gorbachev was prepared to let the countries of the Eastern bloc go their own ways, which he hoped would be his way, and after he retracted the infamous Brezhnev Doctrine of "limited sovereignty," the specter of Soviet intervention disappeared. Central Europe suddenly had become a real political option. Gorbachev was going to let countries get out of the old Soviet version of Eastern Europe; the term "Central Europe" was suddenly in vogue. However, it appeared in confusing, different contexts and combinations: Central Europe, Central/Eastern Europe, Central and Eastern Europe, Eastern and Central Europe, East Central Europe. No one was really sure what the parameters of this region were, but if it meant getting out of the Soviet Empire, it was a good idea.

Left to their own devices, the peoples of the Eastern bloc each had their own revolutions in 1989: at different times, with varying objectives, and under dissimilar circumstances. The Berlin Wall fell, German unification suddenly appeared on the political agenda, and all sorts of confederative plans for the new democracies of Central Europe were in the air. Central European states would have to cooperate with one another to offset the influences of a unified Germany and the Soviet Union in the future. The region would come into its own.

Things in Central Europe have not turned out the way that many people expected during that heady and optimistic year of 1989. (This also is true for the newly independent states that emerged from the former Soviet Union after 1991.) Yugoslavia has deteriorated into a series of states and a series of wars, and the newly independent states of the former Soviet Union are confronted with several Yugoslavias within their frontiers. Czechoslovakia has fallen apart. There has been no "Marshall Plan for Eastern Europe." The transformation of planned economies into market economies is proving to be much more difficult than many Western economists assumed. Democratic institutions and traditions are weak in the "new democracies." The ugliest forms of nationalism are resurgent not only in Central and Eastern Europe but also in the West. Too many people are thinking of solving the problems of the outgoing twentieth century with nineteenth-century ideologies.

The term "Central Europe" is used in two different contexts today. A broad historical definition of the region includes Austria and Germany; a narrower definition based on usage influenced by the former East–West division of Europe does not. For example, both Germany and Austria also readily define themselves as "Central European" states today, if this means that they are the easternmost representatives of Western Europe (or the European Union) or that they have special historical relationships with their eastern neighbors and obligations to help them. But if Western Europe is coextensive with the European Union, then the term "Central Europe" usually refers to those countries of the former Eastern bloc that have higher per capita incomes and are at higher levels of economic development than the "new democracies" on the Balkan Peninsula or in the former Soviet Union. Intergovernmental agencies like the Organization for Economic Cooperation and Development (OECD) or the World Bank therefore distinguish in practice between "Central Europe"—Poland, the Czech Republic, Slovakia,

Hungary, and Slovenia—and "Eastern Europe."[12] There seems to be a historical constant here: These Central European states are behind the West but still ahead of the East and the Southeast.

Certainly many of Central Europe's current problems are the results of more than forty years of Communism, and in this respect, they are unprecedented. But it is equally important to recognize that many of the contemporary problems of Central Europe antedate Communism. These are *old* Central European problems under *new* Central European circumstances, and the problems, like the idea of Central Europe itself, have venerable traditions. Some of the smaller problems are just five or six decades old. The formidable ones might be at least five or six centuries old, and even if they are not, some Central Europeans at least *think* they are. It is time to go back and look at the beginning of the story.

☆ 1 ☆

Central Europe and
the Roman Christian West

400–1000

Defining the relationships between national, historical, or cultural borders and physical borders is exceedingly difficult. Many geographers, whose job it is to come up with meaningful criteria for defining regions, do not like the term "Central Europe" because it subsumes too many heterogeneous phenomena under one concept. Such methodological reservations do not seem to disturb most Central Europeans, however. Although geologic formations and soil types, average annual precipitation and mean temperatures, and flora and fauna undoubtedly are important scientific determinants, these are not the type of criteria that Central Europeans use to define themselves. Nevertheless, a brief look at the topography of Central Europe is useful because Central Europeans have a propensity to look at their borders in terms of either divine or natural endowments, and the concept of "natural borders" always has been dangerous.

One way to follow the historical flow of events in Central Europe is to look at the land: the mountains as physical obstacles, the plains as the absence thereof, and the rivers as a means of communication within regions or as lines of demarcation between them. The western border of Central Europe traditionally has been the most German river, the Rhine, and the beginning of the eastern border, which is more difficult to define, is the drainage basin of Poland's national waterway, the Vistula. The vast expanses of the Northern European Plain, which stretches virtually unbroken from the French Atlantic to the Ural Mountains, have always been conducive to movement or, conversely, have never provided much natural protection.

Aggressors always have exploited the advantages of the plains: from the Great Migrations in the fifth century or the invasions of the Tatars' eastern

13

hordes in the Middle Ages to the armies of Napoleon and Hitler in the nineteenth and twentieth centuries. Flatness lends itself to transgressions ranging from raids to imperial expansion, and it tends to make decisive battles more a matter of logistics, the mobility of sheer numbers over great distances, than anything else. Russia was the only European country eventually to reach a size that allowed it to compensate for the disadvantages of flatness with vastness, the dimensions of which grow in winter.

Smaller peoples inhabiting the plains, like Lithuanians and Poles, frequently have been at a geographical disadvantage when confronted with larger neighbors, like Germans and Russians. However, all the nations of northern Central Europe, regardless of their relative size, have been fascinated at one point or another in their histories by the possibilities for expansion that have accompanied the wide open spaces, and they all have had empires on the plains. The drive for more space to live, something that German imperialists of the nineteenth and twentieth centuries articulated as a national right to *Lebensraum,* is neither a particularly modern nor a peculiarly German attribute. It may be construed as a historical constant related to the absence of natural borders and barriers in this part of the world.

The landscape of Central Europe south of the Northern European Plain is highly contoured. The plateau of the Bohemian Massif and the mountainous western and northern parameters of the Bohemian Basin initially separated the Czechs from their German-speaking neighbors to the north in Saxony, to the West in the highlands of central Germany, and to the south in the Danube Valley. The Carpathian Mountains, which curve from the eastern end of the Bohemian Massif along the Polish and Ukrainian borders down into Romania, also have separated the inhabitants on the plains north and east of this mountain chain from the peoples living south and west of it: Poles and Ukrainians from Slovaks, Hungarians, and Romanians. This rugged division has naturally helped separate Central Europe into distinct spheres: to the north, the plains, and to the south, the mountains and valleys charted by the course of the Danube River and its 300 tributaries.

The Danube, the only major European river that runs from west to east, traverses 1,770 miles from its source in southwestern Germany's Black Forest, north of the Swiss Alps, to its delta on the Black Sea, east of the Carpathians. Although the Danube's banks are shared by nine contemporary European states and help define parts of five international borders, this river rarely has been a frontier. The Alps in the west and the Carpathians in the east always have been difficult to cross, and the Dinaric Ranges, the rugged chains of mountains that run from the Alps down the Adriatic coast, also contributed to giving this part of the world an "inland" or "Danubian," as opposed to a Mediterranean, orientation. Most of the former Yugoslavia's major rivers empty into the Danube, not the Adriatic. The Adriatic coast also historically belonged to Venice's maritime empire, which is one of the reasons that Mussolini referred to the Adriatic as *mare nostro,* "our sea."

Circumscribed by these different mountain ranges, the plains of the central Danube Valley—from Vienna to Budapest and from Budapest to Belgrade—always have been a means of communication and a site of conflict.

GEOGRAPHIC ZONES

Drainage basin limits of the Danube

The Danube seems to have naturally channeled the energies of the peoples who have inhabited its banks to such a great extent that following the course of the river and its tributaries is indispensable to understanding events in this part of the world as movements up and downstream.

The openness of the Northern European Plain, the northern rim of the Bohemian Basin and the Carpathian Mountains as natural barriers, and the orientation of regions south toward the Danube River Basin are three primary geographical features of Central Europe that have physically contributed to defining two broad sets of historical conflicts in this region. For the millennium preceding World War I, the dynastic contests among Germans, Poles, Lithuanians, and Russians on the plains of the north were frequently peripheral to analogous struggles among Austrians, Czechs, and Hungarians—and later Turks—for the hegemony of the Danube Valley in the south. These historical theaters were separated from each other by mountains which basically served as a natural barrier to expansion from the plains of the north and a natural limit for expansion from the valleys of the south.

Romans and Barbarians: Christians and Pagans

Looking at the history of Europe in terms of the West's defending itself from the East has a long tradition in Central Europe. Disciples of the "East–West" confrontation theory of European history find one of the oldest and most important historical precedents, in the first century A.D., in the Roman fortification of the western banks of the Rhine and the southern banks of the Danube. The erection of the Limes, a system of strategically placed roads, fortified camps, and watchtowers manned by what military people would call "rapid deployment units," marks a turning point in the Romans' conception of their empire. The objective of subjugating and incorporating barbarians into the empire was replaced by the task of keeping them out which the Romans did for three centuries, with varying strategies and decreasing degrees of success. The Goths sacked Rome in 410.

The tribes that inhabited the areas east of the Rhine and north of the Danube, those dark ancestors of Central Europeans, were "barbarians" by the standards of Greco-Roman culture and pagans whose conversion to Christianity drew them relatively late into the sphere of Western civilization. This observation is important because nineteenth-century Romanticism and nationalism coalesced in some cases to create an atavistic pride in this non-Mediterranean heritage. The proponents of this non-Christian national genealogy glorified the fictitious purity of barbarian culture in a manner that depreciated the civilizing influences and accomplishments of the Mediterranean world and, at the same time, postulated the idea of tribal combat—struggles among peoples, nations, and races—as the moving force of history. The nineteenth century fascination with the idea of a national soul or collective primal spirit, something the Germans call *Volksgeist*, was often diametrically opposed to the cosmopolitan spirit of rationality identified with the classical world and reformulated during the Enlightenment. Each Central European nation discovered sooner or later its own *Volksgeist* by imitation or introspection. A concept like the "Slavic soul" may sound less ominous or more romantically benign, but it is not devoid of shadowy recesses.

The deterioration of the Roman Empire contributed to the eventual establishment of the southern and eastern borders of Central Europe. At the beginning of the fourth century, Emperor Constantine moved the political center of the empire from Rome to the shores of the Bosporus between the Black and the Aegean Seas. He gave the empire not only a new capital, Constantinople, a "second Rome" bearing his name, but also a new religion, by converting to Christianity on his deathbed in 337. At the end of the fourth century, the reign of Emperor Theodorus represented the culmination of tendencies manifest under Constantine. Theodorus declared Christianity the official religion of the empire, and in 395 he formally divided the empire into autonomous halves, each of which was ruled by one of his sons. Honorius ruled the Western Roman Empire, which corresponded more or less to our contemporary notion of Western Europe, from Rome and later Ravenna, and Arcadius ruled the Eastern Roman Empire from Constantinople which included the Roman provinces south of the Danube on the Balkan Peninsula and in Asia Minor, the Middle East, and Egypt.

As the political center of the Roman Empire shifted from west to east during the fourth century, the religious center of Christianity shifted from east to west, from Asia Minor to Rome. This reciprocal movement was important because Constantinople and the Eastern Roman Empire provided the basis for the development of the Byzantine Empire and the Eastern Orthodox Church, whereas the fall of the Western Roman Empire in 476 made the Roman Church the single most important carrier of cultural continuity in the West. The Eastern Roman Empire, no longer Roman in the classical, Mediterranean sense of the word but gradually transformed by Greek influences into Byzantium, survived the initial and subsequent onslaughts of the barbarians.

Eastern Christianity gradually developed a symbiotic relationship with Byzantium's autocratic state, as well as theological traditions, rituals, and a religious sensibility that differed substantially from the those of the Roman Church. Although it took Rome and Constantinople centuries to finalize their incompatibility—the Great Schism of 1054 marked the Eastern Church's final rejection of Roman papal authority—the foundations for the "East–West split" of Christendom were laid early and have been enduring.[1] The twentieth-century spirit of ecumenism has made little progress in bridging the dogmatic gaps between the Roman and Eastern Churches.

This brief excursion into the history of the late Roman Empire and early Christianity is important for two reasons. First, the collapse of the Western Roman Empire brought a definitive end to the classical, military-administrative, imperial state in the west, whereas the survival of the Eastern Roman Empire entailed the maintenance of many imperial structures. In the east, the imperial state provided the basis for a higher level of civilization, but it was relatively inflexible. The complete collapse of the imperial state in the west created a chaotic situation, but the long-term task of bringing order to this chaos in Western Europe led to the establishment of a series of smaller and more dynamic polities that ultimately developed into freer societies. Western Europe's emerging civilization relied heavily on imperial Roman traditions, but unlike the civilization of the Byzantine East, it was not stultified by the heritage of an imperial Roman state.

Second, the mission of converting the pagans of Central Europe to Christianity proceeded from two poles: Catholic (or Latin) Rome and Eastern Orthodox (or Greek) Constantinople. The location of each center of Christianity determined their most promising fields of missionary work. The

most important Roman outpost in Central Europe was a diocese established
in 739 in Passau (situated on the Danube on the contemporary Austrian–
Bavarian border), and the decisive Roman Catholic impulses of Christianization emanated from there. Eastern Orthodoxy operated out of Constantinople and eventually gained a firm hold on the southern Balkan Peninsula, along the shores of the Black Sea, and established important centers of
religious devotion and missionary promotion in Kiev and eventually
Moscow. After the Turks conquered Constantinople in 1453, the Russians
claimed the imperial heritage of Byzantium as well as the spiritual patrimony of the Eastern Church. The princes of Moscow began calling themselves
czars, a Slavonic contraction of "Caesar," and Moscow consecrated itself as
the "third Rome."

The importance of the Eastern Church's missionary work is perhaps best
illustrated by the fact that the invention of the Cyrillic alphabet used in the
southern and eastern Slavic languages like Bulgarian, Serbian, Ukrainian,
and Russian, is attributed to St. Cyril and St. Methodius, two Greek missionaries sent from Constantinople to the Greater Moravian Kingdom[2] in
the ninth century. The missionary purpose of inventing of an alphabet for
Slavic languages was to translate the Word of God from Greek into the Slavic vernacular, and it had the concomitant benefit of providing the converts
with the orthographic tools they needed for the transition from an oral to a
literary culture. Christian scribes replaced pagan bards as the recorders and
interpreters of the past.

The Roman Church had Western Europe firmly in its fold, but Rome and
Constantinople competed for the souls of the pagans in Central Europe.
The success of the Roman Church's missionary work is demonstrated by the
dates that Central Europeans use to document "national conversions" to
Western Christianity. The papal coronation of Charlemagne as the Holy Roman Emperor in Rome on Christmas Day in 800 is generally regarded as the
final stage of reorganization and consolidation for the early Western Church
in Germany, and the decisive missionary impulses for the western Slavs came
from the west.

For the Czechs, Wenceslas, a duke of Bohemia who according to legend
was killed by his brother Boleslav I in 929 because of his devotion to Christianity, is a symbol of national conversion. (He is known to most inhabitants
of the English-speaking world through the Christmas carol that calls him a
king and praises his goodness.) It is one of those quirks of history that Do-
bravka, the daughter of Wenceslas' murderous brother Boleslav, was married to Mieszko I of the Piast dynasty in Poland and played a key role in her
husband's—and consequently the Polish nation's—conversion to Christianity in 966.

In 1966 Poland's Roman Catholic Church and Communist state both celebrated the millennial anniversary of this event, although with different rituals and intentions. The state secularly emphasized Poland's historical foundations and its affinity to the Slavic and Soviet east. Among other things,
Communist apologists underscored the fact that the contemporary borders
of Poland correspond well to those that existed a millennium ago: a pecu-

THE "ROMAN WEST" AND CENTRAL EUROPE, 400–1000

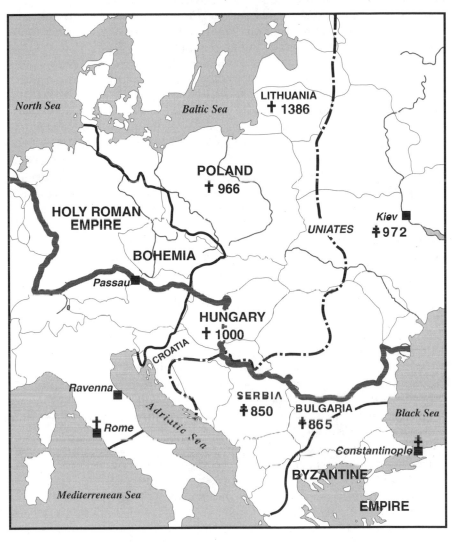

North Sea

Baltic Sea

LITHUANIA ✝ 1386

POLAND ✝ 966

HOLY ROMAN EMPIRE

UNIATES

Kiev ☦972

BOHEMIA

Passau

HUNGARY ✝ 1000

CROATIA

Ravenna

Adriatic Sea

SERBIA ☦850

BULGARIA ☦865

Black Sea

✝ Rome

Constantinople ☦

BYZANTINE

Mediterrenean Sea

EMPIRE

Limes – Frontier of the Roman Empire, ca. 350

Dates of "national conversion"

✝ 966   Roman Catholicism

☦ 865   Eastern Orthodoxy

Frontiers of Holy Roman and Byzantine Empires, ca. 1000

The Roman Catholic/Eastern Orthodox "divide"

liar historical justification for the fact that Poland's enormous territorial losses to the Soviet Union in the east after World War II were compensated by large Polish gains in the west at the expense of Germany. The church religiously celebrated the Catholic identity of the Polish nation along with its Western or "Roman" orientation. The election of Cardinal Karol Wojtyła, the archbishop of Kraków, as Pope John Paul II in 1978 was a spectacular reconfirmation of Poland's westward-looking or "Roman" tradition, and it would be difficult to underestimate the importance of the Polish pope as a source of moral and national inspiration in Poland's struggle with Communism during the 1980s.

The Magyars, a nomadic tribe that made its debut in Europe in 896 by spilling over the Carpathian Mountains onto the Hungarian Plain, were a wild and recent addition to Central Europe's collection of peoples. With distant roots somewhere in the depths of Central Asia, these combative nomads spoke a language from the Finno-Ugric family that was incomprehensible to their neighbors. Their eventual settlement on the Hungarian Plain in the central Danube Basin between the Germans, who had colonized the upper Danube Valley down to Vienna, and the Romanian inhabitants of the Carpathian Mountains completed the separation of the southern Slavs on the Balkan Peninsula from their linguistic relatives to the north. It also took the Magyars quite some time to abandon their nomadic ways. During the first half of the tenth century, they periodically made raids into Germany, France, and northern Italy. However, a decisive defeat at the Battle of Lechfeld (in contemporary Bavaria near Augsburg) in 955 helped them settle down, and the first great Hungarian king, St. Stephen, was responsible for drawing them into the sphere of Western civilization.

St. Stephen, crowned the Apostolic King of Hungary by the pope in 1000, received from the pope the attribute "apostolic" for his kingship, for the efforts he made to convert his subjects to Christianity, an achievement for which he was canonized later on. For Hungarians, the crown of St. Stephen is a symbol not just of Christianity but also of statehood and legitimacy: the obligations of the king to the nation and the union of the nation with its ruler. There is one striking twentieth-century example of the importance of this symbolism. At the end of World War II, the crown of St. Stephen and other Hungarian regalia—the royal scepter, orb, sword, and coronation gowns—were taken out of Hungary, and they eventually ended up in the hands of the U.S. army in Germany. The U.S. government then brought them to the United States and had them deposited in Fort Knox. The fact that the United States returned them to Hungary in 1978, partly as a reward for the relative liberality of the Hungarian Communist regime under János Kádár, was a tremendous foreign policy success for the Communists. Some contemporaries interpreted the return of the crown and the regalia as an implicit recognition of the legitimacy of Communist rule in Hungary; others criticized it as such. (The commonsense approach was that the Hungarian crown should be back where it belonged.)

During the spectacular wave of reforms in Hungary in 1989, which included removing the Soviet red star from the Hungarian national emblem, there was a serious debate whether or not to incorporate the crown of St. Stephen into Hungary's new national emblem. Opponents of this idea called the crown a "reactionary," monarchical, clerical, and even imperialistic symbol, whereas proponents defended it as the only appropriate traditional and national symbol. This heraldic issue, which raised passions in Hungary similar to those seen in the United States when people argue whether burning the Stars and Stripes is a constitutional right or should be prevented by a constitutional amendment, was not settled until the spring of 1990 (in favor of the crown).

Poland's traditional national symbol is an eagle with a crown. When the Communists came to power in Poland after World War II, they removed (or, as many Poles would say, "stole") the crown traditionally borne by the eagle on the national crest. The Polish reform parliament reinstated it in 1989. In 1990, the Czechoslovak reform parliament removed the red star that the Communists had added to the traditional Bohemian crest of a lion in 1948 and then began a long debate about how much space the Czech and the Slovak parts of the republic were to have on a new national crest because the Slovaks were spatially underrepresented on the old one. Equal space eventually was given to the Czechs' lion, the traditional symbol for the historical kingdom of Bohemia; the Moravian eagle, the crest of the duchy of the Bohemian crown located between Bohemia and Slovakia; and Slovakia's patriarchal or double bar cross, a commemoration of the fact that St. Cyril and St. Methodius, the first Christian missionaries in Central Europe, began their work in Slovakia. (This quibbling about heraldics was merely an omen of things to come. Czech and Slovak nationalists succeeded in sabotaging the idea of a federal republic, and on January 1, 1993, independent Czech and Slovak Republics were established.)

The dates of "national conversion" used by Central European nations merely indicate how successful the Roman Church was in spreading throughout Central Europe its interpretation of the Word, its forms of organization, and its Latin alphabet, and it is no mere coincidence that the southern and eastern borders of Central Europe can be determined by the relative strengths of Roman Catholicism or Eastern Orthodoxy as well as the use of the Latin or Cyrillic alphabets. The differences between Croats and Serbs in the former Yugoslavia are a good example of the East–West split in Christendom, because the Balkan Peninsula was an early medieval forum of East–West competition. By the end of the eleventh century, the kingdom of Croatia on the northern frontier of the Byzantine Empire opted for the western form of Christianity, whereas Serbia, under the influence of the Byzantine Empire, had adopted the Eastern Orthodox rite. Although Croats and Serbs learned to speak fundamentally the same language—a standardized Serbo-Croatian constructed by nineteenth-century linguists—the Croats are Roman Catholic and use the Latin alphabet, whereas the Serbs are Orthodox and use the Cyrillic one.

Romanian is another good example of the strength of Eastern religious orientation in this region. Although Romanian is a Romance language, part of the Roman Empire's linguistic heritage of Latin-based tongues, Romanians used the Cyrillic alphabet and a vocabulary with predominantly Slavic roots until the beginning of the nineteenth century. The adoption then of the Latin alphabet helped modernize the language, a process that borrowed heavily from French.

The differences between Poles and Russians or Poles and Ukrainians reinforce the idea that the southern and eastern borders of Central Europe can be drawn using alphabets and religions. Different alphabets and different conceptions of the same religion are useful instruments for drawing cultural borders within Europe, but they do not necessarily promote mutual understanding among the peoples who have them. Each nation in the region—Roman Catholic, Eastern Orthodox, or, later, Protestant—came to regard itself as a "chosen people" with Christian and national missions: defending the True Faith against other Christian heretics and shielding the Christian West against infidels. In the nineteenth century, nationalism drew heavily on the sense of exceptionalism rooted in the Christian and European missions that individual peoples in the region saw themselves as having fulfilled in their histories.

Roman Catholic, Eastern Orthodox, and Islamic Empires:
Charlemagne, Byzantium, and the Rise of the Ottomans

The papal coronation of Charles, King of the Franks, as the Holy Roman Emperor on Christmas Day in Rome in 800 is an event generally regarded as a symbol for the gradual rise of the West. Subsequently called Charles the Great, or Charlemagne, the new emperor, a devout Christian and a gifted warrior, had consolidated control of a territory roughly coextensive with those states that were the founding members of the European Economic Community, Western Europe's current economic empire, in 1958: France, Belgium, the Netherlands, Luxembourg, the Federal Republic of Germany, and Italy.

Charlemagne's accomplishments impressed his Central European contemporaries to such an extent that his name—in Old German Karl, in Old Slavonic Kral—was not adopted as a loan word for the proper name Charles; rather, *kral*, or derivatives of it, became synonymous with "king" or "ruler" in Slavic languages. This shows to what extent the Slavs of Central Europe imitated Western models of feudal organization. Centuries later, monarchs throughout Europe still frequently traced their genealogies back to Charlemagne—and ultimately to the founders of Rome, Romulus and Remus—as a means of fictitiously enhancing their lineage and legitimacy.

The historical importance of Charlemagne's Holy Roman Empire was greater than any of its material achievements. A loose federation of territories he had subjugated personally, the empire declined rapidly after his death in 814, and it was Roman and imperial in name only. It was not ruled by a strong central administration or by Roman law, nor was it defended by legions. Nonetheless, it represented the first of a series of Western renaissances—attempts to resuscitate and rearticulate the lost heritage of Rome—and it was the first major alliance between throne and altar in the West. In this respect, Charlemagne's empire was "holy," and it provided a new model for the concept of dominion. Barbarian chieftains had based their right to rule on tribal precedent and brute force, whereas Christian lords became God's representatives on earth and were responsible for managing a divinely preordained order. Although we should not underestimate the importance of brute force in the medieval world, the rights of Christian rulers were limited by complicated obligations to their subjects which, in comparison with barbarian practices, tempered and perfected the institutions of subordination in feudal society.

By around 1200, the Holy Roman Empire, which had experienced a series of territorial and organizational transformations in the centuries following Charlemagne's death, was a loose confederation of feudal states that covered contemporary Germany (East and West), Silesia in southwestern Poland, Bohemia and Moravia (the contemporary Czech Republic), Austria, Slovenia, parts of Croatia and northern Italy, Switzerland, a strip of eastern France, and the Benelux countries. Although the empire included a considerable number of non-Germans, it became an important vehicle of medieval politics in Germany, an empire of the *natio Germanorum*, a "German nation." It is important to recognize, however, that the medieval Latin concept of *natio*, or "nation," referred to the community of feudal lords both in Germany and elsewhere, not to "the people" in the nineteenth century democratic or nationalistic sense of the word.

This empire was and remained decentralized and weak. The Holy Roman Emperor barely had the means to intervene directly in the affairs of the medieval lords, who became responsible for electing him, and as time passed, the empire increasingly assumed the status of a political fiction. Nonetheless, the imperial title and the claims accompanying it were significant in Central European politics until 1806, when Napoleon's promotion of a revolutionary French empire led to the abolishment of the Holy Roman Empire.

The word for empire in German is *Reich*, and the *Reichsidee*, the "idea of the empire," played an important role in the German speaking world long after the empire had ceased to function politically, as well as after its abolition in 1806. Although Charlemagne was not a German statesman in the nineteenth-century sense of the term, some German historians illicitly interpreted him as such a millennium after his death and, in doing so, turned Charlemagne's early medieval and polyglot empire into a German national empire. (Reinterpreting medieval history using the categories and interests of nineteenth-century nationalism is a bad habit shared by many Central Europeans.)

The Roman territorial concept of *Germania*, Charlemagne's idea of *imperium*, and the medieval concept of a *natio Germanorum* all initially had very little to do with the ideas that pervaded German politics in the nineteenth century, but they were appropriated to serve nationalistic and imperialistic purposes. The unification of Germany under the hegemony of the Prussians and the proclamation of the "Second German Reich" in 1871 made Charlemagne's empire the "First German Reich," and Hitler's "Third German

Reich" articulated its mission with a perverted reinterpretation of the first two. Each of the German empires after the one attributed to Charlemagne progressively distanced itself from the Christian and confederative ideals that the *Reichsidee* embodied. The Second Reich was predominantly Protestant, Prussian, and autocratic, and the Third Reich was pagan, barbarian, and totalitarian. (Given the bad experiences that many Europeans have had with imperial Germany, some of them viewed the unification of West and East Germany in 1990 as the beginning of a "Fourth Reich" that would dominate Europe using banks instead of tanks.)

The Iron Curtain corresponded to the old eastern border of the Carolinian Empire to such a great extent that a Hungarian historian once remarked that "it is as if Stalin, Churchill, and Roosevelt had carefully studied the status quo of the age of Charlemagne on the 1130th anniversary of his death"[3] (at the Yalta Conference in 1945). The idea that Germany historically has been a cultural border of the West is, however, erroneous. The post–World War II or Cold War concepts of East and West often disregarded the historical and cultural orientation of the eastern half of Central Europe: East Central Europe as the region east of the eastern frontiers of German empires yet west of the western frontiers of Russia.

As early as the twelfth century, the term *Europa occidentalis*, "Western Europe," was used to describe the region west of a line that ran roughly from the lower Danube Valley along the eastern Carpathian Mountains and up to the Baltic. This "primordial Iron Curtain"[4] was not politically but theologically inspired, and it corresponded to the spheres of influence of Western Christianity and Eastern Orthodoxy or Rome and Byzantium. As interesting as it may be to seek historical precedents for the terms East and West in medieval Europe, it would be misleading to assume that there was a general awareness at that time of this interior European border. Furthermore, as great as the theological differences between the Orthodox and Roman Churches were, they were secondary in comparison with the differences between the Islamic Orient and the Christian Occident.

The Battle of Tours (on the banks of the Loire River in west central France) in 732 is frequently regarded as the turning point of Christendom's struggle with Islam, but this assumption merely reflects the adoption of a myopic French or Western European perspective. It took centuries to drive the Arabs off the Iberian Peninsula, and the eastern representative of Christendom, the Byzantine Empire, struggled with the Islamic East until the middle of the fifteenth century.

The rise of the Ottoman Turkish Empire at the start of the fourteenth century signaled the beginning of the end for the Byzantine Empire, which successively lost its holdings in the Middle East, in Asia Minor, and on the Balkan Peninsula. The Turks' victory at the Battle of Kosovo on June 28, 1389, was a turning point in the development of their European empire, just as it was a tragedy for the medieval kingdom of Serbia, because for the Serbs it marked the beginning of more than four centuries under Ottoman rule.

The Ottoman Empire's territorial strangulation of Byzantium culminated in 1453 with the siege and fall of Constantinople. The importance of this event for Central Europe was twofold. First, the center of the Orthodox East shifted from Constantinople to Moscow, and the inheritance of Byzantium's imperial claims and the Orthodox religious mission profoundly impressed the Russians. From the Russian and the Orthodox point of view, the czar became the direct successor of the Roman emperors, whereas Western Christians were a collection of heretics and schismatics. As the only legitimate emperors and the only truly Christian sovereigns in Europe, the czars had the duty of maintaining and spreading the faith, which involved, among other things, defending the eastern border of Christendom from the onslaughts of Asian hordes for centuries as well as aspiring to free their Orthodox Slavic brothers on the Balkan Peninsula who had fallen under the "Turkish yoke."

Furthermore, the demise of the Byzantine Empire made the rise of the Ottoman Empire a Central European problem. After the Serbian defeat at Kosovo in 1389, the Kingdom of Hungary eventually assumed responsibility for "defending the Christian West." (This is a standard phrase that all Central Europeans have used to describe their "historical missions" at one point or another in their histories.)

After the fall of Constantinople in 1453, the Ottoman Empire entered a new phase of continental European expansion, and the southern border of Central Europe became a fluctuating military frontier for the next 400 years. The Hungarians attempted to halt the Ottoman advance but failed, as the Serbs had before them. The death of Louis II, the king of Bohemia and Hungary, in the Battle of Mohács in 1526 was a event central to understanding Hungarian history, and it may be used to mark the beginning of the high tide of Ottoman expansion in southeastern Europe. After the fall of Hungary, the Habsburgs of Austria assumed responsibility for defending Occidental Christendom and succeeded—perilously at first. The Turks sieged Vienna in 1529.

The Turks ruled the first empire that threatened the independence of those smaller nations inhabiting Central Europe, and as we shall see, between the sixteenth and the twentieth centuries the experience of being subjugated by foreign empires was something all Central Europeans recurrently had in common. Although it is a bit premature to deal with these events at this point, we should note that the defense of Western Christendom took place on the southeastern borders of Central Europe. Therefore, the southern frontiers of the historical kingdoms of Croatia and Hungary may be used as plausible criteria for defining part of the parameters of Central Europe. South of this frontier, the Balkan Peninsula, which was religiously Orthodox, became politically Turkish for more than four centuries. The differences between Western or Roman Christianity and Eastern Orthodoxy, combined with the extended rule of the Turks over the Orthodox Christians on the Balkan Peninsula, greatly accentuated the differences between Central European and Southeastern European cultures.

Since the end of the Cold War, there also has been a renewed interest in "the cultural division of Europe between Western Christianity, on the one hand, and Orthodox Christianity and Islam, on the other." Samuel P. Huntington advanced the controversial and disquieting hypothesis that the era of political and ideological conflicts rooted in nineteenth- and twentieth-century ideologies, such as the Cold War, has passed and that "the conflicts of the future will occur along the cultural fault lines" based on older and more fundamental criteria such as "history, language, culture, and, most important, religion."[5] Nationalism has made a surprising comeback since the demise of Communism. The fact that wars in the former Yugoslavia have erupted along the millennium-old cultural fault line between the Roman Catholic Croats and the Orthodox Serbs, on the one hand, and that the conflicts in Bosnia-Herzegovina frequently—and in most cases inaccurately—have been portrayed as confrontations between Christians and Muslims, on the other, seem to support this thesis.

⚜ 2 ⚜

Feudal Foundations

1000–1350

One of the peculiarities of Central Europe is that some people from the region consider the Middle Ages to be the high point in their national historical traditions. Therefore, we should examine the period before 1500 because the process of empire building in Central Europe, which gradually led to the demise of the kingdoms of Hungary, Bohemia, and Poland, began shortly thereafter. By the end of the eighteenth century most of Central Europe had been divided among three dynastic powers: Habsburg Austria, Romanov Russia, and Hohenzollern Prussia. It would be a distortion, however, to view the history of Central Europe from the perspective of these three powers at their nineteenth- or early-twentieth-century territorial zeniths, because each of these great empires started small. Around 1300, Berlin, Vienna, and Moscow were the capitals of feudal duchies that were modest in size and negligible in importance when compared with the kingdoms of Bohemia, Hungary, or Poland. The misfortune of these nations with the venerable tradition of having their own kings and lords—the modern but somewhat misleading terminology would be "national self-determination"—was that they became the subjects and vassals of foreign powers. Therefore, one aspect of understanding Central Europe involves developing both a feeling for the real and ideal dimensions of those older Central European kingdoms—which were empires in their own right but were conquered by foreign powers—and the sense of tragedy that goes along with it.

During the nineteenth century, there was a peculiar alliance in Central Europe between the assumptions of liberalism, on the one hand, and the premises of nationalism and Romanticism, on the other, and this wedding of apparently disparate ideas produced very favorable interpretations of the

27

Middle Ages. The concept of nationalism had to be retrospectively articulated in terms of people's "ancient" freedoms, which had been violated or lost, an enterprise that required a Romantic reinterpretation of the Middle Ages as a period of national freedom, at least in comparison with subsequent periods of foreign domination, which had to be reestablished in the spirit of liberalism. This may seem terminologically a bit complicated, but it basically means that visions of the future frequently were versions of the past transformed by Romanticism and liberalism. The freedom and independence of the past that had been lost in the past had to be regained or reestablished in the future.

It is important to avoid confusing the medieval meaning of the term "nation" (*natio*) with its nineteenth-century counterparts "nation," "nation-state," and "nationalism." In the Middle Ages, there were four large political entities in Central Europe: the Holy Roman Empire of the German Nation and the kingdoms of Bohemia, Hungary, and Poland. It would be misleading to call these political bodies "states" in the modern sense of the word. Rather, they were relatively loose confederations ruled by kings who claimed a limited amount of jurisdiction for specific subordinate political and territorial units, each of which, in turn, was ruled by nobles who exercised a high degree of autonomy in their own domains. These nobles had a mutually dependent and ambivalent relationship with their respective kings, who in some cases had a hereditary claim to the throne but, in others, were elected by the nobility. In the medieval world, these nobles were the constituent members of the "nations," a term referring to a relatively small class of blue-blooded persons who held titles and lands, not the population or "the people" in terms of the modern democratic theory of popular sovereignty.

Each of these kingdoms also had its own "constitutional order." The kings and the noble members of the political nation were mutually bound to observe certain rights and execute certain duties, a relationship that embodied an inherent conflict. The kings could not expand or centralize their power without infringing on the lords' traditional rights, and the lords were interested in limiting or reducing royal interference in their affairs. Hungarian historians, for example, like to compare the Golden Bull issued by the Hungarian King Andrew II in 1222 with the Magna Carta of civil and political liberties granted by England's King John in 1215. In both cases, the idea of "ancient rights," "rights of the nation," and the limitation of royal power is important.

One of the peculiarities of the development of Central European kingdoms is that they did not evolve into constitutional monarchies like England's, nor did Central European kings manage to create absolute monarchies at the expense of the nobility, as in France. Poles and Hungarians like to point out the similarities between the constitutional developments of their own historical kingdoms, in terms of the protection of individual rights and the rule of law, and the corresponding developments in England. As promising as the auspicious domestic political development of these kingdoms may have been at the time, it was truncated between the sixteenth and late eighteenth centuries by the intervention of foreign empires. Given the subsequent absence of continuity, it would be exaggerating to speak of "democratic traditions" in the region that reach back to the Middle Ages.

All four of Central Europe's political nations also were multiethnic, in the contemporary sense of the word. There were Czech and German nobles in Bohemia, Poles and Lithuanians in the "Polish nation," and an entire kaleidoscope of ethnic groups among the nobility in the "Hungarian nation." But none of these nobles was a "nationalist" in the nineteenth-century sense of the word. The "national interest"—to use a modern term—consisted of the interests of the nobles. "National freedom" referred to the rights of this privileged group, and the "nation" was coextensive with their domains, which were unified by their common allegiance to a king.

Poles, Czechs, and Hungarians find it easy to look back over long spans of time, because they identify more readily with distant and idealized eras of "national freedom" than they do with the intervening histories of foreign subjugation, regardless of how long they may have lasted. The feudal kingdoms of Poland, Bohemia, and Hungary may seem historically remote, but the apex of each of them—a "golden age" before the Turks and the Austrians or the Germans and the Russians came and conquered—have played a vital role in each of these nations' historical imaginations right up into the twentieth century.

For example, when the borders of Central Europe were redrawn after World War I, many Central Europeans looked at the territorial dismemberment of the Austrian and Russian empires as an opportunity to reestablish their "historical borders" which had been violated centuries beforehand—and not in terms of an ethnically defined policy of "national self-determination" aimed at creating homogeneous nation-states that would require unprecedented new borders. In other words, after World War I, many of the "new" states in the region wanted their "old" borders to be reestablished, and this objective became a source of conflict among neighbors, because the historical borders either had been fluid throughout the ages or did not correspond to national borders in the ethnic sense of the word.

It is important to recognize the vitality of historical imagination in this context. Otherwise, the claims of the Poles in 1918, who looked back to the frontiers of the Polish–Lithuanian Republic of 1772, or the Czechs and the Hungarians, who talked about the historical inviolability of the borders of the medieval kingdoms of Bohemia and Hungary after World War I—the former with and the latter without success—would be incomprehensible.

Croatian and Serbian nationalists provide the best contemporary examples of thinking in these terms. For each of them, the deterioration of Yugoslavia after 1989 represented an opportunity to restore national freedoms that had been long lost. After the death of Zvonimir, the Croatian king, in 1089, the Croatian nobility elected the king of Hungary to the Croatian throne. The personal and dynastic union of these two kingdoms extended the domains of the kingdom of Hungary to the Adriatic and is viewed as a windfall in Hungarian history. The Croats, however, tend to interpret it as an early and tragic loss of national independence which took 900 years to reestablish. For many Serbian nationalists, the current attempts to create a Greater Serbian state can be historically legitimized as "restoring" the medieval kingdom of Serbia. The Turkish victory at the Battle of Kosovo in 1389 ushered in the end of the Serbia's medieval empire on the Balkans, and the Serbs had to wait 600 years to start reestablishing it.

These examples illustrate the extent to which the peoples of Central Europe, who were "independent nations" during the Middle Ages but became subject nations in the following centuries, have an intimate relationship to their distant pasts or tend to think in terms of a longer historical continuum.

The Disunited German Empire

The middle of the thirteenth century provides many examples of the dynamics of feudal politics in Central Europe, and medieval Germany is a good illustration of the centrifugal tendencies inherent in feudal forms of political organization. The kings of Germany, who were elected by a select group of feudal lords, bore the title "Roman King of Germany" after they had been crowned in Aachen, the capital of Charlemagne's former empire, and they received the title "Holy Roman Emperor" if they were crowned by the pope in Rome. Whether or not imperial legitimacy was contingent on papal confirmation was a hotly debated issue among medieval contemporaries. The emperors and their supporters preferred to view the emperor as God's highest representative on earth, a position that the papacy and papal partisans claimed for the pope. This dispute was a constant cause of conflict between secular and ecclesiastical authorities. It also was a source of divided loyalties within the empire, which gave "imperial" and "papal" parties a convenient vehicle for realizing less lofty political interests in the name of principle. It also cultivated attitudes of particularism and helped lay the foundations for an "anti-Roman" sentiment in Germany that was to flourish later during the Reformation.

The practice of papal coronation for the emperor was abandoned in the fourteenth century, which made the title of "Holy Roman Emperor" a secular and German affair instead of a papal and Roman one, and the addition of the qualification "of the German Nation" to the imperial title reflected the scope of the emperor's claims. But the kings of Germany as the "Holy Roman Emperors of the German Nation" never managed to overcome the particularism that prevailed in the empire. On the one hand, the noble lords of the empire's numerous feudal estates were obligated to recognize the regal and imperial claims of the kings they elected, were bound by the codes of chivalry to demonstrate their subordination at court by participating in the rituals of fealty, and were required as knights to go to war under certain circumstances. On the other hand, the kings were technically the patrons and benefactors of the nobles, and on election the kings confirmed the rights of their subordinates to their titles and properties in exchange for their loyalty and services. As the highest temporal authority, the king could recall, for example, titles and properties if one of his vassals were "lawless" or died without legitimate heirs, and regrant them. However, within the empire there was an inherent conflict between the centralizing aspirations of German kings with imperial titles and intentions and the regional interests of the feudal lords, who technically were their vassals but resisted every attempt at centralization as an infringement on their particular rights.

During the thirteenth century, Germany's feudal estates managed to replace the tradition of hereditary monarchy with the institution of electoral monarchy, and the idea of the German empire as a confederation of feudal lords, who considered themselves the authentic representatives of the "German nation," gradually replaced the identification of the empire with the German kings as emperors. This inversion of the idea of sovereignty greatly strengthened the position of the individual feudal estates in Germany and was a turning point in the empire's constitutional history. It made the feudal parts of the empire more powerful than the regal or imperial whole, and this constitutional development helped make German disunity the status quo for centuries.

Although it would be a mistake to underestimate how formidable the empire was to medieval contemporaries, it remained throughout the Middle Ages a decentralized feudal state or, rather, a loose affiliation of fundamentally autonomous feudal states. Thereafter, the German tradition of feudal particularism also was reinforced by the confessional disputes of the Reformation and the Counter-Reformation. All attempts to consolidate the ideal German empire into a real one failed. Despite the theoretical unity of the Holy Roman Empire of the German Nation, which continued to play an important role in the German idea of Germany, the factual disunity of Germany became an established part of the European order until the late nineteenth century. For example, in 1648 when the Peace of Westphalia ended the Thirty Years' War, the last great early modern religious conflict among European Christians, there were more than 300 independent German states and literally thousands of sovereign subentities like "free cities" or "free monasteries." After the Napoleonic Wars at the beginning of the nineteenth century, which led to a considerable simplification of the political map of Germany, there still were forty German states.

In light of these circumstances, retrospective generalizations about "Germany" before the end of the nineteenth century or an identification of "the German" with "the Prussian" thereafter are dangerous because they tend to overlook the strength and diversity of those regional traditions in Germany that have feudal origins. During World War II, for example, Allied planners devised several scenarios for weakening "imperial" Germany, and they seriously considered rejuvenating the German tradition of particularism, by creating a number of smaller German states, each of which would have had a regional identity based on historical precedents reaching back to the Middle Ages. Whether the unification of Germany was (and is) the logical or desirable consequence of German history or a dangerous exception to the German historical rule of disunity is basically a question of the length of historical perspective assumed. The unified German national state that existed from 1871 until 1945 (and was reestablished in 1990) is a historical anomaly compared with the German tradition of disunity.

Central Europeans often view the history of Central Europe in terms of a proverbial and imperial German *Drang nach Osten,* a "drive to the east," or as a series of Slavic–German struggles that may be interpreted as archetypal East–West conflicts. Although it would be misleading to depreciate the long-term importance of German missionary work and settlement beyond the eastern borders of the empire during the Middle Ages, the major foreign policy thrust of German kings then was a "drive to the south"—a series of futile imperial attempts to gain control of Italy, which led to an ongoing struggle between the German kings and the papacy. In comparison with this "North–South" conflict or the various attempts to consolidate the empire from within, the eastern frontier of the empire was, in many respects, a theater of subordinate political importance. On and beyond this frontier, however, several families, the first generation of Central European dynasties, engaged in struggles for hegemony and territory.

Austrian, Bohemian, Hungarian, and Polish Dynasties

During the tenth century, a series of *Marken*—in Old German, *Mark* meant both "province" and "border"—were established along the turbulent eastern frontiers of the Holy Roman Empire to secure its borders, and in 976 a noble German family, the Babenbergs, was entrusted with a duchy in the Danube Valley called Ostarrichi, literally the "eastern realm," which laid the historical foundations for Österreich, or Austria. The Babenbergs gradually worked their way down the Danube and finally established a ducal residence in Vienna, not far from the frontiers of the Kingdom of Hungary ruled by the Árpád dynasty (896–1301), which had its seat in the Hungarian Plain but ruled a multinational empire extending north and east to the Carpathian Mountains (including contemporary Slovakia, part of Ukraine, and Romanian Transylvania), south to Serbia, and southwest to Croatia. North of the Babenbergs' realm, the Přemysl dynasty (895–1306) had consolidated itself on the plateau of the Bohemian Massif, and north of the Kingdom of Hungary the Piasts of Poland (860–1370) had established a loosely knit kingdom on the plains between the Carpathian Mountains and the Baltic Sea in the Vistula Valley.

Each of these four families was confronted with similar problems. On the one hand, they had the task of consolidating their domestic power over their own feudal vassals or estates, whose interests frequently clashed with their own, and on the other, they had to maintain their holdings or extend them at the expense of their neighbors. The outcome of these domestic struggles made negotiable the relationships of feudal kings to their own frequently powerful vassals. Since political power in the medieval world was personally exercised by individuals, not anonymously administered by modern institutions or states, its scope was limited by any contemporary standards. Consequently, the fate of dynasties depended to a great extent on their leading figures' personal mastery of the political skills of diplomacy and warfare.

Feudal borders also were frequently renegotiated after conflicts, and there were many chronic points of friction among these four dynasties. Both the Babenbergs and the Árpáds were interested in rounding out their holdings along the contemporary Austrian–Hungarian border at their respective neighbor's expense. The Czech Přemysls were engaged in an intermittent struggle with the Polish Piasts for control over the territories between the Bohemian Basin and the Vistula Valley: to the southeast, Moravia, which they gained, and to the northeast, Silesia, which often changed hands before becoming part of the Bohemian realm in the fourteenth century.

It also is important to note that there was no medieval "Kingdom of Slovakia." Rather, Slovakia was part of the Kingdom of Hungary from about the year 1000 until 1918, and the Slovaks were predominantly peasants with Hungarian lords. After World War I, Slovakia united with the predominantly Czech lands of Bohemia and Moravia to form the Republic of Czechoslovakia, and the only precedent for an independent Slovakian state is an embarrassing one: a clerical–authoritarian puppet state that collaborated with Nazi Germany from 1939 to 1945. However, the Czechs, who look back at their own royal traditions and a history of comparatively higher cultural and economic development than that of the Slovaks, often view the Slovaks as a culturally underdeveloped "subject nation" of peasants and country bumpkins. Such attitudes contributed to the deterioration of Czechoslovakia after 1989.

This is just one example of an entire series of Central European national stereotypes and prejudices that go back to medieval relationships. There were larger nations that historically had been lords—like the Austrians (as Germans in the medieval sense of the word), Hungarians, Czechs, and Poles—and smaller nations that they viewed as "natural" subjects: Slovenes, Croats, and Serbs in southern Central Europe; Romanians in the southeast; Slovaks in the middle; and Ukrainians and Belarussians in the east. This idea of a hierarchy of nations in Central Europe was reinforced during the nineteenth century, when the amalgam of nationalism and Romanticism popularized the idea that the superiority of some nations had been demonstrated by the roles they had played as historical agents in the past, regardless of how remote, and that the passivity or inferiority of others had been documented by the fact that they could not look back on comparable traditions or achievements. Having been subjects instead of lords or objects instead of agents of history, the "subject nations" were frequently considered to be peoples with "no history."

Bohemia's Imperial Bid:
King Otakar's Thirteenth-Century Empire

In 1246, the death of Friedrich "the Quarrelsome," the last Babenberg Duke of Austria, created one of the first great Central European opportunities for empire building, in the medieval sense of the word. Killed in a border quarrel with the Hungarians, Friedrich had no male heir to assume his title, which left open the question of the succession of his duchy. Technically speaking, the King of Germany had the right to dispose of the titles and territories vacated by Friedrich's death because Austria was a duchy of the Holy Roman Empire, but the empire was in such a state of disarray in the middle of the thirteenth century—two competing kings had been elected by conflicting parties of feudal lords—that the issue remained unresolved. Nonetheless, Otakar II, the king of Bohemia, and Béla IV, the king of Hungary, were not concerned about the legal technicalities surrounding the vacant ducal seat of the Babenbergs, and they both were interested in the real opportunities that Friedrich's death and the ensuing power vacuum presented. Béla acted quickly and seized the southern half of the Babenberg holdings, the province of Styria, where he placed his son Stephen as ruler.

Otakar's entry into Austria was more diplomatic. He negotiated with the Babenberg vassals in the Danube Valley, who were tired of the conflicts and insecurity the interregnum had caused and prepared to accept Otakar as their lord, and then in 1251 he married Friedrich von Babenberg's sister, Margaret, a woman more than twenty years his senior, in order to strengthen the legitimacy of his acquisitions. He began calling himself *dux Austriae,* Duke of Austria, and he consolidated his new holdings by using a policy of resolutely punishing disobedience and generously rewarding loyalty.

During 1254/1255 Otakar participated in a crusade led by the Order of the Teutonic Knights against the indigenous pagan inhabitants of Prussia on the Baltic coast, which exposed him to the possibilities for expansion in the plains of the north, but his immediate interest was rounding out and consolidating his holdings in the south. In 1261, he drove the Hungarians out of Styria, gained the allegiance of the Styrian estates, and, in the process of negotiating a peace settlement with the Hungarians, arranged an engagement with Kunhata, a granddaughter of the Hungarian king. This interdynastic marriage, so typical of medieval politics, was facilitated by a papal dispensation he received to divorce his wife, Margaret, who was too old to bear the children he urgently needed as successors, and was designed to help cement the peace with the Hungarians. Although Otakar needed to establish stability on the eastern borders of his realms in order to pursue his interests in the north and the south, his marriage to Kunhata could not overcome the long-standing Bohemian–Hungarian rivalry or repress his newly acquired Hungarian in-laws' desire for revenge.

Motivated by a vague papal promise of attaining "perpetual dominion" over heathen territories in Lithuania, Otakar undertook a second crusade in 1267 to assist the Teutonic Knights in their allegedly Christian mission of converting eastern Central Europe's last stronghold of infidels—the modern military term for these crusades would be "pacification"—and he entertained the idea of establishing a territorial base of operations on the Baltic that would eventually allow him to exercise more influence over the fragmented holdings of the Polish Piast dynasty. This aspiration never left Otakar, whose interests turned south once again, where he gained control of Carinthia and Carniola, two duchies in contemporary southern Austria and Slovenia. Otakar's political vision was, as one medieval chronicler observed, to extend his power *ut a mari usque ad mare,* "from the Baltic Sea to the Adriatic Sea," *et terminos orbis,* "and the limits of the world,"[1] and some historians see his plans as the first manifestation of the idea of a "Danube confederation," or multinational Central European empire.

Otakar's plans were challenged in 1273 when Rudolph von Habsburg, a nobleman with holdings in southern Germany and Switzerland, was elected king of Germany. One of Rudolph's first royal acts was to reclaim the duchies of the empire that had been illegally occupied before his election, among them Otakar's acquisitions, in order to enhance his own holdings. Although Rudolph had the law of the empire on his side, Otakar was squatting on the properties in question, and he initially tried to bargain with Rudolph, a situation complicated by the fact that Otakar technically was Rudolph's vassal because Bohemia was part of the Holy Roman Empire. Otakar wanted to make his recognition of Rudolph as king contingent upon Rudolph's recognition of Otakar's hereditary titles and holdings in Bohemia as well as the holdings he had illegally acquired in the past twenty-five years, but Rudolph showed no willingness to negotiate. In 1276, Rudolph organized an army with the help of cooperative German lords and dissatisfied Austrian ones, and he managed to mobilize the Hungarians against Otakar. (The use of national terminology here may be a bit misleading. In this context, Germany, Austria, Bohemia, and Hungary should be treated as geographic and, in some cases, dynastic concepts, not as primordial national states. Rudolph von Habsburg, for example, was a German from Switzerland who ruled in Austria without being German, Swiss, or Austrian as we usually understand the terms. Medieval power was not "national.")

Rudolph marched on Austria and forced Otakar to renounce his claims. Otakar's preparedness to reconcile himself with Rudolph was merely a tactical ploy, however. Outnumbered in 1276, he appealed to the interests and fears of his Slavic neighbors to the north in Silesia and Poland by vividly describing the Germans' territorial greed in terms of their "never satiated mouths," "filthy hands," and "vile desires." Within two years Otakar felt that he had organized enough support to settle his score with Rudolph, who relied on loyal members of the German and Austrian estates and an alliance with the Hungarians to defend his claims. In accordance with the code of chivalry, Otakar and Rudolph agreed on a time and place to do battle, and their armies, ranging from knights on armored horses to archers, each allegedly 20,000 strong, met on the Marchfeld Plain north of Vienna on August 26, 1278.

When the opposing armies clashed on the battlefield, Otakar's troops held their ground and then appeared to be gaining the upper hand. Although the only honorable form of knightly combat was frontal, Rudolph had made provisions for a tactically brilliant but chivalrously despicable surprise attack, an ambush on one of Otakar's flanks, which was executed so effectively by a small group of fully armored knights that it threw Otakar's troops into disarray. They panicked and fled, and once Otakar recognized the hopelessness of the situation, he followed them. Although the exact circumstances of his death have never been completely clarified, he apparently was taken captive by personal enemies—some of his own disgruntled

Czech vassals—disarmed, and murdered. After Rudolph's battlefield tactics, this was the second great violation of the code of chivalry that day.

In the nineteenth century, there was a tendency to see Otakar as a primordial representative of Pan-Slavism or, conversely, to regard Rudolph's success as a "German victory" over a "Slavic threat," but these are basically examples of the type of nationalistic pathos and chauvinism that can accompany the interpretation of key medieval events. Rudolph's victory was a turning point in the history of Central Europe, nevertheless, in that it established the Habsburgs as a contender in the Danube Basin. Aside from demonstrating greater longevity than any other European dynasty—the Habsburgs ruled for 640 years, from 1278 until 1918—they eventually realized their own version of a Danube empire some centuries later.

Although it is tempting to say that Bohemia's imperial aspirations died on the battlefield with Otakar, this was not the case. In 1298, Otakar's son Wenceslas II arranged an engagement between his nine-year-old son, Wenceslas III, and Elizabeth, a daughter of Andrew III, the king of Hungary, and in 1300 Wenceslas II was also crowned king of Poland, not as an act of Slavic solidarity, but in an attempt to find a strong man from the outside to overcome the fragmentation of the Polish kingdom. When Andrew III, the last male in the Hungarian Árpád dynastic line, died in 1301, the Přemysls made their claim to the crown of Hungary, but they met the resistance of the Hungarian magnates and the pope, who promoted the interests of an even more distant foreigner: Charles Robert from the Neapolitan line of the French Anjou dynasty, who was crowned king of Hungary in 1308.

As provocative as the vision of unifying the Bohemian, Polish, and Hungarian crowns may have been, it was as unrealistic as it was short lived. The Přemysl dynasty had neither the resources nor the support it needed to realize such ambitious plans. Wenceslas II died in 1305, and the Přemysl dynasty expired one year later when his son Wenceslas III was murdered under unclear circumstances on his way to assert his interests in Poland. Contemporaries attributed the regicide to agents of the king of Germany, his own disgruntled Czech vassals, or Hungarian or Polish nobles. The Habsburgs of Austria immediately tried to seize the Bohemian throne vacated by Wenceslas III's death, a move reminiscent of Otakar's old aspirations, though with reversed roles, but the newly elected king of Germany, Henry VII von Luxemburg, managed to negotiate his son John onto the vacant throne by arranging a wedding with a Přemysl princess and cajoling the Bohemian nobility.

The Middle Ages were a period devoid of nationalism in the modern sense of the word, but even so, Central Europeans alternately interpret medieval history in a spirit of cosmopolitanism or through the spectacles of nationalism. In the cosmopolitan vein, for example, Czechs look back at success of the Luxemburg dynasty in Bohemia between 1310 and 1437 as one of the high points in their history, although the Luxemburgs were foreigners and "Germans" in the medieval sense of the word. For example, Charles of Luxemburg, King of Bohemia, was elected king of Germany in 1346 and crowned as the Holy Roman Emperor Charles IV in Rome in 1355, two events that made Prague an imperial capital. Charles founded the first Central European university in 1348, not in Germany, but in Prague, and his reign is generally recognized as a period of peace, prosperity, and cultural blossom.[2] Similarly, Hungarians seem to have no problem with the fact that Louis I of Anjou (1326–1382), a king who went down in Hungarian history as "the Great," was a French dynastic transplant via Naples, because he ambitiously consolidated and expanded the Kingdom of Hungary.

Dynastic politics can be construed to represent the beginning of a long tradition of confederative plans for Central Europe. The brief unification of the Bohemian and Polish crowns under Wenceslas II from 1300 to 1305 or the Přemysl's aspirations in Hungary may have been chances to form a union or unions that would have been more successful in resisting the future aggression of larger and stronger neighbors like the Germans and the Russians. (The idea of having missed an important historical opportunity 500 or 600 years ago is very Central European.) Nevertheless, during World War II, leading Polish and Czechoslovak politicians in exile, General Władysław Sikorski and Eduard Beneš, discussed the idea of a Czechoslovak–Polish confederation.[3] In January 1990 both the American security expert Zbigniew Brzezinski and the foreign minister of the new Czechoslovak reform government, Jiří Dienstbier, speculated that a Czechoslovak–Polish confederation could be one means of helping the western Slavs resist in the future the influence of larger neighbors like the Soviet Union and a unified Germany.

Poles and Hungarians also look back fondly at the period between 1370 and 1385, during which Louis the Great, king of Hungary, was also king of Poland, although the long-term viability of this constellation was nil. The fact that the magnates of Hungary elected a number of kings from the Polish dynastic line in the following 150 years and a Hungarian was elected king of Poland in the sixteenth century can be seen as neighborly reciprocal gestures. Many patterns of conflict and cooperation in Central Europe were established in the Middle Ages, and they still play an important role in the Central European historical imagination. The ambivalent relationship that most Central Europeans have to the Germans provides perhaps the best example of this point.

The German "Drive to the East," 1200–1350

It is common to interpret the history of Europe in terms of predominantly Western innovations that moved east. The German-speaking world traditionally has played a formative role in the history of Central Europe because it has been the primary transmitter of Western ideas to its eastern neighbors. In the early Middle Ages, for example, German dioceses and missionaries played a decisive role in converting the pagan peoples of the east to Western Christianity. One of the consequences of these conversions was the adoption of feudalism as a Western form of political and social organization that was in many respects superior to the tribal structures it replaced. Christians tilled the soil, and their lords were constrained, in theory at least, by the rule of law. There are later examples of this West–East pattern of trans-mission in the Middle Ages: German contributions to the development of the east, a gradual movement eastward of the borders of the German-speaking world, and the establishment of German colonies or settlements through-out the eastern half of Central Europe.

The importance of German culture and civilization for Germany's east-ern neighbors and this West–East mode of transmission were established early and proved to be enduring. German influences traditionally have been a source of stimulation and enrichment for their non-German neighbors to the east, and Central Europeans who are prepared to take a dispassionate look at their national traditions readily recognize the substantial influence of German philosophy, literature, science, technology, and investment on their own cultures and countries. But this appreciation is seldom devoid of ambiguity because the Germans not only exercised a congenial culturally enriching influence; they also often came as conquerors and overlords.

Before the nineteenth century, historians showed relatively little interest in the medieval phenomenon that came to be called the German *Ostbewe-gung*, the "eastward movement," or the *Drang nach Osten*, the "drive to the east." However, nineteenth-century nationalism and Romanticism threw a new light on this period, which was amply interpreted by messianic chau-vinists of German culture as an early manifestation of the superiority of Ger-man culture or, conversely, criticized by Slavic historians as the forerunner of German imperialism. The German "drive to the east" was, however, nei-ther an example of cosmic historical forces at work nor a primordial Ger-man imperial conspiracy but basically the result of population pressures in the German empire combined with the presence of personal and econom-ic opportunity outside the German-speaking world. From 1200 until 1350, the year the plague, or Black Death, began taking its toll in Europe, there was a wave of German emigration to the kingdoms of Poland, Bohemia, and Hungary.

During the twelfth century, a medieval agricultural revolution provided the basis for an unprecedented population boom. The transition from a two- to a three-field system of cultivation, a French innovation based on the in-troduction of winter crops, and the improvement of the most primitive forms of agricultural technology—like the metal plowshare, the scythe in its current form, and the use of horses instead of oxen—made agricultural pro-duction more intensive and extensive, and the consequential growth in pop-ulation in Germany provided the human material for "colonies" or settle-ments in the less densely populated east.

Enterprising feudal lords recognized that their own prosperity depend-ed on their subjects' productivity, and they invited groups of German farm-ers and burghers, which medieval chronicles called *hospites*, or "guests," to cultivate their lands and trade in their towns and cities. The *Theutonici*, or "Germans," were enticed by the legal conditions of land tenure or com-merce which were more favorable than those prevailing in the German em-pire and less restrictive than the local or traditional laws "hosts" applied to their indigenous subjects. During the nineteenth century, German historians made quite an affair out of the introduction of the *ius Theutonicum,* the so-called German law, used to attract settlers as well as the adoption of German municipal corporate charters based on the "Law of Magdeburg" by cities outside the German-speaking world, because these innovations fit well into their conception of the Germans as "carriers of culture" to an eastern wilderness. German dioceses had played an important role in the initial Christianization of Central Europe, and then German law "civilized" it.

German law was not exclusively German in origin, nor was it solely applied to Germans. Rather, it was part of the package deal that lords were willing to offer settlers from Germany, other "guests," and sometimes their own subjects if they were willing to relocate, in exchange for prospects of participating in the fruits of settlers' labor in the future and as compensation for the hardships of pioneering, like draining swamps and felling forests. Self-interest was a primary motive for hosts and guests alike. German settlers offered to their hosts not only manpower but also the transfer of technology and know-how in their rudimentary forms, and "the East" had a function for medieval Germans that was analogous in some respects to that of "the West" for nineteenth-century Americans. One thing the histories of both these otherwise disparate frontiers have in common is the role they played in the formation of similar national myths. German historians later stylized the "eastward movement" into a "taming of the wilderness" and a Teutonic form of "manifest destiny."

The history of German settlement in the east and the various organizational forms developed to promote it is an intricate topic.[4] A few generalizations must suffice here as points of orientation. There were a number of different patterns of settlement. In some cases, German settlers gradually displaced or absorbed the indigenous populations. The gradual Bavarian settlement of the Danube Valley and the eastern Alps between 800 and 1000 created a German-speaking peninsula in the Slavic world and laid the foundations for Austria. (Whether the Slavic population was displaced or assimilated is not clear.) Between 1000 and 1200, Germans gradually settled the areas coextensive with contemporary East Germany, which made Bohemia a Slavic-speaking peninsula in the German-speaking world. Between roughly 1200 and 1350, there was a virtual boom of settlement in areas farther east like Silesia and along the Baltic coast: parts of contemporary Poland. The borderlands of Bohemia and Moravia also became relatively homogeneous German-speaking areas during this time and represented another German "penetration" of the Slavic-speaking world.

A second common pattern of development was the establishment of "linguistic islands"—German-speaking towns, villages, and farming communities of varying sizes—scattered throughout the medieval kingdoms of Poland, Bohemia, and Hungary and as faraway as the Ukraine. The German or "Saxon" colonization of Transylvania in the Carpathian Mountains, which the kings of Hungary vigorously encouraged during the thirteenth century, is a good example of a large "island" that maintained its German linguistic and cultural identity right into the twentieth century. Although German "guests" also assimilated into their host cultures, many scattered, smaller "islands"

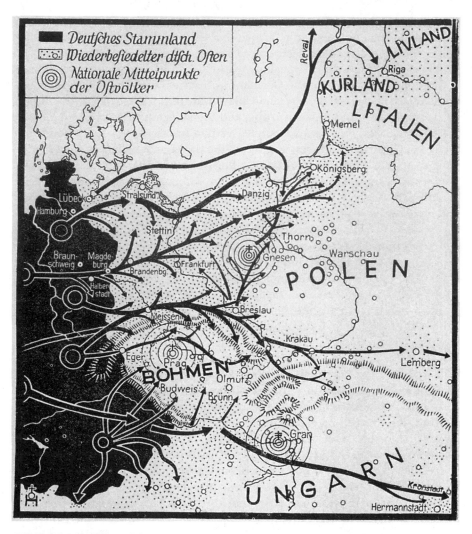

With the exception of the Teutonic Order, German settlement in various regions in East Central Europe from the thirteenth through the eighteenth centuries was a peaceful process overall. However, starting in the nineteenth century Geman nationalists began to portray it as a conquest just as the non-German nations of the region began to perceive it as age-old aggression. Black areas represent German "core territory"; arrows, the patterns of the German "drive to the East"; dotted areas, the "resettled [*sic*] German East"; and concentric circles, the "national centers of the Eastern peoples." ("The Greatest Colonial Achievement in History: The German Resettlement [*sic*] of the East from the 12th to the 14th Centuries," map from a National Socialist tract by A. Hillen Ziegfeld, *1000 Jahre deutsche Kolonisation und Siedlung* [1000 Years of German Colonization and Settlement] [Berlin: Edwing Runge Verlag, 1943], p. 15; Austrian National Library)

also retained their ethnic homogeneity and identity. In other cases, German burghers established themselves as a trading class in foreign towns and cities, along with the Jews. (The emigration of Western European Jews to East Central Europe increased steadily after the thirteenth century, but the motives for the Jewish migration were different from those of the German "pioneers." That is, Western European Jews were expelled from the west or fled to the east—in particular to the kingdom of Poland—to escape religious persecution.)

The initiators of the German settlement were royal or noble non-German hosts, not the German guests, and so we should not assume that the Polish, Czech, or Hungarian nobles who invited the German settlers were either "teutonophiles" or in a position to anticipate the long-term "national consequences" of their policies. In other words, neither they nor the German settlers had the extensive prejudices regarding themselves and foreigners that nineteenth-century nationalism produced; they did not think in terms of nations or states in the modern sense of the word. German colonization also cannot be construed as some kind of German "national policy" or a teleological movement of *das deutsche Volk*. On the contrary, it was a question of foreign invitation and individual initiative.

German settlers had a predominantly symbiotic relationship with their host cultures, from the Middle Ages until the nineteenth century, which eventually poisoned the traditions of cohabitation with nationalism. German historians began exalting the process of medieval settlement as a "heroic deed of the German people" or the "greatest colonial achievement in history," just as Czech historians, for example, began to describe the Germans as a bunch of foreign parasites or predators who unscrupulously enriched themselves at the cost of the Czechs.

The physical presence of millions of Germans outside Germany,[5] combined with an exaggerated German nationalistic interpretation of the Middle Ages in the nineteenth century, also contributed to the elaboration of the concept of Central Europe as a German *Sprach- und Kulturraum*, a "linguistic and cultural space." This idea depreciated the autonomous cultural achievements and traditions of the non-German peoples of Central Europe, and these nineteenth-century attitudes helped lay the foundations for Adolf Hitler's twentieth-century ideology of race and space.

The Germans were not, however, the only inhabitants of the Northern European Plain that have shown a historical propensity for eastern expansion. For centuries, proponents of the French imperial idea regarded the Rhine as the eastern "natural border" of France in a manner similar to the spirit in which German imperialists viewed the Vistula. Poland had a long tradition of eastward expansion, and Russia eventually extended its empire from the Ural Mountains to the Pacific Ocean.

Some historians and geographers have explained this phenomenon as the inherent tendency of states to expand in the direction of least resistance, and they have often supplemented this theory with a chauvinistic and foreboding doctrine of cultural types based on the assumption of a West–East *Kulturgefälle*, a "cultural gradient" or "decline," or the inherent ability of "su-

perior" Western cultures to overcome "inferior" Eastern ones.[6] However, in
the context of Central Europe, "the East" always has been a concept used
relative to national frontiers. For the French, the East as the beginning of a
"cultural decline" started in Germany, but for the Germans it began in Bohemia or Poland. For the Czechs it began in Slovakia, and for the Poles in
Ukraine, Belarus, or Russia. A regional variation of the same type of pattern
can be found in southern Central Europe: As "Germans," many Austrians
looked down on Hungarians, and at their worst, Austrians and Hungarians
shared a disdain for their Slavic neighbors to the south on the Balkan Peninsula, to the north in Bohemia, Moravia, and Slovakia, and to the east in
general.

Stemming the German Tide?
The Battle of Grunwald

Although the medieval German settlement of the east was a peaceful process
overall, there was one notable exception that played an important role in
the historical imagination of the Poles and the Germans in particular: the
activities of the "Order of the Hospital of the Blessed Virgin Mary of the German House of Jerusalem," better known as the Teutonic Knights. This order was a product of the Crusades; the fall of Jerusalem in 1187 and the failure of the Third Crusade forced them to relocate their activities to Europe,
where they were reconstituted as a chivalric order that offered its services to
any ruler who was willing to pay them to fight pagans and infidels. Their
Central European career began with a brief stint in Transylvania under the
patronage of the king of Hungary in 1224 and 1225, but then he released
them, allegedly because of the lack of loyalty they showed their royal patron.

   The Teutonic Knights did draw themselves to the attention of Conrad of
Mazovia, a Piast prince who ruled a realm in central Poland. Conrad was engaged in an ambitious operation, the conversion and subjugation of his pagan neighbors to the north in Prussia, but he was short of manpower. In
1226, he offered to give the Teutonic Knights the district of Chelmo (or
Kulm), which would provide them with a base of operations and reward
them for their efforts, and shortly thereafter the Teutonic Knights appeared
on the scene to assume their "Christian duty." For the next six decades they
converted the Prussians using military instead of missionary methods, the
sword instead of the Gospel, and they established a well-organized realm
that they stocked with German settlers from the West. Much to the consternation of their original Polish hosts, the Teutonic Knights became a formidable continental power in their own right and skillfully managed to have
their operations sanctioned by the pope and the German emperor. They
also had the audacity to pocket Gdańsk, a vital port on the mouth of the Vistula, which they called Danzig, as well as its hinterland of eastern Pomerania. The acquisition of these territories effectively sealed off the Poles from
free access to the sea and helped create a problem that was to last for centuries.

At the peak of its development around the end of the fourteenth century, the Order of the Teutonic Knights controlled Prussia, Estonia, and Latvia.[7] They continued their crusading in the east in an attempt to "convert" and subjugate Lithuania, the last pagan stronghold of Central Europe, and they became embroiled in intermittent conflicts with the Poles. Then, a Polish–Lithuanian interdynastic marriage in 1386, one of the conditions of which was the conversion of Lithuania to Christianity, robbed the Teutonic Knights of their missionary legitimacy as crusaders, in addition to laying the cornerstone for the Jagiellonian dynasty: a personal union of the kingdom of Poland with Lithuania that lasted for centuries and initially functioned as an anti-Teutonic coalition.

There were a number of long-standing points of contention between the Teutonic Knights and their Slavic neighbors: the control of the Vistula, disputes over borders, and the Teutonic Knights' ambitious policies of acquisition and colonization. The day of reckoning came on July 15, 1410, near the village of Grunwald in Prussia. The king of Poland, Władysław Jagiełło, had organized a motley "Pan-Slavic" army of some 39,000, consisting of Poles, Lithuanians, Czechs, and Ukrainians and supported by Tatars and troops from as far away as Romanian Wallachia. These troops engaged the Teutonic Knights, a force 27,000 strong under the leadership of the order's Grand Master, Ulrich von Jungingen, on the battlefield near the village of Grunwald. Given the sources, the course of the battle and the relative merits of each "national contingent" of the Polish army are rather difficult to summarize, but by the end of the day approximately half the Teutonic Knights were dead, and the other half had been taken prisoner for ransom. As resounding as the defeat may have been, the conditions of peace were rather mild. The Teutonic Knights agreed to withdraw from part of Lithuania, and they guaranteed free trade on the Vistula. These relatively minor concessions were completely disproportionate to the enormity that the Battle of Grunwald later assumed in the Polish historical memory.

During the nineteenth century, the Teutonic Knights played a central role in Polish historical poetry and literature, which usually made little or no distinction between them and the Germans in general and depicted them as a pack of bloodthirsty, sadistic, and unscrupulous invaders, an image diametrically opposed to the contemporary German Romantic depiction of the Teutonic Knights as those noble representatives of Christian culture and German chivalry who heroically civilized the east. One of the first Polish medieval poems commemorating the Battle of Grunwald compared it with a Polish David's victory over a German Goliath, and Adam Mickiewicz, the Polish national poet of the nineteenth century, saw the Polish conflict with the Order of the Teutonic Knights as a metaphor for the struggles of smaller oppressed nations like the Poles against larger tyrants like the Germans and the Russians. There also is a long Polish tradition of regarding the Teutonic Knights as the precursors of future German aggression and oppression, like the Prussian participation in the division of Poland after 1772 or the German occupation of Poland during World War II. The Battle of Grunwald also frequently has been stylized into a national or even racial struggle between Germans and Slavs. In Soviet mythology, for example, the Teutonic Knights were the medieval forerunners of Hitler's armies, which made the Battle of Grunwald the medieval Slavic counterpart of stemming the German tide at Stalingrad in 1942/1943.[8]

Neither the Order of the Teutonic Knights nor the Battle of Grunwald, which the Germans refer to using a different name, Tannenberg, played the central role in German history or historical literature that they did for the Slavs in general or the Poles in particular. Nonetheless, the Germans interpreted their victory over the Russians on the eastern front at the beginning of the World War I as a modern Battle of Tannenberg and a belated rectification of the historical record. In addition, Hitler commemorated this victory by giving his plans for the German invasion of Poland in 1939 the code name Operation Tannenberg. Even though the activities of the Order of the Teutonic Knights never reached into Russia, the Nazis also drew parallels between the order's medieval conquest and settlement of the east and their invasion of the Soviet Union in 1941. *Blitzkrieg* and *Lebensraum* were merely the modern versions of the Teutonic Knights' "eastern mission"—German swords and plowshares as the means of civilizing the eastern heathens and providing the German people with more space to live. The fact that one SS division was named after the Order of the Teutonic Knights merely demonstrates to what extent the Nazis used and abused historical precedents for their purposes.

Historians have done a tremendous amount of work in recent decades in an attempt to portray the role of the Teutonic Knights in an manner devoid of nationalistic and Romantic prejudices, and this enterprise has been complemented by a balanced attempt by all the nations involved to evaluate dispassionately the role of German settlement in East Central Europe in the Middle Ages in general. However, this has been an uphill battle because something as academically remote as the discoveries of professional medievalists does not immediately debunk national myths so dear to the people who believe in them.

The Great Late Medieval Kingdoms

Poland and Hungary, 1350–1500

When Czechs, Hungarians, and Poles look back on their histories, they share a sense of tragedy related to those events leading up to the loss of "national freedom," and for the Hungarians and the Poles, this feeling of loss is often intensified by reminiscences about extensive territories lost as well. If the old historical kingdoms of Poland and Hungary were "organic wholes" to the same extent that many Poles and Hungarians feel they were, the sensations they experience are akin to the phantom pain that amputees have after having lost a limb. They know that what has been lost is gone for good, but neurological quirks sometimes allow them to feel pains in the missing extremities.

The Czechs are perhaps an exception to the other peoples of Central Europe because they generally do *not* think in "imperial" dimensions (although many Slovaks might contest this statement, because they feel that the Czechs did not treat them as equal national partners as long as they were living together in one state). The grand visions of the last three representatives of the Přemysl dynasty—Otakar; his son, Wenceslas II; and his grandson, Wenceslas III—were medieval and ephemeral, and the kingdom of Bohemia reached its modest territorial zenith in the fourteenth century under the Luxemburgs, by contractually securing the previously contested duchy of Silesia from Poland and briefly ruling the duchy of Brandenburg farther north.

After that point, the Czechs never made any major territorial demands on their neighbors, and the relatively small size and stable borders of the kingdom of Bohemia is one explanation for the fact that the idea of a "Greater Bohemia" has never played a pronounced role in the Czechs' historical imagination or perception of themselves. When Czechs look back, their sense of national loss is not intensified by the recollection of territorial sacrifices as well. This characteristic distinguishes Czechs from Hungarians and Poles, whose sense of loss is exacerbated by the fact that they ruled multinational empires substantially larger than their twentieth-century states. Historical magnitude—the idea of having been great—is an important part of the Central European mode of national self-perception as well as a form of retrospective psychological compensation for smaller states. The rise of the kingdom of Poland or the history of the kingdom of Hungary at its zenith in the late fifteenth century serve as good illustrations of this point.

The Wedding of Poland and Lithuania, 1386

Most people, with the obvious and understandable exceptions of Poles and Lithuanians, do not realize that Poland and Lithuania were a joint continental superpower at one point in their histories. During the fifteenth century, the unified kingdoms of Poland and Lithuania were the largest European power, and the genesis of the Polish–Lithuanian union in 1386 is a good example of how dynastic politics and primal "national alliances" functioned in late feudal and early modern Central Europe.

Toward the end of the fourteenth century, the Polish Piast dynasty expired, but it did so under auspicious circumstances. The reign of the last Piast, Casimir the Great (1333–1370), marked the end of nearly two centuries of fragmentation and the beginning of a phase of "national consolidation," in the medieval sense of the word. Casimir reasserted the crown's authority over the nobility, which had exploited its past weakness, and he expanded his kingdom's holdings to the east and southeast using a skillful combination of warfare and diplomacy. Casimir gave Kraków, the historical capital of Poland, the political and architectural status of a European capital, and he founded Central Europe's second oldest university there in 1364. According to the chronicles, he was loved by his people and respected by his contemporaries, but his long list of achievements unfortunately did not include a legitimate male heir.

The fate of the Piast dynasty hinged on Casimir's procreational misfortune. None of his three legal marriages produced male offspring, and the three sons he did sire, who were the results of amorous adventures with other married women, had no legitimate claim to his patrimony. Like many great politicians, Casimir also preferred to leave unresolved the question of his succession. Although there were a number of options concerning possible lines of succession, the crown was assumed by Casimir's nephew, Louis of Anjou ("the Great"), the king of Hungary, who was a product of a previous interdynastic marriage between Casimir's sister Elizabeth and Charles Robert of Anjou, the first "Neapolitan" king of Hungary.

Modern observers, who are accustomed to thinking in neat categories like nations that correspond to states, and vice versa, or who project modern national identities into the past, are frequently misled or confused by the patterns of interdynastic marriage because they appear to be nationally incompatible. But it made just as much sense to the Polish contemporaries involved to have a Hungarian king of Poland as it did for Hungarians to have a French king of Hungary from Naples, because the nobles of the feudal estates, who elected the kings, considered their particular interests to be the interests of the "nation," in the medieval sense of the word. They had no problem electing a foreign king if they thought he would promote their interests, because the virtual absence of the kinds of attitudes produced by nineteenth–century nationalism made politics a much more cosmopolitan affair.

After the first generation of Central European dynasties expired, the question of succession was resolved in each case by electing "foreigners" as kings instead of choosing "domestic" candidates from among the indigenous nobility. After the Babenberg line died out in Austria in 1240 and Otakar's interregnum, the Austrian estates recognized Rudolph von Habsburg's claims. When the Hungarian Árpád dynasty ended in 1301, the Hungarian magnates were prepared to elect an almost exotically foreign king from Naples, just as the Czech nobility were willing to ally themselves with the powerful but equally foreign and "German" House of Luxemburg after the Přemysl dynasty died out in 1306.

In this respect, the personal union of Hungary and Poland under Louis of Anjou from 1370 until 1382 was no great exception. Before Louis, the kings of Bohemia had also been kings of Poland (1300–1306), and after him there were Polish kings of Hungary (1440–1444, 1490–1526). The crowns of Bohemia and Hungary also were personally united between 1419 and 1459 under Sigismund of Luxemburg, Albrecht von Habsburg, and Albrecht's son Ladislas V, and they were reunited from 1490 until 1526 under a Polish prince from the Jagiellonian dynasty who had been elected to both thrones, Vladislav II, and his son, Louis II.

In each case, there were relative advantages and disadvantages to having a foreigner on the throne, and there seemed to be alternating patterns of benefit and abuse that depended on the personalities, interests, and skill of the respective foreign kings. In some cases, they put the regal resources of their "home kingdoms" at the disposal of their "second kingdoms" and new subjects, or they were the source of beneficial innovation. Exploitation or neglect, however, were also inherent possibilities in such a constellation.

In Hungary, Bohemia, and Poland, the nobility also had a certain logic in turning to foreigners to resolve the domestic crisis of succession that accompanied the expiration of a dynasty. Each indigenous caste of nobility had centuries of experience in infighting, protecting local interests, and resisting royal centralization. Therefore, nobles generally were not interested in seeing someone from their own "national" ranks succeed to a position of royal predominance, because domestic alliances of ambition, jealousy, or greed might upset the delicate balance of interest and self-interest that feudal nobles traditionally cultivated among themselves.

When foreigners were elected king, they frequently made generous concessions to the indigenous nobility. Coronation ceremonies included the guarantee of the newly chosen king to respect the nobility's "ancient rights"

Dynastic Transitions, "Foreign" Kings, and Joint Kingdoms

Archdukes of Austria	Kings of Bohemia	Kings of Hungary	Kings of Poland
Babenberg dynasty († 1248)	Přemyslid dynasty († 1306)	Árpad dynasty († 1301)	Piast dynasty († 1370)
Habsburg dynasty (1278–1918)	Luxemburg dynasty (1310–1437)	Anjou dynasty (1307–1382)	Casimir "the Great" (1333–1370)
		Louis the Great, King of Hungary (1342–1382) — *nephew* → and King of Poland (1370–1382)	
son-in-law → Sigismund of Luxemburg, King of Bohemia (1419–1437)		and King of Hungary (1387–1437)	Polish–Lithuanian union under Władysław Jagiełło I, Jagiellonian dynasty (1386–1572)
Albrecht of Austria → King of Bohemia (1437–1439)		and King of Hungary (1437–1439)	
son →	Bohemian interregnum (1439–1443)	King of Hungary (1440–1444) and	Władysław Jagiełło III, King of Poland (1434–1444)
	Ladislas V, King of Bohemia (1443–1457)	and King of Hungary (1445–1457)	Casimir IV, King of Poland (1446–1492) — *son*
	George Poděbrady (1458–1471) Last Bohemian "national king"	Matthias Corvinus (1458–1490) Last Hungarian "national king"	
	Vladislav II (Jagiellonian) King of Bohemia (1471–1516) and King of Hungary (1490–1516)		
	son → Louis II King of Bohemia (1516–1526) and King of Hungary (1516–1526)		
brother-in-law Ferdinand I Archduke of Austria (1521) → King of Bohemia (elected 1526) and King of Hungary (elected 1527)			

and "ancient freedoms." The kings had to swear that they would—to use a modern term—"uphold the constitution," and one of the peculiarities of the constitutional development of these kingdoms was that the nobility remained much stronger, much longer than in Western Europe. If there was one thing the noble estates of Hungary, Bohemia, and Poland had in common, it was their interest in having kings who would not interfere excessively in their affairs. The large size of these kingdoms' noble classes, which ranged from lesser nobility with little more than titles to magnates and barons with vast estates, also was a comparative structural peculiarity. In the Middle Ages, 4 to 5 percent of the population were "noble" in Hungary (and 7 to 8 percent in Poland), whereas the average in Western Europe was about 1 percent.[1] This kind of noble overrepresentation in the population made them a more formidable special interest group and a greater royal problem than elsewhere.

It is an irony of history that the Hungarian, Bohemian, and Polish nobles, who considered themselves the true representatives of their respective nations, promoted political institutions based on the weakness of central authority, and exactly this characteristic—the persistence of feudal structures—proved to be an enormous deficiency in the future because it reduced the ability of these kingdoms to resist their neighbors (and enemies), who had adopted comparatively modern and more efficient forms of centralized political organization.

The Angevin line of Louis the Great, the king of Hungary and the king of Poland, suffered the same fate as that of his Piast predecessor, Casimir the Great. Having failed to produce a male heir, Louis made arrangements for a female succession and received the assurance of the Hungarian and Polish nobility that the elder of his two daughters, Maria, who was married to Sigismund of Luxemburg, was to succeed him as queen on both thrones. When Louis died in 1382, the Hungarian crown passed via Maria's marriage to Sigismund into the hands of the Luxemburgs for a generation, but the Polish nobility saw that it would be in their best interest not to become part of this powerful constellation and chose instead to elect Louis's younger daughter, the ten-year-old Jadwiga, queen of Poland. After her election, their next task was to find a husband for Jadwiga who would be a suitable king for themselves. Although Jadwiga was technically already engaged to Wilhelm von Habsburg, a prince from Austria whose family was later to base an entire empire on a series of successful interdynastic marriages, the most influential factions of the Polish nobility chased him out of Kraków when he arrived to claim his bride. They decided that another marital scheme would be more advantageous and opted for a conjugal and political relationship with the grand duchy of Lithuania instead of Austria.

Around the turn of the fourteenth century, Lithuania, a country of 25,200 square miles today, was at the peak of its development. It stretched from the shores of the Baltic Sea east toward Moscow and southeast through Ukraine to the shores of the Black Sea and encompassed approximately 350,000 square miles. (Just for the sake of comparison: It was 100,000 square miles larger than France or the U.S. state of Texas.) The Lithuanians, the last pagans of Europe, were a robust and disciplined tribe of warriors, who had managed to exploit the indigenous weakness of the various principalities of European Russia to their own advantage, and they ruled their extensive holdings with a circumspective policy of demanding modest tribute and exercising sufficient tolerance.

Jogaila, Grand Duke of Lithuania (ca. 1351–1434), was realistic enough to recognize that paganism was not a religion with a future. Confronted with Christianity in the form of the crusading Teutonic Knights and in the neighboring kingdom of Poland, whose own expansion to the east was a source of bilateral conflict, he realized that Roman Catholicism was bound to come sooner or later. In any event, the prospects of voluntary conversion and a marriage to the virgin queen of Poland, a union laden with political opportunities, were much more promising than the probability of forced conversion at the receiving end of the swords and lances of the Order of the Teutonic Knights. The knights had successfully subjugated the indigenous pagan inhabitants of Prussia and the Baltic coast and were in the process of using their crusaders' mandate to batter Lithuania's western frontiers.

Polish and Lithuanian matchmakers negotiated a package of conditions that were incorporated into Jogaila and Jadwiga's marriage contract: Jogaila's baptism before the wedding; the conversion of his pagan subjects to Roman Catholicism; the release of Polish prisoners and slaves; and the coordination of operations against a mutual enemy, the Teutonic Knights. On February 15, 1386, Jogaila was baptized. Three days later, he married Jadwiga, and their joint coronation took place in March. The new king of Poland accepted the Christian name Władysław, and his Lithuanian name was polonized as Jagiełło. He returned to Vilnius, the historical capital of Lithuania which also received a new Polish name, Wilno, decreed the abolition of the pagan gods, and began the mass conversion of his subjects. One of the most important short-term consequences of this marriage was that Poland assumed responsibility for propagating Catholicism among the Lithuanians, which deprived the Teutonic Knights of their legitimacy as Christian crusaders. It also laid the foundations for a political alliance that was to bring to a halt the Teutonic Knights' eastward expansion.

This Polish–Lithuanian marriage also had many far-reaching consequences. It established a personal union of the Kingdom of Poland and the Grand Duchy of Lithuania, and for the next 186 years, the Jagiellonian dynasty directed the two kingdoms like a team of horses pulling a common chariot. (This affiliation can be compared with the union of the kingdoms of Scotland and England under the Stuarts at the beginning of the seventeenth century, which eventually led to the establishment of the United Kingdom.) After 1569, Poland and Lithuania formed a constitutional union, a commonwealth or "united kingdom," that prevailed until the first partition of Poland 200 years later in 1772.

The greatest benefactors of the personal and then the constitutional unions of Poland and Lithuania were the nobles, who managed to maintain their feudal or "ancient freedoms" for centuries after they had ended elsewhere in Europe. In other words, while the modern, centrally administered

CENTRAL EUROPE, ca. 1500

North Sea

Baltic Sea

TEUTONIC ORDER

Vilnius

GRAND DUCHY of LITHUANIA

HOLY ROMAN EMPIRE

KINGDOM of POLAND

Prague

BOHEMIA

Kraków

Vienna

KINGDOM of HUNGARY

HABSBURG AUSTRIA

Budapest

Mohács 1526

MOLDAVIA

VENICE

FLORENCE

Adriatic Sea

Nicopolis 1396

Varna 1444

Kosovo 1389

OTTOMAN EMPIRE

Black Sea

PAPAL STATES

NAPLES

Constantinople 1453

Mediterrenean Sea

SITES OF MAJOR TURKISH VICTORIES

Based on Paul Robert Magocsi, *Historical Atlas of East Central Europe* (Seattle: University of Washington Press, 1993)

state was evolving—as either despotism in czarist Russia or absolutism in France, Prussia, and Austria—Poland became a dual anachronism characterized by the weakness of its crown and the strength of its feudal estates. Poles, however, prefer a more poetic and patriotic interpretation of this phenomenon, like the island of freedom in the sea of tyranny.

The Polish–Lithuanian union also drew Poland politically into the East where it became the most influential representative of the West. The participation in Western European traditions is one of the most important criteria for qualifying to be Central European, and in this respect, the eastern frontiers of the Polish–Lithuanian Commonwealth represented the greatest extension of Western European civilization in the European East. Furthermore, the westward expansion of imperial Russia in the eighteenth century interrupted the "Western development" of this region by politically incorporating it into the East. The establishment of the Baltic republics and the reestablishment of Poland after World War I make the interwar period a short-lived "return to the West" for the region, but it was reincorporated into the East by the creation of the Soviet bloc after World War II.

Before the establishment of the newly independent states (NIS) in 1991, one scenario for the deterioration of the Soviet empire, which was frequently dismissed as unrealistic, was that those non-Russian republics that had been Christianized by the Teutonic Knights—Estonia and Latvia— or historically had been part of the Polish–Lithuanian Commonwealth— Lithuania, Belarus, and perhaps Ukraine[2]—would abandon the Soviet Union or "imperial Russia" and thus reinstate the borders of "the West" roughly along the frontiers of Poland-Lithuania before it was partitioned at the end of the eighteenth century. It would be misleading to overestimate how "Western" the Estonians, Latvians, Lithuanians, Belarussians, or Ukrainians are, but this should not detract from the fact that the deterioration of the Soviet Union occurred roughly along the lines of the historical frontier just described.

The Poles were the senior partners in the Polish–Lithuanian union. The Lithuanian nobility were gradually assimilated or polonized to such an extent that the term "Polish" came to represent the joint interests of the Polish and Lithuanian nobility (similar to the way in which the umbrella term "British" came to epitomize the common or national concerns of England and Scotland—and with the same asymmetry). In the long run, two ethnically different groups of nobles identified themselves with one cultural tradition and as one "political nation," in the medieval sense of the word.[3]

The union of Poland and Lithuania also added a new national dimension to the two-tier order of feudal society in the east. In western Belarus and western Ukraine, the educated, middle, and administrative classes and the landowning gentry became predominantly Polish and Roman Catholic. The urban centers were polonized and had considerable Jewish populations (due to the high level of Jewish immigration to Poland-Lithuania from Western Europe). The lower classes and the rural population of serfs were Eastern Slavs and Orthodox. For example, cities like the Lithuanian Vilnius or the Ukrainian L'viv became "Polish" to such a great extent that Poles eventually regarded them as essentially Polish, and it was common for Polish landowners to rely exclusively on the labor of Belarussian or Ukrainian serfs.

Although tolerance was one of the political keys to ruling an ethnically diverse and religiously heterodox kingdom, the Poles had a propensity to regard their Western, Catholic, and national culture as superior to the indigenous Eastern Slavic and Orthodox cultures over which they ruled. The fact that Polish rule of the "subject nations" in vast regions of the European East was more tolerant and benevolent than the iron fist the Russian czars (and then the Soviets) later imposed obscures the Polish lords' attitudes toward their non-Polish subjects, some of which still exist in contemporary Polish nationalism. From the Polish point of view, there is a tendency to look back at the Polish–Lithuanian union as one big happy family. But the national perspectives of the former subject nations of the Poles like the Belarussians and the Ukrainians are not quite so rosy or sentimental.

The long-term consequences of the Polish engagement in the east after 1400 also were analogous in some respects to those of the medieval German "drive to the east" before 1350. The Poles, who perceived themselves as standing at the threshold of a West–East "cultural gradient," came to consider themselves as "carriers of culture" to less developed civilizations and regions. Although the Polish settlement of regions eastward was never as extensive as the medieval German "colonization" of its east, the development of a fundamentally Polish ruling class and the formation of Polish "linguistic islands" in urban centers created a situation that made the drawing of national borders along ethnic–territorial lines virtually impossible in the future. This fact was amply demonstrated by the problems surrounding the establishment of Poland's eastern frontier after World War I and its revision during World War II.

One of the combined results of these phenomena was that Polish nationalists later assumed that eastern Central Europe and considerable portions of Eastern Europe historically belonged to a Polish "linguistic and cultural space," a notion that had an uncanny similarity to the German nationalistic concept of Central Europe as a *deutscher Sprach- und Kulturraum*. Although Polish variations on this idea of national and cultural space were relatively benign in comparison with the German ones, they were not devoid of equally condescending or chauvinistic undertones.

Both Poles and Lithuanians look back on the personal union of their countries under the Jagiellonian dynasty and the subsequent creation of the Polish–Lithuanian Commonwealth as the golden ages in their histories. Together they stopped the German expansion to the east at the Battle of Grunwald. They held the Russians at bay for centuries, and at the same time, they defended Christian Europe from the onslaughts of eastern hordes.

Poles and Lithuanians have never forgotten the historical magnitude of these achievements or the former dimensions of their kingdoms, but as the easternmost representatives of the cultural sphere that defines itself as "the West," they feel that the importance of their role has never received the recognition from the West that it deserves. Although there is a certain amount of retrospective resentment among Lithuanians, who have recognized that the Polish–Lithuanian affiliation benefited the Poles at the expense of Lithuania, neither Poles nor Lithuanians have forgotten their legacy of collaboration. As the Eastern bloc crumbled in 1989 and the aspirations for national independence by the republics of the Soviet Union climaxed thereafter, some Poles saw the historical precedent of a Polish–Lithuanian association as the basis for some kind of future cooperation, but this vision has not materialized.

The Greatest Hungarian King:
The Reign of Matthias I, 1458–1490

When Hungarians look back on their history, they have a large, multinational kingdom in their mind's eye. At its peak, the Kingdom of Hungary stretched from the Carpathian Mountains and Slovakia in the north through the central Danube Valley to Serbia in the south and from Transylvania in the east across the Danube Valley to Croatia on the coast of the Adriatic in the west. As elsewhere in medieval Europe, the idea of ethnicity barely played a role in formulating the concept of the Hungarian "political nation." Its constituent members, feudal lords, were not only Hungarian but also Romanian, Serbian, and Croatian, and they even included a few magnates of French and Italian origin, who had been benefactors of the crown. These nobles conducted their business with one another and with the crown in Latin, and regardless of their differences of ethnic origin or mother tongue, they all regarded themselves as members of the *gens Hungarica* or *natio Hungarica*, the "Hungarian nation."

Despite this cosmopolitan tradition, some Hungarian historians have not looked back favorably on the "foreign kings" who ruled this multinational kingdom after the death of Louis of Anjou, "the Great," in 1382. Louis's successor and son-in-law, Sigismund of Luxemburg, who was elected Holy Roman Emperor of the German Nation and King of Bohemia after assuming the Hungarian crown, is best remembered for a combination of arbitrariness and ruthlessness when he was in Hungary, or absenteeism and neglect when he was not. The following reign of Sigismund's son-in-law, a Habsburg, Albrecht of Austria (1437–1439), and the tenure of a Polish king from the Jagiellonian dynasty, Władysław III (1440–1444, known as Ulászló I in Hungarian history), were too brief to be of any lasting consequence.

Subsequent kings from these foreign dynasties had poor reputations, according to the Hungarian historical record. Vladislav II (Ulászló II for Hungarians), a Jagiellonian prince who had been elected king of Bohemia before assuming the Hungarian crown in 1490, and his son, Louis II (1516–1526), were responsible for presiding over a period of national decay that culminated in a resounding Hungarian defeat at the hands of the Ottoman Turks in 1526, a catastrophe that was merely a prelude to the Turkish occupation of most of Hungary for the next 160 years. Ferdinand I, a Habsburg, was elected king of Hungary in 1527, and his family turned the crown of St. Stephen from an elected national institution into a hereditary foreign possession for the next 391 years, until 1918.

Under these circumstances, there is a certain temptation to make foreigners responsible for Hungary's national tragedies. From this perspective, the bumbling of Polish kings contributed to the demise of Hungary, which Western Christendom abandoned to the Turks, with the sole exception of the Habsburgs, who benefited from Hungary's predicament. Given the relationship between foreign rule and national calamity in Hungarian history, it is no mere coincidence that the brief interlude of "national independence," between 1444 and 1490, during which Hungary was ruled by

Hungarians, was the last "golden age" in Hungarian history. This era is identified with the career of a Hungarian general, János Hunyadi, and his son Matthias, the only "national" king to rule Hungary between the expiration of the Árpád dynasty in 1301 and the demise of the Habsburg Empire in 1918.

The career of János Hunyadi was nothing less than meteoritic. Not a "high-born" magnate but a member of the lesser Hungarian nobility from Transylvania, Hunyadi made a name for himself by brilliantly serving the Hungarian crown.[4] He also accumulated more than 4 million acres of land in the process, which made him the largest landowner in Hungarian history. Raised at the court of Sigismund of Luxemburg, Hunyadi put his considerable strategic and military skills at the disposal of Albrecht von Habsburg, the Austrian duke and son-in-law of Sigismund, who had assumed his father-in-law's multiple titles and holdings as Holy Roman Emperor, King of Bohemia, and King of Hungary.

Albrecht, who was the type of dynastic material out of which empires were made, entrusted Hunyadi with organizing the defense of Hungary's southern frontier which, after the Turks' decisive victory over Serbia in 1389 at the Battle of Kosovo, had become Western Christendom's front line of defense against the Ottomans' expanding Islamic empire. But Albrecht's brief two-year reign showed how ephemeral imperial visions were in those days. Albrecht contracted dysentery in the course of a military operation against the Turks in Serbia and died in 1439, leaving behind a pregnant wife instead of a successor.

The Hungarian nobility then elected Władysław III, the Jagiellonian king of Poland, to the Hungarian throne, and he as well relied on Hunyadi's skills in the field. Hungary's turbulent southern frontier also turned out to be the scene of Władysław's demise. Hunyadi considered offense to be the best defense, and he made plans to expel the Turks from Europe with the help of the peoples they had subjugated—Serbs, Romanians, and Bulgarians—who, in turn, would confederate with Hungary in the future. During an offensive Hunyadi organized to push the Turks back down the Balkan Peninsula, Władysław fell in the Battle of Varna on the Black Sea coast of Bulgaria in 1444. (He is remembered as "Władysław of Varna" in Polish history. This heroic attempt to stop the Turkish advance later became, for Poles, the national achievement of a Polish king and, for Hungarians, of a Hungarian king.)

Left with a vacant throne for the third time in seven years, the Hungarian nobility elected the five-year-old Ladislas V, the son that Albrecht of Austria's wife bore shortly after Albrecht's death, and they simultaneously designated Hunyadi as "regent," a position that entailed the guardianship of the child-king and the interim government of Hungary until Ladislas came of age.

During his regency, Hunyadi promoted centralization, ostensibly to mobilize the resources he needed to continue the defense of Hungary's southern frontier, but chronic infighting among the various factions of Hungarian nobility and the fact that they suspected him of exploiting his powerful position to further his personal interests instead of those of the nation undermined the kind of national unity that a concerted military effort required. Hunyadi's regency ended in 1453 when Ladislas came of age (and the Turks finally took Constantinople, an event marking the end of the Byzantine Empire).

Hunyadi crowned his career by lifting the Turkish siege of the border fortress of Belgrade in 1456, but he scarcely had an opportunity to enjoy the fruits of his victory because he fell victim to a plague that had broken out in the Hungarian camp. The magnitude of Hunyadi's achievement, which was perceived as a decisive victory over the Turks, impressed his contemporaries to such an extent that the pope ordered Christian churches to ring their bells daily at noon, a practice still observed in many Roman Catholic countries today. The death of the sixteen-year-old Ladislas V, unwed and childless, in the following year facilitated the rise of János Hunyadi's son Matthias, who, despite a series of intrigues against him and his family, managed to organize the noble support he needed to be elected king of Hungary in 1458.

Matthias Hunyadi, also called Matthias Corvinus, embodied the ideals of the Renaissance ruler. (Corvinus is a Latin derivative of *corvus*, "raven," the animal adorning Matthias's coat of arms.) As a humanist, he combined personal erudition with a generous patronage of the arts. His collections, library, and court were renowned throughout Europe. As a politician, he used Machiavellian cunning to achieve his objectives, and he did not shy away from methods that were nothing less than despotic. Matthias understood that his royal power was limited by the traditional strength of the Hungarian nobility, and so he pursued a straightforward and ruthless strategy of augmenting the former by diminishing the latter.

Matthias's plan for strengthening the central authority of the crown was to curtail the feudal privileges of the powerful nobility or "magnates," a measure that—along with carefully orchestrated propaganda praising his wisdom and magnanimity—won him the sympathies of the people, who preferred the new forms of regimentation he introduced to the old ones he replaced. Matthias initiated a more equitable system of justice and taxation and instituted a relatively effective administration for executing them, and he reinvested the income he gained as a result of more effective tax collection in projects that produced political capital. The instrument he devised for executing and enforcing his policies was Central Europe's first standing army, a troop of well-paid mercenaries frequently clad in black armor or chain mail, estimated to be 30,000 strong and under Matthias's personal command. With his "Black Army," Matthias Corvinus bypassed the king's traditional feudal reliance on the nobility for military support, a medieval practice that had constantly weakened the crown because the nobles often used their "ancient rights" to withhold it. The Black Army was a lethally effective tool for dealing with domestic resistance as well as an agile military detachment that could respond quickly to foreign threats.

During the first part of Matthias's thirty-two-year reign, he reassumed his father's mission of crusading against the Turks. However, he soon recognized that Hungary's resources alone would never be sufficient for this task, so he made peace with the Turkish sultan in order to stabilize Hungary's southern frontier. Then he turned his attention to the northwest, Bohemia and Austria, and spent the last twenty years of his life trying to establish a "Danubian empire" under the hegemony of the Hungarian crown. Hungary had always played an important role in the southern Central Europe's various imperial schemes, so Matthias was no great innovator in this respect. Otakar of Bohemia, Sigismund of Luxemburg, and Albrecht of Austria each had considered founding a Danubian empire, and the interdynastic marriages among the ruling houses of Poland, Bohemia, Hungary, and Austria throughout the Middle Ages were attempts to achieve some kind of larger and lasting union at the nuptial altar instead of on the battlefield.

The first phase of Matthias's imperial plans brought him into conflict with the kingdom of Bohemia, a prosperous realm torn by decades of confessional strife between the Roman Catholics and the Hussites. The Hussites were the followers of that forerunner of the Reformation and "Bohemian Luther," Jan Hus, whom Catholic authorities had condemned as a heretic and burned at the stake at the Council of Constance in 1415. The Bohemian nobles were divided into Catholic and Hussite factions, which correspondingly supported or resisted the crown, and the king of Bohemia, George of Poděbrady, tried in vain to find a politically acceptable solution to the problem of religiously inspired rebellion. The fifteenth-century Bohemian predicament of religion and rebellion, war and reconciliation, was merely a small-scale preview of the types of problems Central Europe was to face on a grand scale in the following century.

Matthias had no political reservations about exploiting the problems of George of Poděbrady, and although Matthias was a devout Catholic, he supported the rebellious faction of Hussite nobility by invading Moravia in 1468. The following year, the Hussite opposition elected him as a schismatic "king of Bohemia," and Matthias took this political mandate as a pretext for extending his holdings into Silesia. George of Poděbrady died the following year. (Poděbrady was the last Czech king of Bohemia, just as Matthias was the last Hungarian king of Hungary. Consequently, Poděbrady enjoys a position in Czech national history similar to that of Matthias in Hungarian history. However, Poděbrady never was as successful as his adversary.)

The subsequent election of a new and legitimate king of Bohemia, the Jagiellonian prince Vladislav II, by the Czech nobility who had remained loyal to the crown, changed the composition of the political fronts that Matthias faced, and he spent most of the rest of the decade battling the Catholic king of Bohemia, a Pole who could rely on dynastic assistance from home. In 1478, Matthias sought a compromise to consolidate his holdings and offered to recognize Vladislav's titles and holdings in Bohemia if Vladislav were willing to recognize those of Matthias in Moravia and Silesia. Vladislav, who later earned the nickname *Dobre*, Czech for "good" or "OK," because he was so complacent, was neither politically nor personally strong enough to do otherwise and accepted the deal. Satisfied for the time being with what he had achieved in Bohemia, Matthias next turned his attention to the Habsburgs' holdings in Austria.

At the end of the fifteenth century, the Habsburgs' domains were roughly the size of contemporary Austria. After the struggle with Otakar of Bohemia and the assumption of the duchies of the Babenbergs in 1278, the family had fared quite well and had expanded their holdings from the east toward the Adriatic and through the Alps to the west. The House of Habsburg, however, also had been plagued by the episodes of internal strife that accompany any family business, and compared with other Central European dynasties, they were not among the major players in the game of power politics. Matthias's antagonist, the archduke of Austria and Holy Roman Emperor, Frederick III (1416–1493), may have laid the foundations for the rise of the Habsburg Empire by arranging a fortunate marriage between his son, Maximilian I, and Maria of Burgundy, but he was no formidable opponent himself. Frederick III, who was renowned for his combination of indecisiveness and persistence, never defeated Matthias; he merely outlived him.

Matthias started his operations against Austria in the spring of 1480 by invading the duchy of Styria (in contemporary southern Austria) and began working his way north to Vienna. Castles and fortified towns fell one after the other, and Matthias, who came to conquer, not to plunder, gave orders to his Black Army to treat the local populace diplomatically, which basically meant curtailing to a certain extent the standard pastimes of soldiers, like rape, pillage, and arson. In five years, Matthias occupied eastern Austria, took Vienna by siege, and settled there apparently with intention of making the city the capital of his empire. Frederick III retired to the city of Linz, about a hundred miles upstream from Vienna on the Danube, and did what he could, which apparently was not too much. In his capacity as Holy Roman Emperor, Frederick III solicited support from the noble estates in Germany and received an amount reflecting the modesty of the powers inherent in the imperial crown and title he bore: a weak army of knights that Matthias's Black Army scattered without trouble. Otherwise, Frederick waited.

In the meantime, Matthias made himself comfortable in Vienna. He donated a new roof for Vienna's central landmark, St. Stephen's Cathedral, and he cultivated the allegiance of the fickle Viennese in particular and his Austrian subjects in general by using circumspection and generosity. His only son, Johannes Corvinus, was the product of a love affair he had with Barbara Edelpeck, the daughter of a Viennese commoner, and Matthias had every intention of securing his son's succession to the Hungarian throne and his empire. But then Matthias died suddenly in Vienna in 1490 at the age of forty-seven after a short and mysterious illness, and his empire, which had been held together by his ambition and authority, disintegrated into its previous parts.

The death of Matthias in his prime and the mysterious circumstances surrounding it—some forensic historians think he was poisoned—has traditionally been treated as a tragedy in Hungarian history, although Matthias had made more than enough enemies in the course of his career. He took half the kingdom of Bohemia away from Vladislav, which angered loyal Bohemians and the Jagiellonian dynasty, and he fought with the Hussites against the Catholics, which aggravated the pope. He was squatting on Habsburg territory, and many Hungarian magnates saw his superabundant power as a threat to their own vital interests. Under these circumstances it would have been easy to find a villain with a vial of poison, if there was one, either at home or abroad.

Analyses of Matthias and his political achievements vary. Was he was a Hungarian national patriot, whose plans were a farsighted and noble attempt to gain control of the resources and manpower he needed to defend Hungary and Western Christendom from the Ottoman threat, or was he merely a rapacious and cosmopolitan dynasty builder, who was discouraged by his lack of success in the south and inspired by the more promising prospects for expansion elsewhere? The historical truth is perhaps to be found somewhere in between. Hungarians have traditionally assessed Matthias Corvinus as "the greatest of Hungarian kings."[5] His defense of the peasants and lesser nobility against the magnates made him popular, a "people's king." The national importance and popularity of Matthias in Hungarian history also is undoubtedly related to the fact that before (and after) his reign, the kingdom of Hungary was (and remained) an object of foreign imperial acquisition. Under Matthias, however, Hungary was the center of an empire. He reversed the established historical roles and, for a change, made Hungary, the traditional prey of foreign empires, an imperial predator.

Matthias's conquest of Vienna is viewed as a high point in Hungary history, and some Hungarian cynics regard it as the most recent one. It even is mentioned in the third strophe of the Hungarian national anthem, a nineteenth-century epic national poem by Frenec Kölcsey: "and the proud fortifications of Vienna groaned under King Matthias's dark (or 'black') army."[6] His death in 1490 marked the beginning of the end of this brief, proverbial "golden age."

The Hungarian nobles' decision to elect to the Hungarian throne the Jagiellonian prince and king of Bohemia, Matthias's former adversary Vladislav, partly because Vladislav's incompetence was in their own interest, marks the beginning of the downward curve in the nation's fortunes. The death of Vladislav's son and successor, Louis II, in the Battle of Mohács against the Turks in 1526 was a national tragedy. Given the intricacies of dynastic politics in Central Europe, the fact that the grandson of a Polish king was simultaneously the king of Bohemia and the king of Hungary should be no surprise at this point, but in order to explain why his death in 1526 was a national catastrophe for Hungary—as well as Bohemia—and an enormous windfall for Austria, we must examine one more piece of the Central European mosaic: the rise of the Habsburgs.

Empire Building at the Altar: Habsburg Marital Diplomacy, 1477–1515

For European dynastic families, whose business was ruling, children were political capital. Marriages were investments or the diplomatic equivalent of mergers. Warfare was one of the vicissitudes of the market, and the inability to procreate amounted to bankruptcy. Like modern multinationals, these families had home offices and foreign subsidiaries, and they ran their oper-

The Habsburgs' Three Generations of Interdynastic Marriage

**** marriages   ━━━━━ hereditary line of succession

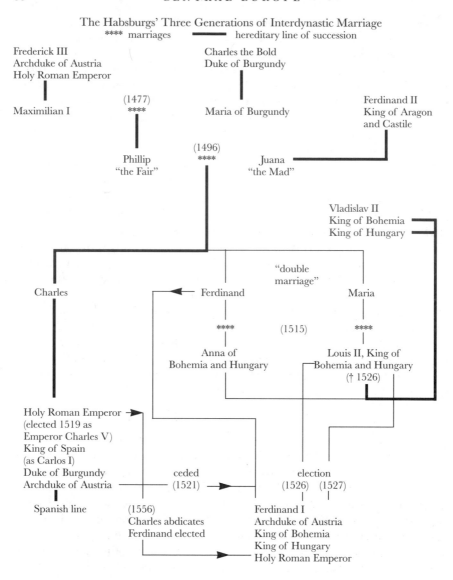

ations on an international scale. It would be a moot point to argue which European dynasty ran the best business, but it is an indisputable fact that the Habsburgs stayed in business the longest, from 1278 until 1918. They saw the local competition like the Anjou and Luxemburg dynasties go bankrupt, and they watched big foreign concerns fold, like the English Tudors or Stuarts or the French Bourbons. The key to the Habsburgs' success was not fighting wars to force their competitors out of the market but arranging marriages, which positioned them well within it. Three generations of dynastic intermarriage from 1477 until 1515 changed their family business into a global concern.[7]

Frederick III, who had been so ineffectual in stopping Matthias Corvinus from realizing Hungarian imperial plans, laid the foundation for the Habsburg Empire by arranging a marriage between his son, Maximilian I, and Maria of Burgundy, the only child of Duke Charles "the Bold" and the sole heiress to a flourishing principality that encompassed vast stretches of contemporary eastern France, Belgium, and the Netherlands. The Burgundian court, perhaps the most luxurious and sophisticated in all of Europe at the time, merely reflected the prosperity of the realm over which Charles ruled. Maximilian and Maria married in 1477, and even though Maximilian had to fight a series of wars to defend his claims in Burgundy, their marriage was a happy if brief one. Maria bore him an all-important son, Philip, before her tragic death in 1482 when she, late in her second pregnancy, fell from a horse, killing herself and her unborn child.

The death of Maximilian's father, Frederick III, in 1493, brought the Habsburgs' Austrian holdings into his hands, and three years later Maximilian managed to arrange a marriage between his twelve-year-old son, Philip, and Juana of Aragon, the daughter of the king of Spain. As fate or fortune would have it, Juana's older brother, the heir apparent to the throne, and her older sister, a vehicle for female succession, died young, and their deaths made Philip "the Fair" heir to the vast Spanish holdings on the Iberian Peninsula and in southern Italy and Sicily. Although Philip died relatively young at the age of twenty-eight, and Juana, who had a depressive disposition, eventually went insane and accordingly was known as Juana "the Mad," this couple managed to produce six children. The three eldest, Charles (known as Carlos in Spanish history), Ferdinand, and Maria, provided their grandfather with the human capital he needed to pursue the next phase of his nuptial diplomacy.

Although Maximilian's greatest success had been in the west, he never lost sight of the importance of the east, and he negotiated carefully with Vladislav II, the Jagiellonian prince who had been elected king of Bohemia after the death of George of Poděbrady in 1471 and king of Hungary after the death of Matthias Corvinus in 1490. Maximilian proposed a double engagement. The first nuptial bond was a straightforward deal: His granddaughter Maria was to marry Vladislav's son and heir, Louis II. The second had a male option clause. One of his grandsons, either Charles or Ferdinand, was to marry Vladislav's daughter Anna. Which husband Anna was to have, however, would be determined by the Habsburgs at a later date. The preengagement, engagement, and marital contracts that were negotiated over a decade were enormously complicated, and they included the mutual guarantee that if one of the dynasties were to expire, the other was to inherit the rights to its titles and holdings. Therefore, the potential Bohemian–Hungarian regal in-laws of the Habsburgs had something to gain from their Austrian in-laws under certain circumstances, and vice versa. This entire deal was closed in Vienna in 1515 with the famous "double marriage" of four preadolescent children. Ferdinand von Habsburg married Maria of Bohemia and Hungary, and Louis II of Bohemia and Hungary married Anna von Habsburg.

Marital diplomacy was the key to the rise of the Habsburgs. In *The Family of Emperor Maximilian I* (1515), portrait by Bernhard Strigl, are depicted Maximilian (left), Holy Roman Emperor and archduke of Austria, with his son Philip, whose marriage established a claim to the Spanish throne (center), and Maximilian's wife, Maria of Burgundy. In the foreground are his grandchildren Ferdinand (left) and Charles (center) with Louis II, king of Bohemia and Hungary (right), who was wed to Maximilian's granddaughter Maria. Charles inherited all titles and lands from his father and grandfather but ceded the Austrian holdings to his brother Ferdinand, who, after the death of his brother-in-law Louis II in the Battle of Mohács in 1526, became king of Bohemia and Hungary. (Kunsthistorisches Museum, Vienna)

Due to the institution of primogeniture, the prospects for Ferdinand as the second-born son were not especially good. When Maximilian I died in 1519, Charles added his grandfather's Austrian and Burgundian holdings to the substantial Spanish ones he had inherited from his father, Philip, in addition to being elected king of Germany and Holy Roman Emperor of the German Nation as Charles V. As a Habsburg raised in Burgundy and at home at the Spanish court, Charles, who traveled extensively during his reign, was a truly cosmopolitan figure. He had accumulated such an enormous amount of power that he was the last German emperor to take seriously the medieval concept of a *monarchia universalis*, the idea of a unified Christian European empire dating back to Charlemagne. But he did cede his Austrian holdings to his younger brother by 1522, a fraternal act that established within the Habsburg dynasty a western Spanish line and an eastern Austrian line.

The two branches of the family worked closely together. For example, when Charles V abdicated as German emperor in 1556, he engineered the election of his brother, Ferdinand, to the position he had vacated, and the Habsburgs gradually turned the office of the Holy Roman Emperor of the German Nation from an elected position into a hereditary entitlement that the Austrian line controlled until 1806 when Napoleonic imperialism led to the dissolution of the remnants of what Germans retrospectively called the "First Reich." The division of the House of Habsburg into a Spanish and an Austrian line also established a pattern that for centuries was to determine the dynamics of continental politics. The rise of France involved conflicts with both "national" branches of the Habsburg dynasty: a Spanish empire and a growing Austrian one.

Charles's fraternal generosity, Maximilian's prenuptial agreements, and Ferdinand's wedding band laid the foundation for the rise of the Habsburg Empire in Central Europe, and the death of Ferdinand's brother-in-law, Louis II, king of Bohemia and king of Hungary, at the Battle of Mohács in 1526 provided an occasion to erect the superstructure. Looking back at the three generations of Habsburg marital diplomacy, it is easy to understand the old saying "Bella gerant alii, tu felix Austria nube" (Let the others fight wars; you, lucky Austria, marry). These marriages, however, also led to wars. Charles, the most powerful Catholic ruler in Europe and the Holy Roman Emperor, became inextricably entangled in Christianity's civil war, the Reformation, and after Ferdinand assumed the Hungarian crown, he also inherited the responsibility for defending Western Christendom against the Islamic infidels of the Ottoman Empire.

❧ 4 ❧

The Bulwarks of Christendom

Religion and Warfare, 1400–1550

"Bulwark" is a military term with heroic connotations like valor, fortitude, and self-sacrifice. It also is a historical metaphor for the role that almost every Central European nation sees itself as having played at one time or another in history, from the Middle Ages right up to the present. The larger context of the bulwark metaphor is the assumption that the history of Western Christendom—or Western Civilization or "the West"—is analogous to the chronicle of a fortress that has had a succession of different enemies at its gates. Consequently, the "fortress of Europe" has had a number of bulwarks, each of which has assumed a specific tactical function in the overall strategy of defense at a given time. The descendants of the defenders of the Croatian, Hungarian, Austrian, German, and Polish bulwarks, each of which was constructed using different historical materials, tend, however, to look back on the achievements of their particular national bastion instead of the overall historical architecture of the European fortress. The occupants of one bulwark always seem not to have appreciated the achievements of the inhabitants of the other bulwarks because nationalism has limited their field of vision.

The use of the bulwark metaphor, as well as synonyms like "bastion," "battlement," and "rampart," dates back to the Middle Ages. The term *antemurale christianitatis* (from medieval Latin *ante* [pre- or fore] and *murus* [wall]), "the Bulwark of Christendom," was commonly used to describe Central Europe's (or Western Christendom's) frontiers with oriental infidels like the Tatars and the Turks or with the Eastern schismatics of the various Orthodox denominations. Significant national claims to having championed the Pan-European cause of Christianity at one time or another in history differ because the nature of the oriental or Eastern threats changed throughout the ages.

64

Before the Ottoman Empire gained a foothold on the Balkan Peninsula during the fourteenth century, the Eastern threat came from Asia. The Mongols, nomadic warriors from the depths of Central Asia, appeared on horseback in Europe in 1240 and cut a swath of destruction through Ukraine, Russia, southern Poland, Silesia, Moravia, Hungary, and the Balkan Peninsula. With their speed and agility, they decimated every military force of cumbersome armored knights that the various rulers of medieval Europe could mobilize. Although they withdrew the following year as unexpectedly as they had appeared, some of them, the Tatars, settled in the Volga River Basin and the Crimea along the northern coast of the Black Sea.

Historians generally agree that the Mongols had the potential for virtually destroying Europe in 1240/1241—Hungary, for example, lost an estimated 60 percent of its population—and that the Mongols' unexpected withdrawal to the east was a stroke of good fortune. The residual Tatar threat after their departure never was of comparable dimensions. On the contrary, the subsequent expansion of the kingdoms of Poland and Lithuania to the southeast made the Tatars' periodic raids and demands for tribute an almost exclusively Polish problem. The Tatars' conversion to Islam, however, added a religious dimension to this conflict which, combined with the memories of the Mongols' original conquest, rhetorically and psychologically turned a Polish national problem into the Polish defense of Western Christendom.

The use of the term *antemurale christianitatis* also referred to Christendom's front line of defense against the Ottoman Empire, and the history of this military frontier from the end of the fourteenth century, the Turks' resounding victory over the Serbs at the Battle of Kosovo in 1389, until the end of the seventeenth century frequently is portrayed as a series of futile attempts to stop the Ottomans' advance interspersed with periods of peace during which the Turks consolidated their gains. If one adopts a definition of Europe as coextensive with Christianity, the Orthodox East represented the West's front line of defense in its conflict with Islam, and the kingdom of Serbia, and before it Bulgaria, defended the West in this respect.

After the fall of Serbia, the responsibility for this task fell to Hungary. Although the Hungarians launched various crusades and preventive wars against the Turks, these operations cost more than they gained, but the Hungarians held their own for well over a century: until the Battle of Mohács in 1526. Before taking a look at the consequences of the Turkish capture of the Hungarian bulwark, it is useful to recall a few of the crucial events that transpired beforehand inside the fortress of Western Christendom. The Reformation not only undermined the unity of the Christian West; in the process, it also changed the entire idea of the "Bulwark of Christendom."

The Crack in the Foundation:
Jan Hus and the Bohemian Precedent

The conventional event and date that historians use to designate the beginning of the Reformation is the posting in 1517 of Luther's "Ninety-five Theses on Indulgences" on the doors of the Palace Church in Wittenberg. From the Czech point of view, the Reformation began a bit more than a century earlier, with the career of a Bohemian priest, Jan Hus (1369–1415), whose theological, liturgical, and ecclesiastical reforms anticipated those of Martin Luther (1483–1546).

It would be unwise to overestimate how innovative or modern Hus was. His ideas were influenced by other fourteenth-century theologians, the Englishman John Wycliff in particular, who wanted to "renovate" the church, and he stood clearly in a late medieval theological tradition lacking the existential spirituality characteristic of Luther. Hus's work, like that of his German successor, culminated in a critique of a church he considered insufficient. His reformation of the liturgy, rejection of ecclesiastical hierarchy, introduction of the vernacular instead of Latin in worship, and belief in the primacy and immediacy of the Gospel were concerns and innovations echoed later in Luther's works. In both cases, the logical consequence of their theological quests was to doubt the adequacy and the legitimacy of the Roman Church as a vehicle for Christian salvation. Their interpretation of the Bible and their understanding of the relationship between man and God led them to question the idea of Roman authority in matters ranging from the nature of the sacraments to the question of how a community of believers should be organized.

Although neither Hus nor Luther intended to split the Christian church or to change the worldly order of lords and subjects that God had ordained, they did destroy the traditional symbiosis between Roman Christianity and worldly authority, thereby pitting denominations of Christians against one another in civil war. In some cases, their teachings inspired Christian subjects to rise up against their ordained superiors, who, in turn, fulfilled their God-given duties as Christian lords by slaughtering their insubordinate and schismatic subjects. Hus's followers pitched Bohemia into five decades of intermittent internal strife (1419–1470), and Luther's teachings precipitated a series of wars among noble factions in the German empire (1522–1555), as well as a major uprising of peasants against the nobility (1524–1526). The unity of Western Christendom, based on the venerable tradition of "one, Holy, Catholic, and Apostolic Church,"[1] deteriorated as Christians fought Christians in the name of God and True Religion.

Hus's career ended when he was called to the Council of Constance in 1414, one of the periodic synods of ecclesiastical authorities the Roman Church organized to formulate doctrinal and organizational policy. Hus responded as a devout Christian and went prepared to defend his teachings. Sigismund of Luxemburg, the Holy Roman Emperor and king of Hungary, also provided Hus with an imperial assurance of safe conduct and immunity. In Constance, however, Hus refused to recant, and Sigismund reneged on his imperial guarantees. The ecclesiastical authorities then dealt with Hus as a heretic and burned him at the stake on July 6, 1415. In the process, they also created the first anti-Catholic martyr of the Reformation and a Czech national hero.

Hus's religiously motivated rejection of the Latin ritual and the Roman Catholic Church later became archetypical symbols of Czech aspirations for

The Bohemian theologian Jan Hus was burned at the stake on July 6, 1415, after being condemned as a heretic by Roman Catholic authorities at the Council of Constance. Woodcut from a fifteenth-century chronicle by Ulrich von Richental. (Austrian National Library, Picture Archive)

national independence which, translated into the spheres of culture and politics, were historically manifested as a struggle against German and Roman Catholic domination. The perfidious conduct of Sigismund of Luxemburg also became a national symbol illustrating the extent to which Czechs could rely on Germans to protect Bohemia's national interests. The election of Sigismund of Luxemburg, the "murderer" of Hus, to the Bohemian throne in 1419 precipitated the outbreak of the Hussite wars.

The Hussite faction, fortified by faith, was led by Bohemian nobles who were willing to fight their German and Roman Catholic king. They were defending the freedom of the Bohemian nation, on the one hand, and their own freedom of conscience, on the other. For the first time in history (and according to some observers, the last) the Bohemians also showed an exceptional amount of military initiative and ingenuity, and they scored impressive victories in the field. However, unresolvable theological differences, which had political implications, between radically minded social utopians and more moderate Hussites weakened this "national movement" which eventually degenerated into a state of civil war, and the moderate Hussites eventually sided with their Catholic enemies to eliminate the residual threat that the Hussite fundamentalists represented.

Anti-German sentiment among Bohemia's nobles helped elect George of Poděbrady, the first "national king" of Bohemia since the extinction of the Přemysl dynasty in 1306 and the last Czech king of Bohemia, in 1458, but he did not manage to overcome the cleavages that the Hussite wars had created. After the Habsburgs procured the Bohemian crown in 1526, the Czechs increasingly perceived this Roman Catholic and "German" dynasty as a dual threat to the Czech nation, which defined itself using Hus as a national hero and forerunner of the modern Czech struggle for national recognition and independence.

In the Czech historical tradition, Hus became a nationalist and a democrat, but a Czechoslovak Communist interpretation described those followers of Hus as propagating a radical form of Christianity, not as protodemocrats, but as proto-Communist social revolutionaries. Under the Communist regime, May 9, the commemoration of the liberation of Prague by the Red Army in 1945, was the official national holiday. Then in May 1990, the Czech "national" parliament—a "state" legislature for the Czech half of the Czechoslovak federal republic—declared July 6, the day of Hus's martyrdom in 1415, as the new Czech national holiday, whereas the parallel Slovak body adopted July 5, the feast day of St. Cyril and St. Methodius, the first Christian missionaries in Central Europe, as their national holiday. Because of their Roman Catholic traditions, Slovaks generally do not identify themselves with Hus.

The execution of Hus inflicted such a deep wound on the Bohemian national soul that the Czech Roman Catholic Cardinal Beran raised the issue of Hus at the Roman Catholic Church's twentieth-century synod of ecumenism and liturgical reform in the early 1960s, the Second Vatican Council, which incidentally introduced the vernacular as the language of worship 550 years after Hus had done so.[2] Czechs see Hus's fate as an expression of one of the tragic paradoxes of their history. Czech ingenuity, the Czech quest for national freedom, or a combination of both have repeatedly been frustrated by historical circumstances. Hus was doomed to fail because he was ahead of his times, and Luther's later success in Germany overshadowed the importance of Bohemia's historical precedent.

Western Christianity Divided: The Reformation

If Czechs overestimate the importance of Hus for Luther, then Germans underestimate it, but these tendencies are to be expected when people deal with their own national heroes. One of the most striking differences between the biographies of these two reformers is that Hus defied the Roman Church and ended up at the stake; Luther did the same and died in his own bed at the age of sixty-three. To understand the origins of Luther's defiance, we shall briefly explore one of his early theological insights.

On the surface, Luther's Ninety-five Theses were a critique of the Roman Church's practice of selling indulgences, or ecclesiastical dispensations for sinning in exchange for cash. Although the purchase of an indulgence may not appear to be a "good work," it was one of those worldly acts through which people tried to attain salvation and, in this respect, comparable to other worldly acts of a much more positive nature, like brotherly love. Luther's fundamental insight was that no worldly act could save a person's soul because faith, and faith alone, was the prerequisite of salvation. Luther assumed that if people listened to the Word of God and were prepared to submit to his Will, they would open their soul for the gift of Divine Grace, which exhibited itself as faith. Although faith, in turn, could manifest itself as good works, good works were not necessarily a manifestation of faith. Therefore, Luther developed the doctrine of justification by faith alone.

One of Luther's central theological insights was to make salvation solely an affair between individual believers and their God (provided that they had access to the Gospel, which, as the Word of God, was the sole source of faith). Luther explicitly rejected human merit in this world as the vehicle of salvation and implicitly denied the necessity of an intermediary between individual Christians and their God. Because of the emphasis Luther placed on the subjectivity or "inwardness" (*Innerlichkeit*) of the religious experience, historians have called him the father of modern subjectivism and individualism and made him responsible for that peculiarly German propensity for soul-searching and introspection. But the direct result of Luther's "inwardness" combined with his belief in the immediacy and profound simplicity of the Gospel was to question the entire legitimacy of the Roman Church, with its emphasis on "external" rituals and doctrines which, according to Luther, had distanced themselves enormously from the original spirit of the Gospel and had nothing to do with faith.

It is also an indisputable fact that at the beginning of the sixteenth century, the Roman Church was in a sad state of disarray and a negligent shepherd of souls. Luther felt that by selling indulgences and neglecting pastoral work, like the propagation of the Gospel, the Roman Church was stealing people's money with the deceitful promise of heaven and abandoning their souls to hell at the same time, and he responded to this injustice with wrath reminiscent of biblical prophets. The Roman Church was nothing more than an instrument of the devil, and the pope was nothing less than the Antichrist personified.

Luther, whose initial aspiration was to reform the church, had no grand designs to change the worldly order, but the disparity between his intentions and the consequences of his teachings was enormous. Luther was a conservative in many respects, although the full implications of his political or social conservativism were by no means apparent to his contemporaries and became clear only after Protestantism was established under the patronage of Protestant sovereigns. For example, Luther believed that God, in his Providence, had assigned each Christian a station in life. Since salvation was a spiritual affair between God and man, there was no point in attempting to change the worldly order of things in God's name, and doubting God's Providence was a sign of an absence of faith, that all-important prerequisite for salvation. Luther's theology of spiritual subjectivity consequently supported conformity or a recognition of the political and social status quo as divinely ordained. Good Christians used their conscience in private and fulfilled their Christian duty at a divinely appointed station in public.

Two important phenomena have their origins in this teaching. First, Luther helped change the entire concept of work from a biblical curse—the Roman Catholic–Mediterranean interpretation of Genesis—into a Christian duty by elevating every person's task to the status of a divine "calling": doing one's Christian duty in life. In his famous study *The Protestant Ethic and the Spirit of Capitalism,* Max Weber concluded that Calvinism's radical transformation of the Lutheran idea of providential vocation provided one of the foundations for the development of the "Protestant work ethic" that contributed to the "rise of capitalism."[3]

Second, Luther's teachings were one of the origins of the German tradition of subordinating the individual to the state. This phenomenon is partly related to the manner in which Lutheranism and, later, the various Reformed churches became politically established. In northern and central Germany especially, the advocates of Protestantism among the German nobility initially provided this religion with a worldly haven in their political domains, which led to the establishment of "territorial churches," and these lords also used Protestantism as a conviction, or a pretext, to legitimize their conflicts with the Roman Church and the (Catholic) Holy Roman Emperors of the German Nation. The subjective personal and public political identification of German nobles and their subjects with Protestantism, which owed its initial organizational survival to the protection it received from secular rulers, regionally elevated the religion of the "territorial churches" to the status of a "state religion," on the one hand, but political patronage also gradually led to a subordination of Protestant churches to the Protestant state, on the other. Although the reasons for the historical and structural subordination of the Protestant Church to the Protestant state were not primarily theological, Luther's theological subordination of the individual to the status quo justified this phenomenon in principle. The subordination of the German Church to the German state and the German Protestant as a Christian individual to the German state had devastating consequences in the future.

During the nineteenth century, a German "religion of the state" evolved out of the tradition of Protestantism as a "state religion" and Luther's theology of "inward" spirituality and external conformity. The rise of Prussia before 1870, the Second German Empire thereafter, and the Third Reich each may be used to illustrate this point. At first it may appear contrived to make Luther's apolitical form of German devotion responsible for the later German worship of the godlike state. But there is no overlooking the fact that under the leadership of political deities like the Kaiser or the Führer, many good Germans religiously served the imperial German state by using their consciences in private and doing their duty in public. The affinity between this phenomenon and Luther's theological paradigm of good Christians serving the Lord by serving their lords is too strong to be overlooked.

Attempts also have been made to interpret Luther as a revolutionary, although the term and the concept were completely foreign to him and his contemporaries. Luther stood at the end of a long medieval tradition of Christian reform characterized by concepts like *renovatio, restauratio,* and *re-*

formatio, which implied a return to a more pristine and authentic form of Christianity. Nevertheless, Marxists, for example, saw Luther as a representative of an "early bourgeois ideology" and interpreted the Reformation as a social upheaval caused by the transition from feudalism to capitalism.

In this context, Thomas Müntzer, initially an ally of Luther and then his antagonist, is of particular interest because he abandoned Luther's premises and understood the Christian mission as the establishment of a more just and equitable social order, here and now. Müntzer's radical theological and political program was that "the first shall be last and the last shall be first." He was one of the ideological and organizational masterminds behind the peasants' uprising of 1525, which shook the southern German-speaking world with its attempt to erect the kingdom of God on earth. Needless to say, the feudal lords put down this uprising with ruthlessness and bloodshed, and in a tract he composed especially for this occasion, Luther gave them his blessing for doing their Christian duty.

For Marxists, Müntzer was the founder of a revolutionary tradition that the "other Germany," the German Democratic Republic, used for forty years in its futile attempt to create a separate national identity for a "socialist German fatherland." (If the historical personalities that a country uses on its currency are an indication of their national importance, we should point out that Müntzer adorned East Germany's smallest bill, the five-Mark note, a place of prominence analogous to George Washington on the U.S. dollar. Karl Marx was on the East Germany's one-hundred-Mark bill.)

Müntzer could be regarded as a predecessor of Marx because he believed in the perfectibility of human society and recognized the necessity of mass action to achieve it. He can even be construed to have anticipated Lenin because Müntzer understood that revolutionary action required a radical program and a revolutionary organization, a group of specially selected and self-sacrificing believers. Although his ideology was "historically conditioned" by Marxist standards, Müntzer anticipated the revolutionary role that the masses were to play in the future. From the dual perspective of a history of the oppressor and a history of the oppressed, the genealogy of "capitalist" Germany ran from Luther to Bismarck to Hitler, and to the Federal Republic of Germany; the heritage of the "other" or socialist Germany ran from Luther to Müntzer to Marx, and to the antifascist tradition of the Communist Party of Germany (KPD) during the Nazi era, and it culminated in the German Democratic Republic.[4]

This example shows how divergent the interpretations of Luther and the Reformation can be. Of course, to his contemporaries, Luther was anything but conservative. His theological assault on the Roman Church and the papacy had enormous worldly consequences and brought him into conflict with Charles V, the Holy Roman Emperor, a Habsburg who saw himself as a Catholic defender of the faith. Luther's critique of the Roman Church resulted in an official condemnation of his writings and his excommunication in 1520, but the "heretic" responded with an unprecedented act of defiance by burning a copy of the papal bull in public and calling it the work of the devil. Ecclesiastical authorities expected the secular supplement to excommunication, an imperial ban, from the emperor, but German nobles sympathetic to Luther's cause implemented some of the empire's venerable legal stipulations, basically feudal forms of due process, to insist that the accused had the right to be heard before being condemned. After having received an imperial guarantee of safe conduct—Luther undoubtedly had in mind the fate of his predecessor Hus under similar circumstances—he appeared in 1521 at the Imperial Diet in Worms, a convocation of the German feudal estates. In the presence of the emperor, however, Luther refused to recant.

These acts of defiance made Luther a national hero in both the modern and the medieval sense of the word. Various representatives of the empire's feudal estates, members of the *natio Germanorum* or "German nation," disliked papal and imperial intervention in their secular affairs just as much as Luther disdained them in his theological and spiritual ones. For Luther, nothing less than salvation or eternal damnation was at stake. His interest in Christian freedom was neither an invitation to sectarianism nor a call for insubordination, although some of his contemporaries interpreted it as such. Although he believed that the conflict of Protestant subjects with their Catholic lords or Catholic and Protestant lords among themselves was unjustifiable, the Will of God would determine the outcome. Although Luther encouraged Protestant lords to obey their Catholic superiors, he did not hesitate to advise them to use the sword to combat the schismatics of other Reformed churches as well as the sedition of their subjects.

Luther's teachings left in their wake a series of insurrections and wars, but it would be difficult to sort out concisely the motives for the individuals or groups who participated in them. They ranged from religious messianism to calculating pragmatism. For the empire's feudal estates, Luther's teachings represented an opportunity to maintain or augment the traditional liberties they had, owing to the chaotic constitutional state of the Holy Roman Empire of the German Nation. In this respect, Protestantism provided a theological justification for the realization of immanently worldly interests. The conflicts of the feudal lords of the German nation with the Roman Church and the Holy Roman Emperor, a Catholic Habsburg raised in Burgundy and the king of Spain whom the German estates regarded as an alien with ambitious dynastic aspirations, also gradually assumed all the terminological characteristics of a national struggle against foreign subjugation. This conflict was not a national struggle of the German people in the nineteenth-century sense of the word, but the nineteenth-century interpretation of the Reformation retrospectively turned it into one.

The terminology that Luther used in his acrid attacks on the Roman Church contributed to the mutually exclusive use of the term "German," which was identified with attributes like authentic and legitimate, and the terms "Latin" or "Roman," which were associated with characteristics like debasement, degeneration, and foreign domination. One of the best examples of the Reformation as a "Latin–German" conflict concerns the liturgy and dealt with the language of worship: Latin, the linguistic manifestation of the universality of the Roman Church but incomprehensible to the layperson, versus German, an example of the vernacular understood by everyone. Luther's translation of the Bible into German was not only a milestone in the development of the German language; the Word of God *auf deutsch* also opened a completely new realm of religious experience for his contemporaries. This is one credible spiritual or psychological explanation for the subsequent success of the Lutheran and Reformed churches in Germany and elsewhere.

The identification of the German word with the True Word of God, German religion with True Religion, and the German church with the True Church appear to follow almost naturally, and the Second German Empire later provided one of the most plastic examples for how Germans later interrelated the ideas of religion, exceptionalism, and nationalism. Erected between 1893 and 1905, the Cathedral of Berlin, reminiscent of Michelangelo's original plans for St. Peter's Cathedral in Rome and with a small-scale emulation of its dome, symbolized Berlin and Germany's position as the global center of the Protestant world.

Although the motives for Luther's deprecating attitude toward all things Latin were theological, his Latin–German terminology had its political counterpart during the Reformation in the Protestant German estates' "national" struggle against all things "Roman": papal and ecclesiastical authority and intervention, on the one hand, and "foreign" (Habsburg and Catholic) imperial power, on the other.

With the support of classical texts, Ulrich von Hutten, a German humanist and contemporary of Luther, added a new dimension to the use of these terms. The Roman poet Tacitus, for example, had described the Teutonic tribes that initially inhabited *Germania* as noble, courageous, peace-loving peoples and valiant warriors, and von Hutten interpreted the conflicts between these primordial inhabitants of Germany and the Roman Empire as a classical precedent explaining the present. The pope and the emperor, Roman and imperial, were the joint descendants of Caesar and the contemporary representatives of the age-old "Latin" aspiration to subjugate the German world.

Although we should not overestimate the impact of von Hutten's comparison—simply because most of his contemporaries were illiterate—we should note that he developed a form of argumentation at the beginning of the sixteenth century based on the rhetorical disparity of German culture with Latin or Mediterranean civilization, which went far beyond Luther's theologically motivated distinction between Rome and Germany. In the future, von Hutten's reasoning was taken literally to extremes. In the nineteenth century, Germans classicists began ignoring the great importance of Semitic and Egyptian influences on Greek culture and started postulating that the origins of Greek culture were "Aryan" (and hence proto-German).[5] These assumptions were coupled with the deprecating attitude that Roman civilization represented a debasement of the classical Greek world.

Some historians even associated German culture in its purest form with the primordial Teutonic inhabitants of *Germania,* thereby reducing Christianity to a historically acquired attribute that was essentially foreign to the genuine nature of *das deutsche Volk*. The proponents of this genre of national genealogy, which reached perverse dimensions in Nazi Germany, questioned the idea of a genuine nexus between Christianity and Germanness (*Deutschtum*) altogether. They extolled, for example, the assertive values of combative Teutonic paganism, criticized the "submissiveness" inherent in Christianity as foreign to the true nature of Germans, and denounced the Judeo-Christian tradition, owing to its historical origins in the eastern Mediterranean world, as "oriental" or "foreign to the Nordic species."[6]

The "Luther-to-Hitler" interpretation of German history is problematic. Luther and the Reformation contributed to the early development of a friend–foe metaphor that postulated rectitude and authenticity to be integrally "German" attributes and simultaneously identified the concepts of "Latin" or "Roman" as symptomatic of debasing or threatening foreign influences. Proponents of nineteenth-century German Romanticism and nationalism also later adopted and transformed the friend–foe terminology of the Reformation for their own political purposes. In this context, Luther was retrospectively assigned the role of having been the "savior of the German nation," and the Reformation was turned into something it initially had not been: the beginning of a long struggle of the German nation for a free and unified Germany.

The conflicts following the Reformation actually did more to promote German disunity than perhaps anything else, because they added a new denominational dimension to the well-established feudal traditions of particularism that existed in the Holy Roman Empire. Both Protestant and Catholic parties eventually recognized that the denominational issue could not be solved by force, and so they agreed in 1555 to call a halt, for the time being at least, in the Religious Peace of Augsburg which established the principle of *cuius regio, eius et religio*, literally, "whose rule, his religion." This pact, which recognized only Roman Catholicism and Lutheranism and denied the legitimacy of various other Reformed churches, gave the empire's numerous secular lords the right to choose their religion as they saw fit and to make that religion binding on their subjects as well. The Religious Peace of Augsburg was basically a recognition of the status quo, which contained the religious problems without solving them, as the Thirty Years' War (1618–1648) was to demonstrate later.

The Reformation weakened the traditional "bulwark of Christendom" by dividing it, and if one is prepared to bypass the various periods and patterns of conversion and reconversion, the following generalizations about the confessional landscape of Central Europe toward the end of the sixteenth century are possible. In the German-speaking world, Bavaria and Austria were thoroughly Protestant, although they later were vigorously reconverted to Roman Catholicism, and outside a sprinkling of Catholic strongholds in west central Germany, the rest of the German-speaking world, interspersed with pockets of Calvinism, became predominantly Lutheran. The Reformation established a North–South denominational watershed that eventually led to the development of two different German cultures: a "northern" and Protestant one, in which Hohenzollern Prussia eventually assumed a leading political role, and a "southern" and Roman Catholic one under the ascendancy of the Habsburgs of Austria and seconded by Bavaria. Northern Germany became a bulwark of the Protestant form of Christianity, and Austria and Bavaria became dual bastions of the Roman Catholicism in the southern part of the German-speaking world.

Because of Hus's influence, the Czechs in the kingdom of Bohemia were predominantly Protestant before the official German beginning of the Reformation, and the Reformation only reinforced the development of a distinctive form of Czech reformed devotion, the Bohemian Brethren. The doctrines of Luther and Calvin also made substantial inroads in the kingdom of Hungary, and they established a few smaller niches in the kingdom of Poland, which was and remained a paradigm of religious tolerance during Europe's various confessional conflicts. Due to its large holdings in the (Orthodox) East, only about half the population of the kingdom of Poland was Roman Catholic, and one of the reasons for the considerable size of Poland's pre-Holocaust Jewish population was that the Polish–Lithuanian Commonwealth served from the thirteenth century onward as a traditional haven for Europe's religiously persecuted. The primary pattern of Jewish migration in medieval Europe was west to east, and the Jews fleeing Christian pogroms in Western Europe in the Middle Ages, were followed by Protestants fleeing Roman Catholic persecution in the seventeenth century. The Reformation also helped reinforce the bulwark idea as a Roman Catholic national metaphor in Poland, because thereafter the country was surrounded by schismatics—German Protestants in the west and the Russian Orthodox in the east—in addition to being threatened by infidels—the Tatars and later the Turks.

The Reformation ended the unity of Western Christianity. It subdivided the idea of the "bulwark of Christendom" among various denominations and nations, and the creation of smaller bastions out of the materials that previously had been nominally cemented by one religion helped weaken those southeastern "bulwarks of Christendom," Hungary and then Austria, which were responsible for defending Western Christendom from the Islam of the expanding Ottoman Empire. Therefore, we should take a brief look at the consequences of this Christian disunity for Western Christendom's battle on its southeastern frontier.

Western Christianity Threatened: The Rise of the Ottomans' European Empire

The medieval Christian world had a long tradition of crusading, and if there was one thing Christians shared with Muslims, it was the conviction that God, like Allah, looked favorably on the idea of holy wars. The various crusades organized during the Middle Ages to regain the Holy Land were relatively futile quests, and the expansion of the Ottoman Empire in the fourteenth century onto the Balkan Peninsula provided an occasion for Western Christendom to launch what could be called its last crusade. Sigismund of Luxemburg, the king of Hungary, organized this operation to help secure the southern frontier of his kingdom, which had come under the increasing pressure of the Ottoman Empire after the defeat of Serbia in the Battle of Kosovo in 1389. Married to the daughter of Louis "the Great," the last Angevin king of Hungary, he used his wife's family ties to inspire French and Burgundian nobles with the idea of driving the Turks out of Europe, and defending the faith was the kind of project the popes had repeatedly encouraged. The flower of the French nation participated in this crusade, which ended in 1396 when Christian forces numbering about 8,000 engaged an estimated 12,000 to 20,000 Turks in the Battle of Nicopolis south of the Danube in Bulgaria. Bewitched by the ideas of chivalry, honor, and glory and nonchalant about details like reconnaissance or tactical planning, the noble French knights—against all the good Hungarian advice they received to the contrary—plunged ardently into a battle that ended in a debacle, which Sigismund of Luxemburg barely escaped.

The manner in which the Ottoman sultan, Bajazet I, treated his vanquished Christian enemies was responsible for making a deep, lasting, and bad impression on Western Christendom. Sultan Bajazet, enraged by his losses on the battlefield and indignant about the fact that the crusaders had massacred Turkish prisoners from a preliminary engagement, decided to take vengeance. Several thousand French prisoners, who were either not young enough to become slaves or not prominent enough to hold for ransom, were stripped naked, bound together at their hands and necks in groups of three or four, and marched in front of the sultan. Then from early morning until late afternoon, executioners decapitated them, one by one, in the presence of the sultan and the French nobles being held for ransom. Although crusaders were notorious for conducting themselves barbarously in the lands they traversed to and from their Christian missions and were usually just as ruthless with their enemies, Western Christendom was shocked by this "oriental" bloodbath. Indeed, incidents such as these provided the basis for the later Western perception of the Turkish threat.[7]

Each Hungarian king after Sigismund had to devote more and more attention to the Turkish problem on the southern frontier. Sigismund's next two successors on the Hungarian throne, Albert of Austria and Władysław III, died there; János Hunyadi and his son Matthias Corvinus managed to hold the front; Vladislav II inherited this problem; and his son Louis II lost his life there. Louis II's antagonist was Suleiman the Magnificent, the sultan under which the Ottoman Empire reached its peak. Before the conquest of Hungary, the Ottoman Empire stretched from Belgrade to Baghdad and controlled Egypt and the eastern Mediterranean. Both its resources and despotism, a superior form of organization that facilitated marshaling such resources, made the confrontation with Hungary an unequal match.

Suleiman's army of 150,000 marched up the Danube and met the forces of Louis II, who had managed to gather 24,000 knights, mercenaries, and auxiliaries, on the plains of southern Hungary near the small village of Mohács on August 29, 1526. The Hungarian strategy was straightforward, chivalrous, and, from a tactical point of view, somewhere between stupid and suicidal. The hopelessly outnumbered knights charged frontally into the

The Battle of Mohács in 1526, which the Hungarians lost to the Turks, was a national catastrophe. Detail from a Turkish miniature with Hungarian forces being led by King Louis II (mounted, upper left), who was killed; Turkish artillery and Turkish troops (right). After Mohács, the Turks occupied most of Hungary for more than 150 years. (Austrian National Library, Picture Archive)

THE OTTOMAN THREAT, 1526–1683

Based on Paul Robert Magocsi, *Historical Atlas of East Central Europe* (Seattle: University of Washington Press, 1993)

—————— International frontiers, ca. 1500

████████ Frontier of the Ottoman Empire at its peak, 1683

— — — Borders of Ottoman vassal states

⚔ *1683* Sites and dates of major Habsburg victories

After the Ottoman Turks decisively defeated the Hungarians in the Battle of Mohác, in 1526, the kingdom of Hungary was divided into three parts for more than 150 years. The Ottomans occupied most of Hungary; the Habsburgs, elected kings of Hungary in 1527, ruled a small strip of territory, "Royal Hungary," on the north-western frontier of the kingdom of Hungary; and Hungarian nobles ruled a semi-independent vassal state of the Ottoman Empire in Transylvania. In the sixteenth century, the Ottoman Empire also expanded up the Black Sea coast into Ukraine, opening up a theater of direct Polish–Ottoman conflict. In 1683, the fortunes of the Ottoman Empire turned dramatically when Polish, German, and Habsburg forces lifted the Turkish siege of Vienna. During the following thirty-five years, Habsburg center of the Turkish lines, which feinted flight to their flanks in order to give the artillery positioned behind them an open field of fire, and then the Turkish troops converged on the Hungarian forces to finish off what was left. Twenty-two thousand members of what chroniclers proverbially called the flower of the nation left their lives on the battlefield. Louis II, extracted from the melee by a group of noblemen, fled. Whether he drowned crossing a river or his noble escorts vengefully murdered him has never been clarified. In any event, the path to Hungary was open for the Turks, and the throne of Hungary was vacant for the Habsburgs.

Hungarians view the Battle of Mohács as the central tragedy of their history because it marked the loss of national independence and the beginning of a series of foreign occupations. After 1526, Hungary was a defeated nation, occupied alternately by the Turks and the Habsburgs. (The Habsburg's initial occupation of Hungary did gradually evolve into a partnership.) The Hungarians' national response to defeat and occupation never was complete capitulation or total assimilation. On the contrary, one of the recurring themes of Hungarian historiography and literature has traditionally been the survival of the Hungarian nation despite the tragedies and hardships of foreign occupation.

After their decisive defeat at Mohács, the Hungarians mastered the arts of revolt, accommodation, and survival. Given the absence of great victories in the past 500 years of Hungarian history, the commemoration of defeats in the spirit of national martyrology, like the Battle of Mohács in the sixteenth century or Hungary's abortive revolutions of 1848 and 1956, has played a central role in articulating the nation's history as a tragic struggle. The commemoration of a defeat, however, simultaneously functions as a celebration of national tenacity—a will to resist and an ability to survive—and this is an attribute that the Hungarians share with the Poles and, to a lesser extent, the Czechs.[8]

Before 1989, Hungarians used to tell a joke that compared the consequences of the Turkish victory in 1526 with those of the Russian one in 1945. The Turks did not force the Hungarians to celebrate Mohács every year (the commemoration of the advent of the Bolshevik Revolution was a national holiday in Communist Hungary), nor did they make Hungarians learn Turkish (learning Russian was mandatory in Hungarian schools). Furthermore, the Turks did not constantly tell the Hungarians that they were their brothers and that they were going to live with them in perpetual friendship.

If Mohács represents a central national tragedy for Hungarians, Austrians simultaneously see it as a windfall in their own history because it was the birth of the Habsburgs' Central European empire. With the exception of a small strip of territory along Hungary's western and northern frontiers and

---

imperial armies launched a series of campaigns against the Ottoman Empire that culminated in the liberation of the kingdom of Hungary. By 1720, the Habsburg Empire had succeeded in regaining most of those territories of the "Christian West" that had been lost to the "Islamic East" after the Battle of Mohác in 1526.

Transylvania in the east, the Turks eventually occupied the central Danube basin. The death of Louis II vacated the Bohemian and the Hungarian thrones, and the advance of the Turks certainly helped inspire the Bohemian estates to elect the archduke of Austria, Ferdinand I, king in 1526, because they sought formidable allies.

Although Ferdinand also had a technical claim to the Hungarian throne, election by the Hungarian nobility was a prerequisite for legitimacy. One faction of Hungarian nobles elected Ferdinand von Habsburg as the king of Hungary in 1527, but another group chose János Zápolyai, the voivode of Transylvania, for the throne. Which king was the legitimate one, the foreign Habsburg or the Hungarian Zápolyai, depends on the national perspective assumed. Austrians opt for Ferdinand, and Hungarians choose Zápolyai. (This claim to the crown was eventually abandoned without recognizing the legitimacy of the Habsburgs, and a series of princes from the Hungarian stronghold of Transylvania—István Báthori, István Bocskai, Gábor Bethlen, Ferenc Rákóczi—well known to Hungarians but virtually unknown to everyone else, continued the struggle for independence.) Tripartition—a Habsburg in the west, the Turks in the middle, and the Hungarians in the east—characterized the situation of Hungary for the next one and a half centuries and created a triangular conflict on the Christian–Islamic frontier.

As the kings of Hungary, the Habsburgs were confronted with two problems: the Turkish occupation of Hungary and the assertion of their rights and titles in unoccupied Hungarian Transylvania. The Hungarians in unoccupied Transylvania also were confronted with two problems: the Turkish occupation of Hungary and the maintenance of the relative independence of unoccupied Transylvania as a base of operations against the Habsburgs and the Turks, who treated Hungarian Transylvania as a vassal state. The Habsburgs fought alternately with the Hungarians and the Turks, depending on whether the insubordination of their Hungarian subjects or the menace of the Ottoman infidels temporarily appeared to be the greater threat, and the Hungarians oscillated between trying to play off the Turks against the Habsburgs, and vice versa, depending on which of the two foreign powers momentarily appeared to be the lesser evil.

The fact that a specifically Hungarian strain of Calvinism also became established in eastern Hungary during the Reformation added another dimension to this triangular conflict. In the future, Protestant Hungarians allied themselves with their fellow believers in the German empire against the Catholic Habsburgs in confessional conflicts, which illustrates how interdenominational conflict in the Christian West affected the Habsburgs. As a bulwark of Catholicism, they were confronted with Protestantism, and as the bulwark of Christendom, they were confronted with the Turks. The relationship between Western Christendom's internal conflicts and its external defense is perhaps clearest on this point. Protestants hesitated to give the Habsburgs the money or the support they would have needed to retake Hungary or to combat energetically the Turks, simply because they were not sure whether those resources would be used against the infidels or themselves.

There is a striking difference between the way in which Austrians and Hungarians view what happened after the Hungarian "bulwark of Christendom" fell in 1526. From the Austrian perspective, when they assumed the Hungarian crown, the Habsburgs also shouldered the responsibility for defending Western Christendom, a burden that was complicated by Hungarian sedition on the frontier and Protestant ingratitude behind it. For the Hungarians, the beginning of the Turkish occupation and the Habsburgs' expropriation of the Hungarian crown marked the beginning of a futile struggle for national liberation that ended 160 years later when the Habsburgs finally defeated the Turks and "liberated" Hungary in the process. (Liberation is a very ambiguous term in Central Europe, and Central Europeans use it with irony. The Habsburgs' liberation of Hungary from the Turks entailed putting down a Hungarian national insurrection. Therefore, the Hungarians were "liberated" from one empire only to be subjugated by the next. Likewise, the Soviet Union "liberated" East Central Europe from National Socialism and then incorporated it into its own empire.)

The Turkish occupation also uncoupled vast parts of Hungary from the orbit of Western civilization for more than one and a half centuries. This fact can be used as one explanation for the subsequent lag, by Western standards, in the country's development. Some Hungarian historians have argued, for example, that the gap between Hungarian and West European levels of development widened noticeably after 1526. Because of the Turks, the Hungarians missed out on some 175 years of Western European development that they otherwise would have participated in had the Turks not been in Hungary.

Furthermore, Hungarian economic historians were among the first in the old Communist East to popularize the term "East Central Europe" in the 1970s. One of their reasons for doing so was the attempt to describe the structural peculiarities of this region and the consequences of its Turkish occupation. In this context, there were indeed important differences between the concepts of Southeastern Europe, western East Europe, and East Central Europe. The term "western East Europe" implies, for example, a Hungarian affinity to Russian (and ultimately Soviet) patterns of development, whereas East Central Europe terminologically and methodologically dissociates Hungary (and Slovakia and Poland) from "the East" by formulating the concept of "Central Europe" as a region that, after the end of the fifteenth century, no longer kept up with "the West" but continued to draw its primary impulses from there.[9] This concept is both important and useful, as we shall see, but it also is a bit unusual insofar as its counterpart, "West Central Europe," never was adopted or articulated by Austrian, Czech, or German historians. One reason for this may be that the old East–West terminology of the Cold War did not permit thinking of Europe in terms of a middle that was neither East nor West.

Southeastern Europe may be used to describe the Balkan Peninsula as a region whose indigenous development was different and later was influenced by a prolonged Turkish occupation. The magnitude of the consequences of Turkish occupation also increased in proportion to the length of its duration. Therefore, they were more profound farther south and added deep-seated structural differences to the initial denominational differences between southern Central Europe and the lower Balkan Peninsula. For example, Hungarians and Croats, adherents of Roman Christianity, spent much less time under Ottoman rule than did their Orthodox neighbors to the south, like the Serbs, Romanians, and Bulgarians, and the extended Turkish presence on the Balkans is frequently used to explain the legacy of underdevelopment in those regions. By Western European standards, Turkish occupation hindered the economic development of this region, although its lag in modernization after the Turks were gone cannot be solely attributed to its Ottoman heritage.[10]

The prolonged Turkish occupation of the Danube Basin and the Balkan Peninsula also helped complicate the ethnic map of the region. War, migration, and resettlement campaigns contributed to the establishment of Serbian minorities in Croatia, the Albanian majority in the historically Serbian province of Kosovo, Croatian and Hungarian minorities in Serbia, and the Croatian–Serbian–Muslim patchwork of Bosnia. Many Serbs attempted to escape the hardships of Ottoman rule by moving north, or they were actively recruited to serve as "frontiersmen" on the Western or Habsburg side of the military frontier. As a result, Eastern Orthodox Serbs played an important role in the defense of Western Christendom. The migration and Habsburg recruitment of Serbs to serve as militia-farmers on the military frontier created new "linguistic islands" of Serbs in the kingdoms of Croatia and Hungary. Albanians in turn filled the vacuum left by Serbian migration in the province of Kosovo. There were also many converts to Islam in the southern regions. Later Germans settlers, Hungarians, and Croats also moved south as the Habsburgs pushed the Ottoman Empire back down the Balkan Peninsula.

The confrontation with the Ottoman Empire was geopolitically a North–South conflict on the Balkan Peninsula, but it was an East–West confrontation in ideological terms: the Islamic Orient or East versus the Christian Occident or West. Although contemporaries may not have recognized this, historians now tend to agree that the magnitude of the Turkish threat was never as great as the contemporary portrayals of it. There also were two natural bulwarks containing the Ottoman expansion northward, Austria's Alps and the Carpathian Mountains on Poland's southern frontier, and there do not seem to be any indications that the Turks ever seriously planned to cross either of them. On the one hand, the expansion of the Ottoman Empire along the shores of the Black Sea and inland from there brought it into peripheral contact with the kingdom of Poland and eventually opened a subsidiary theater of Christian–Islamic conflict in Ukraine. But the Polish heartland never was threatened. On the other hand, the Ottoman Turks would have liked to have rounded out their holdings by taking Vienna, which they besieged in 1529, but the premature onset of winter and a plague in their camps evidently encouraged them to abandon an operation that otherwise would apparently have been a success.

Although the Ottoman threat then subsided until the second Turkish siege of Vienna in 1683, in the interim, Habsburg propagandists enjoyed praising the dynasty as a paragon of courage and as the bulwark of Christendom, and the frequent exaggeration of the Turkish threat was a means of amplifying the Habsburgs' achievements and importance. Overstatement also helped mobilize support at home and abroad, by implying that if the Habsburg bastion fell, the Turks would first slaughter the Habsburgs' own uncooperative subjects and then proceed up the Danube to the Rhine or Paris and do the same to the Habsburgs' Protestant and French enemies. In this respect, the propagation of the idea of a common menace contributed to bridging denominational gaps and consolidating the Habsburgs' domestic and international position by emphasizing their indispensability.

One contemporary description of the eastern front demonstrates the type of hyperbole used: "The Austrian countryside, far and near, is strewn with dead bodies, and its waters are colored with blood. The fields are devastated, villages and market-towns burnt, and our Holy Religion mocked and ridiculed."[11] The themes of barbarism and sacrilege abound in the chronicles of the times which, aside from making the "Infidel Turk" responsible for pillage and plunder and dragging Christians into slavery, portrayed as common Turkish practices, quartering children or raping pregnant women and then cutting open their stomachs and tearing the unborn children out of their bodies. It would be unwarranted to make light of the people's suffering, but Turkish warfare was usually not any more or less ruthless than its contemporary Christian counterpart.

Despite periodic conflicts between the Habsburgs and the Ottomans, the military frontier between the Christian West and the Ottoman East was relatively stable. Nonetheless, the Ottoman reconnaissance units (Akindshi), which were called "runners and burners" because they lived off the land, wreaked havoc whenever they crossed the frontier. Strategically speaking, they were a nuisance, not a threat, but they did remind the Habsburgs and their subjects that Austria was the bulwark of Christendom.

The conflicts of the sixteenth century among Western Christians as well as the confrontation between the Christian West and the Islamic East consolidated the bulwark as a metaphor that the nations of Central Europe repeatedly used to define their respective roles in European history as well as their relationships with one another, and there are many examples of the multipurpose use of the bulwark metaphor in the twentieth century. When Nazi Germany occupied and annexed Austria in March 1938, Hitler called Austria "the newest bulwark of the German Reich." In the early 1950s, the Hungarian Stalinist Mátyás Rákosi—using that peculiar Communist mixed metaphor of "struggling for peace"—called Hungary "a bulwark on the front line of peace." Poland was a "bulwark of Catholicism" in Communism's atheist East. East and West Germany were the respective "bulwarks" of the Warsaw Pact and NATO. And Croatia and Serbia became bulwarks in the war that erupted in the former Yugoslavia in 1991.

One may question the value of military metaphors as a mode of national self-perception because they do not promote peaceful coexistence but, on the contrary, can be a source of conflict themselves. The Czechs are an exception to this rule because the bulwark metaphor never really made its way into their national vocabulary. This fact is strange, because the Czechs appear to be the only Central Europeans topographically entitled to use the bulwark metaphor to describe their country. The Bohemian Basin is surrounded by mountains. But apparently it would never occur to a people surrounded by so many other bulwarks to call themselves one.

❧ 5 ❧

The Counter-Reformation

The Roman Catholic Church and the Habsburg

Dynasty Triumphant, 1550–1700

The idea of reform inspired Protestants and Catholics alike with an apocalyptic sense of urgency that led them to see the world as a battlefield for the agents of God and the devil. Even though religion was often misused as an ideological pretext for the cynical realization of pragmatic political objectives, spiritual conviction was, for better or worse, a motive for action. Habitual Christians of all denominations today have trouble understanding what was at stake because the passions involved are so foreign to our contemporary way of life. The liberal tradition of the separation of church and state, the achievements of post–World War II ecumenism, and the vacuity of the allegedly postideological world in which we live make religious fervor a relatively rare phenomenon.

The Counter-Reformation was nothing less than a spiritual battle for souls, a psychological battle for hearts, and an intellectual battle for minds, and it also became a physical battle for bodies. If the Catholic Church failed to win one of the first three, it did not hesitate to destroy the fourth—the bodies of those whose souls and hearts were possessed or minds recalcitrant. Religious zeal was not a peculiarity of the Roman Church, which, like its Protestant counterparts, existed in a world still populated by demons and devils, who frequently manifested themselves as fanatics and heretics.

It would be difficult to try to ascertain retrospectively whether the Catholic zeal for reconversion, which infamously displayed itself in the Spanish Inquisition's torture and burning of heretics, was any worse than the Protestant fervor that produced witch-hunts in Germany. The doctrinal and organizational centralization of the Roman Church, however, made the excesses of its crusaders qualitatively different from Protestant ones, and it also demonstrated that the Roman Church was better equipped for conflict than any of its numerous Protestant opponents were. The Roman Church rejuvenated the tradition of the "one, Holy, Catholic, and Apostolic Church," and Catholic apologists never tired of emphasizing that Protestantism was divisive and partial instead of "one" or universal, innovative instead of apostolic, and sinful instead of holy. Because the Roman Church was unified and the Protestant churches were not, it did not have to pursue the ancient Roman imperial strategy of divide and rule; it merely had to find a means to conquer the divided.

If the posting of Luther's Ninety-five Theses is conventionally used to mark the beginning of the Reformation, then it is equally conventional to use the Roman Catholic Church's Council of Trent (in northern Italy, from 1545 until 1563) as the inauguration of what German Protestant historians pejoratively called the Counter-Reformation, but people more sympathetic to Roman Catholicism have referred to as the Catholic Reformation. The former term insinuates that the Catholic Church merely reacted to the beating it had taken during the Protestant Reformation, whereas the latter places this episode in the broader tradition of Catholic reform as one of those periodic returns to the original purity and strengths of the doctrine from which it had strayed. The Counter- or Catholic Reformation was undoubtedly both. But since the Protestant term for Catholicism's reform enjoys greater currency than the Roman Catholic one—just as the Protestant interpretation is more popular in the German- and English-speaking worlds than the Catholic one—it will be used here without necessarily being a categorical endorsement of the Protestant position.

At the Council of Trent, the Roman Catholic Church did not attempt to refute the individual points of Protestant criticism. Indeed, the shortcomings of the Roman Church were apparent to devout Catholic men of God, who recognized that the institution of the church was in dire need of reform. Nonetheless, the Roman Church made few concessions on the theological front. On the contrary, it reaffirmed just about everything Luther and his contemporaries had criticized. Luther's rejection of scholastic philosophy and theology had led him to call reason a whore; a renaissance of neoscholastic rigor was the Roman Church's response. Luther rejected the entire spectrum of intermediaries and rituals that Catholicism placed between people and their God, from the Virgin Mary and the saints to the pope, the ecclesiastical hierarchy, priests, and the Roman sacraments and liturgy; the Roman Church posited them as indispensable means of Salvation in addition to making the Protestants' subjective conviction of being saved or chosen by God a cardinal sin. The Protestant spirituality of "inwardness" led to a rejection of the traditional artistic and architectural accoutrements of worship, ranging from relics and processions to magnificently designed and adorned houses of God, because they merely distracted the soul or fell into the category of worshiping false idols. The Roman Church propagated a sensuous and dramatic new form of expression that rejuvenated the tradition of *ad majoram gloriam Dei*, "for the greater glory of God," and intended to give Christians a glimpse of his glory, the Baroque.

The Counter-Reformation was originally a Mediterranean phenomenon because Italy—the home of the papacy and the Baroque style—and Spain—the birthplace of the Roman Church's most effective counterinsurgency organization, the Society of Jesus, or Jesuit order—were the two Roman Catholic countries least affected by the Reformation. The most important Mediterranean political agent of the Counter-Reformation was Habsburg Spain, and the Habsburgs of Austria, who received the full support of their Spanish dynastic relatives, Rome, and the Jesuit order, eventually assumed this role north of the Alps.

Before 1600 the progress of the Counter-Reformation in the north was limited. The Jesuits spearheaded the Roman Church's efforts and eventually assumed a leading role in education as a battle for hearts and minds, but the Habsburgs were not necessarily predisposed to become the papacy's vehicle in the battle for bodies and lost ecclesiastical terrain. Ferdinand I, the Habsburg who, as the archduke of Austria, king of Bohemia, king of Hungary, and (after 1556) Holy Roman Emperor of the German Nation, personally embodied the rise of the House of Austria to a major power, felt that tolerance was the best means of dealing with the issue of denominational diversity.

His successors between 1564 and 1619—Maximilian II, Rudolph II, and Matthias—individually confronted the religious issue with an open sympathy for Protestantism, incompetence, and pragmatism, in that order. The ascendancy of Ferdinand II to the Bohemian throne in 1617 and his assumption of the Austrian titles and Hungarian crown along with his election as Holy Roman Emperor in 1619, however, changed the complexion of the situation because he was prepared to ally himself with Rome and its agenda. Ferdinand II was renowned for his personal devotion, and he identified with loyalty the divinely ordained mission of the House of Habsburg with the Roman Church and Roman Catholicism in a manner which made heresy seditious or sedition heretical. The Catholic piety of the Habsburgs gave their dynasty a mission and an absolutistic ideology; the Counter-Reformation presented them with an opportunity to combat Protestantism and consolidate their realms in the name of God.

Breaking Bohemia's Back:
The Battle of White Mountain, 1620

Ferdinand II perceived Protestantism as the primary political problem inside and outside his immediate realms. As Holy Roman Emperor, Ferdinand took seriously the Roman Catholic obligations he saw as part of his Roman imperial title, and he viewed the gradual Protestant erosion of the political–denominational status quo, which had been established by the Religious Peace of Augsburg in 1555 but undermined by the conversion of the subjects of Catholic lords to Protestantism, as a process that had to be reversed.

The domestic situation that Ferdinand II confronted in his own realms when he came to power also was complicated.[1] The union of the Habsburgs' various realms was dynastic or personal, not constitutional, and the Habsburg Empire never completely lost its character of being a collection of feudal estates. For example, Ferdinand had a series of titles and domains, each of which had its own constitution. He was the archduke of Austria *and* the king of Bohemia *and* the king of Hungary, and so on. Each of these realms had its own feudal estates with its own historical traditions and institutions and particular regional interests, and the dynasty could increase its power only at the expense of these respective feudal estates. In addition, the majority of Ferdinand's subjects were Protestants, and Protestant apprehension about Roman Catholicism reinforced the feudal estates' traditional aversion to royal attempts at centralization. The rebelliousness of his Protestant Hungarian subjects in Transylvania was a good example of how these religious and feudal interests coalesced, and Bohemia became one.

A conflict between Bohemian nobles and the representatives of the crown in 1618 over the violation of a royal guarantee ensuring freedom of religion, made by one of Ferdinand II's vacillating predecessors on the Bohemian throne, provided an occasion for the Counter-Reformation to turn into a Central European military conflict. A group of enraged Bohemian nobles threw two of Ferdinand II's appointees, responsible for managing royal affairs in his absence, and their secretary out of one of the windows of the Hradčin, the royal castle in Prague. (They survived their fall of more than sixty feet by falling onto a heap of compost, *vulgo*, or in the Czech oral tradition, horse shit.)

This act of defenestration—from Latin *de* (out) and *fenestra* (window)—is a symbol of enormous historical importance for the Czechs. In 1419, the Hussite wars, which nineteenth-century Czech historians viewed as the first "national struggle" against German–Catholic hegemony, began when Hussites threw Catholic councilmen out of a window of the Prague town hall. The "Prague defenestration" of 1618, which Czechs traditionally have seen as the beginning of a second national struggle in the spirit of the first Hussite one, was to have ruinous consequences for Bohemia. The third defenestration in 1948—when the Czech foreign minister, Jan Masaryk, a non-Communist in Czechoslovakia's recently formed Communist government and the son of Thomas Masaryk, the founding father of the Republic of Czechoslovakia in 1918, was found dead beneath the open window of his office—symbolized a political and a personal break with Czechoslovakia's interwar tradition of independence and democracy. (According to the Communist authorities, Masaryk's death was a suicide, but all evidence unearthed since then clearly points to murder.)

In 1618, the Bohemian nobility decided that Ferdinand had violated the rights of the estates he had solemnly sworn to observe when assuming the Bohemian crown, so they retracted the crown and established a directory of thirty nobles to rule the land. Then they elected a Protestant prince from the duchy of Pfalz in Germany, Frederick V, king of Bohemia, an act that eventually dragged German Protestants and Catholics into the affair.

A nation's fate never hinges on a single event, but there always are relatively isolated incidents, like battles, that may be used to symbolize auspicious or ominous turning points. The Battle of White Mountain (Bilá hora) outside Prague in 1620 plays a role in the Czech historical memory analogous to the one that the Battle at Mohács in 1526 does for Hungarians, because it symbolizes the beginning of a national tragedy. The Bohemian estates were determined to fight for their liberties and organized an army of 20,000 men. Ferdinand II resolved to reassert his rights and sent a legion of 25,000 mercenaries under the leadership of a Catholic Spanish-Flemish nobleman, Field Marshal Johann Tserclae von Tilly, to restore order in the lands of the Bohemian crown. The Battle of White Mountain had none of the epic qualities one would expect from confrontation with such profound consequences. More of a skirmish than a clash of cosmic forces, it lasted less than an hour. Tilly's professional soldiers of fortune scattered their poorly organized opponents, and Ferdinand II proceeded with the work of dismantling Bohemian independence.

Czech nationalist historians and Habsburg apologists have argued whether Ferdinand was vengeful or merciful to the point of exhaustion. Twenty-seven leaders of the uprising were arrested, put on trial, and beheaded on the square outside Prague's town hall. After 1918 twenty-seven white crosses were inset in the plaster there to commemorate these martyrs of the Bohemian nation, which incidentally included a number of German nobles. Distinguishing between the Bohemian nation and the Czech nation is important in this context. The Bohemian nation in the medieval sense of the word consisted of Czech *and* German nobles who fought the crown to maintain their own freedoms and privileges, not those of "the people." The Czech nation as a linguistic, cultural, and eventually political entity arose in the nineteenth century, and nineteenth-century Czech nationalists tended to reinterpret retrospectively the old Bohemian nation in modern Czech national terms. This led to distortions and turned the feudal or religious conflicts of German kings with Bohemian nobles or German Catholics with Bohemian Hussites into ethnic conflicts between Germans and Czechs.

Ferdinand II's imperial strategy for breaking resistance once and for all in the kingdom of Bohemia was ruthlessly straightforward. He expropriated the rebels, reconverted the lands of the Bohemian crown to Catholicism, and eventually demoted the relatively independent kingdom of Bohemia to the status of a dynastic province by turning its crown from an elected privilege into a hereditary possession. Czech historians later referred to the period starting with the Bohemian defeat in the Battle of White Mountain as *doba temna*, "the time of darkness."

Approximately 150,000 people emigrated from the lands of the Bohemian crown to escape religious or political persecution, among them 185 noble families and other traditional carriers of Czech culture like urban bourgeoisie, ministers, and professors. More than 50 percent of the land, and an even higher percentage of the larger landed estates, changed hands in the course of these confiscations.

The greatest benefactors of the Habsburg policies were the *soldatesca*—the officers of the international pack of mercenaries whom the Habsburgs had recruited to fight their wars for them and who were paid in land instead of cash—and the established Bohemian nobility that had remained loyal to the Roman Church and the Catholic crown. These measures changed the makeup of the Bohemian estates by ennobling foreigners—Spanish, Irish, Italian, Flemish, and German mercenaries patronized by the Habsburgs—or by increasing the holdings of the indigenous Catholic Bohemian nobility. Bohemia's large class of nobles, which was predominantly Czech, Protestant, and recalcitrant, was replaced by a smaller one, which was "German," Catholic, and loyal to the Habsburgs. (In 1918 the Republic of Czechoslovakia confiscated eighty estates that were larger than 25,000 acres, the majority of which belonged to aristocrats who had long records of serving the Habsburgs.)

The power of these nobles not only was enhanced by their loyalty to the Habsburgs or the magnitude of their estates—by the mid-seventeenth century eighty-five families controlled more than 60 percent of the country's peasants—but also was augmented by the development of practices usually subsumed under the term of "second serfdom," a phenomenon that had little to do with the Habsburgs or the Counter-Reformation but temporally coincided with them. The development of "second serfdom" in Bohemia and also in eastern Austria, Hungary, Poland, and parts of eastern Germany consisted basically of lords' reassertion of feudal rights over peasant-serfs at a time when, farther west, the restrictions of medieval or "first serfdom" were gradually disappearing because of the development of money-based or cash economies that made it more profitable for lords to extract money, rather than goods or services, from their tenant-serfs. "Second serfdom" restricted rural mobility by binding peasants to the land and by increasing the burden of traditional labor obligations that they owed their lords.

It might lead too far astray to delve into the complexity of this issue. In brief, however, "second serfdom" became a characteristic of vast regions of Central Europe, and one of its consequences was that it helped maintain hierarchical, predominantly rural forms of social and economic organization, which inhibited in the long run the development of more mobile or prosperous societies. Old forms of subjugation reasserted themselves under new conditions of dominion in Central Europe, whereas the deterioration of old forms of subjugation in Western Europe gradually led to the acquisition of new freedoms, both economic and political. It would be difficult to overestimate the long-term consequences of this kind of development, because Central Europe's neofeudal political structures reinforced relative economic backwardness, and vice versa. In other words, "in East-Central Europe the period from the sixteenth to the eighteen centuries cannot be regarded as an era of transition from feudalism to capitalism but rather a peculiar, belated feudalism. Medieval conditions, instead of waning, were consolidated."[2]

This pattern of postponed or retarded development in Central Europe was established early on and was enduring. A rift between the levels of economic development in Western and Central Europe—East being a term reserved for Russian developments—may have existed as early as the twelfth century, and it began to widen considerably in the seventeenth century. The consequences of Western Europe's "dual revolution"—a term E. J. Hobsbawm used to describe the (British) Industrial Revolution of the eighteenth century and the French (political) Revolution of 1789[3]—also manifested themselves later and to a lesser extent in Central Europe than in Western Europe. Although it is a bit too simplistic to couple the evolution of capitalistic or industrial societies with the rise of liberalism and democracy, the development of Central Europe was characterized by the persistence of its precapitalistic or preindustrial economies as well as the perseverance of its neofeudal and, later, absolutistic political traditions and institutions.

A brief digression on the ensuing peculiarities of the development of Central Europe's economic and social structures is perhaps necessary here. Economic historians have investigated the reasons for the "West–East developmental gradient" in Europe and the phenomenon of "backwardness," and they distinguish among the various regions based on criteria related to urbanization, capital accumulation, commerce, industrialization, the development of market relations and real incomes, and the like, which usually are summed up under the concept of "modern economic growth." Economic historians also employ variations on a threefold division of Europe: an Atlantic region and its hinterland reaching from the French coast across the Netherlands to the North Sea; a Mediterranean region; and a Continental region. Central Europe belonged to the Continental region of economic development, and by the eighteenth century, there were wide economic disparities between the economically more dynamic regions of northwestern or "Atlantic" Europe and the Continental regions, which increasingly regressed toward the (Russian) east and the (Ottoman) southeast.

Another characteristic of this economic development was its "unevenness." The most advanced part of Central Europe was its small "Atlantic region": the northern Rhine Valley, which had a long Hanseatic commercial tradition and hence possessed the structures conducive to industrialization. Otherwise, there were great disparities in the patterns of development in western Germany between the northern and southern regions, such as Bavaria. A more important regional frontier was a west–east one that ran along the Elbe River, roughly corresponding to the border between Prussia in the east and a plethora of German states and estates in the west (or, to use a more contemporary frontier, to the former frontier between East and West Germany). Large landed estates and second serfdom were characteristic of the economic organization on the Northern European Plain from the Elbe River deep into Russia, and they had their counterparts to the south in Bohemia, eastern Austria, and Hungary. Although there were notable exceptions in Bohemia, Silesia, and parts of Austria, agrarian "backwardness" or retarded economic growth (using the Western European or Atlantic standards of commercial capitalism and industrialization) later became one of the characteristics of Central Europe. The longer that the venerable economic structures prevailed and the farther east that one went, the greater the gap became. In terms of their development, Prussia, Bohemia, and Austria were less backward than Poland and Hungary which, in turn, were ahead of Russia or the Ottoman Empire.[4]

Back to the consequences of the Habsburg victory in the kingdom of Bohemia in the seventeenth century: It is difficult to determine whether the victory of Ferdinand II's Habsburg imperialism over the indigenous Bohemian nobility merely accelerated a number of processes that had already begun, like the accumulation of lands into larger estates, second serfdom, or a homegrown Bohemian Counter-Reformation started by the Jesuits, or to what extent it instigated them. The formation of an upper class of wealthy aristocrats, who were assimilated into the Roman Catholic and German-speaking court culture of the Habsburgs and became their most reliable representatives and agents in the kingdom of Bohemia, inhibited for centuries the development of the Czech language and culture, just as the reestablishment of Roman Catholicism as the religion of the land robbed the Czechs of their particular form of devotion. During the nineteenth century, the retrospective pathos of nationalism merely amplified these injuries.

Confronted with the choice of staying and conforming to the Habsburg, German, and Roman Catholic culture or leaving, many members of the Bohemian national elite left, and the term "Bohemian" initially appeared in various European languages to describe the abject state in which these émigrés lived. Only later did it assume the poetic connotations of Puccini's *La Boheme.*

Unlike the Hungarians or Poles, whose histories also are characterized by protracted periods of imperial occupation but interspersed with uprisings and revolts or "struggles for national freedom," the Czechs never seemed to assume a confrontational course with their Habsburg subjugators. Consequently, by Hungarian or Polish standards, there is an absence of open conflict and rebellion in Czech history, and Hungarians and Poles have criticized the Czechs for this fact.[5]

Poles tend to forget that the Roman Catholic Church, which was the spiritual backbone of the Polish nation in times of occupation and duress, remained alien in many respects to the Czechs, because of the manner in which it was forced on them during the Counter-Reformation. Roman Catholicism was a German-Habsburg religion, not a Czech one. Hungarians often overlook the fact that their nobility was never expropriated, exiled, or "Germanized" to the great extent that the Bohemian nobility was, and the kingdom of Hungary retained (and eventually regained) a fair amount of real political autonomy under the Habsburgs that the kingdom of Bohemia lost and lost for good in the seventeenth century. Thereafter, the Czechs did not have a traditional class of aristocrats who could act as the carriers of the "national cause" as the Hungarians or the Poles did.

The fact that the Bohemian nation was effectively decapitated in the seventeenth century had enormous consequences for the evolution of Czech political culture in the future. Poland and Hungary were "gentry nations" in the seventeenth century and continued to be so until the nineteenth century. However, Bohemia ceased to be a "gentry nation" because it lost its aristocratic "national leaders" in the seventeenth century. In Bohemia during the nineteenth century, the Czechs had to constitute themselves—from scratch and from the bottom up, so to speak—as a linguistic, cultural, and political nation. Therefore, Czech nationalism was "bourgeois, democratic, fairly egalitarian, rational, and pragmatic," whereas Polish and Hungarian nationalism, in part due to its feudal origins, was aristocratic, more defiant, and romantic.[6] Surprisingly, the Habsburgs' destruction of Bohemia's feudal nation in the seventeenth century contributed to the evolution of a more modern and democratic Czech political culture in the long run.

Nevertheless, in order to create the impression of some kind of national continuity, some Czechs have maintained that there was a psychological strategy for national survival that people adopted in the seventeenth century and that was operative until the twentieth century. But the attempt to construe continuity here is not especially convincing, because after the seventeenth century the "Czech nation" consisted basically of illiterate peasant-serfs. According to this version of the story, the development of a Czech double standard, or "double life," was allegedly one means of dealing with foreign occupation. Public life was putting up with the trials and tribulations of subjugation and the demands of collaboration, whereas private life was an "inner emigration": an attempt to maintain as much personal integrity and decency as possible under such circumstances. In other words, behind a facade of external conformity, Czech authenticity continued to exist. The psychological mechanisms of overt resilience and covert resistance helped the Czechs as a nation survive and eventually flourish under the Habsburgs until 1918, and it facilitated their survival under other foreign empires in the future: the Germans from 1939 until 1945 and the Communists and Soviets thereafter.

In 1979, one Czech dissident described the everyday attitude of the contemporary Czech citizen living under neo-Stalinism as "the choice of a politically disengaged pursuit of private welfare, purchased by a formal loyalty vis-à-vis power, and the illusion of decency within the limits of a private existence."[7] These are attitudes that pessimistically describe the Czech tradition, and they also have a certain affinity to the features of one of the champions of Czech national literature (but a figure hardly known outside the country), Jaroslav Hašek's "good soldier Svejk."[8] After World War I, Hašek, a humorist of high caliber, wrote a series of novels describing the adventures of Svejk, an outspoken Czech who constantly got himself into and out of trouble. He ended up in the Austro-Hungarian army during World War I but confounded his superiors by always *literally* following orders. In doing so, Svejk illustrated the absurdity of the military in particular and war in general and also managed to avoid participating in the insanity and barbarism around him.

Svejk is an ambiguous figure because he conformed and collaborated, and it is not clear whether or not his servitude was feigned, his dull wittedness simulated, or his mistakes part of a calculated strategy of subversion. Svejk was petty bourgeois, not the stuff out of which heroes are made. But critical Czechs are perhaps the first to admit that they do not have a heroic national tradition of resistance.

Winners and Losers:
The Peace of Westphalia, 1648

The Habsburg conquest of Bohemia started as a regional confessional conflict between a Catholic lord and his Protestant subjects, but it spilled over into Germany as the protagonists of Roman Catholicism and Protestantism took sides (and arms) for and against Ferdinand II, the Holy Roman Emperor of the German Nation. The dynamics of the escalation of this conflict, which led to a series of wars over the next thirty years, are too complicated to be discussed in detail here, but the Habsburg–Bohemian confrontation developed into a Pan-European power struggle that had very little to do with religion. The Habsburgs of Spain and Austria, allied with the Catholic states and estates of Germany, championed the causes of the Counter Reformation and the (Catholic and Habsburg) Holy Roman Emperor. The Protestant and anti-imperial estates of Germany allied themselves with the Catholic but anti-Habsburg France, the Protestant maritime powers of England and the Netherlands, and the Lutheran Sweden, whose king, Gustavus Adolphus II, was not only a champion of the Protestant religious cause but also wanted to establish his own Baltic empire.

The Thirty Years' War was Europe's first "world war," but none of the parties involved were victors in the sense that they vanquished their enemies. They merely fought one another to a state of exhaustion that led to the Peace of Westphalia in 1648. Battered at sea by England and the Netherlands, overextended on land, and plagued by domestic problems, Spain was the big loser in this conflict, and the beginning of Spain's demise as a major European power made France the big continental winner. France extended its "sphere of influence" eastward, and after 1648, France claimed the role of being the *protector Germaniae*, "protector of Germany." This ostensibly anti-Habsburg pretense barely veiled France's interest in a weak, disunited Germany and aspirations to establish its "natural border" on the Rhine River.

Habsburg Austria won at home and lost abroad. The Habsburgs consolidated their control of Bohemia and Austria, which were thoroughly reconverted to Catholicism, and the Protestant powers promised not to interfere in the future in the Habsburgs' internal religious affairs. As the traditional bearers of the office of the Holy Roman Emperor of the German Nation, however, the Habsburgs effectively lost their ability to intervene in the affairs of the German empire because the Peace of Westphalia recognized a multitude of German states as sovereign entities. In this respect, the Habsburgs and the idea of the German empire as some kind of cohesive whole were losers, whereas the numerous German states and their rulers were winners because they factually and formally were emancipated from the venerable constraints of the emperor and the empire. This event not only marks the beginning of the Habsburgs' long but gradual departure from a position of predominance in German politics, but the idea of "territorial sovereigns" also cemented the German tradition of particularism and disunity for the next two centuries.

Among the biggest losers in the Thirty Years' War was the "civilian" population of Germany, and the Thirty Years' War was a "modern" conflict in this respect. For decades, the various armies of foreign mercenaries had lived off the land like locusts, and between 1618 and 1648 the classic agents of Malthusian population control—war, famine, and plague—reduced the total population of Germany by about 35 percent, from 21 million to 13.5 million, and regionally up to 90 percent in areas of the Rhine Valley and Bavaria, which often were battle zones. As a result, it took approximately a century for Germany to regain its prewar population.

The lands of the Bohemian crown were the biggest loser in just about every respect. The Czechs lost their crown, most of their nobility, and their religion, in addition to about 70 percent of a population of 3 million; by 1648, only 5,000 of the country's previous 35,000 prospering towns still existed. Between 20 and 25 percent of the peasants' lands had been abandoned by 1650, and the gaps that emigration and the war had created in the Czech population were frequently filled by German-Catholic immigrants. This represented the second wave of the "Germanization" in Bohemia, which had begun in the Middle Ages.[9] The toll of the Thirty Years' War was enormous, but it was the last great religious war that representatives of Western Christendom fought among themselves, although it was not Western Christendom's last great religious war.

Defeating the Infidel, or Poland Saves the West: Lifting the Turkish Siege of Vienna, 1683

Between the first Turkish siege of Vienna in 1529 and the second one in 1683, the Christians of the west spent more time and energy combating one another than the infidel Turks. Despite all the rhetoric about the Turks as a Pan-European threat, the Ottoman Empire was basically a problem for the easternmost representatives of Western Christendom, the Habsburgs of Austria and the kingdom of Poland. The Turkish threat also was a godsend for denominational and dynastic opponents of the Habsburgs: Protestants inside and outside their realms and the Bourbons in France. France, for example, consistently allied itself with the enemies of Habsburg Austria, because any energy the Habsburgs expended on the infidels in the east detracted from their potential to intervene in the affairs of the west. After the initial Ottoman advance at the beginning of the sixteenth century, the military frontier between the Habsburg and Ottoman empires was relatively stable. Further Ottoman expansion in Europe had followed the lines of least resistance—along the coast of the Black Sea to Romania and into southern Ukraine—and although contemporaries did not recognize it, the Ottoman Empire was suffering from one of those diseases that befalls all imperial giants: overextension.

The expansion of the Ottoman Empire into (Ukrainian) Poland and the machinations of French diplomacy also added new elements to the well-established triangular struggle among the Habsburgs, Hungarians, and Turks on the eastern frontier. Under Louis XIV, France supported the Ottoman Empire against the Habsburgs; interceded on behalf of Poland in Istanbul in order to help establish peace on the Polish–Ottoman front in Ukraine; and then appealed to the king of Poland, Jan Sobieski, whose wife was French, to funnel French support into Hungary. In 1678, after soliciting French and Turkish patronage, Hungary began one of its intermittent revolts against the Habsburgs, the Kuruc uprising. Imre Thököly, one of the Hungarian national heroes that the Magyar struggle with the Habsburgs produced, was the mastermind of the so-called Kurucs, a Hungarian word derived from the Latin *crux*, the "cross" that the crusaders wore in combat against the infidels and that became a term for Hungarian national crusaders against the Habsburgs. For the Habsburgs, the Kuruc uprising added the problem of internal insurrection to the task of external defense.

This situation merely demonstrates to what extent other considerations were at work behind the Baroque stage settings of the drama of Western Christendom versus the Oriental infidel. For the Hungarians who were interested in regaining independence, the Ottoman Empire appeared not only to be stronger than the Habsburgs but also the lesser of two evils, and the vision of a unified Hungary under Ottoman patronage animated the Hungarians' plans. For Jan Sobieski, the idea of a future reunification of the Polish and Hungarian crowns may not have been out of the question. After all, there were a number of historical precedents: Louis the Great from the Anjou dynasty, the king of Hungary (1342–1382), was also the king of Poland from 1370 until 1382; Władysław Jagielleo III, the king of Poland (1434–1444), was the king of Hungary (as Ulászló I) from 1440 until 1444; and Stephan Bartory, a Hungarian prince of Transylvania, was the king of Poland from 1576 to 1586. Finally, for the Catholic French and the Islamic Turks, anything that was bad for Habsburg Austria was good for them.

Retrospective self-justification is an important function of national historiography. Austrian historians, who consider themselves the heirs to the Habsburg tradition of defending Western Christendom, criticize the Poles and Hungarians for surreptitiously or blatantly participating in French machinations that benefited the Ottoman infidels. Polish and Hungarian historians, who think of their histories in terms of national struggles for emancipation from imperialists like the Habsburgs, emphasize its pro-French aspects and, as good Westerners, play down its direct benefits for the Turks. It is fruitless to argue, therefore, whether the French dagger in the imperial back of the Habsburgs was better or worse than the Ottoman scimitar in their stomachs.

The second Turkish siege of Vienna in 1683 changed the situation because Sobieski, the king of Poland, decided that the defense of Western Christendom was more important than anything else. His conviction destroyed the diplomatic house of cards the French had built and eventually made Sobieski and Poland the "saviors of the West." The West received a generous advance notice about the intentions of the Ottoman Empire because Islamic tradition required that a "holy war" had to be ceremoniously proclaimed in Istanbul. Festively gathering men and matériel in Istanbul and then formally sending them off on their crusade was another part of this ritual, which coincidentally contradicted the rationale of logistics like the advanced deployment of supplies or heavy war matériel. Historians are unsure why the decision to take Vienna was made, because it violated the practices of coexistence and cooperation that had been established on the Austrian–Ottoman frontier, but many attribute it to the personal ambitions of Kara Mustafa, the grand vizier and, next to the sultan, the most powerful man in the Ottoman Empire.

On March 31, 1683, Kara Mustafa sent a formal declaration of war to the Austrian emperor, Leopold I, in Vienna, and he left Istanbul with his troops, a force of around 180,000, on the same day. Mustafa's strategy was to reach Vienna as soon as possible in order to shorten the amount of time the Habsburgs would have to organize their defense, but this plan turned out to be a momentous error because the heavy-siege artillery that would have been necessary to shell into submission the fortified city of Vienna could not be moved as fast as the troops. Nonetheless, Mustafa's army made good time by contemporary standards. They were at the gates of Vienna three and a half months later and surrounded the city on July 14. Emperor Leopold did not exactly raise the morale of the Viennese by fleeing the city with his entire court a week before the Turks arrived, supposedly to organize support in the German empire, but he set an example that many wealthy Viennese followed.

The massive walls and bastions of Vienna, state-of-the-art seventeenth-century fortifications, and an international contingent of 12,000 troops were responsible for holding the Turks at bay until relief could be organized, but the city took a terrible beating in the process. After the Turks gave up hope that Vienna would capitulate, they dug a network of trenches that led up to the city's fortified walls; tunneled underneath them to deposit explosives, which they detonated to breech the fortifications; and then stormed the gaps that had been torn in the walls. By the beginning of September, two-thirds of the original 12,000 defenders had fallen, and the remainder had been weakened by hunger and disease.

The relief of Vienna contained all the elements of a Christian crusade. Pope Innocent XI called on all Christians to defeat the infidels and, more important, generously helped finance the operation. Emperor Leopold appealed to his own estates, German duchies, and Poland for help, and three different relief armies of approximatelyly equal size collected during the summer and began to converge on Vienna. Contingents from the German empire—Bavaria, Saxony, Brandenburg, Hannover, and Württemberg—marched down the Danube and joined forces upstream from Vienna with the Austrian imperial corps under the leadership of Duke Charles of Lorraine and the Polish troops under Jan Sobieski, who was given the honor of being the commander in chief of some 75,000 men, half infantry and half cavalry. On September 12, the relief forces gathered on Kahlenberg, a small mountain overlooking Vienna on the banks of the Danube, and then swept down the slopes to engage the Turks, who were not only exhausted from the protracted siege but also tactically ill prepared to deal with the assault. The entire day was spent in battle.

A contemporary engraving of the Turkish siege of Vienna in 1683: in the background, flanked by Turkish tents, is the network of trenches that the Turks dug to reach the city's fortifications, the besieged city, and the Danube. (Historisches Museum der Stadt Wien)

Which leader merits the official title of the "savior of Western Christendom" is an issue that historians of different national dispositions have debated for the last three centuries. Austrians like to emphasize the importance of Duke Charles of Lorraine's leadership and troops, but the absence of either the German or the Polish contingents undoubtedly would have reduced the strength of the relief forces so much that a victory would have been improbable. The fact that the Polish cavalry under the command of

Sobieski formed the spearhead that broke through the Turkish lines at a critical point in the battle also is important. The Poles were the first to storm the Turkish camp and consequently had the great honor of taking the tent of the grand vizier, Kara Mustafa. In the ensuing confusion Kara Mustafa fled, and the Turkish resistance collapsed.

The following night Sobieski wrote his wife from the grand vizier's tent, where he had set up his headquarters: "Our Lord and God, Blessed of All Ages, has brought unheard of victory and glory to our nation. All the guns, the whole camp, untold spoils have fallen into our hands. Having covered the trenches, the fields, and the camp with corpses, the enemy now flees in confusion." He also noted that Duke Charles of Lorraine, the duke of Saxony, and the commander of the forces defending the city of Vienna "embraced me, congratulated me, and called me their saviour."[10] Sobieski harvested the greatest glory (and according to some of his comrades in arms a disproportionately large chunk of the Ottoman booty) in Vienna, and he entered the nearly vanquished city before Emperor Leopold I arrived, a violation of protocol that led to rather cool relations between the Habsburg emperor and the Polish king. Nevertheless, before returning home, Sobieski and his Polish troops participated in a pursuit action that led to another resounding Turkish defeat in Hungary.

Conjectures about what would have happened if the Turks had taken Vienna are futile but provocative. Historians tend to agree that the expansion of the Ottoman Empire at the end of the seventeenth century beyond Vienna was improbable or that the loss of Vienna would not have resulted in a collapse of the Habsburg Empire. But contemporaries were not aware of the inherent weaknesses of the Ottoman giant, and sensitized by more than a century of propaganda and hyperbole, they perceived the Turks' invasion as an appalling threat to Western Christendom. The triumph of Western Christendom at Vienna in 1683 and subsequent victories in the following years, such as the liberation of Budapest in 1686, therefore made a correspondingly profound impression on everyone at the time. The victory at Vienna was the pinprick that deflated the Ottoman Empire's imperial balloon in southeastern Europe, and it marked the beginning of a new phase of expansion and consolidation for the Habsburg Empire.

With the victory over the Turks, both the Austrians, who consider themselves the legitimate curators of the Habsburg heritage, and the Poles claimed to have saved the West. For the Poles in particular, it would be difficult to overestimate Sobieski's and Poland's accomplishment because it is portrayed and perceived by Poles as one of the zeniths in their nation's history, documenting how unselfishly Poland has served the idea of the West. Most people outside Poland do not know that Poles repeated the achievement of saving the West in the twentieth century when Polish troops led by another great Polish military man, Marshal Józef Piłsudski, defeated the Red Army in the Battle of Warsaw in 1920. Although Bolshevik Russia in 1920, like the Ottoman Empire in the late seventeenth century, was not strong enough to pursue an expansive policy in the West, Poland saved the West in 1920 in a way similar to how it saved Western Christendom in 1683.

The Consolidation of the Habsburg Empire

The Habsburgs established Central Europe's first modern empire. After the momentous victory in Vienna in 1683, the wars the Habsburgs fought are a good indication of where they made their gains. In the east and southeast, expansion was at the expense of the Ottoman Empire and rebellious Hungary. Austria's imperial armies fought a series of wars against the Turks (1683–1699, 1716–1718, 1737–1739) and put down a major uprising in Hungary (1703–1711), which, after having been liberated from the Turks by the Habsburgs, attempted to liberate itself from its liberators. These external and internal conquests pushed the border of the Habsburg Empire down the Balkan Peninsula approximately to the southern periphery of the historical kingdom of Hungary, a frontier that ran from the Adriatic coast north of Belgrade to Transylvania.

The Habsburgs consolidated their power in Hungary by using a strategy similar to the one they had pursued in Bohemia. Along with the introduction of an energetic program of reconversion to Roman Catholicism, the Habsburgs expropriated recalcitrant nobles and generously patronized those aristocratic families who were willing to serve the dynasty loyally. Their strategy was to forge a community of interests among the Roman Catholic Church, the dynasty, and the indigenous aristocracy. The Habsburgs did not succeed in Hungary to the extent they did in Bohemia, however, because many of the nobility's "ancient rights" remained intact along with the Hungarian crown as a nominally electoral institution. As a result, the Hungarians later became the strongest and most influential minority in the Habsburgs' multinational empire.

The 160 years of Turkish occupation, uprisings, and Habsburg–Ottoman wars had greatly weakened Hungary and taken a heavy toll on its population, which dropped from around 4 million in 1500 to 3.5 million in 1700. The Habsburgs also promoted a German-Catholic settlement of vast regions of the central Danube Valley that had been depopulated. During the eighteenth century more than a million settlers, many of them from the southern German province of Swabia but also including emigrants from the Rhine Valley, Tyrol, Belgium, and France, relocated there, and they were subsequently called "Danube Swabians." As in Bohemia after the Thirty Years' War, this modern phase of German "colonization" created new "linguistic islands" similar to those that initially had been established in the Middle Ages. Croats and Serbs, who fled north to escape from living in the Ottoman Empire, and Slovaks, who moved south, also added new dimensions to the ethnic composition of Hungary, whose population may have been up to 75 percent Magyar in the Middle Ages but was only around 40 percent Magyar by 1800.[11]

In the west, Habsburg Austria's major antagonist was Bourbon France, and the major fields of conflict between these two imperial dynasties were Germany and Italy, regions that consisted of a series of smaller disunited states and hence were the kind of power vacuums that lent themselves to foreign intervention and expansion. The War of the Spanish Succession

(1701–1714), which was precipitated by the extinction of the Spanish line of the Habsburgs and conflicting Austrian and French claims to the vacant throne, eventually led to the Habsburgs' acquisition of Spain's "eastern" territories on the Continent: the Spanish Netherlands and holdings in Italy, which established Habsburg predominance in the northern part of the country. Between 1683 and 1740, the Habsburgs more than doubled the size of their realms, from a domain of approximately 115,000 square miles, an area a bit smaller than the British Isles, to an empire of more than 230,000 square miles, somewhat larger than contemporary France, and they later acquired a considerable portion of Poland.

This comparison is perhaps misleading insofar as the Habsburg Empire was not a cohesive kingdom. Outside their acquisitions in Italy and the Netherlands, the Habsburgs' hereditary "Austrian" holdings, the kingdom of Bohemia, and the kingdom of Hungary formed the territorial tripod on which their Central European empire rested. These realms were held together by neither a constitutional apparatus comparable to that of the United Kingdom nor a centralized state bureaucracy similar to that of absolutistic France, and they were by no means as ethnically and linguistically homogeneous or "national." On the contrary, the Habsburg Empire was a collection of different kingdoms and domains, many of which were multinational (or multiethnic) but personally unified by the dynasty although otherwise laterally unrelated. The hereditary Austrian holdings were predominantly German but included Slovenes and Italians; the lands of the Bohemian crown were predominantly Czech but included a great number of Germans; and the kingdom of Hungary encompassed Magyars, Slovaks, Ukrainians, Rusyns, Romanians, Germans, Serbs, and Croats. The inhabitants of Tyrol, for example, had very little in common, with the exception of their Habsburg ruler, with the Czechs in Bohemia or the population of Hungarian Transylvania.

Although none of these peoples thought in the categories of nineteenth-century nationalism, in each part of their empire the Habsburgs were confronted with different political (or feudal) institutions, religious (or Protestant) traditions, and ethnic (or non-German) groups. They used an ideology of dynastic imperialism and absolutism that the Roman Catholicism of the Counter-Reformation reinforced—one ruler, one religion—in their attempts to consolidate these heterogeneous holdings, but it was difficult to apply uniformly because of the various forms of feudal and denominational particularism. The Habsburgs broke the various forms of resistance they encountered the best they could, but incompletely. Their imperial and Roman Catholic ideology commanded the allegiance of their subjects at the expense of turning some of them into enemies.

The consolidation of the Habsburg monarchy drew the veneer of one upper-class civilization—cosmopolitan and imperial, aristocratic and German-speaking, Roman Catholic, and supranational—over the surfaces of heterogeneous regions that were particularistic and neofeudal, ethnically and linguistically polyglot, subservient, and outwardly conformist. The proliferation and density of Baroque monasteries, churches, and religious monuments in the Habsburgs' realms attest to the outward success of the Counter-Reformation and the idea of the Church Triumphant. Politically, the Habsburgs carried the Roman Catholic Church's victory over heresy and the infidel, and the idea of the Dynasty Triumphant found its visual expression in a building boom of Baroque palaces that celebrated the achievements and grandeur of the dynasty and its aristocratic attendants. The Habsburgs' court, which was their prime instrument of government, created an unusually cosmopolitan forum for the careers of aristocrats—Germans, Czechs, Hungarians, and Italians, all "Austrians" in the imperial sense of the word—who were prepared to identify their interests with the concerns of a dynasty that defined itself in terms of its imperial and Catholic supranationalism. In serving the imperial whole, they stood above the empire's constituent parts.

Despite this cosmopolitan touch, German was the language of assimilation and dominion in the Habsburg Empire, and the consolidation of the Habsburgs' power in the historical kingdoms of Bohemia and Hungary eventually contributed to the idea of defining southern Central Europe as part of the "German linguistic and cultural space." The Habsburgs' German and the Roman Catholic Church's Latin also became symbols of foreign subjugation for many of the empire's non-German and Protestant subjects. The dynasty's violation of the venerable feudal rights of their subjects, the Bohemian and Hungarian nations in particular, and the Roman Church's simultaneous smothering of Protestantism created a reservoir of resentment that nineteenth-century nationalism later tapped so successfully.

The Habsburgs may have succeeded in consolidating their realms from the top down, but they failed to create a mode of consolidation that worked from the bottom up. This lack of integration perhaps did not diminish the initial strength of the Habsburg Empire, but it created a heritage of latent dissatisfaction that weakened it internally and eventually helped tear it apart. Nevertheless, the rise of the Habsburgs' Danubian empire at the expense of the kingdoms of Bohemia and Hungary and the Ottoman Empire ended the first phase of empire building in Central Europe.

ᵈ 6 ᵈ

Absolutism as Enlightenment

1700–1790

The rise of continental European absolutism during the seventeenth and eighteenth centuries and the concomitant development of the stream of thought called the Enlightenment may appear to be incompatible in theory, but they were compatible in practice. Although the various philosophers of the Enlightenment agreed on a few basic methodological principles like a faith in reason instead of revelation, a critical analysis of tradition and authority, and the scientific spirit, there is really no point in arguing who the best representatives of the Enlightenment were because each nation seems to have its own. In the British tradition, for example, John Locke or David Hume are representative figures. In France, Voltaire and Rousseau are generally regarded as the respective moderate and radical representatives of the Enlightenment. Among professional philosophers and most Germans, Immanuel Kant, the professor from Königsberg in East Prussia, generally is recognized as the consummation of the Enlightenment. (A cursory glance at the biographical dates of Locke, 1632–1704; Voltaire, 1694–1778; and Kant, 1724–1804, illustrate the West–East transmission or British–French–German sequence of the Enlightenment.)

Prussian, Austrian, and Russian rulers interested in enlightenment could not rely on much indigenous critical philosophy because seventeenth-century Prussian Protestant piety, Austrian Counter-Reformation Catholicism, and Russian Orthodoxy did not provide fertile soils for freethinkers. Therefore, the best representatives of the eighteenth-century Enlightenment in Central and Eastern Europe were not homegrown philosophers but monarchs, and these monarchs looked to France for political and philosophical inspiration.

The philosophy of the Enlightenment, like the French (political) and

(British) industrial revolutions that followed in its wake, was initially a Western European innovation that gradually moved eastward with proportionately decreasing amounts of success. In light of the insularity of British developments, they should perhaps be bracketed out of consideration here. British political institutions somehow escaped the ruthless scrutiny of Reason as they evolved into a parliamentary system. The British tradition of Enlightenment also was more empirical and skeptical than the French tradition, which was influenced to a much greater extent by rationalism and the assumption that it was both feasible and desirable to plan and execute projects on a grand scale.

In France, the Bourbons used the idea of enlightened progress—a more rational organization of the state and society—in order to enhance the power of the dynastic state as well as to justify the monarchy's infringement on the venerable (or backward) feudal rights of the nobility and the church, which had limited it for centuries. A more effective and larger professional bureaucracy for the administration of public affairs ranging from the military to the construction of roads and canals or the collection of customs, taxes, and duties; the codification of laws; the propagation of new agricultural and industrial technologies or foreign trade; the guarantee of religious toleration; and the improvement and extension of education as well as its secularization, which involved breaking the Jesuit monopoly on universities, are just a few examples of how enlightened absolutism simultaneously benefited the state and the population as a whole. Each increase in the health, wealth, and intelligence of the absolute monarch's subjects was an incremental gain in power and potential for the absolutistic state, and in this respect monarchs recognized the benefits of enlightenment, which was ambiguously altruistic and obviously authoritarian. As modern forms of organization and technology, rationality and progress placed new instruments of dominion at the disposal of enlightened monarchs, who used them to pursue their age-old dynastic interests, the enhancement of power, but still saw themselves as representatives of God's divinely preordained order on earth.

As a technique for augmenting control, enlightenment enhanced the power of the Bourbon dynasty and French state, but at the same time the (liberal English and radical French) philosophical presuppositions of enlightenment gradually eroded the Baroque foundations of French absolutism. The standard interpretations of the dynamics of the Enlightenment usually emphasize that enlightened philosophy lent itself first to absolutism's destruction of old and obstructive feudal freedoms but then, carried on to its logical conclusions, became an expression of the rising middle or bourgeois classes' interest in more intellectual, political, and economic freedom. This development, in turn, eventually led to the revolutionary demise of absolutistic monarchy. This is not the place to expound on the relationship between philosophical enlightenment and political revolution or the problematic issue of the economic preconditions for both. Nonetheless, in Western Europe there were two broad patterns of enlightenment: one absolutistic form that the dynastic state instigated and administrated "from above" and one democratic form that the rising middle class initiated and articulated "from below." In the former case, the enlightened dynastic state thought for the people, and in the latter, the enlightened people thought for themselves.

Enlightenment in Hohenzollern Prussia, Habsburg Austria, and Romanov Russia was quite different from its Western or French precedents. By around 1700, all these ruling dynasties knew that they were either falling behind or were backward to start with, and so they turned to foreign ideas and experts in order to do something about it. However, "enlightenment from above" was not accompanied to a comparable extent by "enlightenment from below," and the Central and Eastern European enlightenment of absolutism as a "revolution from above" was not succeeded by a liberal democratic "revolution from below." On the contrary, secularization and centralization "from above" frequently met the violent resistance of religious traditionalists and feudal particularists, particularly in Romanov Russia and the Habsburg Empire, who felt that enlightenment was merely a violation of venerable religious customs, just as absolutism was an encroachment on revered traditional rights.

The Enlightenment ushered in a new age of freedom. Poles, however, are in the peculiar position of identifying the Enlightenment with their loss of freedom because the Polish–Lithuanian Republic became a victim of enlightened absolutism.

Triangular Conflict in the East:
Poland-Lithuania, Sweden, and Russia

Despite the legendary importance of Jan Sobieski and Poland's intercession in lifting the siege of Vienna in 1683, Poland appears to have been only marginally involved in major sixteenth- and seventeenth-century Central European conflicts: the Reformation and Counter-Reformation, which were basically a struggle between northern German Protestants and southern German Catholics, or Western Christendom's struggle with the Ottoman Empire, which for the most part was a burden for the Habsburgs of Austria. In accordance with its tradition of religious tolerance, Poland refrained from participating in the excesses of the Reformation and Counter-Reformation, and Poland's conflict with the Ottoman Empire in Ukraine also was basically a venerable struggle with an old enemy, the Crimean Tatars, who were vassals of new lords, the Ottoman Turks. Therefore, one might be tempted to delegate Poland to some kind of peripheral position outside the mainstream of Central European events which appear to have been centered on the Rhine and the Danube Valleys. But Poland was the pivot on which the conflicts on the Northern European Plain hinged. If Poles are asked to identify the archenemy they have constantly battled throughout their history, it would be geography, because every point of the compass marks a different adversary that at some time or another swept across the Polish plains: the Swedes from the north, the Tatars and the Turks from the south, the Prussians from the west, and the Russians from the east.

It is difficult to call Swedes Central Europeans because their abstention from Continental conflicts for the past few centuries made them a paragon of European neutrality or Scandinavian isolationism. During the late sixteenth and early seventeenth centuries, Sweden tried to establish an empire based on nothing less than a *dominium maris Baltici*, a "dominion of the Baltic Sea," and it intended turning the Polish–Lithuanian Republic, Russia, and Brandenburg Prussia into permanently landlocked countries. The first phase of Sweden's imperial expansion was in the eastern Baltic. Finland, a Swedish vassal state, was the scene of direct Swedish–Russian conflict, whereas the struggle for the hegemony of contemporary Estonia and Latvia was a triangular affair among Swedes, Russians, and Poles, who fought in a series of rotating two-against-one alliances, coalitions that depended on exploiting the fluctuating strengths and weaknesses of the parties involved. The reign of Gustavus Adolphus II (1611–1632)—the "Lion of the North" and Swedish king who entered the Thirty Years' War on the side of German Protestantism for the sake of defending the faith—marked the beginning of the second phase of Swedish expansion, and Gustavus Adolphus added substantially to the realization of a Swedish *dominium maris Baltici* by seizing Polish Baltic ports in addition to acquiring a territorial foothold along the coast of northern Germany.

If the seventeenth-century rise of Sweden's Baltic empire and the western expansion of Russia's empire under the Romanovs toward the Baltic and in Belarus was the source of one "northern" triangular conflict for the Polish–Lithuanian Republic, then the gradual Russian encroachment on Ukraine and expansion toward the Black Sea during the same period provided the basis for a second triangular conflict in the south, in which Poland-Lithuania, Russia, and the Ottoman Empire alternately fought among themselves. The fact that Russia gradually forced the Ottoman Empire out of the Crimea (north of the Black Sea) and Moldavia (east of the Carpathians) merely indicates the extent to which the Polish–Lithuanian sphere of influence in the region had deteriorated. The Russian–Ottoman conflict also reinforced the idea of Russia as the bulwark of Orthodox or Eastern Christendom.

The Polish–Lithuanian Republic was in the worst possible geopolitical position because Russia and Sweden each had more to gain from Polish losses in the Baltic north and in the Ukrainian south than they could hope to gain through Polish alliances. The two stronger powers systematically exploited the weakness of the third, which began to play an increasingly negligible role in the Swedish–Russian struggle for hegemony, aside from providing a convenient, centrally located battlefield. In 1655, for example, the nephew of Gustavus Adolphus, Charles X, invaded the Polish–Lithuanian Republic, ostensibly to check Russian advances in the east, and as a result of this Swedish intervention, Poland's last effective resistance to its enemies in the east collapsed. The six years of confusion that followed are known in Polish history as "the Deluge." Swedes romped up and down the Vistula Valley from the Baltic to the Carpathian Mountains; at Sweden's invitation, Calvinistic Hungarians from Transylvania joined the action; and Russia made substantial gains in the east and Ukraine.

The Great Nordic War (1700–1721), a conflict in which Sweden's King

Charles XII (1697–1718), "the last Viking," and Russia's Czar Peter the Great (1698–1725) were the major antagonists, conclusively resolved the struggle for Baltic hegemony. Charles was an ingenious field marshal but a poor politician, and his diplomatic incompetence offset his military ingenuity. Therefore, he was eventually confronted with a coalition of virtually any and everybody who had something to lose by his success or to gain by his failure. Russia; Poland-Lithuania; the German states of Saxony, Prussia, and Hamburg; Denmark; and Norway joined forces against him. This conflict raged along the Baltic coast, in Denmark, and throughout Poland, and it extended into Belarus and down into Ukraine. The turning point of this war was deep in Ukraine at the Battle of Poltava in 1709.

Charles was the first modern "imperialist" who shipwrecked on the vastness of Russia (and apparently neither Napoleon in 1812 nor Hitler in 1941 learned from the lessons of their predecessors). Greatly weakened, Charles nevertheless continued his struggle for the next nine years, but his death during the siege of the Danish castle of Frederiksborg in 1718 punctuated the end of the idea of a Swedish Baltic empire, and the victors divided the Swedish spoils among themselves. Russia, which gained control of Estonia and Latvia as well as Finland, and Prussia, which reestablished itself on the Baltic coast, were the biggest winners. Poland-Lithuania, nominally among the short-term victors in the denouement of the Baltic conflict, was actually one of its long-term losers because the new Baltic power constellation—an expansive Russia and an expanding Prussia—eventually led to its demise.

Although the maintenance of a Swedish–Baltic empire certainly would have influenced future events in Central Europe and provided a geopolitical alternative to the development of the Prussian and Russian empires that began to come into their own after its collapse, conjectures about what could have happened if Sweden had retained its predominance in the Baltic region fall into that futilely provocative realm of historical speculation. Estonians and Latvians look back on the seventeenth century with fondness. As coastal people on the Baltic, their "natural" business partners were in Sweden, Hamburg, or Amsterdam. They would have benefited more from a western, Protestant Swedish-Baltic empire than the eastern, Orthodox, and Russian one that absorbed them. But Russian and German expansion and East–West conflicts determined the political dynamics of Central Europe from the eighteenth century until the end of the twentieth, and if there was one country caught fatally in the middle of this field of contention, it was Poland.

The Polish Paradox:
Freedom Without "Enlightenment"

Both parliamentarianism and absolutism were inherent in the constitutional struggle between lords and vassals in European feudal societies. In Western Europe, medieval monarchy, which was based on a complicated system of mutual rights and contractual obligations that regulated the relationships between kings and nobles as well as nobles and their subjects, developed in two relatively distinct directions. One historical trend, which could be called the British or parliamentary path, entailed the expansion of the venerable rights of the nobles at the expense of those of the crown and the extension of those rights to commoners. It culminated in a liberal democratic tradition characterized by ideas such as parliamentary representation, limited government, the sovereignty of the people, government by the consent of the governed, and catalogs of civil rights. Medieval monarchy's other pattern of development, which could be called the French or absolutistic path, strengthened the crown at the expense of the historical rights of the nobility and centralized power in the hands of the monarch or state.

Both distorted versions of the British parliamentary pattern of development and imitations of the achievements of French absolutism applied to Central Europe. The Polish–Lithuanian Republic, for example, experienced a peculiar, truncated form of British development, which resulted in a weak crown and a parliament controlled by a large and relatively free and strong nobility, whereas its neighbors, Prussia, Russia, and Austria, followed the French pattern of absolutistic development with varying degrees of success. During the eighteenth century, the Poland–Lithuanian Republic became a political anachronism that was simultaneously more free and less modern than its Prussian, Austrian, and Russian neighbors, whose absolutism was based on the elimination of feudal freedoms that had previously limited the centralization of political power.

The Hohenzollerns of Prussia, the Romanovs of Russia, and the Habsburgs of Austria divided the Polish–Lithuanian Republic among themselves in three phases at the end of the eighteenth century (in 1772, 1793, and 1795), and after the final partition, Poland effectively disappeared from the political map of Europe for 123 years. The initial demise of Poland came relatively late in comparison with the downfalls of the historical kingdoms of Bohemia and Hungary, which were incorporated into the Habsburg Empire at the beginning of the sixteenth century and "Austriafied" to a certain extent by the end of the seventeenth century.

It is a moot point to argue whether or not the Polish loss of independence was any more or less tragic than the corresponding Czech or Hungarian forfeitures of national freedom at much earlier dates. But it was much more complete. The kingdoms of Hungary and Bohemia remained formally intact as component parts of the Habsburg Empire—the Habsburgs were the kings of both Hungary and Bohemia—whereas the historical kingdom of Poland virtually ceased to exist. It is one of those paradoxes of Polish history that the Polish nobility's love of their "golden freedoms" contributed to their loss. A few observations about the anomalous development of the Polish–Lithuanian Republic explain this point as well as why the country was so ill equipped to face the absolutistic challenges of its "enlightened" neighbors.

The formal establishment of a parliamentary system in Poland dates back to 1493. The great achievement of the Polish Diet, or Sejm, the representative body of the nobility, was to limit royal prerogative. The precedent of *nihil novi*, "nothing new" without the consent of the Diet, was established in 1505, and in 1569 Sigmund II August, the last representative of the Jagiellonian dynasty, succeeded in turning the Polish–Lithuanian Commonwealth from two hereditary domains personally united by one dynastic family into one constitutionally united "republic" with a freely elected monarch. After the extinction of the Jagiellonian dynasty in 1572, each subsequently elected king of the Polish–Lithuanian Republic had to swear solemnly to respect and protect the existing laws of the country, and this ritual merely symbolized to what extent the idea of sovereignty had been transferred from the king to the nobles, the constituent members of the "political nation." The interests of the "Polish nation" were the interests of the nobles, and they, in turn, preferred weak kings to strong ones.

The institution of electoral monarchy turned out to be less fortuitous for the Polish–Lithuanian Republic. Only three of the ten kings elected in the two centuries between the expiration of the Jagiellonian dynasty in 1572 and the first partition of Poland in 1772 were Poles.[1] The introduction of an electoral monarchy greatly increased the importance of Warsaw, because a small village in its immediate proximity, Wola, was chosen as the site for royal elections simply because it was more centrally located than the historical capital of Kraków in the south, and at the beginning of the seventeenth century the royal seat was moved to Warsaw. One of the procedural peculiarities of Polish politics was that both the election of kings and the passage of legislation in the Sejm (Diet) were based on the principle of unanimity, which in turn rested on the assumption that minority parties would recognize their moral obligation to submit to the will of the majority. As unusual as this traditional practice may seem, it functioned well as long as the participants in the political game were willing not to take advantage of its inherent formal flaws.

For example, when anywhere between 10,000 and 15,000 nobles converged on Warsaw to participate in a royal election, the usual instruments of intuition, persuasion, cajoling, threats, and bribery normally led to unanimity. Periodically, though, there also were times during which the failure to agree or the election of competing kings meant that the election had to be settled on the battlefield. The legislative or parliamentary counterpart of unanimity was the so-called *liberum veto*, a device allowing any single member of the Diet to halt the proceedings. This veto had traditionally been used as a means of clarifying certain points or as a vehicle for lobbying. However, after the middle of the seventeenth century, it degenerated into an instrument of parliamentary obstruction. The *liberum veto* gave Polish nobles, who were willing to act as the agents of foreign powers, the opportunity to block legislation and lame innovation in the Diet, on the one hand, and it gave foreign powers ample opportunity to criticize Poland as an anarchic and unruly country, on the other.

Another peculiarity of the Polish situation was that an inordinately large percentage of the population was involved in the political process. Approximately 10 percent of the population—ranging from powerful barons with enormous holdings to penniless and propertyless petty gentry—enjoyed the "golden freedoms" by virtue of their titles and standing, and this class of nobles and gentry was two to ten times larger than any of its Western European counterparts. Given the power the nobles had acquired and their sheer strength of numbers, it is easy to understand how the idea of Poland-Lithuania as a "republic of nobles" evolved. The nobility also demonstrated attitudes that appear to be modern, such as a reliance on using legal precedent, a belief in protecting individual rights, and the importance of limiting central government, but in fact they were feudal. The Polish nobility consistently used their "golden freedoms" to protect and promote their particular feudal interests in a manner which prevented the republic from developing into a more modern and viable centralized state. Then the partitions of Poland at the end of the eighteenth century transformed the venerable vices of the gentry into national virtues in the nineteenth century. For example, the old habit of opposing royal power expressed itself as the will to resist foreign oppression; feudal conservativism was transmuted into a determination to preserve national traditions; and the idea of a restoration of Poland lent itself to revolutionary interpretations.

There are nominal and formal affinities between the modern freedoms we associate with the liberal democratic tradition and the "golden freedoms" of the Polish–Lithuanian Republic, and there is also a long Polish tradition of drawing parallels between the constitutional development of Poland-Lithuania and the United Kingdom—such as a reliance on legal precedent, the protection of individual rights, and a Polish form of habeus corpus. The similarities of these two traditions are important to Poles because they can be used to demonstrate how venerable Poland's "democratic tradition" is. However, they also obscure the fact that despite Poland's freedom-loving traditions, it has virtually no tradition of modern representative or parliamentary democracy, nor did it ever have the type of advanced capitalistic economy that provided the basis for economic and political liberalism in the West.

Poland may have been a relatively free country by the standards of eighteenth-century absolutism, but not by modern standards. The Polish nobility, for example, enjoyed the "golden freedoms," whereas nine-tenths of the population, which was subject to backward forms of feudal tenure and control, did not. In this respect, waxing poetic about how free Poland was before the partitions is a bit problematic. Furthermore, as the representatives of the "political nation," in the medieval sense of the word, the Polish–Lithuanian nobility was a multinational and religiously heterodox class that defined itself in terms of its hereditary rights or position in the political process and not by the modern ethnic, linguistic, or religious criteria of "Polishness": Polish born, Polish speaking, and Roman Catholic. The language of politics, Latin, merely reflected the cosmopolitan nature of the medieval idea of the "Polish nation."

The feudal ideas of freedom and nation were different from modern-democratic and ethnically Polish concepts of both, just as the national freedoms that were lost in the partitions of the Polish–Lithuanian Republic at the end of the eighteenth century were different from those that Poles aspired to achieve in the nineteenth century.[2] A reinterpretation of the feudal past in the spirit of nineteenth-century liberalism and nationalism, which produced distorted idealizations of the "golden age" as more free and more national than it had been, was a trait that the inhabitants of the "historical kingdoms" of Central Europe—Czechs, Hungarians, and Poles—shared. Nevertheless, the idea of "regaining" the freedoms of the past played an important role in each of these people's visions of the future.

Frederick the Great and Prussian Pathology

Hohenzollern Prussia provided the regional model for Central European enlightenment, which Romanov Russia and Habsburg Austria imitated because it was most successful in the implementation of the French enlightened absolutistic strategy. The reigns of both Prussia's Frederick Wilhelm I (1713–1740), "the Soldiers' King," and Russia's Peter "the Great" (1689–1725) were typical of the first generation of enlightened absolutists because they were marked by a pragmatic interest in technical and organizational inno vations for the sake of military development and state administration, not in the philosophical trappings of enlightenment as a means of justifying absolutism. Frederick Wilhelm resolved most elegantly and efficiently the inherent and age-old conflict between the centralizing aspirations of the crown and the particular feudal interests of the landed nobility. Instead of fighting Brandenburg-Prussia's strong class of landowning nobility, the Junkers, he effectively enlisted them into the service of the state by making careers in the military or the bureaucracy part of the duties and status of that class. Aristocracy became part of the state bureaucracy.

Frederick Wilhelm was above all a military man, and he was one of the first regents of Europe to make the uniform of the commander in chief the centerpiece of a regal wardrobe. In addition to turning the Prussian army into a professional organization during his reign, the emulation of military discipline in all realms of public life accompanied the standard repertoire of enlightened reforms aimed at improving public administration, which enhanced the power of the dynastic state. Coupled with the indigenous Prussian strain of Calvinistic piety, these innovations led to the development of austere values: The religious concepts of Christian vocation and Calvinistic virtue coalesced with the military values of authority, service, and duty and the demands of rational organization. *Zucht, Ordnung, und Pflicht*—"discipline," "order," and "duty"—became the cardinal virtues of Prussian military organization, the state, and society. The subsequent rise of Prussia from a second-rate to a major European power, which also developed Europe's most effective standing army for a state of its size, merely demonstrated how compatible Protestantism, absolutism, militarism, and "enlightened" rationality were with one another.

The reign of Frederick the Great (1740–1786), the son of the "Soldiers' King," represented the classic age of enlightenment in Prussia. Unlike his father, who was primarily interested in the pragmatic benefits of rationalization, Frederick the Great was a full-fledged intellectual apostle of the French form of enlightened absolutism. He imitated all the irrational high Baroque extravagance of the court of France's Louis XIV (but on a smaller scale), and he adopted French philosophy to legitimize the enhancement of dynastic power. Frederick added an elegant French veneer to the austerity characteristic of his father's reign. For example, he corresponded extensively with Voltaire, who spent two years at Frederick's court, and he had a summer palace, San Souci, a miniature version of Versailles, constructed in Potsdam, outside Berlin.

Frederick recognized that expanding Prussia's territory and influence would ultimately be at the cost of the Polish–Lithuanian Republic and the Habsburg Empire. At the beginning of his reign, he conspired with the French and the Bavarians against Habsburg Austria and started a war that led to the acquisition of Silesia, an exceptionally prosperous part of the domains of the Bohemian crown that the Habsburgs held. Then in 1772, he masterminded the first of the three partitions of Poland. Frederick was the first Prussian politician to recognize that the rise of Prussia to a position of predominance in Germany was contingent on forcing the Habsburgs as the Holy Roman Emperors of the German Nation out of the sphere of German politics. It took more than a century to achieve this objective, but the legendary Prussian foreign minister Otto von Bismarck did so brilliantly between 1860 and 1870 and established Prussian-German predominance in Central Europe in the process.

It is difficult to talk about the attributes of the German national character because German and anti-German propaganda during the two world wars relied on the propagation of stereotypes. The Prussian spiked helmet is an ominous symbol. But the identification of "the Prussian" with "the German" does injustice to other fundamentally different German traditions reflecting the regional diversity and feudal heritage of Germany, like Hanseatic cosmopolitanism, the republican traditions of the Rhineland, or Bavarian Catholicism. The term "Prussian" nevertheless can be used to describe one German national characteristic insofar as the unification of Germany under the auspices of Prussia in 1871 led to a "Prussian-ification" of Germany. One explanation for the success of Germany and one of the roots of the aggressive nature of German nationalism in the late nineteenth century and in the first half of the twentieth century can be found, psychoanalytically speaking, in the authoritarian structures propagated by Prussian-German states.

Social cohesion in all societies is based on authority, and the more rigid, unquestionable, or, politically speaking, absolute authority becomes, the more hierarchical and repressive societies tend to be. Subordination to a strict authority, whether it be embodied in the stern father of a family or, analogously, in a powerful leader in an absolutistic state, makes tremendous psychic demands on individuals, especially if obedience is elevated to the status of the primary moral obligation in private and public life. It does not allow an individual to disobey—that is, to ventilate the aggression or dissatisfaction that subordination inevitably induces—in a socially or politically acceptable manner.

The high degree of personal identification with authority that accompanies its "internalization" and the perception of authority as both morally binding and inherently good alleviate to a certain extent some of the conflicts inherent in subordination, by making obedience or service—doing one's duty—into a source of personal gratification. Subordination has the concomitant benefit of relieving the individual conscience from having to make moral decisions, by transferring responsibility for them to figures of authority. The natural tendency to ventilate aggressions on subordinates also becomes problematic as soon as obedience is recognized as a binding and overriding moral virtue to be rewarded on all levels of the social and political hierarchy. Thus it is most economical to export or project the aggressions that accompany subordination onto "enemies" or "scapegoats" outside the authoritarian hierarchy or social group. The degradation or dehumanization of these scapegoats, simultaneously accompanied by an idealization of the individual or collective self to increase the distance between the scapegoat and the self, helps turn them into objects on which aggressions can be ventilated without creating conflicts of conscience.

Such psychological mechanisms can be found in all peoples and cultures, and clinically speaking, every nation has its own psychopathological profile. The "aggressive–subservient personality type" is not a peculiarity of German tradition; however, as the German psychoanalysts Alexander and Margarete Mitscherlich observed in *The Inability to Mourn*, their study of the post–World War II German psyche, this personality type "is no foreigner to our national culture."[3] As national attributes, the phenomenon of "anticipatory obedience" (*vorauseilender Gehorsam*), the expectation and execution of dictates or commands even before they are explicitly stated; a "subordination mentality" (*Untertänigkeitsmentalität*); and the prevalence of the "authoritarian personality type" indicate a high degree of identification with authority and its internalization, a phenomenon that has been a constant source of concern for observers of Germany as well as among Germans themselves.[4]

Although the psychopathology of groups is a controversial way of looking at history, the relationship between subservience and aggression can be used to illustrate the dynamics of Germany's development. One of the keys to the success of authoritarian or totalitarian German states was their ability to marshal social and economic resources effectively, because most of their subjects identified themselves with, accepted, or acquiesced to the authority of the state and understood obedience, service, or "doing their duty," a concept that can be traced back to Protestant and "enlightened" Prussian traditions, as an overriding moral *and* rational obligation. The domestic function of German imperialism was to consolidate disparate social groups, whose divergent interests were a potential source of conflict in the Reich, by providing them with common "foreign" objectives.

The expansive nature of German imperialism can also be explained as a means of focusing and exporting the aggressions that authoritarianism produced in German society. In this respect, nationalism and racism, the idealization of the German nation (or collective self) and the degradation of alleged enemies can be explained as psychological mechanisms. The device of negative integration was a characteristic of imperial German nationalism: the ability to portray "internal enemies"—Communists; Socialists; Catholics; Jews; and Polish, Danish, and French minorities—and "external enemies" as so subversive or threatening that "good Germans" would close ranks against them.

Prussian enlightened absolutism and the various forms of German "absolutism" that succeeded it in the Second German Empire (1871–1918) and the Third Reich (1933–1945) or the German Democratic Republic (1949–1990) are qualitatively different from other Central European forms, like Austrian or Russian absolutism and neoabsolutism in the eighteenth and nineteenth centuries and Soviet Stalinism in the twentieth century, due to the high degree of individual identification with authority they engendered in their subjects. Although it would be misleading to ignore the traditions of the German Left or to draw too monolithic a picture of German authoritarianism, many Germans viewed political dominion as service and accepted the logic of absolutism.

There really was no inherent conflict between the old Protestant idea of vocation and the new enlightened idea of submitting to the demands of rational organization. As a matter of tradition and conviction, Prussians not only accepted and followed the rules, but they also excelled in doing so. (The German sociologist Max Weber defined "discipline" as "finding a specifiable number of people who in virtue of a habitual attitude will obey a command in a prompt, automatic, and unthinking manner" or as "uncritical and unresisting obedience."[5] For Weber, discipline was not a peculiarity of the German national psyche; it was part of the structural rationale of modern industrial economies and modern bureaucratic states characterized by hierarchical structures and an extensive division of labor.)

It would be unwise to overlook the differences between National Socialist and Communist ideologies and the roles they played in articulating and implementing political policies, but there was no real break in the authoritarian tradition in East Germany after World War II. National Socialism was followed by "Prussian Stalinism." East German historians appropriated the Prussian tradition of enlightened absolutism in order to give the German Democratic Republic its own "progressive" yet authoritarian national history along the lines of "from Frederick the Great to Erich Honecker." For example, in the mid-1980s a statue of Frederick II, which had been removed from its place on Unter den Linden in East Berlin after the war because it was a symbol of old Geman nationalism, was returned to its original site as a symbol of a new Eastern German nationalism.

Nationalism, which was a cohesive force in Germany, was a corrosive influence in the multiethnic and multidenominational empires of Austria and Russia. In comparison with Prussia before 1870 and the German empires thereafter, the subjects of the Austrian and Russian empires never identified themselves with state authority to the same extent that the Prussians and later the Germans did. Therefore, submitting to the will of the state was not experienced as service but as servitude.

Compared with the Germans in their national empire, the subjects in the multinational empires of the Habsburgs and the Romanovs resented authority more than they internalized it, and instead of learning to follow the rules, they developed strategies for bending or evading them. Understanding the distinction between following rules and not breaking them (duty and deceit) is important to appreciating Central European political culture. It explains, for example, why the use of coercion was more important in the "disorderly" Austrian and Russian empires than in the German one. Not duty but duplicity was typical of the Austrian and Russian subjects: a humiliating but feigned deference and respect for authority in its presence, coupled with an opportunistic disregard of it in its absence.

The authoritarian use of coercion in the Austrian and Russian empires not only created a reservoir of resentment and aggressive potential; the lack of identification with authority also undermined social and political cohesion. Both these features could be found among the various minorities of Austria and Russia's multiethnic and religiously heterodox empires, where there were an immediate abundance of local enemies or scapegoats, as the propensity to ventilate national aggressions on the minorities that were lower down on the respective social, ethnic, or denominational ladders. If German absolutism often produced individuals with a masochistically compulsive sense of "duty" and order, then the most negative manifestation of the Austrian and Russian use of coercion to maintain order were those latent sadists who waited for an opportunity to live out their aggressions.

It will be important to recall later this short digression on the psychology of absolutism and authoritarianism, as it is one reason for the lethal effectiveness of the Third Reich as a pathological yet normal German state as well as an explanation for the sheer nastiness of Central and Eastern European nationalism. However, the deep-seated fears and hates of Adolf Hitler were not a product of the northern Central European Protestant–Prussian–German tradition, which provided an efficient instrument for the execution of Nazi ideology, but the southern Central European Roman Catholic–Austrian–multinational tradition. Hitler was an Austrian or, perhaps more appropriately, a German from the Habsburgs' multinational empire. Born in Braunau on the Inn River just across the border from Bavaria and raised in Linz on the Danube, Hitler called his youth in Vienna, the multiethnic capital of the Habsburgs' multinational empire, before World War I "the hardest, though most thorough, school of my life" in which, he observed, "I obtained the foundations for a philosophy in general and a political view in particular which later I only needed to supplement in detail, but which never left me."[6] In this respect, only half the pathology of National Socialism was "Prussian."

Russia's Westward Turn:
Peter the Great and Catherine the Great

If Prussia's enlightened absolutism was organizationally and psychologically successful in the short and the long run, Russian enlightened absolutism, in comparison, was not. Peter the Great, a czar whose reform policies frequently (and inaccurately) have been cited as historical precedents for Mikhail Gorbachev's glasnost and perestroika, started building the Baltic port of St. Petersburg, that proverbial "window to the West," in 1703. The first secular book in Russian history, a compendium of general knowledge with the misleading title *Arithmetic*, and Russia's first periodical, a journal on technical and military subjects, appeared the same year. These examples show how late Russia's physical access and metaphorical opening to the West was and what kind of information or expertise interested Peter, who identified education or enlightenment with vocational–technical training related to the crafts of war and state administration. They also indicate the belated advent of secularization in the Russian Orthodox East.

We should not assume, however, that Russia's "Westward turn" came overnight. On the contrary, it came hand in hand with Russia's westward expansion at the expense of Sweden and Poland-Lithuania, and there were protagonists of "Westernization" before Peter's reign.[7] Like all the subsequent rulers of Russian empires to date, Peter was confronted with problems inherent in the empire itself: its vastness, underdevelopment, and diversity.

These were the opponents with which Peter and his successors struggled, not the feudal estates occupying the absolutist monarchs farther West. At a relatively early date, the Russian conflict with feudal privilege had been resolved in the interest of a peculiarly Eastern form of "absolutism." At the end of the fifteenth century, the dukes of Moscow created a new "service nobility," which existed parallel to an indigenous one of free estates that was comparable in some respects to its Western feudal counterparts and cultivated the same kind of particularistic interests. However, the new "service nobility" derived its power exclusively from the czar and identified its interests with those of its benefactor because it profited from the growth of his personal dominion as well as the territorial expansion of Russia, primarily in the form of the confiscation of vanquished territory or property. In other words, the Russian czars won the conflict with their old feudal nobility by outnumbering them with the "service nobility," which expanded as the Russian empire did. One of Peter the Great's ingenious innovations was to merge these two noble classes into one uniform aristocratic caste, by making service in the czar's military or state bureaucracy an obligation for all.

Unlike the development of Western European feudalism, in which the nature of power was defined "constitutionally"—that is, by a complicated system of laws or precedents that determined and regulated the rights and obligations of lords and vassals, rulers and their subjects, or, generally speaking, the state and society—the Eastern European or Russian development can be characterized by the maintenance of "archaic" authority: power as a monolithic and personal attribute of the ruler. The Eastern Orthodox or Byzantine tradition of the church's subordination to the state, as opposed to the Western European tradition of the separation of church and state or spiritual and temporal authority, and the absence of the complicated kinds of contractual relations typical of Western feudalism made the Russian czars undoubtedly more despotic, autocratic, and powerful than their royal or imperial contemporaries farther west.

The history of the evolution of Western political institutions can be interpreted as the replacement of "archaic" forms of power by law that regulated and constrained the use of power. Parliamentary or constitutional governments evolved out of feudal struggles between the rulers and the ruled or the state and society, on the one hand, and they were based on the concept of respecting individual rights and freedoms and the rule of law, on the other. In this respect, the Magna Carta was one of the first "human rights documents" of the Western tradition.

One of the primary elements of the "Eastern" or Russian tradition was the lack of inherent constraints on "archaic" power or the relative absence of the idea of the rule of law. The intrinsic tension between the state and society in the West hardly existed in the East because of the lack of traditional constraints on political power as a form of "archaic" or personal dominion. The czars "owned" the state, and the state "owned" society, or, as the Hungarian historian, Jenő Szücs, observed: "The West subordinated society to the state, the East "nationalized" it."[8] If one is prepared to use certain traditions of legality or checks on power as a criterion for European civilization, the Russian political heritage is less European than those of Central European states because it is almost historically devoid of the kinds of constraints on power that characterize "civil" societies.

Theoretical and technical enlightenment was just as compatible with the practice of despotism in Russia as it was with the development of absolutism in the West. However, the transition from a religious to a secular state, as well as from a decentralized to a centralized empire, was by no means as fluid. Religious fundamentalism and peasant insurrectionism—those indigenous forms of Russian traditionalism that inspired resistance to enlightenment and centralization—provided the basis for a "conservative coalition" against the reforming Romanovs until the twentieth century. Imported French rationality never succeeded in winning the battle with these primal manifestations of the Russian soul and the Russian soil. The reign of Catherine the Great (1762–1796), who was perhaps the best example of the "second generation" of enlightened absolutists, can be used to demonstrate this point.

Philosophical contemporaries in the West admired Catherine the Great because she embodied the idea of enlightened absolutism. Personally erudite and intellectually agile, she corresponded extensively with Voltaire, who was one of her great protagonists in the West and wrote a history of imperial Russia praising her brilliance. She vigorously promoted all things French, from fashion to philosophy, among Russian aristocrats and laid the foundations for a class of westward-looking secular intellectuals with a vague disposition for sweeping change. She also got along famously with Frederick of Prussia, and she encouraged the establishment of German settlements in the Volga River Valley in Ukraine. (These settlements maintained their ethnic identity and linguistic integrity until the twentieth century. After the Nazi invasion of the Soviet Union in June 1941, Stalin regarded the so-called Volga Germans to be politically unreliable and deported approximately 1.5 million of them from their traditional homeland in the Volga Valley of eastern Ukraine across the Urals into the Soviet Union's Asian republics.)

Catherine's reign began with a radical vision of enlightened economic and legal reform. These innovations violated the traditional interests and attitudes of the aristocracy and the peasantry to such a great extent that they provoked resistance and revolt, and her experimentation ended in retractions and despotic retaliation. Despite all her programmatic brilliance, very few of Catherine's ambitious innovations endured. The pattern of state-initiated reform "from above," pious or peasant revolt "from below," and the state's retraction of reforms and retaliation against the insurrectionists was repeated regularly in Russian history from the eighteenth century until the twentieth century.

Although the Bolshevik Revolution of 1917 was a radical ideological break with the Russian past, in some respects Lenin and Stalin stood squarely in the Russian political tradition. A monolithic and omnipotent state and the autocratic wielding of power were parts of the imperial czarist heritage incorporated into the Soviet tradition but legitimized using a different ideology: the "dictatorship of the proletariate." Like the czars, Lenin and Stalin were "enlightened" or "revolutionary" despots who, with the support of a minority, had to "revolutionize" Russian society "from above," and they dealt with the resistance their innovations evoked "from below," just as their predecessors did: with brute force.

The "modernization" of Russia—the Russian Civil War (1917–1920) and Stalin's policies of forced industrialization and the collectivization of agriculture in the 1920s—claimed millions of victims. As long as Mikail Gorbachev as a reformer managed to refrain from reverting to the despotic–dictatorial use of force to solve the problems of revolt that "enlightened" reforms traditionally have induced in the Russian empire, he was breaking with historical precedents. His enlightened reforms also provoked an insurrection by the conservative forces in the Soviet Union, but the putsch of August 1991 failed. Unlike his predecessors in Russian history, however, Gorbachev did not manage to reassert his authority. He eventually was swept aside by the democratic and nationalistic forces that his reforms had released. The problems of the newly independent states are in many respects similar to those Russia faced after the first Russian Revolution in February 1917. After disposing of the czar, the provisional government was confronted with the predicament of creating a democracy in a society without democratic traditions.

Habsburg Enlightenment:
Maria Theresia and Joseph II

The Habsburg Empire was a latecomer to the idea of enlightened absolutism. Although the reign of Charles VI (1711–1740) coincided with those of Prussia's "Soldiers' King," Frederick Wilhelm, and Russia's Peter the Great, the Habsburg emperor cannot be counted among the representatives of that first generation of enlightened absolutists. On the contrary, instead of being the Habsburg Empire's first enlightened absolutist, Charles VI was its last Baroque emperor. His reign was the apotheosis of that grandiose and spectacular form of Roman Catholic court culture in which the accomplishments of the dynasty and the Church Triumphant mirrored each oth-

er. Charles VI, who was not a bad amateur composer, had a greater personal penchant for Italian music than the kind of military administration that
fascinated his Prussian and Russian contemporaries. He enjoyed basking in
Baroque glory.

The worst of all possible dynastic fates befell Charles: He had no male
offspring. But he did spend a great deal of time and energy during his reign
negotiating the so-called Pragmatic Sanction with the other ruling houses
of Europe. This was the recognition of his daughter Maria Theresia as an
extraordinary but legitimate vehicle of succession, coupled with a guarantee of the indivisibility of the Habsburgs' hereditary titles and holdings.
(Maria Theresia married Duke Francis Stephan of Lorraine, and the dynastic line subsequently bore the name Habsburg-Lorraine.) By the time
Charles VI died in 1740, he had received all the reassurances he needed, but
treaties, like words, can be cheap.

As soon as his twenty-three-year-old daughter nominally assumed power,
the plans for dividing up the Habsburg Empire came out of diplomatic draw-
ers throughout Europe. For example, Prussia's Frederick the Great prompt-
ly occupied and annexed Silesia, a prosperous and predominantly German-
speaking realm that historically had belonged to lands of the Bohemian
crown that the Habsburgs wore, and he conspired on a grand scale against
the Habsburg Empire with the Bavarians and the French. However, Maria
Theresia succeeded in asserting herself in the men's world during the War
of the Austrian Succession (1741–1748). The Habsburgs' realms—minus
Silesia, which she futilely attempted to regain in two later wars with Prussia—survived intact.

Maria Theresia was raised in the Habsburgs' family tradition of Roman
Catholic piety and devotion at her father's Baroque court, and she had no
great personal disposition for the philosophy of the Enlightenment. The
wars she fought at the beginning of her reign, in particular, the great successes achieved by Prussia, a kingdom much smaller than her own, convinced her that her realms had to be reorganized in order to allow her to
marshal their resources more effectively in the future.

Unlike her contemporaries on the Prussian and Russian thrones, Frederick the Great and Catherine the Great, Maria Theresia did not embrace
the philosophical program of the Enlightenment. She never indulged in the
kind of philosophical discourse for which Frederick and Catherine were
renowned. As the pious mother of sixteen children, who allegedly used
more maternal instinct in her reform strategies than enlightened philosophy, Maria Theresia was a bit doughty by the standards of stellar enlightened
absolutists like Frederick and Catherine, who barely veiled their contempt
for her. Nevertheless, she also executed a "revolution from above" in her
realms, and the problems she faced—indigenous conservatism, economic
underdevelopment, and the sheer diversity of the Habsburg Empire—were
analogous in some respects to those that Catherine confronted in Russia.

The project of enlightened absolutism in Austria could be called a
"*counter*-Counter-Reformation."[9] If the alliance of interests among the dynasty, the Roman Catholic Church, and the nobility in the Habsburg Em-

pire had been the key to its initial consolidation in the seventeenth century, reforming the Habsburg Empire in the eighteenth century included revising the traditional domestic balance of power among these interest groups in favor of the dynasty. The dynastic centralization of power and the creation of modern centralized bureaucracies for state administration and defense had to be executed at the expense of the venerable rights of the church and the nobility, both of which had loyally served the dynasty.

Neither the heritage of the Roman Catholic Counter-Reformation nor the feudal diversity of the Habsburgs' holdings were conducive to the execution of an enlightened absolutist policy that attempted to replace the empire's old raison d'etre—the conservative, Catholic doctrine of dynastic loyalty—with a progressive, secular ideology of state efficiency. Secularization jeopardized the interests of the church in a manner similar to the way centralization threatened the age-old particularistic interests of the multinational nobility that the Habsburgs had drawn into their service.

The Protestant traditions of northern Germany provided a political environment and an intellectual atmosphere that were more receptive to enlightenment than the Roman Catholic ones that prevailed in the Habsburg Empire. During the Reformation, German rulers in the north subordinated the Protestant Churches to the state, whereas in the Habsburg Empire the universal interests of papal Rome stood behind the alliance between the dynasty and the church. Owing to the emphasis on the inwardness and personal nature of the religious experience, a certain tolerance or individualism became attributes of the Protestant sensibility, and this frame of mind provided a more fertile environment for freethinkers. Conversely, the Catholic Counter-Reformation emphasized authority and dogma, and the Roman Church had institutions for squelching deviation and heresy, both religious and secular.

Northern German Protestants developed a philosophical and literary culture of *Dichter und Denker*, poets and thinkers, which had some of its roots in the Protestant tradition of the interpretation and propagation of the Word and the "inwardness" of the religious experience, whereas Southern German Catholic culture was more visually and sensually inclined. Baroque music, theater, painting, and architecture flourished in the German Catholic south and the Habsburg Empire, under the patronage of ecclesiastical and secular lords who relied on the spectrum of Baroque effects to portray their visions of divine or dynastic glory. Roman Catholic Baroque church architecture, for example, fell into the realm of false idols from the Protestant biblical perspective, but to the adherents of Roman Catholic piety, Baroque churches were not contemporary versions of worshiping the Golden Calf but built for the greater glory of God (*ad majoram gloriam Dei*) with the intention of giving worshipers a glimpse of his glory.

One of the origins of the Protestant work ethic was the belief that serving successfully in this world was indicative of having been chosen by God for the next, a conviction that human action had intrinsic meaning and merits and that success was a sign of having been chosen by the Lord. The tradition of Baroque Roman Catholic religiosity, in comparison, emphasized the omnipotence and glory of God and the vanity of human endeavor, and it contributed in this respect to transmitting values that could be called Mediterranean. German Protestants believed in serving the Lord and Duty; Catholics in southern Germany and the Habsburgs' realms believed in man's inability to interpret the ways of the Lord and the ways of the World, the transient nature of human existence, and Death.

Abraham à Santa Clara, a renowned preacher of the Austrian Counter-Reformation, once observed in a sermon that "the body is meat that soon stinks, and life is a little ship that soon sinks." The casual, roundabout way of doing things or the ability not to take life too seriously—the phenomenon usually described as *Gemütlichkeit*—is one criterion for distinguishing southern German Catholics, like Bavarians or Austrians, from northern German Protestants, and it can be traced back to attitudes rooted in the traditions of Baroque piety. The Protestant work ethic was based on postponed gratification; the Catholic ethic of *Gemütlichkeit* obviously was not. Perhaps Catholicism also contributed to the economic backwardness of the Habsburgs' realms because it did not theologically promote capital accumulation.

Furthermore, Roman Catholicism appears to have provided a more fertile ground for the development of subservient personality types in that the Catholic tradition of Providence (as opposed to predestination) justified the arbitrary ways of the worldly lords as the ways of the Lord. The Protestant tradition, however, contributed to the development of a different breed of authoritarian personality type in that the concepts of vocation, predestination, and duty produced different attitudes toward order. Protestant authority had a logic that Catholic authority lacked. Despite these sweeping generalizations, it is obvious which of these sensibilities was more prone to the cool, technical rationality of the Enlightenment. The fact that the program of enlightened absolutism violated the Baroque sensibility engendered by the Roman Catholic Counter-Reformation in the Habsburg Empire is one explanation for the resistance it met.

During her reign, Maria Theresia and her advisers introduced a broad spectrum of judicious administrative, legal, and educational reforms.[10] Her son and successor, the "revolutionary emperor" Joseph II (coregent with Maria Theresia from 1765 to 1780, emperor from 1780 to 1790), had a more ambitious and radical program, and the problems he confronted show how difficult it was to reform the Habsburgs' Catholic and neofeudal empire. Joseph's motto was "everything for the people, nothing by the people." He based his program on a rational bureaucratic reform of society "from above" which may appear to have been liberal but was in effect absolutistic. Its primary aim was not to promote or protect the rights of individuals but, rather, to modernize society and expand the power of the state.

During his decade of reform, Joseph abolished perpetual serfdom, which violated the interests of the nobility, and changed the traditional obligations of tenured serfs to their lords for the use of their land, from payment in goods or services to payment in cash. This innovation, in turn, created problems for the serfs. Like his mother Maria Theresia, who had removed one of the last formal vestiges of Bohemian independence by suspending the Court Chancellery of the Bohemian Crown in Prague and transferring the administration of Bohemia to Vienna, Joseph wished to limit the historical autonomy of the kingdom of Hungary. This raised the ire of the Hungarian nobility because it violated their historical rights.

Joseph's proclamation of German as the administrative language of the empire also broke with established traditions and created resistance. But it was basically a relatively straightforward measure of rationalization: the use of a modern language instead of Latin. Joseph's introduction of German turned a linguistic question into a political one, and the issue of which language was to be used officially in the Habsburgs' realms became a problem that was to afflict the empire periodically throughout the nineteenth century. This is just one indication of how difficult it was to create a modern centralized state out of an imperial conglomeration of feudal ones.

Joseph's subjects welcomed the anticlericalism that was part of his policy toward the Roman Catholic Church more than they did the consequences of his programmatic antifeudalism. Joseph pursued an ambitious policy of secularizing the state and public life. For example, he suspended some 700 monasteries and convents of contemplative orders that were not engaged in useful public activities like education, caring for the sick, or agriculture—approximately one-third of the monastic institutions in his realms—and liberally confiscated their properties. He also began his reign with the so-called Patent of Tolerance that guaranteed his Protestant subjects religious freedom and laid the foundations for the eventual equality of the Jews, which was to give them an avenue of assimilation in the future. He took censorship out of the hands of the church and established freedom of the press, although after writers began taking the liberty of criticizing the emperor himself, he restricted it.

The results of Joseph's decade of radical experimentation were rather short lived. Although his important decrees concerning religious toleration, monastic suspensions, and the abolition of serfdom endured, he either withdrew most of his reforms shortly before his death, or his brother and successor, Leopold II (1790–1792), did so shortly thereafter. (Incidentally, Joseph chose to have an epitaph describing his failure engraved on his coffin.) Both his contemporaries and historians agree that he simply tried to do too much, too fast. His radical solutions to the empire's indigenous problems created new problems without solving the old ones first.

Nonetheless, during the nineteenth and twentieth centuries, various political ideologies adopted the reign of Joseph as a historical precedent. Liberals looked back on his propagation of economic freedoms; socialists saw him as a forerunner of the welfare state; and both liberals and socialists appreciated his anticlericalism. National Socialists praised his Germanness, commended his authoritarian leadership, and maintained that he was a precedent for the *Führer* and the totalitarian German state. After World War II, Austrian Communists even cautiously attempted to reconcile Joseph II's enlightened absolutism with Joseph Stalin's "progressive" form of centralized state administration.[11]

These examples briefly illustrate how ambiguous the Central European tradition of enlightened absolutism can be. Nevertheless, if the absolutistic experiment with enlightenment was most successful in Prussia and least effective in Russia, the results in the Habsburg Empire were somewhere between these extremes. The Enlightenment started later in Central and Eastern Europe than in the West, and it occurred under less auspicious circumstances. It was truncated to a great extent by the French Revolution and the Napoleonic Wars, which merely demonstrated to monarchs what happened when enlightenment (and France) got out of hand. For a number of reasons, the relative poverty of liberal democratic traditions was and remained a characteristic of Central European political culture. Economists have observed that the mercantile economy in the region was underdeveloped. Therefore, the most important agent of change, the middle class, was smaller than that in Western Europe. The persistence of neofeudalism or absolutism itself can also be blamed for stunting the development of more liberal societies. One way or the other, old structures and old ideas prevailed longer in Central Europe than in Western Europe.

Immanuel Kant defined enlightenment as man's responsibility for freeing himself from a self-inflicted state of ignorance caused by cowardice and laziness, and he used a classical exhortation to describe the task of enlightenment: Sapere aude! "Dare to know!"[12] If the Enlightenment encouraged people to think for themselves, the Central and Eastern European political variations on this maxim could be characterized by the qualification "but not too much."

∗ 7 ∗

Nations Without States,
States Without Nations

1790–1848

If reason and revolution are concepts frequently used to characterize those eighteenth-century trends that culminated in the French Revolution, then Romanticism and reaction are concepts regularly employed to describe the early-nineteenth-century responses to the Enlightenment and the upheavals that shook France and then the rest of Europe after 1789. The French Revolution abruptly ended royal and imperial experimentation with enlightened reform in Central and Eastern Europe. Systematic searches for revolutionary sympathizers or radical conspirators in Vienna, Berlin, and St. Petersburg produced negligible results, and as the French Revolution began to devour its own children, enthusiasm for it evaporated among those enlightened reformers who initially sympathized with its objectives. The execution in 1793 of the French king, Louis XVI, and his wife, Marie Antoinette—a daughter of Maria Theresia and the sister of the Habsburg emperors Joseph and Leopold as well as a personal friend of Russia's Catherine the Great—and Robespierre's Reign of Terror during 1793/1794 shocked the ruling elites of Europe. It was not because regicide or the bloodletting that accompanied revolts was so foreign to them, but because they represented a political program based on systematically destroying the old order.

The dynamics of the French Revolution and its relationship to the rise and demise of the Napoleonic empire are complicated. Generalizations about the period between the outbreak of the French Revolution in 1789 and its diplomatic denouement in 1814/1815 at the Congress of Vienna, which established a new Continental balance of power based on old anti-revolutionary precepts, tend to oversimplify the conflicts of this era along the lines of France and the principles of the Revolution versus everybody else—

the Continental powers plus Britain—and tyranny. Instead of describing the military campaigns or the complicated diplomatic carousels of conflict and collaboration during this period, we shall examine a few of the enduring consequences of the revolutionary era for Central Europe.

From 1792 until 1815 Europe was constantly in a state of war, in which the antagonists of France's revolution and Napoleon's subsequent empire alternated between anti-French coalitions and pro-French alliances. The various principalities of Germany, Prussia, and Russia fluctuated between military adversity and diplomatic advantage by fighting against France, with France, or remaining neutral. Austria, the only power to participate in all four anti-French coalitions, and Britain were France's most consistent enemies.

One important and lasting Napoleonic contribution to revising the map of Europe was a "rationalization" of the political order in Germany, which was still, at the beginning of the nineteenth century, a multifarious feudal patchwork of kingdoms, principalities of various sizes, and independent city-states. Napoleonic reforms reduced to forty the 200 states that had been the constituent members of the Holy Roman Empire of the German Nation. At the peak of its power in 1810, France directly governed the Netherlands, Belgium, and Luxembourg; all of Germany west of the "natural border" of the Rhine; northern Germany eastward to Lübeck (roughly the German–Danish border); and it established a client association of German states, the Confederation of the Rhine, which reached from the Alps to the Baltic Sea but excluded Prussia and Austria. Although French imperial occupation and intervention in Germany activated nascent German nationalism (and Francophobia became one of the constituent attributes of German nationalism in the nineteenth century), many of the smaller German states found cooperation with France to be a convenient means of pursuing their traditional interests, like weakening the power of the Habsburg-Austrian Holy Roman Emperor of the German Nation. It also gave them a vehicle for gaining territory and offset the interests of larger rivals like Prussia. Napoleon played rather well the old French imperial role of *protector Germaniae.*

Although the Confederation of the Rhine was a short lived, Napoleonic imperial construction, its establishment in 1806 marked the end of the Holy Roman Empire of the German Nation, on the one hand, and the beginning of Germany as a "de-imperialized" confederation of states, on the other.[1] At the Congress of Vienna in 1815, Europe's diplomats and peacemakers reformulated the idea of a confederative Germany, which included Prussia and Austria as well as the German principalities that had been temporarily annexed by imperial France. The main international function of the German Confederation, a loose association of forty German principalities under the seniority of Austria, was not to replace the old German empire but to provide a forum for maintaining the new status quo of fewer but nevertheless disunited German states, and it did so well for the next five decades. However, the two largest members of the German Confederation, Austria and Prussia, had conflicting interests. Austria wanted to maintain the status quo which, in turn, placed severe restrictions on Prussia's ambitions. The long-term Prussian strategy for establishing its own empire involved forcing Habsburg Austria out of its venerable position of factual and titular predominance in the sphere of German politics.

At the Congress of Vienna, the diplomats of the victorious powers—England, Russia, Austria, and Prussia—treated France reasonably and divided the spoils of victory fairly. They established a European balance of five powers that proved to be enduring. Although it would be an exaggeration to call the nineteenth century a period of general peace, there was no general European war between the Congress of Vienna and World War I. With the sole exception of the Crimean War of 1854–1856, which was geographically peripheral, none of the thirteen European wars between 1815 and 1914 involved more than two of the five major powers or seriously jeopardized the traditional balance of power. However, the rise of Prussia and the unification of Germany at the respective costs of Austria and France redistributed how European power was balanced. In Central Europe, the antirevolutionary sentiment and absolutism cemented the cooperation of the Prussian, Austrian, and Russian empires for the greater part of the nineteenth century. Their rear-guard actions against liberalism and the nationalism of their indigenous minorities lasted until the end of World War I.

The Partitions of Poland, 1772–1795

Given the central position of the French Revolution in world history, it is difficult to believe that the partitions of Poland at the end of the eighteenth century impressed Europeans just as much as the upheavals did that began in France in 1789. Most contemporaries, however, showed an insufficient appreciation for what was transpiring in France. The immediacy of events always makes it difficult for witnesses to anticipate how important they are or how they will be evaluated in the future by a retrospective discipline like history. In any event, our understanding of the French Revolution today did not fit into the political and historical categories of the late eighteenth century. Traditional concepts like sedition and revolt or regicide and war were at first sufficient for interpreting what was happening in France. The relationship between the Enlightenment as a *révolution d'esprit* and the transformation of France as a *révolution politique* eventually became clear, but this causal nexus was not evident to contemporary observers, many of whom viewed the revolution as a historical aberration instead of the historical necessity it became.

A traditional approach to European history, which could be called "Western Eurocentric," reduces the study of European history to the investigation of the allegedly most advanced representatives of the West: England and France. A "major powers" interpretation of European history may be a bit more sophisticated because it includes Germany, Russia, and, to a certain extent, the Habsburg Empire. From the Western Eurocentric perspective, the partitions of Poland appear to be of peripheral importance, especially in comparison with the magnitude of the French Revolution. From the major powers perspective, the partitions of Poland are a relatively small subchapter in the imperial histories of Russia, Prussia, and Austria.

It would be a mistake, however, to underestimate the great impression that the partitions of Poland made on contemporaries throughout Europe and the permanent impression they made on Poles. An 800-year-old kingdom was not merely territorially truncated or temporarily occupied by its more powerful enemies and neighbors; it virtually ceased to exist. "For the first time in modern history," British historian Lord Acton stated in 1862,

> a great State was suppressed, and a whole nation divided among its enemies. . . . Thenceforward there was a nation demanding to be united in a State,—a soul, as it were, wandering in search of a body in which to begin life over again; and, for the first time, a cry was heard that the arrangement of States was unjust—that their limits were unnatural.[2]

Despite the affinities among the Polish, Czech, and Hungarian national experiences as parts of foreign empires, the Polish case is exceptional in many respects. After 1526, the kingdoms of Bohemia and Hungary continued to exist as "occupied" territorial and political entities, and they gave their inhabitants a certain amount of regional autonomy or sense of historical continuity, even though the kings of Bohemia and Hungary were Habsburgs.

During the nineteenth century, the Hungarians, for example, were eventually able to reassert their "historical rights." In 1867 a political compromise between the Habsburgs and the Hungarian nation led to the creation of the Dual Monarchy of Austro-Hungary, and the Kingdom of Hungary regained a considerable amount of autonomy. From the Czech perspective as well, the Kingdom of Bohemia may have been occupied and subjected, but it did not cease to exist. After World War I, the Czechs used the centuries-old historical and territorial continuity of the kingdom of Bohemia as one argument for successfully negotiating part of the borders of the Czechoslovak Republic. Poland was not occupied or incorporated into one dynastic state but partitioned by three. Therefore, Poles could not look back on the continuous existence of a Polish state. Their only real point of orientation was a historically extinct precedent that became more and more remote with each passing year: the Polish–Lithuanian Republic of 1772.[3]

It irks Poles that Voltaire, a consummate representative of the Enlightenment, made frequent and almost uniformly hostile remarks about Poland, which he considered to be backward and anarchistic. (Rousseau, another luminary of the Enlightenment and the father of Romanticism, was one of the few contemporaries who commented favorably on Poland's traditions of freedom.) From the perspective of the various apologists for enlightened absolutism, the partitions of the Polish–Lithuanian Republic were a sign of progress: the imposition of rationality and order on chaos. The Polish nobility's maintenance of their "golden freedoms" had created a "republic of anarchy" that had no chance to defend itself. It lacked the modern, centralized institutions of authority, finance, administration, or defense that would have been necessary to do so.

The background of each of the partitions of Poland is complicated, but the overall results can be summarized. Prussia's Frederick the Great masterminded the first partition in 1772, and Russia's Catherine the Great initiated the second and third ones in 1793 and 1795. Historically, the Habsburg Empire had no real designs on Poland, but it did gain territory through the partitions.

Before the first partition, the Polish–Lithuanian Republic was a kingdom of formidable size: more than 286,000 square miles, larger than contemporary France. The first partition of 1772 reduced the republic's territory by roughly 30 percent; the second partition two decades later lopped off another 40 percent; and the remaining 30 percent was divided up in 1795. When it all was over and done with, Prussia and Austria each had incorporated a bit less than one-fifth of the territorial booty into their domains, and Russia absorbed the remaining lion's share of three-fifths. Although Napoleon reestablished a short-lived Polish client state—the Grand Duchy of Warsaw from 1807 until 1815—Poland effectively ceased to exist as a political entity. The partitioning powers found fine names for the pieces of the Polish–Lithuanian Republic they incorporated into their empires. Prussia created the Grand Duchy of Posen, and Austria created the Kingdom of Galicia and Lodomeria. Two Polish client states—Austria's Republic of Kraków and Russia's Congress Kingdom of Poland, named after the Vienna Congress that created it in 1815—initially enjoyed some autonomy, but they were abolished by their respective imperial keepers in 1846 and 1864.

The fact that Maria Theresia had severe reservations about participating in the first partition of 1772 and that the Austrian empire's subsequent imperial administration in Poland was never as effective or as ruthless as its Prussian or Russian counterparts helped make Austria and the Habsburgs the most benign of the three culprits in the Polish historical memory. The liberality of the Austrian imperial administration toward the end of the nineteenth century eventually made the Habsburgs a symbol of political and religious tolerance which, given the hardships of foreign occupations by the Germans and the Soviets in the twentieth century, also became a source of nostalgia for the good old days in southern Poland. Some inhabitants of the part of contemporary southern Poland that belonged the Austrian imperial province of Galicia, especially the residents of Kraków, maintain that the prolonged Austrian presence influenced the southern Polish mentality. For example, confrontations between opposition movements and Communist authorities in the 1970s and 1980s never seemed to be as bloody or violent in Kraków as they were in Warsaw (in the former Russian partition) or Gdańsk (in the former German partition). Some people attributed this fact to the Austrian penchant for avoiding confrontation or bending the rules: a certain residual *Gemütlichkeit* from the good old days.

The temporal coincidence of the second and third partitions of the Polish–Lithuanian Republic in 1793 and 1795 with the pre-Napoleonic or republican phase of the French Revolution also helped give Poland a prominent position in that realm of political imagination called "the struggle for freedom." The partitions of Poland represented a victory of the old order of dynastic imperialism in Central Europe at a time when the democratic

Between 1772 and 1795, Russia, Prussia, and Austria divided the entire territory of Poland among themselves in three partitions. In an engraving portraying the First Partition of Poland in 1772, situated (from left to right) around a map of Poland, are Catherine the Great of Russia; Stanislaw August Poniatowski, king of Poland, attempting to hold on to his crown; Emperor Joseph II of Austria (coregent with Maria Theresia at the time); and Frederick the Great, king of Prussia. (Austrian National Library, Picture Archive)

principles of the French Revolution—liberty, equality, and fraternity—began to emerge in the West: "Poland was partitioned on the eve of the birth of Nationalism and Liberalism and thus became a symbol of all those people for whom self-determination and the consent of the governed provide the guiding principles of political life."[4] Subsequently there was a tendency among Poles to interpret the Polish national cause as a universally valid symbol for the struggle of oppressed peoples for freedom.

The term "freedom" lends itself to equivocal use. After the partitions, some Poles wished to regain the "golden freedoms" of the past and were not necessarily interested in the liberal democratic values propagated by the French Revolution. Nevertheless, Polish Romanticism managed to obscure the difference between these two different kinds of freedom during the nineteenth century, and it turned the Polish–Lithuanian Republic into a greater democracy than it ever had been.

Polish Romantics also compared the fate of Poland to the Passion of Christ: A chosen nation, Poland was scourged, crucified, and buried, but it would rise in glory from the dead. The political ideals of the French Revolution and the messianic vision of the Resurrection became the leitmotifs of Poland's national struggle. For example, after an uprising in the Russian partition of Poland in 1863, which was brutally squelched, the Polish eagle mounted on a black cross—Poland crucified—became a national symbol that women wore as jewelry on chains around their necks, and after the proclamation of martial law by the Jaruzelski regime ended the initial phase of the Solidarity movement in December 1981, women started wearing this Polish cross again.

Poles flocked into the Napoleonic armies because they identified their national cause with the French revolutionary principles of liberty, equality, and fraternity. Nonetheless, the Poles did not fare any better under the auspices of the Napoleonic empire than they did under the Prussian, Russian, or Austrian ones. Poland was merely a pawn that Napoleon ruthlessly exploited in his imperial strategy, and he had no reservations about abusing the Poles' freedom-loving potential. In 1801, for example, Napoleon sent a legion of Polish volunteers to Haiti in the Caribbean to put down a rebellion of black slaves. Ironically, the Poles contributed to Haiti's independence by contracting swamp fever and dying nearly to the last man.

Central European Soul: Volksgeist

If one had to identify a thinker responsible for giving Central European nationalism its peculiar twist, it would be Johann Gottfried Herder (1744–1803), an innovative philosopher who exerted tremendous influence on the development of German Romanticism. Although Herder had several predecessors, he was responsible for popularizing the idea of the *Volksseele,* or *Volksgeist,* the "soul" or "spirit" unique to each people.[5] His observations and generalizations about collective attributes of the various peoples of Europe, as well as his prescriptions for discovering and preserving their respective "national souls," made a profound impression on his contemporaries.

As a proto-Romantic, Herder rejected many of the fundamental principles of the rationalistic version of the Enlightenment and also the Francophile and cosmopolitan form of civilization it propagated. He had great reservations about the mechanical and linear idea of progress because he saw it as a destructive agent that was leveling the differences between peoples, each of which had its own authentic nature or soul. Enlightened absolutism showed how homogeneous and restrictive new forms of rationality could be, and the modern centralized state was robbing people of their natural freedoms. Manifestations of unadulterated human nature and "soul"— like the emotive spontaneity of empathy or the creativity of the artist—were the supreme expressions of humanity for Herder, not enlightened reason, science, or technology. Herder came to view civilization and culture as concepts almost antithetical in this context, and the most genuine manifestations of a culture were to be found in its least "civilized" representatives: common men and women living traditional ways of life.

Each people had a unique collective soul, a *Volksgeist*, which was manifested in their collective voice: not merely in a common language, but also in the poems, stories, songs, and melodies of the common folk. Herder emphasized the role of language and tradition in the formation of collective or "national" souls, and he popularized the idea of different "linguistic and cultural nations" without propagating the creation of nation-states. The modern state was a perfect example of a rational—and hence "artificial"—form of organization for Herder, who entertained arcadian ideas about life in organic, smaller communities. Herder also helped popularize the assumption that the common folk who lived traditional ways of life were the most pristine carriers and the most important curators of national culture.

Herder's fascination with language as a nation's creative medium and collective voice, as well as his conviction that the most authentic manifestations of a people are to be sought in those traditions that had distanced themselves least from the original nature or historical heritage of a people, made a deep impression on his Central European contemporaries. Herder's aesthetics of populism and romanticism added a strong retrospective and introspective dimension to the idea of belonging to a particular nation. He inspired work in the fields of historical philology, the history of national literatures, medieval history, comparative ethnology, and an unprecedented interest in folk music and lore throughout Central Europe: all those things of which national traditions are made.

It would be difficult to underestimate the breadth and the depth of Herder's impact. Sir Isaiah Berlin, the famous British historian of ideas, maintained that "all regionalists, all defenders of the local against the universal, all champions of deeply rooted forms of life, both reactionary and progressive, both genuine humanists and obscurantist opponents of scientific progress, owe something, whether they know it or not, to the doctrines which Herder . . . introduced into European thought."[6]

It is important to distinguish here between Herder's intentions and the consequences of his work, because he was the sort of genius whose insights could easily be misinterpreted. Herder, a Protestant minister, Christian humanist, and pacifist, thought that a natural harmony among all peoples and cultures based on empathy and understanding was possible. He was one of the first modern champions of cultural pluralism, or "diversity," and a forerunner of the contemporary multiculturalism. The critique of the white European and Eurocentric version of *civilization* by contemporary multiculturalists is based to a considerable extent on the early-nineteenth-century, German Romantic concept of *culture*, or "roots." Around 1800 Herder designed the methodological tools used for the discovery or rediscovery of ethnic identities in the second half of the twentieth century. In this respect, he was, for example, one of the intellectual fathers of the African American rediscovery of "Mother Africa."

Herder was convinced that no one culture could be measured or judged by the standards of another and that to "brag of one's country is the stupidest form of boastfulness."[7] But Herder's terminology and his observations about the various peoples of Europe often were abused. In this respect, he helped create national stereotypes and those national feelings that, once hurt, were to provide a breeding ground for conflict in the future.

For example, Herder recognized that the Germans had played an ambiguous role in European history, or, as he formulated it, "more than all others have contributed to the weal and woe of this continent."[8] Some of the attributes that led to German success, often at the expense of their neighbors, were "their tallness and bodily strength, their bold, enterprising hardiness and valor, their heroic sense of duty that moved them to march after their chiefs wherever they might lead and to divide countries as spoils of war." (This passage merely shows how easy it was for the Nazis to draw up a national genealogy "from Herder to Hitler.")

Although he disapproved of war, Herder described the "warlike constitution" of the Germans in terms of their national character. Germans had been conditioned by a host of geographical and political circumstances initially related to the Romans' inability to subjugate Germany and subsequently by Germany's glorious role as "a living wall against which the mad fury of Huns, Hungarians, Mongols, and Turks dashed itself to pieces." He also recognized that the Germans' eastern neighbors, "the poor Slavs," frequently were on the cutting edge of the Germans' warlike disposition, and he showed a great deal of compassion for them.

Herder admired the ancient Slavs as "charitable, almost extravagantly hospitable, devoted to their rustic independence, yet loyal and law-abiding and contemptuous of pillaging and looting." However, given the unfortunate position of the Slavs between the Germans and the various threats from the east, Herder observed: "All of this was no use to them against oppression, it conduced it." It is one of those quirks of history that a German was one of the most influential figures in the development of Slavic historiography. Herder popularized the idea of peace-loving and protodemocratic Slavs as the victims of the aggressive, warlike, and autocratic Germans. Consequently, he played an essential role in the way the Slavs came to view their own history, as a national struggle against German aggression that culminated in the loss of ancient Slavic freedoms, and he envisioned a day when these "submerged peoples that were once happy and industrious" would rise from their "long, languid slumber" and be "delivered from their chains of bondage."

Herder also exerted great influence on Hungarian historiography. He felt that smaller peoples such as the Magyars were endangered by the threat of extinction via assimilation, a conjecture and insult that stimulated Hungarian nationalism. The Hungarians also used Herder's precepts to interpret their "conquest" of the Danube Basin at the end of the tenth century as a world historical event. The Magyars' interpretation of their *Drang nach Westen* had certain affinities to the Germans' rendition of their *Drang nach*

Osten, and Hungarians found all sorts of similarities between their own noble traditions and martial virtues as warriors and victors and the German ones. The glorification of national achievements and a sense of cultural superiority became primary characteristics of Central European nationalism, and in this respect the Magyars were like the Germans, just smaller.

Romanticism was politically ambivalent. Generally speaking, the progressive and revolutionary aspects of Romanticism were and remained particularly strong in France. After the French Revolution and the Napoleonic occupations of Germany, however, the precepts of Romanticism evolved into a set of a conservative, anti Enlightenment, and antirevolutionary attitudes in the German-speaking world. Historians "discovered" the virtues of the political and social order of the Middle Ages, and antimodernism became a fashionable attitude that helped justify reactionary political measures. Czech political romanticism had more affinities to the French version, whereas both strains existed in the Polish and Hungarian traditions: a conservative one for the aristocrats and magnates who glorified the freedoms lost and wanted to restore the old order and a progressive or liberal one that aimed at the creation of democratic national states.

The coalescence of romantic nationalism with the precepts of nineteenth-century liberalism allowed the "historical nations" of Central Europe— Czech, Polish, and Hungarian to interpret their histories as a continuous struggle for freedom and against foreign, and in particular German, hegemony. Historical references to the Middle Ages and the ancient freedoms that had been lost had the important function of equivocally legitimizing the national struggles for modern freedoms that were substantially different, but freedom nonetheless. Herder's assumption that the Slavs lost their "ancient freedoms" because their peace-loving dispositions made them unable to contend with German aggression transformed those feelings of national or cultural inferiority engendered by the history of German predominance—and the Habsburgs were just as German as the Prussians from this perspective—into sentiments of moral superiority that helped define national identities in the future.[9]

Herder's observations could be ambiguous. Taken out of context, a statement like "The Slavic peoples occupy a larger space on earth than they do in history" is full of devastating potential. Furthermore, although Herder's conception of *Volk* was not biological or racial—the introduction of racial categories for nations was one of the dubious achievements of the late nineteenth century—Herder interwove the concepts of nation, *Volk,* and *Kultur* in a manner that later lent itself to a racial interpretation. In one respect, it contributed to the rise of modern anti-Semitism. Jews could not fulfill the linguistic, cultural, or genealogical criteria for belonging to a nation, because they spoke Yiddish or worshiped in Hebrew; possessed cultural and religious traditions that were foreign to the larger national communities in which they lived; and had their roots, however remote, in the eastern Mediterranean world. Bastardizations of Herder's historical observations about relationships between "dominating Germans" and "submissive Slavs" also led to the development of the concepts of "superior" and "inferior" peoples which culminated in the Nazi terminology of a *Herrenvolk* and *Sklavenvölker*: a German "master race" and the Slavic "slave races."

Despite Herder's positive intentions, the Herderian model had disastrous consequences in the long run. Each people in Central Europe assumed that it had the task of discovering or recovering its own soul, and since Herder and his German Romantic contemporaries were among the first to do so, they established a paradigm that other Central European nations imitated. In this respect, the various national manifestations of the Slavic or Hungarian soul were ethnic imitations of the German *Volksgeist*, or to put it simply, some of the subsequent theoreticians of Slavic and Hungarian nationalism used a German paradigm in an attempt to out-German the Germans by making their national traditions at least as glorious and chauvinistic as the those of the Germans. Very few people exercised the type of compassionate tolerance or empathy Herder had envisioned; no one was interested having a national past that did not surpass others in greatness; and Central Europeans have rarely demonstrated an ability to view themselves as equals.

From Nations to Nationalisms

Inhabitants of the United Kingdom or the United States of America rarely refer to their sense of allegiance to the political institutions of their countries or the sentiments that go along with them as nationalism. British subjects and citizens of the United States may consider themselves patriotic— "God Save the Queen" and "God Bless America"—but not nationalistic. Nationalism is foreign to the Anglo-American understanding of democracy, and in English, the concept is imbued with negative connotations. Nationalism is a "Continental" phenomenon.

Part of the problem here is terminological. In English (as well as in French), the concept of nation is intimately associated and, in some cases synonymous, with the term "state." Nationality refers to state citizenship and the sense of allegiance to national institutions that goes along with it. Virtually anyone can become a U.S. citizen, as the history of emigration to the United States has amply demonstrated. The institutions of Great Britain unite the English, Welsh, and Scottish subjects of His or Her Majesty, despite their differences, and in France the idea of the republic has gone hand in hand with the concept of the French nation.

The genealogy of modern nationalism is a complex topic,[10] so it will have to suffice here to observe that the liberal democratic Anglo-American and French revolutionary republican traditions identified the people's allegiance to the institutions of the (democratic) state and the (democratic) political principles on which they were based as the primary criteria for being a member of the nation, whereas the Central and Eastern European ones did not. In other words, the Western European equations of state equals nation equals people (the presence of political institutions interested in promoting that mode of national identification from the top down) and people equals nation equals state (the development of democratic traditions promoting a participatory mode of national identification from the bottom up) did not apply to the Central European experience. In Central Europe, nations either were divided among various states or had been incorporated into multinational empires. Therefore, they developed divergent perspectives on nations and nationalism. A few Central European examples of the problematic relationship between nations and states will illustrate these points.

If one is prepared to accept a fundamentally *political* definition of nationalism as "primarily a principle which holds that the political and the national unit should be congruent,"[11] Central Europe's two problems were that there were either too many states or too few, on the one hand, and that the patterns of conquest, settlement, and migration from the Middle Ages until the eighteenth century had made multinational the formerly independent feudal "nations," like the kingdoms of Bohemia, Hungary, and Poland-Lithuania, as well as the empires that swallowed them.

Germany and Poland were nations divided among states, although under different circumstances. At the beginning of the nineteenth century, the German nation was divided among forty different sovereign states. All these states, despite their regional traditions, were equally German because the old feudal idea of the "German nation" came to be understood as a "linguistic and cultural nation"—a *Sprach- und Kulturnation*—that historically had many parts—the constituent members of the Holy Roman Empire of the German Nation—but transcended their numerous political borders. Poland was divided among three foreign empires between 1772 and 1795, and Poles became citizens of three imperial states: Prussian Poles, Austrian Poles, and Russian Poles. But the extinction of a Polish state did not destroy the Polish nation; on the contrary, the experience of the partitions contributed to its modern development.

The Habsburg, Ottoman, and Russian empires were dynastic states made up of different nations. The Austrian emperors, Ottoman sultans, and Russian czars each had incorporated a multifarious congregation of larger and smaller peoples into their multinational empires, and some of these peoples, to use the Austrian empire as an example, had their own venerable traditions as nations. The medieval idea of the political nation provided historical and terminological precedents for the development of modern forms of nationalism for Czechs, Hungarians, Poles, and Croats,[12] whereas other "unhistorical nations"—such as the Slovaks, Ukrainians, Romanians, and Slovenes—were in the process of articulating some kind of national awareness or autonomous cultural identity. Consequently, the nineteenth century was one of national quests and questions: the "German Question" and the creation of a second German Reich, the "Polish Question," the "Nationalities Question" (*Nationalitätenfrage*)[13] within the Habsburg Empire, the "Jewish Question," and the "Balkan Question" caused by the deterioration of the Ottoman Empire.

Given the complexity of the relationships between nations and states in Central Europe, generalizations about how nationalism evolved are difficult. However, one standard approach to the development of nationalism is to distinguish among three qualitatively different phases or periods. The first Romantic or protonationalistic phase at the beginning of the nineteenth century was mainly cultural, literary, and folkloristic, and it had no particular or immediate political implications. This phase is a period generally referred to as "national awakening," and it involved the *creation* of national traditions. But it also provided the basis for a second phase, which roughly corresponded to the middle of the nineteenth century, characterized by the preparedness of certain national elites to agitate politically for the "national idea." This second phase culminated in national uprisings or revolutions in 1848: the so-called Springtime of Nations. The third phase of mass nationalism, when national movements began to enjoy the collective popular support that nationalists always maintained they had, came in the last third of the nineteenth century and the beginning of the twentieth.[14]

In this context, it is important to keep a few not so apparent facts in mind. First, "nations do not make states and nationalisms but the other way around."[15] National languages, heritages, and identities did not exist, even remotely, to the same extent *before* nationalism as they did *after* nationalism. Second, nations are, according to Benedict Anderson's formulation, "imagined communities."[16] National traditions had to be created and projected into the past. Then they appeared to have always been there. Therefore, nineteenth-century nationalism was able to invent age-old national identities and conflicts where none had previously existed.

Furthermore, it is important to distinguish between what happened in Western Europe, where states provided the institutional framework for the articulation of nationalism and the process of nation building,[17] and the situation in Central Europe, where nationalism inspired nations in the short or the long run to create (or re-create) their own states. A third and equally important perspective is, as Ernest Renan, a French theoretician of nationalism, stated in 1882: "Historical error is an essential factor in the formation of a nation." Commenting on this observation, the British anthropologist Ernest Gellner pointed out that "a shared amnesia, a collective forgetfulness is at least as essential for the emergence of what we now consider to be a nation."[18] In other words, getting its history wrong, including forgetting what came before nationalism, frequently plays a greater role for a nation in forming its identity than getting its history right.

The Politics of Language

The political importance of the modern standardization of languages can hardly be underestimated because the standardization of the spoken and written word—the linguistic vehicles for the creation of national literary and historical traditions—and public education in the broadest sense of the term were two important preconditions for the propagation of nationalism. During the nineteenth century every incremental increase in literacy, education, and communication contributed to the potential of nationalism. A fictitious but symptomatic example can be used to demonstrate this point.

At the end of the eighteenth century, an illiterate peasant-serf and speaker of an incomprehensible dialect, who worked the same plot of ground that his ancestors had and who lived on a relatively unsophisticated barter or semicash economy, probably never had been farther than a few days' walk from his birthplace, regardless of where he lived. He definitely did not have the vaguest idea what it meant to be a member of something as large and grand as a nation, nor was he willing to kill or be killed for it. However, by the end of the nineteenth century, the great-grandson of this peasant-serf was a small landowner who had a primary education and was literate enough to read a newspaper occasionally. His livelihood depended on the vicissitudes of the European grain market, and he might have had three or four years of compulsory military service. He most likely had ridden on a train, had been to a big city, or had relatives who had emigrated there to join the industrial workforce. This kind of person knew to which nation he belonged as well as who his nation's historical and current enemies were.

There are a number of complicated methodological issues related to how nations are defined and differing opinions as to whether one criterion, like language or ethnicity, or a combination of many, such as language, cohesive territory, a shared history, or common cultural traditions, should be used to define nationhood. Furthermore, although an increase in the feeling of nationalism undoubtedly was one of the characteristics of the nineteenth century, it is difficult to judge how many people from different social groups subjectively identified themselves with the precepts of nationalism at a given time. Here we shall use a few orthodox examples of how Central European nations were made while simultaneously taking into account some of the political peculiarities of the Central European situation.

Two traditional criteria important to classifying a people as a nation are a "historic association with a current state or one with a fairly lengthy and recent past," and "the existence of a long-established cultural elite, possessing a written national literary and administrative vernacular."[19] In Central Europe there were only four historical nations, and none of them was an independent state at the beginning of the nineteenth century: the German nation of the defunct Holy Roman Empire, which included the German-speaking Austrians; the Polish nation, which had been divided among three empires; and the Bohemian nation[20] and the Hungarian nation, both of which had been incorporated into the Habsburg Empire. From the perspective of these "historical nations," the various other nations or peoples of Central Europe were "unhistoric." They could not look back on histories as rulers but merely on the past as subjects.

For all four of Central Europe's historical nations, the literary and administrative vernacular of public life—politics, government, and education—was Latin until the eighteenth century and, in some cases, the nineteenth century. Therefore, the language used for public purposes like politics or administration and the vernacular languages used for private affairs outside the public sphere traditionally were different. For example, when Polish or Hungarian nobles dealt with one another or with affairs of state, they frequently spoke Latin, but when they attended to affairs on their estates they spoke, depending on the location, some regional dialect of Polish, Lithuanian, or Ukrainian with their subordinates and serfs in the first case, or Magyar, Slovak, Romanian, Serbian, Croatian, or even German in the second. In the Habsburg Empire the foreign literate vernacular of the upper, educated, and ruling classes (Latin and German) often was incomprehensible to people who spoke national vernaculars. The common folk were not only illiterate; their vernacular generally consisted of either a variety of dialects or an archaic semiliterate language whose development had been stunted by the traditional use of Latin or the introduction of German.

It is important to distinguish here between what linguists call literary languages and nonliterate vernaculars, or spoken but not written languages. National languages are almost always semiartificial constructs. (The standardization of English spelling and grammar, for example, is relatively recent. The first English-language dictionary was published in 1755; the Oxford English Dictionary did not appear until 1888. One of the characteristics of the intervening period was the development of prescriptive grammar, rules governing how things ought to be said.) Individual Central European languages crossed the threshold from non- or semiliterate vernaculars to literary media at different times and developed at different speeds. Philologists were among the first and most important "national awakeners." They had the task of turning the nonliterate vernacular, the spoken word, or archaic semiliterate traditions into a literate vernacular, a modern written language. In developing languages and literary traditions, they helped create the kinds of national "souls" about which Herder had written.

This project included expanding vocabularies and standardizing spelling, grammar, and, above all, pronunciation. A diversity of dialects had to be replaced by a uniformly written and spoken national language. Furthermore, a standardized national language was the prerequisite for the creation and transmission of national traditions such as the recording of folktales and folk songs or the writing of national literatures or histories, a fact demonstrating the relationship of literacy, education, and nationalism.

When people became members of a larger literate and linguistic community, they crossed the threshold from regionalism to nationalism. Only after the various languages of Central Europe were established as legitimate and functional literary and cultural media could their public use for administrative, educational, and political purposes become an issue, and given the hegemony of German, the use of national languages became a political problem of increasing magnitude in the nineteenth century, especially in the Habsburg Empire.

The non-German nations of Central Europe crossed the linguistic threshold from non- or semiliterate to literary languages at different times and under different circumstances. To begin with an exception: the Poles possessed a relatively highly developed literary language before the partitions. The partitioning powers then pursued assimilatory policies of Germanization and Russification with more or less equal rigor during the first half of the nineteenth century. Although Austrian censors prohibited Polish words like "freedom" (*wolnosc*) and "fatherland" (*ojczyna*) from appearing in print, the rigor of the Austrian imperial administration slackened in the second half of the century to such an extent that the Austrian portion of partitioned Poland became a center of Polish culture.

During the same time span German and Russian were introduced as the official languages in the public offices and schools of the Prussian and Russian partitions. The policies of the partitioning powers contributed to the creation of a mode of national identification with the Polish language that had not existed beforehand and that was reinforced by the great works of Polish Romantic poets, like Adam Mickiewicz, who wrote in exile.

As part of his reform and modernization strategy, the Habsburg emperor (and king of Hungary) Joseph II issued an imperial decree in 1788 that replaced Latin with German as the language of state administration and higher education in the kingdom of Hungary. The enlightened rational behind this was to replace an antiquated language, Latin, with a modern one, German, used elsewhere in the empire for administrative purposes.[21] But the Hungarian nobility, as representatives of the old *natio Hungarica*, saw this as a violation of their "historical rights," and they successfully insisted on the restoration of Latin. Some five decades later, Magyar successfully displaced Latin as the language of public life. (Meetings of the Hungarian Diet, the kingdom's parliament of nobles, and lectures at the University of Budapest were held in Latin until 1840 and 1844, respectively.)

The transition from Latin to Magyar—and the demands that modern education and administration placed on Magyar as a basically archaic vernacular—induced a linguistic reform and renewal in Hungary that included the invention of literally thousands of new words,[22] and this process of linguistic renewal fueled the "awakening" of the modern Hungarian nation. The same cultural milestones can be used in Central Europe to document the rise of national awareness: the first collection of folk songs, the first dictionary or grammar book, the first national newspaper, the first national theater, the first national opera, and so forth. However, given the multinational composition of the populace of Hungary—Hungarians, Germans, Slovaks, Ukrainians, Romanians, Serbs, and Croats—and the fact that over half of the population was not Hungarian, the rise of Magyar to the status of a public language, along with the aspiration of some Hungarian nationalists to make it the only public language for administration and education—to Magyarize the minorities, who were the majority—reproduced the old problem of a dominant language under new circumstances.[23]

The development of Hungarian nationalism in the nineteenth century is a good example of how the old political idea of a feudal nation, the *natio Hungarica*, was used to legitimize the new idea of a linguistic nation as the basis of a state (that is, people living in Hungary should speak Magyar) as well as to justify policies of assimilation from above that were less ruthless in execution but similar in spirit to the autocratic ones the Prussians and Russians had introduced in Poland. In other words, after the Habsburgs abandoned the idea of linguistically "Germanizing" Hungary, the Hungarians pursued the idea of Magyarizing it. A certain affinity between Hungarian nationalism and German nationalism cannot be overlooked here. As a "historical," linguistic, and cultural nation, many Hungarians considered themselves to be superior to the various national minorities living in the kingdom of Hungary, just as many Germans considered their language and culture to be superior to non-Germanic ones.

The creation of Serbo-Croatian is a superb example of how modern, artificial languages were constructed out of regional dialects. The Catholic Croats used the Latin alphabet and spoke three major dialects, two of which had developed literary versions and one of which was easily comprehensible to Serbs. Orthodox Serbs also had a number of regional dialects and used the Cyrillic alphabet. However, Serbs and Croats managed to make a bilateral linguistic compromise.

Vuk Karadžić (1789–1864), a Serbian writer, philologist, author of a grammar and a dictionary, and collector of folk songs and poems, exercised the greatest influence on the development of literary Serbian. He chose *sto*, the most widespread Serbian dialect, which was closely related to one of the Croat dialects, as the basis of his standardization of Serbian. Ljudevit Gaj, a Croat who propagated the idea of the cultural unity of southern Slav nations, spoke and wrote in one of the Croatian dialects more remotely related to Serbian. But then he began writing in the Croat dialect closest to *sto*, the one Karadžić had chosen as the basis for literary Serbian. As a result, Serbo-Croatian developed as one literary language after the middle of the nineteenth century, although it was written in Latin characters by the Roman Catholic Croats and Cyrillic ones by the Orthodox Serbs. (We will not address the status of Slovene as a "Yugoslav" language here. But in brief, Slovenes can passively understand Serbo-Croatian, whereas Serbs and Croats cannot read or understand Slovene without special training.)

The selection of these dialects and their standardization was to have enormous political implications in the future. In one respect, it represented an attempt to construct a common southern Slav cultural heritage capable of offsetting German and Hungarian influences, and it often was combined with the vague Romantic conception of an ancient southern Slav kingdom stretching from the Alps and the Adriatic to the Black Sea. (In Serbian and Croatian, *jug* means "south"; hence the term "Yugoslav.") Because language was viewed as the essential criterion for nationhood, the standardization of Serbo-Croatian inevitably promoted the idea that "all South Slavs were basically one people and that, by implication, they should form a political unit."[24] Furthermore, it deprived Croat nationalism of a linguistic justification and provided Serbs with a convenient excuse for expansion in the future, insofar as some Serbian nationalists regarded all people who could comprehend the *sto* dialect, which Karadžić had chosen as the basis for the standardization of Serbian, as members of an ancient Serbian nation. In this respect, the idea of the cultural unity of "southern Slav" nations could be used as a vehicle for the realization of Greater Serbian aspirations.[25] (After the establishment of a Yugoslav state in 1918, many Croats felt that Serbo-Croatian was hegemonic, insofar as Serbs had the political control over standardization. Since the deterioration of the former Yugoslavia in

1991, both Croats and Serbs feel constrained to emphasize how different their languages are.)

The development of literary Czech and literary Slovak provides one last example of how linguistic issues became cultural and political ones in the nineteenth century and remain so in the twentieth. The fact that one of the many fathers of the creation of modern literary Czech, Josef Dobrovský (1753–1829), wrote his works on Czech philology and the history of Czech literature in Latin and German is merely one indicator for the then current inadequacies of the Czech vernacular or the position of cultural hegemony that German had attained in Bohemia.

The publication of Josef Jungmann's Czech–German dictionary (1835–1839) marks another milestone in the development of the language. František Palacký, the first great modern Czech historian, initially published in German his monumental, five-volume *History of Bohemia* (1836–1857), which was based on the Herderian premise that the history of Bohemia was "a ceaseless battle between the German and the Slav elements."[26] (It appeared later in Czech.) Each incremental step in the development of literary Czech and the national awareness (produced by literary and historical works written in that idiom) increased the tension in Bohemia between Czechs and the Habsburg-German ruling class. During the nineteenth century the public use of Czech for administration and education became a volatile political issue.

The standardization of Slovak initially was frustrated by denominational differences. Anton Bernolák, a Slovak Catholic priest, made the first attempt to introduce standardized Slovak at the beginning of the nineteenth century, by raising a west Slovak dialect, which had the greatest similarity to Czech, to the status of a literary vernacular, but Protestant Slovaks rejected this initiative because their literary tradition was based on the first, fifteenth-century Czech translation of the Bible. Slovak Protestants rejected a contemporary Catholic proposal because it did not correspond to the language of their devotional tradition, a form of medieval Czech substantially different from vernacular Slovak. Later, in the 1840s, a Slovak philologist, Ľúdovit Štúr, made a second and successful attempt to standardize Slovak. He adopted a Middle Slovak dialect as the basis for modern literary Slovak and relied on literary Czech as a model for standardization.

Whether Czech and Slovak are dialects of one language or two separate languages has been a hotly debated issue. Linguists find enough essential similarities in vocabulary, syntax, and word formation to justify classifying both of them in the Czechoslovak subgroup of the Western Slavic languages. But the phonetic differences between Czech and Slovak are so great that Czechs and Slovaks can immediately identify each other after a few words have been spoken. Common structural roots and mutual comprehensibility appear to justify the concept of two modern dialects of one historical language, whereas their historical development and vernacular differences support the idea of two languages, a point that is essential if language is the criterion for nationhood. Whether there is one Czecho-Slovak language or two, Czech and Slovak, is an issue of enormous consequence. In this context, Slovak linguists always have been theoreticians of Slovak nationalism. If Slovaks do not have their own language, they cannot be representatives of an independent culture or nation.

The application of other criteria, like historical association and religion, to nationhood seems to support the idea of separate Czech and Slovak nations. It is important to recall here that after the demise of a "Greater Moravian" kingdom in the tenth century, Czechs and Slovaks never lived together in the same state. Instead, Czechs inhabited the kingdom of Bohemia and Moravia, and Slovakia became part of the kingdom of Hungary. Based on the venerable traditions of the kingdom of Bohemia, Czechs consider themselves a "historical nation"; the Slovaks, as subjects of the Hungarian crown, do not have a comparable history of independence and consequently have been labeled as one of those Central European peoples "without a history."

Czechs and Slovaks also have two relatively distinct religious traditions. The Czechs identify themselves with the Hussite form of Protestantism that developed in the fifteenth century, although many of them reconverted to Catholicism in the seventeenth century. The majority of Slovaks are Roman Catholic.

Furthermore, Czechs and Slovaks were confronted with two different foreign ruling classes. The Habsburgs thoroughly broke the back of Bohemia in the seventeenth century and introduced a German-speaking upper class that demoted Czech to a language of serfs and servants. The Slovaks encountered a predominantly Magyar nobility that pursued their own "national interests" on a regional scale, even though they, in turn, were subjects of the German-speaking Habsburgs themselves. Thus the Czechs had to struggle against Germanization, and the Slovaks had to contend with Magyarization.

After World War I, the Czechoslovak Republic attempted to create a common Czechoslovak national identity, and for decades after World War II the Communists pursued a variation on the idea of unity by promoting the ideology of proletarian internationalism, which made class more important than nationality. After the "Velvet Revolution" in Czechoslovakia in 1989, it gradually became evident in constitutional debates about the future structure of the Czech and Slovak Federative Republic that disparate Czech and Slovak ideas about the objectives and pace of political and economic reform, as well as Czech condescension and the agitation of Slovak separatists, would present a formidable challenge to Czechoslovak unity.

There was an important distinction in the Czech and Slovak Federal Republic between "federal" and "national" powers or, to use American terminology, federal powers and states' rights. There was, for example, no joint or federal ministry for culture in the Czech and Slovak Federal Republic but, rather, two "national" or "state" ministries: one in Prague and the other in Bratislava. The drafting of the new Czech and Slovak constitution was shipwrecked on an acrimonious debate over the division and distribution of federal and national powers between the Czech and Slovak halves of the republic. From the Slovak point of view, the main problem was the Czechs' lack of preparedness to recognize Slovakia as an autonomous and equal partner. The inability of Czechs and Slovaks to resolve their differences ended with the "Velvet Divorce" at the beginning of 1993. Many Czechs felt that the division of the Czechoslovak state into two smaller and independent Czech and Slovak states has enhanced their chances for "returning to Europe." Not many Slovaks feel the same way, but this is part of the ambiguity of their newly gained independence.

The "Jewish Question"

Most European peoples participated in the rise of nationalism during the nineteenth century, but the Jews were an exception. Certainly Jews had understood themselves as a "nation," a chosen people, for centuries. But they did not participate in developing a new collective or national identity during the nineteenth century to the same extent other peoples did. On the contrary, the Jewish consensus on what it meant to be a Jew disintegrated parallel to the development and consolidation of new national identities elsewhere in Central Europe. Jews, instead of becoming more Jewish, assimilated into dominant national cultures by becoming Germans or Magyars or, to a much lesser extent, Czechs or Poles.

The emergence of "Jewish nationalism" and Zionism at the end of the nineteenth century was, comparatively speaking, a belated development. Neither the idea that Jews should be recognized as a linguistic and national or ethnic group (and consequently agitate for their national rights as other national groups had) nor the vision of establishing a Jewish homeland was a product of the type of nation building that other peoples experienced. Rather, these ideas were reactions to the success of modern nationalism among other peoples as well as responses to the rise of modern anti-Semitism. They also were issues on which Jews themselves did not agree. In this respect, the "Jewish question" was considerably different from the other national questions in Central Europe, and it was a major issue because most of Europe's Jews lived in Central Europe.

At the end of the eighteenth century, three-fourths of Europe's 1.5 million Jews lived east of the Elbe River, the overwhelming majority of them in Poland-Lithuania. There is a relatively simple explanation for the density of Jews in this region: In the mid-thirteenth century, Poland-Lithuania established a charter that discriminated against Jews but also defined their station in society and protected the residual rights related to it. Unlike the other Christian rulers of Europe, who retracted the rights of Jews and periodically or systematically expelled them, the Polish kings continued to observe the stipulations of their medieval agreement with the Jews, and this made Poland-Lithuania the safest place in Europe for Jews to live. Therefore, the primary pattern of Jewish migration in Europe until the end of the eighteenth century was west to east, because Poland-Lithuania was Europe's principal haven for the religiously persecuted: Jews who fled Christian persecution starting in the Middle Ages and Protestants who sought refuge from Catholic intolerance thereafter. This does not imply that Jews did not periodically face pogroms and anti-Semitic abuse in Poland-Lithuania, but their status there was the most stable and secure in all of Europe.

Each swell of anti-Semitic persecution in Western Europe produced a new wave of Jewish immigration to the east. The Polish–Lithuanian nobility also welcomed Jewish immigration because the Jews, who came mainly from Western European cities, brought with them commercial know-how, connections, and sophistication, and the nobility protected Jewish interests because they directly or indirectly benefited from the fruits of Jewish labor. In this respect, Jewish immigration, the "flight to the east," served purposes similar to German medieval immigration, *der Drang nach Osten*. The indigenous "hosts" profited from the foreign "guests."

As a result of the partitions of the Polish-Lithuanian Republic in the late eighteenth century, Polish Jews became Prussian (and eventually German) and Austrian Jews or Russian Jews: Central European Jews in the former cases or Eastern European Jews in the latter. Prussia had expelled most of its Jews in the seventeenth century and had only a small Jewish community of a few thousand in Berlin when it acquired 100,000 Jews along with its piece of the Polish–Lithuanian Republic. Despite the periodic expulsions and pogroms that Catholic anti-Semitic zeal had inspired, the Habsburg Empire had a relatively large number of Jews—an estimated 150,000 split between the kingdoms of Bohemia and Hungary—when Poland was partitioned. The Austrian empire incorporated 250,000 Jews into its domain along with its "new" province of Galicia. Czarist Russia, which had previously banned Jewish immigration altogether, absorbed more than 1 million Jews with its portion of territorial booty. The Jewish populations in these empires increased dramatically during the nineteenth century. Shortly before World War I, 617,000 Jews were living in the German empire, approximately 2.5 million in the Habsburgs' realms, and 6 million in Russia.

The Jews who became Prussian and Austrian subjects were in a much more fortunate position than those incorporated into the Russian empire, because tolerance was part of the program of the Prussian and Austrian strains of enlightened absolutism. The philosophy of the Enlightenment and the gradual evolution of political liberalism in Germany and the Habsburg realms paved the way to assimilation and eventually to the establishment of equal rights for Jews in the second half of the nineteenth century. In Russia, however, into the twentieth century, vacillating but systematic discrimination, blatant anti-Semitism, and periodic pogroms were the basis of czarist policies toward Jews.

The Enlightenment dramatically changed the status of Central European Jews. Although various forms of institutionalized anti-Semitism and discrimination were a feature of Christian rule, Jews were in some respects similar to other feudal social bodies, such as estates, corporations, or guilds, in that they had a special status: Their communities and lives were circumscribed by prohibitions and rights unique to them as a group. Enlightened absolutism introduced policies aimed at dispensing with many of the traditional rights, privileges, and obligations of specific social groups. The gradual elimination of traditional discriminatory policies toward Jews—which, next to the abolition of serfdom, is generally regarded as one of the great achievements of enlightened absolutism—actually threatened the traditional Jewish way of life. Dismantling the barriers of discrimination also entailed tearing down the walls that had protected or insulated traditional Jewish communities.

By enlightened standards, the traditional Jewish communities of Poland-Lithuania were "backward": self-contained ghettos steeped in orthodoxy and poverty. Therefore, the "improvement" of the Jews was one of the pedagogical aspirations of enlightened rulers, and throughout the nineteenth century the "Jewish question" revolved around making Jews "normal citizens" and more productive participants in a secular society as a whole. The legal emancipation of the Jews was not a continuous or linear process. In the case of the Habsburg realms, Joseph II's Patent of Tolerance in 1781 marked the beginning of the formal, political emancipation of the Jews because it granted them rights that up to that point only Christians had enjoyed. Emancipation lagged in the first half of the nineteenth century, was fueled by the revolutions of 1848, and was formally completed in 1867 when the Austrian and Hungarian constitutions established the principle of equality for all citizens. The Jewish responses to the challenges of the Enlightenment were ambivalent and complex. Reactions ranged from radical secular "modernists," who abandoned Judaism by advocating complete assimilation, to severe "traditionalists," who pleaded for orthodoxy and self-imposed segregation, and they included many different admixtures of innovation and tradition between these extremes.

The fortunes of Central European Jews were intimately bound with the ideas of the eighteenth-century Enlightenment and nineteenth-century liberalism. Previously the traditional avenue of Jewish assimilation had been conversion to Christianity and baptism; the modern alternatives that enlightenment and liberalism proposed were faith in reason and progress. Enlightened philosophy was imbued with secular humanism and based on the premise that science and rationality would create a new kind of humanity. In this respect, Jewish "backwardness" was not essentially different from the backwardness of other peoples. Education provided everyone with a path out of their figurative ghettos and, for Jews, out of their literal ones.

Some Jews abandoned Judaism altogether and sought their salvation in "enlightened" political ideologies such as liberalism—or, later, socialism and communism—because they were secular and facilitated assimilation. There also were more moderate approaches. At the end of the eighteenth century, Moses Mendelssohn was instrumental in establishing the Haskala, a Jewish school of the Enlightenment in Berlin inspired by German philosophy. Mendelssohn sought to reconcile the benefits of secular enlightenment and German culture with the ethics and humanism of Jewish traditions in a manner that would allow Jews to participate fully in the modern world without completely abandoning their heritage. In other words, if Jews learned to interpret their own traditions in the spirit of the Enlightenment, they would see how enlightened Judaism was. Throughout the nineteenth century, one of the ongoing debates among "modernists" and "traditionalists" in Jewish communities dealt with questions of degree. How much reform or innovation was desirable or tolerable? Some Orthodox Jews also rejected change because they considered it to be sacrilegious and to contribute to the destruction of Jewish institutions and religious traditions.

If enlightenment were based on education, then Central European Jews had to find a school of enlightenment to emulate and a corresponding culture to adopt. The Central European paradigms for science and culture *par excellence* were German: *deutsche Wissenschaft und Kultur*. Linguistic assimilation—abandoning Yiddish and Hebrew for German—was the prerequisite for modern education, and the language of instruction was German at many of the schools that the Habsburg authorities established for Galician Jews, as well as many of the most reputable universities in Central Europe. Education also qualified Jews to participate in the larger literary community of the "German linguistic and cultural nation." The universality of (German) science and the all-embracing tolerance of (German) humanistic culture appealed to modernist Jews, who, in many cases, "Germanized" and understood themselves as members of a German linguistic and cultural nation.

In the nineteenth century, there were two complementary patterns of Jewish assimilation. First, the ideas of German science and culture moved east, making into advocates of "German culture" those "Polish" Jews in the Habsburg province of Galicia who were interested in education, assimilation, and the opportunities they entailed. Second, there was a substantial increase in Jewish migration within the Habsburg realms during the last third of the nineteenth century: west to east from Bohemia and Moravia to Hungary and east to west from Galicia to urban centers in Austria and Hungary. Between 1869 and 1910, for example, the Jewish population of Budapest increased from less than 45,000 to more than 200,000 (from 16 to over 23 percent of the city's population) and in Vienna from 40,000 to more than 175,000 (from 6.6 to 8.6 percent).[27]

Not all these Jews assimilated, and they were spread across the entire social spectrum from paupers and panhandlers to bankers and industrialists. The most successful became members of the middle, upper-middle, and entrepreneurial classes in urban centers. They participated in the economic boom of liberalism and recognized that higher education often led to prosperity and assimilation. Jews accounted for less than 5 percent of the population in the Austro-Hungarian monarchy, but at the end of the nineteenth century, well over a quarter of the students enrolled at the universities of Vienna and Budapest were Jewish. Jews were strongly represented—or, in relation to their overall percentage of the population, overrepresented—in professions such as teaching, law, medicine, and journalism, as well as in business and finance. There also were pronounced differences between the "western Jews," who actively sought integration, and the "eastern Jews" in or from the Galician hinterland, whose traditionalism or orthodoxy prohibited them from doing so. Assimilated western Jews frequently were the most ruthless critics of the "backwardness" and orthodoxy of eastern Jews, and the relationships among nonreligious, Reformed, and Orthodox Jews were often acrimonious.

German language and culture initially played an important role in Jewish assimilation, and they continued to do so for those modernist Jews who lived in Galicia, the German-speaking parts of the Habsburg realms, or Bohemia and Moravia. The identification of Jews with German culture frequently went hand in hand with a strong sense of allegiance to the institutions of the Habsburg monarchy, and some historians have argued that assimilated Jews were among the Habsburgs' most loyal subjects because they shared the humanistic and cosmopolitan assumptions of German culture. These attitudes corresponded well to the dynastic program of the Habsburgs, who maintained that their own interests transcended the narrow concerns of specific ethnic, religious, or national groups in their multinational empire.[28]

There also were alternatives to Jewish Germanization. Many Jews in Hungary, for example, who had been raised on German language and culture in the spirit of Jewish enlightenment, eventually became advocates of Hungarian language and culture in the last third of the nineteenth century. Reform-minded Hungarian Jews developed a fortuitous relationship with those representatives of Hungary's political elite who promoted liberalism, nationalism, and Magyarization as a means of assimilating the kingdom of Hungary's minorities into one linguistic and political nation. In this respect, Jews not only could become Germans; they also could become Magyars. In Bohemia and Galicia, some Jews also sought assimilation into the respective dominant Czech and Polish national cultures.

As long as Central European nationalism was liberal, linguistic, and cultural, it gave Jews an opportunity to assimilate, and one can actually speak of a success story for the Jews and the societies into which they assimilated during the last third of the nineteenth century.[29] By 1900, however, the incorporation of racial theories into nationalistic ideologies, the alliance of modern anti-Semitism with nationalism, and the dynamics of nationalism in the Habsburgs' realms had changed the tenor of politics and the prospects of Jewish assimilation. Assimilated Jews frequently were stranded in between different national fronts. In Bohemia, for example, Czech nationalists attacked assimilated German-speaking Jews as agents of "Germanization," whereas German national anti-Semites insisted that they were not Germans, but Jews. Nationalistic demands for excluding the Jews and the emergence of Jewish strategies of self-exclusion—Jewish nationalism and Zionism—document equally well the faltering of assimilation and the "success" of nationalism on all fronts.

Nevertheless, many of the best representatives of the cultural blossom associated with fin de siècle Budapest, Prague, and Vienna were assimilated Jews. Milan Kundera described them as "the principal cosmopolitan, integrating element in Central Europe: they were its intellectual cement, a condensed version of its spirit."[30] The stellar array of "Habsburg Jews" includes Sigmund Freud, the father of psychoanalysis; Ludwig Wittgenstein, one of

the most important philosophers of the twentieth century; the compos-
ers Gustav Mahler and Arnold Schönberg; the founder of the Austrian Social Democratic Workers' Party, Viktor Adler; and the author Franz Kafka,
who, because of his heterogeneous background, is claimed by Germans,
Austrians, Czechs, and Jews as a "national author." These assimilated Jews
made great contributions to enlightened and humanistic German culture,
and they considered themselves as representatives of German traditions in
the arts, letters, and sciences. But German nationalists, who adopted anti-
Semitic and racist doctrines, adamantly refused to recognize these contributions as German. Rather, they condemned them, along with many of the
precepts of cosmopolitan enlightenment and secular humanism that had facilitated Jewish assimilation, as Jewish.

⊰ 8 ⊱

The Demise of Imperial Austria
and the Rise of Imperial Germany

1848–1890

In 1815 the Congress of Vienna diplomatically sealed the victory of the old European dynastic order over revolutionary France, an event that marked the beginning of thirty-three years of peace and stability in Europe. In the same year, the czar of Russia, the king of Prussia, and the emperor of Austria concluded the "Holy Alliance," an anti-revolutionary pact that obligated them as Christian sovereigns to adhere to patriarchal principles of government, and this triad of absolutists cooperated relatively well until the middle of the nineteenth century. The reestablishment of the old European order also is frequently identified with the career of Prince Clemens Lothar von Metternich, a Habsburg diplomat from Germany who played a central role in restoring and maintaining this order and whose tenure as Austria's foreign minister became synonymous with domestic policies of press censorship, police surveillance, and systematic oppression throughout the German-speaking world.

Henry Kissinger, the most important architect of U.S. foreign policy during the Nixon administrations in the 1970s, maintained in his study of Metternich as a diplomat, *A World Restored: The Politics of Conservativism in a Revolutionary Age*, that neither peace, "conceived as the avoidance of wars," nor justice provides the basis of a stable international order but, rather, "legitimacy." Kissinger defined legitimacy as "the acceptance of the framework of the international order by all major powers . . . [which] does not make conflicts impossible, but it limits their scope," and he admired Metternich as one of the main architects of the "legitimate" European order established after the upheavals of the French Revolution. From Kissinger's foreign policy perspective, the essence of revolutionary power is that it "possesses the

courage of its convictions" and is willing to "push its principles to their ultimate conclusion" in a manner that erodes the "legitimacy of the international order."[1] Armed with the principles of liberty, equality, and fraternity,
revolutionary France and Napoleon shook the very foundations of the legitimacy of the old European order, and Metternich helped restore it, thereby making the nineteenth century a period in which conflicts were limited
in scope.

An analogous diplomatic and historical lesson for Kissinger was that the
"revolutionary foreign policy" of Nazi Germany—the revision of the Treaty
of Versailles—was a direct result of the victorious powers' failure after World
War I to establish an international order acceptable to all of the major powers. The defeat of Nazi Germany also established a completely new European order that had to be legitimized. The Soviet Union as a revolutionary
superpower and the threat of thermonuclear extinction made the potential
consequences of conflict in Europe so ominous that the maintenance of "legitimacy," a balance of power between the East and the West, was the pre-
eminent goal of foreign policy, and this is exactly what Kissinger pursued as
a student of Metternich: détente. Given the possibility of a conflict that
could lead to what strategists call "mutually assured destruction"—the
acronym of MAD is poignantly appropriate for describing the consequences
of a full-scale nuclear conflict—Kissinger and almost all other leading diplomats and statesmen of the West saw their roles in Metternichian terms. The
"legitimacy" of the European order established at Yalta in 1945 and reinforced during the decades of the Cold War appeared enduring because
MADness was one of the possibilities inherent in any future attempts to
change unilaterally the status quo.

Timothy Garton Ash, one of the most astute contemporary observers of
Central Europe, has noted the affinities among the "peace and stability" established by the Vienna Congress in 1815, Metternich's or the "Vienna Europe," and the stable order established in 1945, the Cold War or "Yalta Europe." In his attempt to "find a year in European history comparable to
1989," he arrived at the precedent of 1848, the year a series of revolutions
called the "springtime of nations" shook the dynastic order that Metternich's diplomacy had legitimized.[2]

Although Garton Ash expresses his reservations about brief comparisons
(as any respectable historian is required to do) and does not underestimate
the importance of economic and social factors as motors and motives of
change, he emphasizes the importance of the role that intellectuals, ideas,
and ideals played in the preparation and peaceful execution of the various
national reform-revolutions of 1989. This point is significant because intellectuals and students also were the vanguard of the revolutions of 1848,
which, given the bloody standards established by the French Revolution,
were initiated relatively peacefully. The affinity between the principles of reform promoted by the revolutionaries of 1848—constitutional government,
civil rights, the end of serfdom, liberalism, and nationalism—and the aspirations of the dissidents and intellectuals in the Communist states of Cen-

tral Europe in the 1980s to create "civil societies" embodying the same precepts also is striking.

Although it is too early to tell whether or not the revolutions of 1989 will ultimately lead to more peaceful and prosperous democratic societies, they were a success insofar as they managed to dislodge the Communist regimes. At this point, however, the comparison with the revolutions of 1848 breaks down because they failed to topple the old order. Therefore, understanding the motives of the revolutionaries and the reasons for their failure is important. If the success of liberal democratic revolutions is one of the distinguishing characteristics of the Western European political experience, their relative failure has been an essential attribute of most Central European ones. There were no Central European democracies before 1918, and of the many established following World War I, only Czechoslovakia managed to maintain a democracy throughout the interwar period.

The "Springtime of Nations": The Revolutions of 1848

Events in France provided the revolutionary spark for the various proverbial powder kegs of Europe in 1848. In Paris at the end of February, a classic example of royal crisis mismanagement—using firearms for crowd control—brought the masses into the streets, and the barricades went up. King Louis Philip was the first member of the old European order to go down, and after his abdication, moderate protagonists of political reform and radical adherents of social revolution with dissimilar visions of the traditions of 1789 in their heads began their struggle for domestic power in a new republican France. Disunity among the various promoters of change, programmatic radicalism, the agitation of the masses, and the violence that accompanied it gradually drove the moderate representatives of constitutional government into the arms of the reactionaries, and the revolution ran its course in four months. It ended in June with a bloodbath on the barricades of Paris and a Second French Republic that was much less social and democratic than the instigators of the revolution had envisioned in February.

The Parisian precedent inspired people across Europe. In Germany, for example, a series of uprisings organized by the middle class and students and supported by artisans, workers, and peasants led to major concessions in early March by the rulers of various states in the German Confederation—Baden, Württemberg, Bavaria, Darmstadt, Nassau, Kassel, and Hannover—without much bloodletting, by French standards. The subjects from these states of the old reactionary order wanted to be treated like citizens in a new constitutional one, and the demands they made were not revolutionary in the French sense of the word: constitutional monarchy based on some form of popular representation, freedom of speech, freedom of the press and of assembly, an extension of the right to vote, trial by jury, and arms for the "people" in the form of national or citizens' guards. In Vienna, for example, the first "revolutionary" act was the submission of a petition for change by students and members of the middle class. Imperial troops fired on the crowd, and the barricades went up. On March 13, Metternich resigned and fled to England, and the Austrian emperor, Ferdinand I, yielded to popular demands for reform, among them the right of his subjects *as* citizens to draft a new constitution. Five days later, King Frederick Wilhelm of Prussia conceded to comparable demands under similar circumstances.

The main issues that the revolutions of 1848 raised in Central Europe are interrelated: the revolution of 1848 in the German Confederation, Prussia, and the Habsburg Empire and the subsequent attempts to create a single German state; the Czech response to the idea of a unified German state and the "Austro-Slav" strategy for maintaining the Habsburg Empire; and the Hungarian struggle for national independence.

Although there also was an uprising in Posen, the Prussian partition of Poland, as well as revolts against Habsburg rule in northern Italy, I will not discuss these events here. The Poles were confronted with a different set of problems because of the partitions, and given the magnitude of their uprisings in 1830, 1846, and 1863, 1848 was a subordinate affair instigated by German liberalism and then squelched by German nationalism and Prussian troops. (Norman Davies called 1848 in Polish history the "springtime of other nations."[3]) Austrian Field Marshal Joseph Radetzky also smothered Italian national uprisings in the Habsburg's northern Italian provinces, but his victories were not enduring. The provinces that Radetzky held in 1848 were lost in wars with Italy, which was supported by France in 1859 and Prussia in 1866, and their acquisitions were milestones in the process of Italian unification.

Although there was a broad spectrum of political opinion in Germany, the majority of the German "revolutionaries" of 1848 were not advocates of radical democracy, but of liberal reform. They did not remotely aspire to create the type of turmoil and bloodshed associated with revolutionary France, and they frequently viewed the achievements of England—a constitutionally limited monarchy—with the greatest admiration. When the rulers of the various German states were challenged by the people, they lost their nerve and acquiesced to change, but unlike the historical precedent of Louis XVI after 1789, they did not lose control of their state bureaucracies and armies, nor did they lose their heads on the guillotine. The German revolutionaries of 1848 believed in peaceful reform and legal continuity, and they based their hopes on the somewhat naive assumption that if the people behaved civilly, then the rulers would, too. Above all, they wanted to draft their own constitutions and to participate in the establishment of one German state.

The fact that the term "constitutions" appears in the plural is important. Reformers in Prussia and Austria had their own conventions to work out constitutions for their respective states, and representatives from all forty member states of the German Confederation, including Prussia and Austria, had been invited to meet in St. Paul's Church in Frankfurt to work out a constitution for one German state. It also is important to note that the Austrian Constituent Assembly was multinational. It included representatives from the non-German-speaking nations of the Habsburg Empire outside the kingdom of Hungary: Czechs, Poles, Ruthenes, and Slovenes. The Austrian Constituent Assembly was German national, too, in that it dispatched German-Austrian delegates to Frankfurt.

Although it may appear far fetched, the most adequate formal historical parallel that can be drawn to illustrate the constitutional aspects of the German National Convention in Frankfurt is perhaps the situation of the colonies after America's Revolutionary War. The thirteen colonies had to work out individual state constitutions and to send delegates to the Constitutional Convention in Philadelphia to draft a federal constitution.

Although there was a wide spectrum of political opinion among the 600 delegates at the Frankfurt Assembly—centralists and federalists, monarchists and republicans—the National Convention intended to create one German state with one constitution: a new German Reich, which relied heavily on the old borders and confederative traditions of the old Reich, the Holy Roman Empire of the German Nation, as well as the idea of one modern national state for all Germans. During the initial planning sessions for the German National Assembly, an invitation was extended to the famous Czech historian, František Palacký, to represent the kingdom of Bohemia in Frankfurt, because it had been part of the Holy Roman Empire, but he declined, pointing out: "I am a Bohemian belonging to the Slav group of nations."[4]

Palacký's reply shows how difficult it would have been to use the old idea of the Holy Roman Empire of the German Nation to create a modern German national state because it would have had to incorporate the members of other nations—not only Czechs, but Dutch and Danes in the north, Poles in the east, Slovenes and Italians in the south. His statement also underlines the precarious position of the Habsburg Empire in the entire process of German unification. Approximately half the Habsburg realms had been part of the Holy Roman Empire of the German Nation, but the rest—the kingdom of Hungary, the provinces of Galicia and Bukovina in southern Poland, and some holdings in northern Italy—had not. Moreover, if a modern German state were to include all Germans, it would have to extend as far as the Baltic provinces of imperial Russia as well as down through the central Danube Valley and into Transylvania.

The liberals at the National Convention in Frankfurt, however, were not interested in incorporating non-German territories into a German state, nor for that matter, were the Habsburgs interested in dismembering their empire for the sake of a unified German state. In the process of debating the future frontiers of Germany in Frankfurt, three terms came into vogue: *Anschluss* (literally, "to join"), *grossdeutsch* ("greater" German), and *kleindeutsch* ("small" or "lesser" German). To unify Austria with the rest of Germany was the *Anschluss* or "greater" German option.[5]

This idea was based on the assumption that the German-Austrians would be willing to abandon the Habsburgs' multinational empire (which in the summer of 1848 appeared to be deteriorating into its constituent parts) and that the Habsburg dynasty would assume a leading role in a German state.

The "little" German option would exclude Austria from a German state, which meant that Prussia, because of its size and strength, would assume a dominant position in the new Germany. German nationalists did not really know what to do with the polyglot Habsburg Empire. Needless to say, the Habsburgs were not interested in a deterioration scenario that would allow a greater German solution—German-Austrians in Germany and the rest of the empire gone—although there was some vain speculation about bringing all of Austria's non-German territories into some kind of a confederative German state that would ensure the Habsburgs' hegemony in Germany, not really a greater German state, but a greater Habsburg Empire.

Some representatives of the Slavic nations in the Habsburg Empire also expressed their interest in reforming it on the basis of confederative principles. In June 1848, František Palacký, the Czech historian who had rejected an invitation to the German National Convention in Frankfurt, organized a parallel "counterconference" for Slavs in Prague. Outstanding representatives of the Slavic national groups from the Habsburg Empire attended this international Slav congress, along with a few émigré Poles from the Russian partition, and they discussed the future of the Slavic peoples based on a democratic and federal transformation of the empire. As a Czech nationalist, historian, and student of Herder, Palacký was afraid that a unified greater German state would overwhelm its smaller Slavic neighbors, and so he opposed the greater German solution. But, as a liberal Western Slav, he feared czarist Russia and the imperialistic form of Pan-Slavism that it propagated, as well as the possibility of a "Russian universal monarchy." (Czechs historically have understood themselves as Western Europeans; consequently, their Eastern or Pan-slavist orientation has traditionally been weak, although a small group of Czech intellectuals flirted with the idea of czarist patronage as a means of liberating the Czechs from Habsburg-German dominion.)

According to Palacký, the only chance that the smaller nations living between Germans and Russians had was to consolidate and to confederate. Given the probability of the German threat and the magnitude of the Russian menace, the only viable alternative for Palacký was to reform the Austrian empire by turning it into a federation of semiautonomous and democratic national units held together by some form of central government and administration that would coordinate common concerns like foreign affairs, defense, finance, and trade. At that point in his career, Palacký was a representative of a philosophy called "Austro-Slavism," and his most frequently quoted observation was

> that the South-East of Europe bordering the Russian Empire is inhabited by many nations . . . all of whose ethnic origins, language, history, and traditions vary widely and who, individually, are too weak to resist forever their mighty neighbor in the East; this they can do only if they are united by a strong, single hand. . . . Indeed, had Imperial Austria not existed already for so long, it would—in the interests of Europe, of humanity itself—be essential to create it.[6]

Although the Habsburgs' subsequent inability to solve the nationalities problem in their multinational empire dissapointed Palacký, the revolutionary atmosphere of 1848 made the idea of a confederation of smaller nations appear to be a viable alternative. Austro-Slavism justified the Habsburgs' multinational empire in the age of nationalism, but as A.J.P. Taylor pointed out, "To provide a central Europe neither German nor Russian was the last, and least genuine, of the Habsburg 'missions.'"[7] Palacký eventually became so disillusioned with the Habsburgs' inability to turn their multinational dynastic empire into a more democratic confederation of national states that he converted to Pan-Slavism later in is life and placed his hopes in a liberalization of czarist Russia.

Nevertheless, Palacký played an influential role in those traditions defining Central Europe in terms of smaller nations whose existence has historically been jeopardized by German and Russian imperialism. This narrow definition of Central Europe therefore excludes "imperialists"—Russians, Germans, and Austrians—from being Central Europeans.

It would not be advisable to turn Palacký into some kind of visionary, but the collapse of the Habsburg Empire after World War I created a situation in which both of Palacký's worst-case scenarios came true: first a German Central Europe under Hitler and then a Russian one under Stalin. Variations on the idea of a confederation of smaller Central European nations and states were part of many of the schemes for reforming the Habsburg Empire into a "United States of Central Europe" before World War I; they were discussed by East Central European politicians and Allied strategic planning staffs during World War II; and they enjoyed a brief renaissance in Central Europe after 1989.

The first international congress of Slavs was theoretically and historically important but politically impotent. Minor clashes between Czech nationalists and Austrian imperial troops in the streets of Prague provided the commander of imperial forces, Prince Alfred Windischgrätz, with the pretext he needed to dissolve the congress by force. The shelling of Prague showed that the representatives of the old order still had the army at their disposal and that they were prepared to use it. Meanwhile, the National Convention in Frankfurt drew up a constitution for a vaguely defined but nonetheless unified Germany, and reformers in Vienna and Berlin worked on turning dynastic monarchies into constitutional ones. In theory, Frankfurt was the most important scene of events because the National Convention had been recognized as a supreme body whose legislation was to be applied to all German states. In practice, however, the most important political decisions were made in Vienna and Berlin because the Habsburgs and the Hohenzollerns were the revolution's most formidable opponents.

In the summer of 1848, the city of Vienna gradually fell under the control of radical democratic elements. They demanded greater political and social reform, and the revolutionary apparition of 1789 displaced the moderate visions of legal reform and continuity that most of the 1848 liberals continued to entertain. The Habsburg court fled the city, and in October imperial troops under the command of Prince Windischgrätz, the "victor of Prague," marched on Vienna and, despite the valiant attempts of the revolutionary elements to defend it, took the city by force. The advisers of Austria's Emperor Ferdinand, a dull-witted ruler at best, permitted the moderate reformers and would-be parliamentarians of the Constituent Assembly, who also were shocked by the violence of the masses and the imperial troops, to withdraw to a provincial site in Moravia to continue their work on a constitution. This tactical ploy gave the imperial advisers time to prepare to end the revolutionary interlude.

Then Emperor Ferdinand abdicated in order to give young blood an opportunity to rule. In December 1848, his nephew, the eighteen-year-old Francis Joseph I, assumed the imperial throne, a position he filled conscientiously if unimaginatively for the next sixty-eight years. Shortly after coming to power, Francis Joseph ended constitutional experimentation, despite his initial promises to allow it, and he had Austria's Constituent Assembly in the provinces dispersed by force. Then the emperor issued by decree a new imperial constitution that had been hastily prepared by his advisers. Francis Joseph thus gave the people a constitution, but neither one they designed for themselves nor one based on the sovereignty of the people, and even this constitution he retracted shortly after it was decreed. Neoabsolutism became the basis of the "new" order that violated the "historical rights" of the constituent parts of the empire in an attempt to create a modern centralized state.

The corresponding victory of the old order in Prussia followed the same pattern, although it was faster and less bloody. The transfer of the constitutional convention to the provinces, the proclamation of martial law, and the declaration of a new Prussian constitution hastily drawn up by the king's ministers all took place within a month, between the beginning of November and the beginning of December 1848. From the perspective of the Hohenzollerns and the Habsburgs, two-thirds of Germany's revolutionary problem had been solved, and the remaining one-third was the National Convention in Frankfurt, which clung to the vision of a constitutionally unified German monarchy, an idea scuttled by machinations of the restored orders in Vienna and Berlin. Heroic but futile attempts to salvage the accomplishments of the revolution by organizing armed resistance ended with bloody victories of the Prussian army in the summer of 1849. The vision of a unified German constitutional state evaporated and the political status quo ante, the forty states of the German Confederation, was reestablished. However, the Revolution of 1848 made perfectly clear to contemporaries the problems of German unification, a "little" or a "greater" Germany, and the precarious position of imperial Austria as a German yet multinational state. Nothing illustrated this point better than the Hungarian Revolution of 1848/1849.

The kingdom of Hungary enjoyed a privileged status among the Habsburgs' conglomeration of lands because as kings of Hungary the Habsburgs continued to observe certain traditions. For example, the Hungarian Diet, the representative body of the nobility or the "Hungarian nation," ceremoniously crowned the Habsburgs as kings, and it retained a number of legislative powers. The concessions that Emperor Ferdinand made to his subjects when the Revolution of 1848 broke out in March in Vienna had immediate consequences for Hungary which was pregnant with the same spirit of dissatisfaction with imperial rule and desire for liberal reform.

Furthermore, age-old Hungarian aspirations for greater independence coalesced with nineteenth-century liberalism and nationalism. A combination of imperial panic and Hungarian initiatives led to the recognition in mid-March of the Hungarian Diet as an autonomous legislative body. Less than one month later, when Emperor Ferdinand sanctioned the Diet's first wave of reform legislation (including the final abolition of serfdom, an achievement of the revolutions of 1848 throughout Central Europe), he effectively recognized Hungary as a separate state. The Habsburg Empire was thus split in two. As emperor of Austria, Ferdinand had to contend with the representatives of constitutional reform in Vienna, and as king of Hungary, he had to deal with the liberal and national aspirations of the Hungarian Diet. Between the intentions of those German nationalist Austrians who wanted to abandon the Habsburgs' multinational empire for the sake of a greater German state and the designs of Hungarian liberals and nationalists who wanted increasing amounts of independence, the prospects for the dynasty were not promising.

The dynamics of the Hungarian revolution were complicated.[8] Hungarian liberals, who recognized that some type of accommodating relationship with the Habsburg dynasty was necessary, were initially responsible for governing Hungary, and they were confronted with two great domestic problems, insubordination and insurrection. First, Croat nationalists from the kingdom of Croatia-Slavonia, a subordinate state that had been incorporated into the kingdom of Hungary at the beginning of the twelfth century, started making demands for more independence, arguing that they wanted for Croatia from Hungary what Hungary had achieved for itself in Vienna, and the Hungarian revolution produced one great Croat national hero: Josip Jelačić.

A rebel by Hungarian standards, Jelačić was the imperially appointed governor of Croatia, who first sought to assert the "historic rights" of Croatia against Hungary and then allied himself with the Habsburg imperial forces in their subsequent invasion of Hungary. (Croat nationalism has historically been directed against the nation's immediate political overlords. In the nineteenth century, it was more anti-Hungarian than anti-Habsburg, and in the twentieth century it became anti-Serb.[9] Analogously, Slovak nationalism was anti-Hungarian in the nineteenth century before it became anti-Czech in the twentieth.) Second, Hungary's own national minorities—Germans, Slovaks, Ruthenes, Romanians, and Serbs—became increasingly restive, and in the ethnic and religious mosaic of southern Hungary, Hungarian and Serbian nationalists managed to inspire people who had lived peacefully together for centuries to start massacring one another.

As the relationship between Vienna and Hungary deteriorated during 1848, Louis Kossuth, a radical democrat and protagonist of Hungarian independence, emerged as the leader of national resistance. After having militarily settled matters with the revolutionaries and reformers in the Austrian half of the empire, the Habsburgs dispatched the imperial armies that had been successful in reinstating the old order in Italy, Bohemia, and Vienna to deal with the Hungarians at the beginning of 1849. However, a hastily organized Hungarian "revolutionary army" initially held its own against the imperial forces, and in April 1849, the Hungarian Diet revoked the crown from the Habsburgs, proclaimed independence, and appointed Kossuth as Hungary's governor-president.

Kossuth, the greatest national hero that the Hungarian revolution of 1848/1849 produced, was a passionate patriot and inspiring leader. But the time for a compromise with the Habsburgs had long passed, and Hungary's prospects for success were illusory. The imperial court in Vienna turned to czarist Russia for assistance, and the combined operations of the Austrian and Russian imperial armies in the summer of 1849 brought the Hungarian revolution to a quick and bloody end. Kossuth fled the country to agitate for Hungarian independence as an émigré until his death. He never abandoned the notion of breaking completely with the Habsburgs. Later in his life, he considered the idea of a confederation of states along the Danube— Hungary, Romania, Serbia, and Bulgaria—that would ensure Hungarian independence and prevent German-Habsburg or Russian-czarist encroachment on the Balkans.

Along with their revolution, the Hungarians lost all their old historical privileges, but their sacrifices did pay off in the long run. After several futile attempts at centralization, the Habsburgs sought a compromise with the Magyars, the most influential non-German nation in their multinational empire, and this led to the reestablishment of the kingdom of Hungary with considerable autonomy as well as the reorganization in 1867 of the Austrian empire as the Dual Monarchy of Austria-Hungary. In other words, the Hungarians lost the revolution of 1848/1849, but they eventually won the compromise of achieving a special status within the empire as a nation that enjoyed political parity with the German-Austrians.

This national experience was repeated under much different circumstances in the twentieth century. The Hungarian revolution of 1956 also was a brief and bloody struggle for national independence that ended with a Russian military intervention, but the sacrifices were not in vain. Thereafter, Hungary enjoyed an exceptional status within the Soviet empire that allowed Hungarian Communists to exercise a certain amount of liberalism and to experiment with domestic reform in a way not tolerated elsewhere in the Soviet bloc.

The Hungarian historian Iván Berend observed in the mid-1980s that one of the primary differences between the histories of Hungary and Poland was that the Hungarians had lost their revolutions (in 1848/1849 and 1956) but had "won" the compromises with the victors (the Austrians in 1867 and the Soviets after 1956). The Poles, however, lost their revolutions (in 1830, 1846, and 1863 and the "Solidarity Revolution" of 1980/1981) and lost the compromises as well, insofar as the revolts produced either greater repres-

"Farewell to the Fatherland": Louis Kossuth (mounted), flanked by the leaders of the Hungarian Revolutionary Army, emigrated after the failure of the Hungarian Revolution in 1849. (Austrian National Library, Picture Archive)

sion or, in the short term at least, negligible results. (This comparison ceased to be valid in 1989 when the Polish opposition spearheaded by Solidarity literally forced the Jaruzelski government to the "round table" negotiations marking the beginning of the end for the Communist regime.)

After 1848, the next year of revolutions in Central Europe was a long time in coming; 1918 was not an expression of the principles of liberalism as 1848 was but the result of the empires' exhaustion at the end of World War I. According to A.J.P. Taylor, in 1848 "German history reached its turning-point and failed to turn."[10] The implication (or insinuation) here is that if German history had turned at this point in the nineteenth century and Germany had become a more liberal and democratic state or, analogously, if Austria had succeeded in transforming itself into a more democratic federation of nations, Europe perhaps could have been spared two world wars in the twentieth century as well as the experience of National Socialism and Communism.

Although the neoabsolutistic dynasties in Prussia and Austria gradually made considerable concessions to the spirit of liberalism in last third of the nineteenth century, the "exceptional path" (*Sonderweg*) of German history—characterized by the presence of a developing industrial economy and modern capitalistic society; the relative absence of liberal democratic institutions and values in public life; and the persistence of traditional national elites, autocratic political structures, and authoritarian attitudes—began with the failure of the revolution of 1848. If the rise of a modern capitalistic and industrial economy unleashes social forces that promote democratization, as many historians assume, then German history in the nineteenth century was an exception. That is, Germany produced a modern economy and society without developing correspondingly modern liberal democratic attitudes and institutions.

The Prussian Unification
of Germany, 1866–1871

The processes of Italian and German national unification had a number of parallels. They were promoted by individual states: Piedmont-Sardinia in Italy and Prussia in Germany. Ministers with an exceptional amount of diplomatic cunning and skill masterminded these operations: Camillo Cavour for Piedmont-Sardinia and Otto von Bismarck for Prussia. In each case, the first phase of national unification forced the Habsburgs out of the one of their traditional spheres of interest: for Piedmont-Sardinia, northern Italy, which the Habsburgs had ruled since the early eighteenth century, and for Prussia, Germany, where the Habsburgs had played a leading role since the Middle Ages.

Piedmont-Sardinia relied on the *assistance* of other major European powers to achieve Italian national unification. France supported Piedmont-Sardinia in a war against the Habsburg Empire in 1859 which led to the acquisition of the northern Italian provinces of Lombardy, Tuscany, Modena, and Parma, and a Piedmontese alliance with Prussia in 1866 resulted in the Habsburgs' forfeiture of Venice. Conversely, Prussia relied on the *inactivity* of other major European powers to achieve its goal, the establishment of Prussian hegemony in Germany and the unification of Germany into one Prussian-dominated state. In 1866, Prussia trounced the Habsburg Empire in a brief war and then booted the venerable dynasty out of the realm of German politics. The fruit of the Prussian victory in the Franco-Prussian War of 1870/1871 was a unified German imperial state with a Hohenzollern emperor. Neither England nor Russia came to the aid of Austria in 1866 or France in 1870/1871. Prussia's rise to the status of a major European power was nothing less than meteoric. The unification of Germany did not take centuries or even decades; it was accomplished in a few years by Bismarck's consummate foreign policy and realpolitik.

If one is prepared to use "greatness" as merely a descriptive term for influencing the course of events, the "great German" politicians cited most often are Frederick II of Prussia (1740–1786), Otto von Bismarck (1815–1898), and Adolf Hitler (1889–1945). (Helmut Kohl, the "unification chancellor" of the Federal Republic of Germany, will inevitably will be included in this list sometime in the future; death is usually a prerequisite for such an honor.) Frederick the Great was the enlightened absolutist responsible for modernizing Prussia and laying the foundations for its future expansion; Bismarck, the Prussian minister responsible for unifying Germany, was the diplomatic founding father of the Second German Empire; and Hitler, the inaugurator of the Third Reich, "restored" the German empire in 1933.

These examples merely show how nationalistic terminology tends to distort the facts. The primary interests of Frederick the Great and Bismarck were Prussian, not German. Frederick was an extraordinary Francophile who showed very little interest in German culture, and he believed in Prussia, not Germany. Bismarck's primary loyalty also was to Prussia and its dynasty, the Hohenzollerns, not to the German national idea. Although German historians have conventionally celebrated Bismarck as the "unification chancellor," the unification of Germany was a by-product of his expansion of Prussian hegemony, not a goal of his foreign policy. Moreover, Bismarck did not want to unify Germany so much as he wanted to "Prussianize" it. The most infamous German, Hitler, was not a German but a German-Austrian, whom the Germans nevertheless have claimed and many Austrians prefer to disown.

One thing that each of these three "great Germans" recognized was that the avenue to German greatness led through Austria, and accordingly, the Austrian historian Friedrich Heer called them the "great destroyers of Austria."[11] Frederick the Great actively conspired against Maria Theresia, and he expanded Prussia's holdings by instigating a war against the Habsburg Empire in 1740 that led to the Prussian annexation of the prosperous Habsburg province of Silesia. Bismarck maneuvered the Habsburg Empire into a war in 1866 and out of German politics shortly thereafter. The subsequent absence of the Habsburgs in the sphere of German politics was the precondition for a "little" German solution to the problem of creating one unified German national state. Hitler's expansion of the Third Reich began with the occupation and annexation of Austria, the *Anschluss*, and the proclamation of a "greater German Reich" in March 1938.

After the revolutions of 1848, Austria and Prussia, the two largest members of the German Confederation, had substantially different concerns in Germany. The Habsburgs were intent on maintaining their traditional interests and seniority in the Confederation which, in turn, placed severe restrictions on Prussia's ambitions. In September 1862, one week after his appointment as the Prussian foreign minister, Bismarck gave a speech renowned not for the size or importance of his audience—he was wrangling with a budget commission for more money for the Prussian army—but for a single formulation:

> Prussia must gather and consolidate her strength in readiness for the favorable moment, which has already been missed several times; . . . not by means of speeches and majority verdicts will the great decisions of the time be made—that was the great mistake of 1848 and 1849—but by iron and blood (*Eisen und Blut*).[12]

A disciple of the Prussian military theoretician Karl von Clausewitz, who defined war as the pursuit of political goals using military means, Bismarck successfully used the iron and blood of the Prussian army during the first half of his career, as the foreign minister of Prussia (1862–1871), and then he consolidated his achievements during the second half of his career, as the chancellor of Germany (1871–1890).

Bismarck contested Austria's historical and factual seniority in German affairs by insulting Austrian prestige and challenging Austrian power. In 1866, he promoted the idea of a revised German Confederation that would exclude Austria, knowing that the issue would have to be settled on the battlefield. Austria and Prussia, each with sundry allies from the smaller German states, took to arms, and the Prussians demonstrated the technical and organizational superiority of their armies in a war that lasted seven weeks.

The most decisive battle was near Königgrätz in northern Bohemia (Hradek Kralové in the contemporary Czech Republic). The Austrian imperial troops suffered a devastating defeat owing to the superiority of Prussian leadership, logistics, training, and, last but not least, firearms: breechloading rifles with firing pins and cased shells that allowed the infantry to fire more shots.[13] Austrian casualties outnumbered by six to one those of the Prussians, and the concept of "German" military superiority, based on the dual virtues of organization and technology, was born. Europe was shocked that Prussia, a smaller state and a political upstart, had managed to dispatch so easily an opponent as large and as venerable as the Habsburg Empire.

Not only the Prussians but also the Italians and the Hungarians were the big winners of 1866, a turning point in Central European history that is frequently underestimated. Prussia demanded Austria's withdrawal from German affairs, which was a prerequisite for the potential creation of a Prussian-dominated kleindeutsch or "little" German state, but Bismarck did not increase the humiliation of defeat by demanding territorial concessions from Austria, because he realized that he would need the Habsburgs as allies in the future. However, Italy, which in 1866 had simultaneously allied itself with Prussia and gone to war with Austria, profited from Prussia's victory, even though Italian troops were unsuccessful on the battlefield, because Prussia demanded the Habsburgs' forfeiture of Venice as a reward for its Italian allies.

Furthermore, in 1866 the Hungarians employed their old strategy of exploiting the Habsburgs' problems in the west to their own advantage in the east. As the German historian Golo Mann explained, "A German victory—a Habsburg defeat—was a Hungarian victory."[14] The Hungarians pressed for more national autonomy at a time of Habsburg imperial weakness, and they managed to achieve the so-called Compromise of 1867 based on the principle of "dualism." Imperial concessions to Hungarian demands for more autonomy effectively divided the empire into two semiautonomous states. As belated rewards for the revolutions of 1848, Austria and Hungary received new, liberal constitutions, and the parliaments in Vienna and Budapest assumed responsibility for the "domestic affairs" of the respective halves of the monarchy. However, Austria and Hungary were "personally" unified by Francis Joseph, who was the emperor of Austria in one half of his realms and the king of Hungary in the other, and they were politically united by the "imperial and royal" ministries for foreign affairs and defense that were responsible for handling the external affairs of Austria-Hungary as a whole.

The Compromise of 1867 and the establishment of the Austro-Hungarian monarchy satisfied long-standing Hungarian demands for more national autonomy without answering the "nationalities question," because it did not address the status of other national minorities in Austria or Hungary. On the contrary, it merely divided the problem in two, and neither the Magyars nor the German-Austrians managed to satisfy the future demands of their respective national minorities. The Magyars, who were literally outnumbered by the various national minorities in the kingdom of Hungary, pursued a policy of Magyarization. German-Austrians were reticent about recognizing the claims of the national minorities in their half of the Dual Monarchy, and the relationships between German-Austrians and the national minorities seeking greater equality or more autonomy, particularly the Czechs, became increasingly acrimonious.

After the Battle of Königgrätz, the Habsburgs assumed a subordinate role in German politics and turned their attention to the Balkan Peninsula, the only possible avenue left to them for political expansion. Victorious Prussia annexed outright several smaller northern German states and founded the Northern German Confederation, which bound the others asymmetrically to Prussia in a federation that was federal in name only. Bismarck left intact the independence of the predominantly Roman Catholic southern German states—Bavaria, Baden, Württenberg, and Hesse—but he secretly negotiated defensive and offensive alliances with them stipulating that their armies would fall under Prussian command in case of war. Nevertheless, the Prussian achievement of hegemony in northern Germany was just an intermediate station on the path to unification, which was a direct result of the Franco-Prussian War of 1870–1871.

The event that brought French–Prussian rivalries to a head in the summer of 1870 was that some Spanish politicians speculated about offering the vacant Spanish throne to a distant relative of the Hohenzollern dynasty, Prince Leopold from the southern German Catholic house of Hohenzollern-Sigmaringen. Even though this German prince also was remotely related to France's emperor, Napoleon III, French national apprehension about some kind of "German" encirclement rose. France insisted that the German prince renounce any intention of accepting the throne. Through a series of carefully orchestrated provocations, Bismarck raised to the level of a frenzy anti-French sentiments in Germany as well as anti-German sentiments in France. He consolidated the independent southern German states with Prussia and incited France to declare war as a matter of national prestige on July 19, 1870.

Under the command of the legendary Prussian General H.K.B. von Moltke, a carefully planned, precise, and powerful German offensive threw the insufficiently prepared, ill-equipped, and poorly led French armies into a state of disarray, and on September 2, 1870, the French suffered a devastating defeat at Sedan when the Germans captured an entire French army along with Emperor Napoleon III. (The new German Reich subsequently chose September 2—the commemoration of the German victory and the French humiliation—as a national holiday.) The French domestic response

to this German victory was the deposition of Napoleon III and the proclamation of the republican Government of National Defense. The forces of
the new republican France, however, proved to be as insufficient as those of
Napoleon III's imperial France. A series of defeats in the field during the
fall of 1870 preceded a protracted siege of Paris during the winter of
1870/1871, and France's provisional government signed an armistice at the
end of January. Four months later a newly elected French National Assembly accepted the final terms of peace, including the German annexation of
the border provinces of Alsace and Lorraine, which had mixed French and
German populations.

Germans used historical, national, military, and vindictive arguments to
legitimize the annexation of these provinces. Alsace and Lorraine had been
part of the "old" German Reich; their annexation brought Germans into the
Reich (while also creating a new French minority that was conveniently overlooked); their acquisition improved Germany's defensive posture in the
event of a future war with France; and France had to pay for its "aggression."
The German annexation of Alsace-Lorraine also substantially contributed
to poisoning German–French relations in the future.

Historians have argued that Bismarck used the war with France to pursue German unification and that he also needed German unification in order to pursue the war. Regardless of whether military or national concerns
were his higher priority, one of the consequences of the German armies' victories in the field was an atmosphere of national intoxication that made the
process of German unification appear to be inevitable, and the treaties that
initially bound the various German states into a military alliance against
France provided the basis for the foundation of a new German Reich. The
rulers of the various German states outside Prussia agreed to offer the imperial German crown to the king of Prussia in state that had been conceived
as a federation of monarchies with an emperor at its head. On January 1,
1871, while German armies besieged Paris, a new German Reich with the
king of Prussia, Wilhelm, as its inaugural emperor was proclaimed in the
Hall of Mirrors in the Palace of Versailles. The French perceived the time
and place of the proclamation of the German Reich as a further national
humiliation.

In 1848, German reformers and revolutionaries had envisioned a unified German federal state and constitutional monarchy tempered by liberal
and democratic principles, such as parliamentary government and the sovereignty of the people. Although the popular sentiment among Germans in
1871 was overwhelmingly for unification, the new German Reich made few
concessions to the federal, liberal, and democratic ideals that had inspired
the visions of unification in 1848. Germany was not unified democratically
from the bottom up by the people but, rather, autocratically from the top
down by the Prussians.

Prussian centralism, instead of genuine federalism, was one of the organizational characteristics of the new Reich. The German empire had a constitution, but it did not put effective constraints on imperial prerogative. The
position of emperor became a hereditary entitlement of the king of Prussia;

the German army was effectively placed under his command; and he retained the right to declare war. Important ministerial and administrative posts were staffed by members of Prussia's traditional elite of officer-aristocrats. The sheer size of Prussia guaranteed its preeminence in the Bundesrat, a "house of lords" in which the heads of state from the various federated states were represented. The German parliament, or Reichstag, a "house of commons" elected on the basis of limited suffrage, could not introduce legislation, and there was no parliamentary control over the ministers of the government, who were neither elected by the Reichstag nor responsible to it, but were appointed by the emperor.

Bismarck unified Germany without liberalizing it. The continuity of authoritarian, illiberal, and antidemocratic structures despite the subsequent development of Germany into a modern industrial power—or the survival of traditional political elites parallel to the creation of new economic ones—was one of the distinctive characteristics of the new German empire. Conservative historians often emphasize the subsequent liberalization of imperial Germany, whereas their adversaries underscore the persistency of autocratic attitudes and institutions. One of the underlying issues at stake here is the extent to which Bismarck's Kaiserreich laid the foundations for Hitler's Third Reich.[15]

Imperial German Geography: Mitteleuropa

Mitteleuropa, literally "middle Europe," is an ambiguous German concept. Before 1871, Germans traditionally viewed themselves as inhabiting *das Land der Mitte*, "the country in the middle," and in this context middle Europe was a relatively benign descriptive term describing Germany's geographical position between the east and the west, or Russia and France. But, after the establishment of the Kaiserreich in 1871, *Mitteleuropa* gradually evolved into a term describing German imperial ambitions to dominate Central Europe and, in some cases, all of Europe. It also played a terminological and conceptual role in the foreign and occupational policies of the Third Reich. Therefore, the term *Mitteleuropa* is full of pejorative connotations for those Central European peoples who were victims of German imperialism in the twentieth century. (Some German speakers are sensitive enough to the connotations of the term *Mitteleuropa* to use *Zentraleuropa*, "Central Europe," instead. The meaning of *Mitteleuropa* is also, to a great extent, contextual. For example, if an Austrian uses the term in Prague or Budapest or Kraków, it inevitably conjures up relatively nostalgic, Habsburg-imperial associations; but when a German uses it, people start thinking about imperialism.)

Friedrich Naumann's book *Mitteleuropa*, which was published in 1915, was a classic formulation of the German imperial concept of Central Europe.[16] Naumann's *Mitteleuropa* was the projection of a new economic and political order for Europe, and he envisioned *Mitteleuropa* as an association of states in which Germany was to play a central role. Naumann proposed an economic union based on a grand division of labor in which Germany would function as an industrial center, technological innovator, and financial manager whereas adjoining or peripheral states and regions would specialize in agriculture and the production of raw materials or semifinished goods in addition to providing secure markets for German industrial products. He also proposed a political association based in theory on equal membership, although it was clear to him and his contemporaries that Germany would dominate any such constellation in practice.

For Naumann, the borders of *Mitteleuropa* were negotiable insofar as they were contingent on the success of the German war effort and the nature of the postwar settlements. But he thought that the minimal core for a projected "middle European" union had to begin with the creation of a common market between the German and the Austro-Hungarian Empires—an economic transformation of the Central Powers' military alliance—and that adjacent countries would voluntarily seek to associate themselves with this bloc. More ambitious and imperialistic versions of the *Mitteleuropa* idea included the affiliation of a reestablished Poland detached from Russia, substantial parts of the Russian empire itself, and the Balkan Peninsula in addition to Denmark, Belgium, Luxembourg, and France. There was nothing original about Naumann's conception of *Mitteleuropa*, because his projection of a new European order merely reflected the general tenor of opinion among decision makers in the German army, government, and industry at the beginning of World War I, and some of the ideas he expounded can be traced as far back as the first half of the nineteenth century.

The development of imperial German ideology in the Kaiserreich, the role it played in articulating German war aims in World War I, and the continuities and transformations of this tradition in the Weimar Republic and Third Reich is very complicated.[17] But, a few broad generalizations concerning some of the distinctive characteristics of German imperial ideology are possible. The *Mitteleuropa* idea was a composite of global and continental strains of German imperialism that can be roughly circumscribed using terms that gained currency around the turn of the century: *Weltpolitik* ("global politics") and *Lebensraum* ("living space").

The advance of Germany to the status of a major continental power in 1871 provided the political and economic basis for subsequent German claims to being a world power. The beginning of Emperor Wilhelm II's reign in 1888 and the end of Bismarck's diplomatic career in 1890 are the dates conventionally used to mark a hiatus in German foreign policy. The abandonment of the maxims of Bismarck's foreign policy was one of the features of Wilhelm's "global politics." Bismarck believed that the German, Austro-Hungarian, and Russian empires should carefully cultivate their common interests. He orchestrated a grand reconciliation between Germany and Austria-Hungary, and in 1872 he negotiated the Dreikaiser-Bund, the "Three Emperors' Union," which held until 1890. Bismarck also avoided antagonizing British interests in order to encourage the diplomatic isolation or "exclusion" of France from major alliances. But, under Wilhelm II, German relations with both Britain and Russia nonetheless became increasingly antagonistic.

One may argue that global politics was one of the consequences of German unification itself: bolstering economic potential and enhanced national self-esteem. A theoretician and practitioner of *Weltpolitik*, Bernhard von Bülow, the German foreign minister from 1897 to 1900 and then chancellor until 1909, defined global politics as "the support and advancement of the tasks that have grown out of the expansion of our industry, our trade, the labor-power, activity, and intelligence of our people." Von Bülow later recalled, "We had no intention of conducting an aggressive policy of expansion. We wanted to protect the vital interests that we had acquired, in the natural course of events, throughout the world."[18]

In terms of German self-perception, global politics was a form of national entitlement that entailed achieving a position in Europe and the world commensurate with the increased size and prowess of the German Reich, and later conflicts arose as a result of the inability of other powers to recognize the legitimacy of German claims. There was nothing particularly German about the idea of "vital interests" and its relationship to the prevailing concepts of economic imperialism—an industrial center with a protected domestic market that dominated trade with dependent peripheries in order to secure captive markets for its goods and also natural resources for itself—or colonial imperialism, although by British and French standards Germany was a belated participant in staking out colonies in Africa and the Far East.

Furthermore, two frequently cited examples of how *Weltpolitik* directly challenged British and Russian interests were the Germany decision in 1898 to build a navy designed to compete with the British fleet and Germany's technical and financial aid to the ailing Ottoman Empire in 1899 for the construction of a railroad to Baghdad. One vision of global politics was a German sphere of influence "from Berlin to Baghdad" that jeopardized British interests in the eastern Mediterranean and the Middle East and frustrated Russian ambitions in the Balkans, where Germany was partial to the interests of its number one ally, Austria-Hungary.

If *Weltpolitik* described German objectives on a global scale, *Mitteleuropa* was a constituent part of this ideology applicable to continental European objectives. The German conception of *Mitteleuropa* relied on historical, cultural, biological, economic, and political arguments, and one of the most dubious achievements of the German academic community in Wilhelmine Germany was to provide an array of allegedly "scientific" justifications for German imperialism.

The *Reichsidee*, the "idea" of the Holy Roman Empire of the German Nation, exerted a captivating influence on Germans, and some German historians interpreted the establishment of the Kaiserreich in 1871 explicitly in terms of the "mission" of the old Reich in Europe. During the first half of the nineteenth century, German Romantics rediscovered the Middle Ages and identified it as the greatest period in German history. Consequently, the establishment of the German empire in 1871 represented a restoration of Germany to its former position of greatness and a rejuvenation of Germany's "mission" as a promoter and protector of Western Christian culture.

The fact that the Kaiserreich had been established without Austria also

"GERMAN CULTURE AND ITS INFLUENCE"

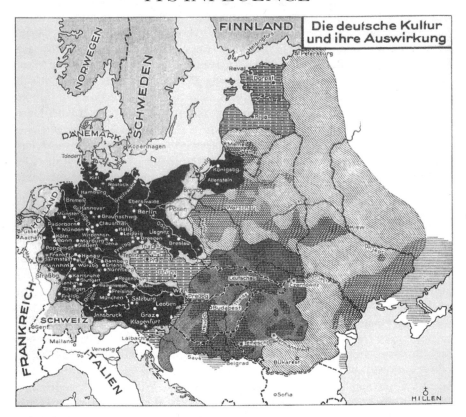

Die deutsche Kultur und ihre Auswirkung

 Territory of the German people (*Volksboden*) that retained its sovereignty and its intellectual centers [Germany and Austria after 1918]

 Border region territories of the German people subjected to foreign powers and its cultural centers [after 1918: Alsace-Lorraine, the Danzig Corridor in Poland, and German-speaking border regions in Czechoslovakia]

 German cultural territory (*Kulturboden*) in foreign states and its cultural centers [Estonia, Latvia, Bohemia, Moravia, and Slovenia]

 Regions that stood under German administration for 100 years and incorporated into foreign states [the Habsburg Empire]

 Major areas of German farmer-peasants and farming culture (*Bauernkultur*) [in parts of Lithuania, Poland, Ukraine, Transylvania, and Serbia]

 German-speaking Switzerland, Luxembourg, and regions of other Germanic languages

 Area in the East where German is used as a lingua franca.

needed some kind of historical justification. Historians described the Prussian and Protestant Hohenzollern dynasty and the *kleindeutsch* German national state as the legitimate heirs to the most glorious and authentic traditions of the Reich or, conversely, downplayed the factual role and historical importance of the Roman Catholic Habsburgs who, as the former emperors of the Holy Roman Empire of the German Nation, were at least titular heirs to German imperial traditions.[19]

Historians also rediscovered the "eastern mission" of Germany—the Teutonic Knights' conversion of the pagans and taming of the wilderness, the *Drang nach Osten*, and the German "colonization" of the East—and they portrayed these achievements in glowing national colors. (German nationalists assigned Habsburg Austria a subordinate role in this historical theater: the "southeastern mission.") The emphasis of German scholars on the "civilizing" historical influence of German missionary work and settlement in the East, enhanced by the accomplishments of "German science and culture" and contemporarily reinforced by exports of German capital and technology, all found their "scientific" confirmation in the concept of a *Kulturgefälle*, a West–East "cultural gradient" that slighted the autonomy and achievements of the Slavic cultures.

From the nationalistic perspective of a German historical mission, *Mitteleuropa* was a German *Sprach- und Kulturraum*, a "cultural and linguistic space," which, given the various phases and forms of German migration to the east and southeast, could be defined as an area that included the Baltic Coast and most of Poland and extended from Bohemia into Ukraine and down the Danube Valley through Austria and across the Carpathian Mountains to the Black Sea.

The development of the pseudoscientific and social Darwinistic theories of race toward the end of the nineteenth century added a completely new racial dimension to the historical, linguistic, and cultural definitions of the Germans as a *Volk* and *Mitteleuropa* as a "German space." As soon as biologists began defining culture as a racial attribute and started using the concept of natural selection—or its social Darwinistic bastardization, "the survival of the fittest"—as a means of distinguishing between allegedly superior and inferior races, historical struggles between Germans and Slavs appeared in a completely new light. Friedrich Ratzel (1844–1904), a German geographer, who popularized the term *Lebensraum*, was just one of many representatives of "German science" whose theories were used to justify imperialism or racism.

Ratzel argued that a given species population (or people) had to expand the amount of space it inhabited in order to ensure its survival. Although the

---

Many of the late-nineteenth-century German imperial assumptions about Central Europe as a "German cultural space" continued to be operative in Germany after 1918 and were incorporated into Nazi ideology. "German Culture and Its Influence" portrays Central Europe as a German "cultural space." (Map and commentary from A. Hillen Ziegfeld, *Geopolitischer Geschichtsatlas* [Geopolitical Historical Atlas] [Dresden: Ehlermann, 1930]; Austrian National Library) combination of Darwinian natural selection with the concept of spatial command was not new, Ratzel emphasized the importance of migration, the biological ability of a people to acquire new and more space, in human geography. Ratzel's theory elevated the displacement of inferior indigenous cultures by superior migrating or "colonizing" ones to a law of nature leading to interpretations that "scientifically" supported colonialism and imperialism.

Ratzel also stressed the historical importance of traditional agrarian societies as the producers of foodstuffs for growing populations and romantically portrayed the members of agricultural societies as the most important carriers and curators of culture. Consequently, it appeared to be a biological necessity for Germany to acquire more territory to accommodate its growing population. Ratzel's theory also had a peculiar antimodern twist: He maintained that agricultural colonization was the most appropriate means of acquiring "living space," and he assumed that the resulting increase in rural population would offset the culturally injurious influence of urban centers: the denatured habitat of liberals, socialists, and Jews.

Generally speaking, the *Weltpolitik* version of *Mitteleuropa* was based on a modern industrial and commercial strategy of economic imperialism—achieving a commanding position on the continental market as a basis for the conquest of the global market—whereas the *Lebensraum* variant of *Mitteleuropa* had autarkic, conservative-nationalist, and racial implications: the creation of a self-sufficient "economic space" on the Continent that would eliminate German dependence on foreign trade and simultaneously give the German people the living space they needed to grow and prosper.

Frequently based upon the idea of German "colonization" on the Continent, this version of *Mitteleuropa* appealed to a broad spectrum of radical conservatives, romantic Pan-Germans, and antimodern agrarianists in Wilhelmine Germany. These groups hailed the virtues of preindustrial agricultural society, feared the cosmopolitanism inherent in industrial civilization as culturally degenerative, and reformulated Germany's historical *Drang nach Osten* in the biopolitical terms of *Lebensraum*. It was clear to the various proponents of the *Lebensraum* theory that the well-being of the German people could not be secured without large-scale annexations in the east and that a major war was the prerequisite for these annexations.

It would be contrived to describe *Mitteleuropa* as a coherent ideological concept. It was malleable enough to provide room for the visions and interests of disparate groups like German industrialists and agrarianists, liberals and conservatives, or believers in Germany's cultural and historical mission as a Christian power as well as atheistic social Darwinists and racists. One of its common denominators, however, was the projection of a substantially expanded German empire into a new European order. Although there was a broad spectrum of opinion concerning the organizational details and aims of this grand design, it was an objective shared by the imperial strategists of both the Kaiserreich and the Third Reich. Adolf Hitler was obsessed by the idea of *Lebensraum*, and many non-German Central Europeans identify *Mitteleuropa* with the instruments he employed to acquire it: war, mass deportations, and genocide.

≹ 9 ≹

World War I and
National Self-Determination

1914–1922

There was a great disparity between the motives and aims of the initial belligerent powers in World War I and the principles and objectives embodied
in the various peace settlements after the war. When the war broke out at
the beginning of August 1914, the Entente Powers of France, Russia, and
England pursued traditional objectives. They sought to defend themselves
against "German aggression" and wished to defeat the Central Powers of
Germany and Austria-Hungary resolutely enough to prevent a recurrence
thereof in the future, but they had no clearly articulated set of joint aims.
The fact that Britain and France, the foremost representatives of Western
Europe's parliamentary and republican traditions, had allied themselves
with Russia, the most despotic power in Europe, did not prevent the Western powers from maintaining that they also were fighting for freedom and
democracy, but these appeals to political principle were not especially convincing. The German violation of Belgian neutrality, part of the Schlieffen
Plan for the invasion of France, provided Britain with a plausible moral justification for entering the conflict, but Britain had a number of other scores
to settle with German *Weltpolitik*.

Aside from weakening Germany and breaking up the German–Austro-
Hungarian alliance, the Entente Powers had no grand designs for a new Europe. Certainly some borders would have to be rectified after the war. Russia had vaguely formulated as an objective the liberation of Ukrainian
minorities in the eastern realms of Austria-Hungary, and the czar had other traditional imperial Russian ambitions such as dominating the Balkans or
gaining control of the Dardanelles Strait. France wanted to recover the
province of Alsace-Lorraine, which it had lost to Germany in 1871. The En-

tente Powers promised neutral countries like Italy and Romania substantial territorial gains in Austria-Hungary in order to draw them into the conflict as allies. Although by the fall of 1915, most of Serbia had been occupied, its armies continued to operate from Greece on the southern front. The future status of a Serbian state, which Russia wanted to see substantially enlarged after the war, was for Britain and France a subordinate point on the agenda. At the beginning of World War I, Entente generals and politicians still envisioned the future postwar order of Europe in terms of its traditional pentarchy of powers: Britain, France, Germany, Austria-Hungary, and Russia.

Although Austria-Hungary would be required to make territorial sacrifices, the importance of the Habsburgs' Dual Monarchy in the European balance of power was unquestioned at the beginning of the war, and neither Britain nor France considered reestablishing an independent Polish state to be one of their war aims. On the contrary, in the midst of the conflict there was no point in making proposals that would either aggravate or weaken their Russian ally. Two sets of events in 1917 radically changed the ideological complexion of the war: Russia's "democratic" and Bolshevik revolutions in February and October, respectively, and the United States' entry into the conflict as an associated power in April.

For the first time in history, the United States intervened in European affairs on a grand scale, and although Russia subsequently withdrew from European affairs for almost two decades, the Bolshevik Revolution radically changed the nature of Europe's largest power. Woodrow Wilson and Vladimir Lenin, two leaders with completely different visions of a new European and a new global order, made substantial contributions to ending the war and articulating the conditions of peace. Although Wilson, as an apostle of American democracy, and Lenin, as a Bolshevik revolutionary, had very little in common, each of them in his own way helped reformulate the objectives of the war, and if there was one term their otherwise disparate political vocabularies had in common, it was national self-determination.

Austria-Hungary:
The "Prison of Nations," 1914–1918

The assassinations of Archduke Francis Ferdinand, heir to the Austrian imperial throne, and his wife, by Serbian nationalists in Sarajevo, the capital of the province Bosnia-Herzegovina, on June 28, 1914, was not one of the more important causes of World War I, but it provided an occasion for it to begin. Francis Ferdinand was the victim of an irreconcilable conflict between Serbian nationalism and Austro-Hungarian imperial policy. The deterioration of the Ottoman Empire in the nineteenth century, a process that the Great Powers alternately promoted and prolonged, had allowed those nations that had been Ottoman vassals or clients for more than four centuries—Greeks, Serbs, Montenegrins, Romanians, and Bulgarians—eventually to emancipate themselves from the proverbial Turkish yoke. But the various struggles against the Turks for national independence, alternating conflicts over territorial claims among the new states themselves, and the interests of the major powers—Austria-Hungary and Russia on the Balkans, Italy in the Adriatic, and Britain in the Mediterranean—made the region inherently unstable.

Bosnia-Herzegovina was the most recent addition to the Habsburg Empire. A European congress held in Berlin in 1878, the diplomatic denouement of a series of indigenous uprisings against the Turks, sanctioned the Austro-Hungarian occupation and administration of Bosnia-Herzegovina as a protectorate. Because Austria-Hungary had traditionally supported the aspirations of the Serbs against the Turks, Serbia, a small state of 4.5 million, initially viewed the Austro-Hungarian protectorate of Bosnia-Herzegovina as a benevolent custodianship that would eventually make way for the unification of the Serbian nation into one state.

Austro-Hungarian relations with Serbia became increasingly acrimonious, however, as Serbian nationalism grew more ambitious, and Austria-Hungary violated several international agreements in 1908 by unilaterally annexing Bosnia-Herzegovina. Furthermore, Francis Ferdinand and his advisers had discussed some kind of federal reorganization of Austria-Hungary that would accommodate the aspirations of its substantial Slavic populations. Among them was the conversion, however unrealistic, of the Austro-Hungarian Dual Monarchy into some kind of Austrian–Hungarian–southern Slav "Triple Monarchy" as one means of politically integrating the substantial southern Slav minorities into the empire.

The annexation of Bosnia-Herzegovina, combined with this type of imperial scenario, turned Serbia, initially a protégé and client state of Austria-Hungary, into one of its mortal enemies because it categorically frustrated Serbian aspirations for national unification, and the Serbs found an accommodating new patron in the czar.

Serbia also represented an existential threat to Austria-Hungary insofar as smaller states in the past had led campaigns for national unification that had ended with the expulsion of the Habsburgs from traditional spheres of influence. In the 1860s, Piedmont had initiated the drive for Italian unification that led to the expulsion of the Habsburgs from northern Italy,[1] and Prussia had ousted Austria from the sphere of German politics. With its Greater Serbian version of southern Slav unification, Serbia jeopardized Austria-Hungary's only remaining sphere of influence. The idea of forfeiting Vojvodina, a southern province of the kingdom of Hungary that was inhabited predominantly by Serbs, and Bosnia-Herzegovina, or portions of it, for the sake of southern Slav unity or a Greater Serbian national state did not occur to Austro-Hungarian imperial advisers. On the contrary, the militarists among them considered a preventive war, the conclusion of which might include the incorporation of Serbia into the empire itself, as one means of resolving the conflict. Then the assassination of Archduke Francis Ferdinand in Sarajevo on June 28, 1914, gave Austria-Hungary a reason for settling matters with Serbia once and for all.

The events that led to the beginning of World War I are well known. Diplomatic bullying and blundering preceded the Austro-Hungarian declaration of war on Serbia, which started a fatal chain reaction. Austria-Hungary declared war on Serbia, and Russia mobilized to back Serbia. Germany declared war on Russia, which brought France and eventually England into the conflict. The failure of Germany and Austria-Hungary to achieve their initial military objectives of quickly knocking France and Serbia out of the war led to a worst-case scenario: a war on three fronts.

Before and during the war, one of Austria-Hungary's largest domestic problems was the status and claims of its national minorities. Before the war, there were a number of congenial plans for converting the Dual Monarchy of Austria-Hungary into a some kind of "federal union" or federation of national states, and during the war, these reform schemes enjoyed great currency. The Czech historian and father of Austro-Slavism, František Palacký, may be regarded as one of the most important originators of various federal programs. Different versions of the idea of a "United States of Greater Austria," incidentally the title of a book by a Romanian, Aurel Popovici,[2] who sympathized with Archduke Francis Ferdinand's reform plans, were popular both before and during the war, and most of these proposals had two common denominators.

One denominator was the formulation of a supranational "Austrian ideology," which defined imperial Austria as a historically necessary and organically grown community of small nations that needed to live together in order to protect themselves from German and Russian imperialism, and the other was plans for a reorganization of the empire that would satisfy the demands of each of its eleven ethnic groups by creating a series of semiautonomous "national states" associated in a federal union. The concept of dynastic loyalty, with the Habsburgs as the consolidating element for the parts of the whole, played an important part in many proposals, but others dispensed with the dynasty.

Although Popovici's proposal did not overcome the problems of regions with great ethnic heterogeneity or smaller "linguistic islands," he suggested, for example, the creation of fifteen "national states" whose borders had an uncanny similarity to the various international frontiers that existed in the region between 1918 and 1945 or have been created by the deterioration of Yugoslavia and the division of Czechoslovakia since 1989.[3] Oszkár Jászi, one of the leading figures in the Hungarian liberal reform movement before the war, published a lengthy study in Budapest in 1912, *The Formation of the National States and the Minority Question*, in which he proposed a "United States on the Danube" or a "Switzerland in the East" whose ethnic "states" or "cantons" would be united in a democratic federation. In a similar vein, Hugo von Hofmannsthal, an Austrian poet, playwright, and essayist, praised the multinational function of the Habsburg Empire. As late as 1917, in an essay, *The Austrian Idea*, he declared: "The intellectual and spiritual amplitude of this idea surpasses everything the national or economic ideologies of our day can produce." Hofmannsthal concluded that the Austrian idea could provide the basis for a "new supra-national European politics which would fully grasp and integrate the nationality problem . . . This Europe, which wants to reform itself, needs an Austria."[4]

Federal schemes also abounded among Austrian socialists, and the empire's Austrian Social Democratic Workers' Party produced two major theoreticians who wrote extensively on the nationalities question before the war, Karl Renner and Otto Bauer.[5] These socialist democrats already had a supranational or international ideology (a reform-oriented strain of Marxism), and their party existed in a multinational empire. Therefore, they envisioned a democratic transformation of the empire—an empire without an emperor, so to speak—based on the federal reorganization of the monarchy into democratic states that would provide for "national-cultural autonomy." Furthermore, special guarantees for the protection of minorities' rights for those individuals who lived outside their respective "national states" was part of the scheme. The peculiar twist in this socialist conception was that it rejected national separatism as a "bourgeois ideology" and posited the supranational state as an advanced stage of social and political development: a regional realization of the global objective of "Workers of the world unite!"[6]

These examples illustrate that there was no paucity of proposals for dealing with the nationalities question. Even though most historians agree that the Habsburgs' multinational empire was an anachronism in the age of nationalism and portray its demise in terms of the centrifugal forces of nationalism that tore it apart, the Entente Powers initially based their policy toward Austria-Hungary on the maintenance of an imperial status quo, because the empire historically had fulfilled the important function of deterring German and Russian imperial expansion on the Continent. One of the major problems that Britain and France faced in regard to their war objectives was finding a means to weaken Germany and to defeat Austria-Hungary without substantially increasing the power of czarist Russia. But the tactics they employed to draw Italy into the war in 1915 and Romania in 1916, the entry of the United States into the conflict in 1917—as well as Russia's dual revolution in the same year—helped shift the Entente's foreign policy toward Austria-Hungary, and they dramatically changed the climate of opinion among the various national minorities in the Dual Monarchy.

At the beginning of the war, Austria-Hungary was confronted with Pan-Slavic imperialism on one front and the irredentism of border states on three others. The czar had declared the "liberation" of the Ukrainian minorities inhabiting the eastern portion of the Austrian imperial province of Galicia, the Austrian portion of partitioned Poland, to be one of Russia's objectives. But the ruthless manner in which Austro-Hungarian authorities, both civilian and military, conducted themselves in this region as the front moved back and forth across it during the first three years of the war hardly engendered among its population feelings of loyalty toward the Habsburg dynasty.

At the beginning of the war, Serbia clearly stated as its goal the unification of all Serbs into one state, and although the Entente Powers did not endorse this objective, it appeared to give the Serbs living in Austria-Hungary a choice between dynastic loyalty and national liberation. Acrid anti-Serb propaganda, the war against Serbia, and the demeanor of imperial officials, who occasionally treated the empire's indigenous Serbian minorities with a combination of suspicion and contempt alienated many Serbs, who, under circumstances similar to those of the Ukrainians, were among the first to dissociate themselves psychologically from the empire. Despite these two negative examples, however, Austria-Hungary's various national minorities demonstrated substantial dynastic loyalty and multinational patriotism well into the war, which was being fought for the sake of imperial unity or, as the oath went, *Für Gott, Kaiser, und Vaterland*, "For God, the Emperor, and the Fatherland."[7] The situation on the empire's "domestic front" did not begin to deteriorate noticeably until 1917.

Nevertheless, the empire's Italian and Romanian minorities became points of contention and foreign policy deficits during the war. Although Germany and Austria-Hungary, allied since 1879, had signed a treaty with Italy in 1882, which provided for mutual assistance if Italy were attacked by France but otherwise obligated each signatory power to remain neutral in conflicts with other powers, the Austro-Hungarian alliance with Italy was contrived. They were traditional enemies with conflicting interests in the Adriatic, and the Habsburg Empire contained large Italian minorities. Although Italy reconfirmed and observed its commitment to neutrality once the war began, it also used its neutrality as diplomatic leverage in an attempt to compel Austria-Hungary into ceding those territories of the empire that housed Italian minorities. Even though Germany pressured Austria-Hungary to compromise, the imperial authorities wanted to postpone as long as possible making any commitments or establishing any precedents.

This example merely indicates how disparate the objectives of Germany and Austria-Hungary were. Austria-Hungary's primary goal was to win the war on the Balkans and to hold the front in the east in order to ensure its territorial integrity. Germany viewed Austria-Hungary as an auxiliary in its conflict with France and Russia and did not want its ally to become embroiled in conflicts that would draw Austro-Hungarian men or matériel away from the Russian front.

Italy, dissatisfied by the Austro-Hungarian lack of preparedness to make immediate concessions, soon turned to the Entente Powers to see what they had to offer. In exchange for the guarantee of substantial territorial gains not only on the Dalmatian coast and the Istrian Peninsula but also in the German-speaking South Tyrol, Italy signed a secret treaty with the Entente Powers in London on May 3, 1915, and declared war on Austria-Hungary three weeks later. Italy wanted to gain control of Trieste, the empire's vital port, and the strategically important Brenner Pass in the Alps, even if it meant incorporating into Italy more than 200,000 German-speaking Tyrolese. (U.S. President Woodrow Wilson was unaware of this secret Italian–Entente agreement when he formulated the ninth of his "Fourteen Points," which stated that a "readjustment of the frontiers of Italy should be effected along clearly recognizable lines of nationality." To fulfill previous Entente commitments and in direct violation of Wilson's principle of ethnic borders, the Brenner Pass frontier was granted to Italy after World War I.)

Both Romania's relationship with Austria-Hungary and its national interests were similar to those of Italy. Romania had declared its neutrality at the beginning of the war. But it also wanted to incorporate into an expand-

In Treue Fest (In Unwavering Allegiance), a photo montage of Germany's emperor Wilhelm II and Austria-Hungary's Francis Joseph I, emperor of Austria and king of Hungary, on a propaganda postcard at the beginning of World War I. The mass distribution of material of this kind was supposed to mobilize domestic support for the war effort. (Österreichische Gesellschaft für Zeitgeschichte, Photoarchiv, Vienna)

ed Romanian national state the Transylvanian part of the kingdom of Hungary, which was inhabited predominantly by Romanians but had sizable Hungarian and German minorities living in relatively large and cohesive enclaves. Since it was clear to all parties involved that the Hungarians would never sacrifice the sanctity or the territorial integrity of the historical kingdom of Hungary in order to procure Romanian neutrality, Romania waited for a militarily opportune moment to cast its lot with the Entente.

During August 1916, when Austria-Hungary was heavily engaged on the Russian and Italian fronts, Romania negotiated secretly with the Entente Powers, and they made generous territorial guarantees—including all of

Transylvania, eastern Hungary up to the Tisza River, "Austrian" Bukovina northeast of Hungary, and the Banat in the Danube Valley—in order to draw Romania into the Entente alliance. With hopes of doubling its size by halving Hungary, Romania declared war on Austria-Hungary on August 27, 1916. Then, however, the collapse of Russia's military offensive in 1916 and the revolutionary collapse of Russia altogether in 1917 isolated Romania on the eastern front, and it sued for a separate peace in 1918.

Although it would be imprudent to label as peripheral the Russian, Serbian, Italian, and Romanian claims, their realization did depend on the outcome of the war, and they did leave intact the ethnic and territorial core of the monarchy: Croats and Slovenes in the south; German-Austrians and Magyars in the middle; and Czechs, Slovaks, and Poles in the north. However, leading representatives of the empire's non-German and non-Hungarian minorities emigrated to the west shortly after the beginning of the war and began agitating for national independence. The reputations of Thomas Masaryk and Eduard Beneš, the founding fathers of the Czecho-Slovak[8] National Committee in Paris and consequently the Czechoslovak Republic, tend to outshine those of their lesser-known southern Slav compatriots like Ante Trumbić and Frano Supilo, two Croats who founded the Yugoslav National Committee in London. (The intricacies of the Polish situation, which was exceptional because the Poles had to contend with three empires instead of one, will be addressed separately.)

Masaryk and Beneš were instrumental in laying the foundations for a Czech and Slovak state, and they helped pave the way for their southern Slav companions. Masaryk had a very cordial personal relationship with Woodrow Wilson, and the United States' entry into the war gave the Czechoslovak cause a powerful advocate. Beneš organized "Czechoslovak legions" by recruiting Czech and Slovak immigrants as well as prisoners of war and deserters from the Austro-Hungarian imperial army to serve under the Entente's banner. Austrian and Hungarian historians who use the imperial army as an example of one multinational institution that functioned well despite the empire's nationalities problem emphasize that the majority of Czechs and Slovaks served respectably, although there were a few notorious (or praiseworthy) exceptions like the Twenty-eighth Division of Prague, which deserted as a closed formation on the Russian front in 1915. Nonetheless, relatively few Slavic prisoners of war from the Austro-Hungarian army actually responded to the call to fight—around 10 percent—and the Czechoslovak legions, important as they were politically, never numbered more than 60,000 men.[9]

Czech and Slovak legionnaires saw action on three fronts, in France, Italy, and in Russia. The contingents of the Czechoslovak legions in Russia swelled after the February Revolution of 1917 nominally turned Russia into a democracy, but after the Bolshevik Revolution in October, they withdrew from the front and took the long way back to the west, via Siberia to Vladivostock. They did not reach home until 1920 because they became embroiled in a number of conflicts with the Bolshevik forces and assumed the role of a surrogate Allied expeditionary force against the Bolsheviks. (One of the most curious conflicts during the Russian civil war was related to the fact that the Bolsheviks released Hungarian prisoners of war in Siberia when they came to power, and the Czechoslovak legions had occupied portions of the Trans-Siberian Railway. The Hungarian prisoners of war, who wanted to get home and needed the railway to do so, allied themselves with the Red Army in battles against the Czechoslovak legions. More than 100,000 Hungarians fought in the Red Army during the Russian civil war. In many cases, they just wanted to get home, but later Communist historians turned these homesick Hungarian POWs into insurgents with a commitment to world revolution and proletarian internationalism.)

There also were national activists who remained at home—for example, the representatives of the Slavic nations who had been elected to the Reichsrat, the imperial parliament for the Austrian half of the monarchy—and they pursued the same objectives by attempting to use their respective mandates to promote the idea of creating autonomous Czecho-Slovak and southern Slav—Slovene, Croat, and Serb—states within the empire. For example, Czechs from across the political spectrum founded the "Czech Union" in November 1916. Although the Reichsrat was suspended at the beginning of the war, it was reconvened in 1917, and on May 29, 1917, Czech members of the Austrian imperial parliament passed a motion demanding that the historical lands of the Bohemian crown and Slovakia be made into one state and that the monarchy be reconstituted into equal federal states. On the following day, Slovene, Croat, and Serb delegates submitted the same program for a southern Slav state. Both these proposals insisted on ending Austro-Hungarian dualism, and they were constitutionally problematic because they involved territories in the kingdom of Hungary (Slovakia and Croatia) that technically were outside the legislative jurisdiction of the Austrian Reichsrat.

It is important to distinguish in this context between autonomy, a negotiable amount of national self-determination within a federally reorganized empire, and national independence, the creation of individual states at the expense of the empire. Well into the war, the Entente Powers and many of the representatives of the individual national groups within the empire assumed that some kind of democratic and federal, multinational, state would take the place of Austria-Hungary.

In November 1916, the death of Emperor Francis Joseph after sixty-eight years on the throne and the succession of Charles—Charles I as Emperor of Austria and Charles IV as King of Hungary—appeared to give Austria-Hungary one last chance. Charles recognized that he needed to get Austria-Hungary out of the war and simultaneously reorganize the empire to placate the respective demands of its minorities for more national autonomy. But he was neither strong enough to abandon the alliance with Germany, in which Austria-Hungary played an increasingly subordinate role, nor innovative enough to restructure the empire. The February Revolution of 1917 in Russia, which disposed of the czar; the United States' declaration of war on Germany on April 2, 1917 and on Austria-Hungary on December 3, 1917, which turned the conflict into a crusade for democracy; and the Bolsheviks'

October Revolution, which threw Russia into a state of revolutionary civil war, created new ideological and strategic circumstances that had far-reaching implications for the future of Austria-Hungary.

When the czar disappeared as an Entente ally, the scepter of imperial Russian autocracy and a Pan-Slavic threat vanished with him. The disposal of the czar lessened somewhat the western and southern Slavs' traditional apprehensions about Russia. It also deprived Austria-Hungary of its historical mission of preventing czarist expansion and made much more plausible the Entente Powers' assertion that they were fighting for freedom and democracy—and against German and Austro-Hungarian imperial aggression and tyranny. Furthermore, in the American declaration of war Woodrow Wilson underscored the United States' commitment to freedom, liberty, democracy, and the rule of law, which explicitly included protecting and realizing the rights of small nations. Because of shifts in Entente policy and propaganda, Austria-Hungary became what its detractors had claimed it was: a "prison of nations."[10]

Lenin also championed the idea of the rights of smaller nations before and after the Bolshevik Revolution, although in a completely different way. For example, in a 1914 tract, *The Rights of Nations to National Self-Determination*, he advocated the idea of the rights of minority nations in multinational empires to secession and the formation of independent national states as a means of promoting the deterioration of the Russian and Austro-Hungarian empires from within. For Lenin, the idea of national self-determination was a vehicle for social revolution. In 1918, Lenin's propagation of peace; social reform; "complete equality of rights for all nations; the right of nations to self-determination; the unity of the workers of all nations,"[11] and the Bolsheviks' recognition of Finland, Estonia, Latvia, Lithuania, Poland, Ukraine, Georgia, and Armenia made a profound impression on the national minorities in Austria-Hungary.

Although the Bolsheviks recognized these national states in the name of national self-determination, there were less altruistic motives at work, too. In the negotiations preceding the Central Powers' conclusion, on March 3, 1918, of a separate peace with Bolshevik Russia on the eastern front, the Treaty of Brest-Litovsk, the Central Powers demanded that Bolshevik Russia recognize and evacuate Finland, Estonia, Latvia, Lithuania, and Ukraine as well as unconditionally forfeit western Belarus and Poland, which were to fall under German and Austro-Hungarian sovereignty.

This condition was part of an imperial German *Mitteleuropa* strategy. As late as August 1918 strategic planners produced plans for carving up Russia into client states and "colonizing" the east. Russia was to become a "German India" in the Kaiserreich's new empire. Confronted with a foreign war he needed to end and a civil war he had to win, Lenin had to consolidate Bolshevik military and political resources for domestic use. He did so by accepting the unfavorable terms the Germans dictated at Brest-Litovsk and jettisoned those newly formed national states revolutionary Russia could not retain for the time being. He could afford to be generous because he had every intention of getting them back later.

According to the theory of Marxism-Leninism and its practice under Lenin and Stalin, national self-determination did not include the right to reactionary politics. During the civil war between the Reds and the Whites, a disjointed coalition of democrats, nationalists, and czarists, the Bolsheviks reclaimed Ukraine, along with other "republics" that had been established on the periphery of the Bolshevik Russia, like Georgia and Armenia, and they almost repossessed Poland. Nevertheless, Lenin's theoretical appeals to national self-determination before 1917 and his political practice thereof during the initial phase of the Bolshevik Revolution, regardless of his motives, threw a completely different light on the raison d'être of the Habsburgs' multinational empire for its Slavic inhabitants as well as the Entente Powers. Russia's multinational empire appeared to be breaking up into a collection of independent Slavic national states. The old czarist threat had been replaced by a new Communist one, whose containment was to become one of the primary goals of the democratic reorganization of Central Europe.

Wilson's perspectives on national self-determination were, of course, radically different from Lenin's. The famous "Fourteen Points" he outlined on January 18, 1918, to describe the United States' objectives in the war were partly a result of the Entente Powers' inability to articulate their joint war aims. In an attempt to keep Bolshevik Russia in the war, which was in the process of negotiating a separate peace at Brest-Litovsk, Wilson called for the "evacuation of all Russian territory" and the "independent determination of her [Russia's] own political development and national policy." Along with the evacuation and restoration of Romania, Serbia, and Montenegro, he demanded a "readjustment of the borders of Italy . . . along clearly recognizable lines of nationality," and as a novelty in Entente policy, he explicitly put the reestablishment of Poland on the postwar agenda: "An independent Polish state should be erected which should include the territories inhabited by indisputably Polish populations, which should be assured free and secure access to the sea." His formulation regarding "the peoples of Austria-Hungary" was sufficiently vague: They "should be accorded the freest opportunity of autonomous development." However, in the spring and summer, the Entente Powers abandoned the idea of an "autonomous development" for "the peoples of Austria-Hungary" within the empire and adopted the form of national self-determination that émigré politicians from Austria-Hungary had propagated: the creation of independent national states at the expense of the empire.

Austria-Hungary's apparently unwavering commitment to its alliance with Germany, an increasing amount of discontent within the empire itself, and the "Congress of Oppressed Races of Austria-Hungary," which leading emigre politicians attended in Rome in April 1918, all helped convince the Entente Powers that maintaining Austria-Hungary was neither desirable nor feasible. In Rome, the Czecho-Slovak and Jugo-Slav delegations declared that they no longer wanted to live under the auspices of the empire. Czech and Slovak émigrés then proceeded to hammer out an outline for a joint program in Pittsburgh in May 1918. Within the empire itself, social unrest due to the hardships of the war and unfulfilled demands for autonomy un-leashed centrifugal political and national forces.

From the Entente's strategic perspective of weakening Germany, replac-ing Austria-Hungary with a series of smaller, democratic, national states had the concomitant benefit of depriving Germany of its hitherto most reliable ally. During World War I, Entente policy toward Austria-Hungary shifted from accommodation to vacillation before becoming decisive late in the day. The recognition of the Czecho-Slovak National Committee in Paris as an as-sociated belligerent power by France, Britain, and the United States between the end of June and the beginning of September 1918 was a death warrant for Austria-Hungary.

In mid-October Emperor Charles finally issued a manifesto declaring the federal reorganization of the empire along the lines of autonomous na-tional states, but this proclamation was as futile as it was late. The Czecho-Slovak National Committee in Paris already had appointed a government, with Masaryk as president and Beneš as foreign minister. Seeing that the monarchy was falling apart, the German members of the Austrian imperial parliament convened on October 21, 1918, to form the Provisional Nation-al Assembly of German-Austria, in an attempt to exercise national self-determination for German-speaking Austrians, too. This body wanted to erect a state for *all* the monarchy's German-speaking inhabitants, and it ex-pressed its desire to enter into a confederation with the other emerging na-tional states. (None of German-Austria's new neighbors took this offer seri-ously.)

Before the end of the month, the kingdom of Hungary dissolved its as-sociation with Austria and proclaimed complete independence, thus ending the Dual Monarchy; nationalists proclaimed the Czechoslovak Republic in Prague; and the "National Council of Slovenes, Croats, and Serbs" consti-tuted itself in Zagreb, the capital of Croatia, to start forming a southern Slav state in conjunction with the émigrés of the Yugoslav National Committee and representatives of the Serbian government in exile. By November 12, the Entente had signed armistices with Germany and Austria-Hungary; Em-peror Wilhelm II and Emperor Charles had abdicated; and the republics of Germany and German-Austria had been proclaimed. The emperors and the empires were gone, but no one knew what the frontiers of the so-called suc-cessor states were.

The Resurrection of Poland, 1918–1922

One of the few things the Entente Powers' decision to dismember Austria-Hungary had in common with their declaration to reestablish an indepen-dent Poland was that both came late in the war. Woodrow Wilson—who em-phasized the importance of a "united, independent, and autonomous Poland"[12] in January 1917, three months before the United States entered the war—was the only Western leader to take seriously the issue of Polish in-dependence as a matter of principle from the very start, and the United States' entry into the war put it on the Entente agenda. The Western European members of the Entente, who felt that raising this issue would alienate their Russian ally, showed little interest in an independent Poland and instead preferred to tinker behind the scenes with various autonomy schemes which included at one point a Polish kingdom dissociated from Russia and Germany but under Habsburg patronage.[13]

But then, the disappearance of the czar as an Entente ally, Bolshevik Revolution, the declaration of Polish independence as an objective of the United States in Wilson's "Fourteen Points," and the Bolsheviks' abandonment of the Entente alliance all helped make the reestablishment of Poland a politically and tactically desirable alternative for the Western European members of the Entente, which initially were disinclined to consider the issue. On June 3, 1918, France, Britain, and Italy formally endorsed Poland's independence as a war aim, at a meeting of the Entente's Supreme War Council in Versailles. It would be a mistake, however, to say that the Entente Powers "created" Poland; rather, they sanctioned its reestablishment after the fact. Poland emerged from the vacuum created by the collapse of the Russian, German, and Austro-Hungarian empires at the end of the war.

Czechoslovak and Yugoslav protagonists for national independence had it easier in that they had to contend with only one empire, Austria-Hungary, whereas the Polish situation was complicated by the late-eighteenth-century partitions of the Polish–Lithuanian Republic, on the one hand, and the World War I alliance systems, on the other. Poles had to cope with three empires: Russia, Germany, and Austria-Hungary. Russia was a member of the Entente, whereas Germany and Austria-Hungary formed the backbone of the Central Powers. Russia occupied approximately three-fifths of the old Polish–Lithuania Republic, and Prussia and Habsburg Austria had split the remaining two-fifths between themselves. Almost 2 million Poles served as soldiers in the German, Russian, and Austro-Hungarian armies during the war, and the Poles on the offensive side of the line were "liberating" Poland to the same extent that those on the defensive side were "defending" it for one of the emperors or empires. Under these circumstances, the Poles' choice of allies could not have been easy: for autocratic, czarist Russia and the Entente democracies, or vice versa, the Entente democracies which supported autocratic, czarist Russia against Germany and Austria-Hungary; for imperial Germany against imperial Russia; or, perhaps the most desirable alternative, for *Gott, Kaiser, und Vaterland*, the preservation of the relative liberality that prevailed in the imperial Austrian province of Galicia.

The two most famous agitators for Polish independence, Roman Dmowski (1864–1939), a conservative, and Józef Piłsudski (1867–1935), a socialist, held nearly diametrically opposed opinions of how Poland was to be restored. Dmowski, born and raised in the Russian partition, was a representative of the so-called realist school. He thought that Poland could be restored under the auspices of the Romanov dynasty and that the war could facilitate this. However, his proposals fell on deaf ears at the czar's court, and after the Central Powers occupied all of the ethnic Poland, he emigrated to the West, where he agitated for Polish independence (and was seconded by a famous concert pianist, Ignacy Jan Paderewski).

In addition to mobilizing public support among Western European and North American Polish immigrants and their descendants, Dmowski recruited Polish émigrés and immigrants for a small "autonomous Polish army," a unit that fought under the French high command. In August 1917 he convened the Polish National Committee in Paris, which the Western Entente allies recognized as the legitimate representative of the Polish people without committing themselves to reestablishing an independent Polish state. One of the Western Entente's foremost concerns was not to antagonize the Russian governments—be they czarist, democratic provisional, or Bolshevik—with the Polish issue, because it was of supreme tactical importance to keep Russia in the alliance and in the war. The eastern front tied down German men and matériel that otherwise could be deployed on the western front.

In this context, it is important to recall that the German government and high command actively supported the Bolsheviks, based on the assumption that domestic unrest in Russia would detract from the Russian war effort so as to free German forces from the eastern front for deployment in the west. German authorities facilitated the return of Lenin, who was isolated in Swiss exile, and thirty other revolutionaries to Russia via Germany in April 1917, and the Bolshevik Revolution subsequently produced the results the Germans desired: a collapse of Russian resistance on the eastern front. But this happened too late in the war to affect Germany's prospects in the west.

The Bolshevik Revolution and revolutionary Russia's ensuing abandonment of the Entente strengthened Dmowski's position, and he argued that a reestablished Polish state would fulfill the dual function of preventing German and Bolshevik expansion in the future. Dmowski's personal adversary in the politics of Polish reestablishment was Józef Piłsudski, an insurrectionary, romantic, socialist, and passionate nationalist who was convinced that Russia was Poland's primary and natural enemy. Born and raised in a patriotic Polish family in Lithuanian Vilnius, Piłsudski, an innocent bystander to an anticzarist conspiracy in his youth, spent five years in penal exile in eastern Siberia as a young man, an experience that was one source of his anti-Russian sentiments. Piłsudski was above all a military man who saw the war as a vehicle for destroying the partitioning powers, and his role to prepare for the aftermath. His means of doing so was not to collaborate with Germany but to cooperate with Austria-Hungary against Russia in public in the short run and to conspire for Polish independence in the long run.

At the beginning of the war, Piłsudski commanded with distinction one of the three brigades of the "Polish legion" that the Austrian imperial authorities had formed, a military unit whose fame in Polish history is considerably larger than any of its actual achievements. But he soon recognized that neither Germany nor Austria-Hungary was remotely inclined to promote Polish national interests; on the contrary, they were in the process of dividing up those portions of the Russian partition they had conquered as part of a cooperative *Mitteleuropa* scheme. Therefore, he dedicated himself to conspiratorial work, resigned his commission, and, after publicly encouraging Polish troops not to swear an oath of allegiance to the Central Powers, ended up in 1917 in a German jail as a Polish national hero.

By the end of the summer of 1918, it was clear to the members of the German high command that the war could not be won, and in order to prepare for the coming period of transition, they established the so-called Regency Council, composed of a group of Polish representatives, which was theoretically autonomous but actually dependent on the military governor of occupied Poland. On November 10, 1918, one day before Germany signed an armistice with the Entente, Piłsudski was released from prison and returned to Warsaw as a national hero. The Regency Council folded and turned over the affairs of state to Piłsudski, who declared himself the provisional head of state and commander in chief of the yet to be constituted Polish army. The manner in which Piłsudski seized the initiative created a peculiar situation, as neither Dmowski and the Polish National Committee in Paris, which the Entente Powers had recognized as the legitimate representatives of the Polish people, nor the Entente Powers themselves were involved.

The advent of peace in Western Europe coincided with the beginning of war, or a series of wars, for Poland. Piłsudski's fait accompli reestablished Poland, although no one knew where the frontiers of this new state were. Polish elections in January 1919, the joint appointment of Paderewski as both prime minister and foreign minister, the designation of Dmowski as the head of the Polish peace delegation at Versailles, and Piłsudski's position as commander in chief consolidated the domestic political situation in Poland. However, despite the division of powers and offices, Piłsudski assumed the most authority in the immediate postwar years. The Allied Supreme Council in Versailles, made up of representatives of France, Britain, Italy, and the United States, presided over the negotiation of Poland's western and southwestern frontiers with Germany and Czechoslovakia. But, the situation in the east was wide open.

The withdrawal of German and Austro-Hungarian troops from Belarus, Ukraine, and Poland created a power vacuum that both Poland and Russia wanted to fill. Bolshevik Russia, whose withdrawal from the Entente after the separate peace of Brest-Litovsk had ruptured Russian relationships with the West, was in the midst of a civil war and a series of conflicts with nations striving for national self-determination, whose interests alternately coincided and conflicted with those of the White Russians, and it had to combat simultaneously allied expeditionary forces that had been dispatched to punish the Bolsheviks for breaching the alliance. Poland's eastern frontier was thus not negotiated by diplomats; it was established by military force. Consequently, it assumed more the character of a cease-fire line, a perimeter sanctioned after the cessation of hostilities, than a diplomatically arbitrated international border.

The application of the principle of national self-determination to the new states emerging in east Central Europe proved to be a futile task. One of its guiding principles was to create states that were ethnically homogeneous, but the intricate patchwork of peoples made this virtually impossible. Historical frontiers and arguments, topography or "natural" borders as a means of ensuring national security by establishing defendable frontiers, and whether the respective states in question had been allies or enemies of the Entente also had to be taken into account. Furthermore, all these variables had to be calculated into the larger framework of the respective national interests of the victorious powers in the region.

There were two Polish positions on its future frontiers. Dmowski and a series of conservatives favored a straightforward application of the principle of historical national self-determination—a reestablishment of the borders of the Polish–Lithuanian Republic of 1772, which included Lithuania and parts of Latvia, Belarus, and western Ukraine—whereas Piłsudski wanted a federation of countries, in which Poland would undoubtedly play a leading role, roughly coextensive in size with the old Polish–Lithuanian Republic. These aspirations conflicted with the Entente Powers' emphasis on ethnic borders, or, as Wilson envisioned the frontiers of Poland in his Fourteen Points: "territories inhabited by indisputably Polish populations." The application of the ethnic principle to Poland's western frontiers was difficult. It functioned well enough in the Versailles negotiations, in which the Entente Powers had direct influence. But it did not satisfy the parties involved, because ethnically mixed German–Polish regions and hence minorities could not be avoided on both sides of the border. The establishment of the Polish–German frontier—the Danzig corridor, which gave Poland the "free and secure access to the sea" that Wilson had promised, the free city of Danzig, and the large part of Silesia that Germany forfeited—became a constant source of German–Polish tensions. A commission of Entente experts recognized that the application of the ethnic principle would be even more problematic on Poland's eastern frontier, and because of the Russian civil war, there were no official representatives of Russia at Versailles with whom an agreement could have been negotiated.

Piłsudski was a patriot and a man of action, not a diplomat. His vision of Poland and the force of circumstances compelled him to act on his own before and after the process of peacemaking began in Versailles. As a military man he was convinced that the most important decisions would be made on the battlefield, not at the conference table. The end of the Great War marked the beginning of a series of armed conflicts for Poland, the largest being the Polish–Ukrainian war and the Polish–Bolshevik war. When Austria-Hungary broke apart in 1918, Ukrainian regiments occupied Eastern Galicia, the part of the Austrian partition of historical Poland that had a predominantly Ukrainian population, and proclaimed the short-lived Western Ukrainian People's Republic. Piłsudski then organized an offensive that by June 1919 drove them back to the old Austrian imperial frontier and contributed to the collapse of the Western Ukrainian Republic the following month. In February 1919 an unplanned clash between Polish and Bolshevik troops in western Belarus escalated into a full-fledged conflict that lasted for well over two years.

Piłsudski's vision of Poland was based on plans to drive Russia off the ter-

CENTRAL EUROPEAN STATES
AFTER WORLD WAR I

─────── Borders of the German, Russian, and Austro-Hungarian empires in 1914

─────── International frontiers after World War I peace settlements

[dark block] Territories lost by the German Empire

[light block] Territories lost by Russia

[medium block] Territories lost by Austria-Hungary

ritory of the Polish–Lithuanian Republic of 1772, and he was prepared to do everything in his power to achieve this objective. He also encouraged Lithuanian, Belarussian, and Ukrainian aspirations for national independence insofar as they corresponded to Polish interests and claims. Piłsudski suggested several schemes for the creation of a federation or confederation of states, or at least an alliance among them, in which Poland would have a central role. He was convinced that the prospects for Poland's future were proportionately related to the decline of Russia's territory and power in the region, and he wanted to see Russia reduced to its ethnic territorial core, a area roughly coextensive with Russia's preimperial or sixteenth-century frontiers. (Before 1989, the idea of independent Baltic, Belarussian, and Ukrainian states was a feature of one of the deterioration or "de-imperialization" scenarios for the Soviet Union. At that time, most analysts agreed that the Soviet Union might let the Baltic states go but assumed that the Soviets would balk at the idea of Belarussian or Ukrainian independence.)

During the Russian civil war Piłsudski refrained from supporting the White Russians, many of whom were Greater Russian nationalists interested in restoring the territorial integrity of the czarist empire at the expense of an independent Poland, and he initially saw the Bolsheviks, who had made substantial concessions to national self-determination, as the lesser of the two evils. Extreme interpretations of Piłsudski and his intentions are that he was either an altruist who was promoting the independence of other nations seeking national self-determination or a representative of "small-power imperialism"[14] who wanted to polonize the German *Mitteleuropa* idea by moving its capital from Berlin to Warsaw. In any event, Piłsudski's desire to expand Poland's territory and influence at the expense of Russia, and the Bolsheviks' intention of maintaining as much of the empire as they could, led to the Polish–Bolshevik war.

During the first phase of the war, Polish forces under Piłsudski seized the initiative and advanced along a front that extended from Lithuania through Belarus to Ukraine. Allied negotiators in Paris made a number of proposals concerning *temporary* eastern frontiers for Poland, each of which fell short of Poland's historical claims, and in January 1920 Lenin even proposed an armistice with generous territorial terms.

Needless to say, Piłsudski did not trust the Bolsheviks, and Western European attitudes toward the Polish–Bolshevik conflict were split. On the one hand, the French premier, Georges Clemenceau, had formulated the idea of a *cordon sanitaire*, a belt of free states that would insulate Western Europe from the Bolshevik threat. (Furthermore, France needed a viable and reliable ally on Germany's eastern border, so Poland was to assume the function that Russia had fulfilled in this respect.) On the other hand, Britain's prime minister, Lloyd George, wanted to establish an ethnic Poland. His highest priority appeared to be finding a modus vivendi with Russia, and he demonstrated neither patience nor sympathy with the Poles or their problems. A turning point in the Polish–Bolshevik conflict was Piłsudski's decision in 1920 to support the democratic nationalist Ukrainian Republic (not to be confused with the ephemeral Western Ukrainian People's Republic he had dislodged from Galicia in 1919) against the interests and claims of the Bolsheviks.

The virtual collapse of central authority after the Bolshevik Revolution in 1917 created auspicious circumstances for the establishment of Ukrainian independence. Ukrainian nationalists proclaimed a republic in November which the Bolsheviks formally recognized in December. However, they also criticized the Ukrainian People's Republic as "bourgeois" and supported the Ukrainian Soviets. Pressed by the Bolsheviks, the Ukrainian Republic asked for and received support from the Germans against the Bolsheviks—*Mitteleuropa* once again—until the end of the war. Thereafter, it became a battleground for Russian Reds and Whites as well as Ukrainian Bolsheviks and nationalists. Between December 1917 and July 1920, Kiev changed hands five times. Piłsudski's offer to the Ukrainian nationalists was that Poland would help ensure Ukrainian independence by expelling the Bolsheviks from the Ukraine if Ukraine would recognize the 1772 frontier of Poland, in other words, forfeit the Ukrainian minorities living inside Poland's historical borders. The establishment of an independent Ukrainian state also was the first step in Piłsudski's grand strategy for creating a confederation of East Central European states at the expense of Russia.

A Polish expeditionary force invaded Ukraine in June 1920 and achieved its initial objective of dislodging the Bolsheviks, but this adventure nearly ended in a catastrophe. Piłsudski overextended Polish troops and resources, overestimated his Ukrainian allies, and underestimated the Bolsheviks, who launched a furious counterattack all along the Polish–Bolshevik front. By the beginning of August, the Red Army was approaching Warsaw, and Poland's fate seemed to be sealed. Then the Polish forces destroyed three Bolshevik armies in an unexpected and tactically brilliant victory at the Battle of Warsaw. The Red Army had plans to march on to Berlin to "world revolution" by force. Whether Bolshevik Russia's resources would have been sufficient for this ambitious enterprise is questionable. But the fact that the Poles stopped the Bolsheviks in Warsaw is often regarded as the national achievement of "saving the West." (Soviet historians subsequently maintained that the Polish victory was more the result of blunders made by the Red Army than of Polish military ingenuity.)

After the Polish victory at Warsaw, Piłsudski launched a counteroffensive that forced back the Russians all along the front. Both parties were exhausted. Poland proposed an armistice and a neutral place, Riga, the capital of Latvia, for negotiating peace, and the Bolsheviks accepted the offer. The Western powers were not involved in negotiating the Treaty of Riga. It was strictly a bilateral Polish–Bolshevik affair, signed on March 18, 1921, and recognized by other powers after the fact. From the perspective of Poland's claims to its historical frontiers, the treaty was a compromise because it forfeited approximately half of those territories in the east—120,000 square miles—that had been part of the Polish-Lithuanian Republic before the partitions.

The Riga agreement also represented a substantial gain because the Polish frontier was considerably farther east than the ethnic frontier that the

Entente Commission for Polish Affairs had proposed in June 1919 or the so-called Curzon Line that the Western European allies had suggested in a cease-fire proposal to end the Polish–Bolshevik war in July 1920 (named after the British foreign secretary, Lord Curzon, who signed the diplomatic cable sent to Bolshevik Russia offering it as a frontier, along with cease-fire conditions). It was approximately equidistant between the "ethnic" borders the Entente had proposed in 1919 and 1920 and the 1772 frontier Poland wanted to regain.

At the end of the Polish–Bolshevik war, Piłsudski also put the finishing touch on Poland's frontiers by occupying the Vilnius region, which had long been a source of conflict between Poland and Lithuania. Both Poles and Lithuanians had strong attachments to Vilnius. It was the historical capital of the grand duchy of Lithuania, but it had also become a predominantly Polish city and a center of Polish culture (in addition to being Piłsudski's birthplace and hometown). The region's ethnic composition was intricate, and all Piłsudski's attempts to cajole the Lithuanians into some type of federation failed. The occupation of the Vilnius region and its subsequent incorporation into Poland in 1922 was Piłsudski's last accomplishment. The promethean achievements of founding the Polish Republic and defeating the Russians made Piłsudski one of Poland's greatest contemporary national heroes.

Like its remote predecessor, the Polish–Lithuanian Republic, which was half Polish and half Roman Catholic, the Republic of Poland was a multinational and multidenominational state, which was approximately two-thirds Polish and two-thirds Roman Catholic. However, unlike its historical forerunner, the Polish Republic had the ideology of a national state, which made its ethnic and religious minorities a domestic problem or, conversely, made Poland a greater problem for its minorities: 5 million Ukrainians, 3 million Jews, 2 million Belarussians; and 1 million Germans. Furthermore, neither Poland nor its neighbors were satisfied with the Polish frontiers. From the Polish viewpoint, they fell short of the historical frontiers of 1772. From the Entente perspective, they violated the principle of ethnic borders. For the Germans, they were part of the humiliating Treaty of Versailles, whose revision became an objective of German foreign policy after 1919.

The Entente also ceded part of Teschen, a small border duchy to which Poland and Czechoslovakia mutually had laid claims, to Czechoslovakia at the peak of the Polish–Bolshevik war in June 1920, which the Poles considered a stab in the back, and this decision spoiled Polish–Czechoslovak bilateral relations from the start.[15] Bolshevik Russia, reconstituted as the Soviet Union in 1923, viewed the frontiers of Poland as tentative and negotiable, as Stalin was to demonstrate amply in the future.

Dictating Peace and Drawing Borders: The Treaties of
Versailles, St. Germain, and Trianon, 1919–1920

Historians with different national and methodological dispositions have defended or criticized the Versailles peace settlements ever since they were concluded. Versailles refers both to the treaty concluded with Germany on

June 28, 1919, and to the various settlements with the former allies of Germany that also were negotiated in the suburbs of Paris: the Treaty of St. Germain with Austria on September 10, 1919; the Treaty of Neuilly with Bulgaria on November 27, 1919; the Treaty of Trianon with Hungary on June 4, 1920; and the Treaty of Sèvres with Turkey on August 20, 1920. There are differing opinions about how good or bad the Versailles peace settlements actually were and to what extent they helped to lay the foundations for the next world war. However, it is indisputable that the German reception of the Treaty of Versailles was almost unanimously negative. Versailles was a national humiliation.

Germany was not the biggest loser in World War I. Austria-Hungary was, and the dismemberment of the Austro-Hungarian dual monarchy created a power vacuum that Germany was to fill. Since Germany was the biggest *intact* loser of World War I, more attention naturally has been paid to the consequences of the Treaty of Versailles with Germany than to the repercussions of the Treaty of St. Germain with Austria or the Treaty of Trianon with Hungary. Immediately after the war, Austrians and Hungarians felt the same way about St. Germain and Trianon as the Germans felt about Versailles, but as small states, their national discontent did not have the same political import as did Germany's dissatisfaction.

The Entente Powers did not negotiate the peace treaties with the delegations from the Central Powers. The representatives of Germany, Austria, and Hungary, although they functioned as observers and occasionally were allowed to testify, were not partners in the negotiations with the Entente Powers; on the contrary, the defeated states were objects of negotiation among the victors. In this respect, the designation "dictated peace" is an accurate description of the so-called negotiation process, and the various Entente Allies also attempted to realize divergent objectives through the negotiations.

The fact that the conditions of the Treaty of Versailles were harsh is well known, and they poisoned Germany's relations with the victorious powers. Germany had to assume responsibility for the war and to pay reparations, which retarded its postwar economic development. It lost territories in the east to Poland and in the west to France, along with its colonies overseas. The German armed forces were drastically reduced and limited in the future. The French premier George Clemenceau was the driving force behind the vindictive treatment of Germany, which included the exploitation of German natural resources and the demilitarization of the Rhineland, because he was convinced that the security of France would increase proportionately with the diminishment of Germany's potential. He even advanced the idea of a revised French–German frontier—the Rhine River—that would have the advantage of being a "natural" and strategic border (and incidentally coincided with the historical frontiers of Napoleonic France), but this proposal was rejected by the other Allies as too radical. Nonetheless, Versailles helped undermine the chances the Weimar Republic had as a democracy, because the national humiliation that accompanied it fueled a conservative-reactionary backlash.

According to Woodrow Wilson, national self-determination was to be one of the guiding principles in the establishment of the new European order. But the manner in which it was applied created a legacy of discontent among Germans, Austrians, and Hungarians, because they saw it repeatedly violated to their disadvantage. The various commissions that the Entente employed arbitrate the numerous conflicting border claims after World War I were more expert than their later reputations, but they were confronted with insoluble problems created by ethnically mixed regions. The Entente organized plebiscites in some border regions to allow their inhabitants to decide for themselves which state they would prefer to inhabit, but in most cases these plebiscites resulted in the predictable dissatisfaction of the ethnic minority and neighboring state that lost them.

In addition, previous commitments had been made to powers that had fought with the Entente, such as Italy and Romania, and they had to be honored. Associate powers like Czechoslovakia also had a status that had to be recognized. Historical arguments, as well, carried a certain amount of weight if they could be supported by economic and strategic arguments. Therefore, the application of the principle of national self-determination was complex and destined to foster discontent. The negotiation of the Austrian, Czechoslovak, and Hungarian borders provides a number of examples of how inconsistently these criteria were applied.

Unlike the other national groups in the Habsburgs' multinational empire, German-speaking Austrians had virtually no tradition of striving for national independence. Based on the idea of the German nation as a historical, linguistic, and cultural community, German-speaking Austrians considered themselves Germans: not Prussians but Germans, just as the inhabitants of Bavaria or Hamburg were Germans and not Prussians. The foundation of a *kleindeutsch* or "smaller German" Kaiserreich in 1871 without Habsburg Austria had created a political monopoly on the idea of being German as well as an asymmetry between the Habsburg variant of Austrian-German culture and the Prussian imperial concept of "German-German" culture. Furthermore, after 1871, "imperial Germans" began to treat their smaller German-Austrian neighbors and their polyglot empire with a certain amount of condescension. Still, despite the obvious differences in traditions and mentalities, Austrian-Germans nonetheless considered themselves Germans.

By the time the Republic of German-Austria had been proclaimed on November 12, 1918, it was clear that none of its neighboring states was interested in a confederation of democracies that somehow could assume the place of the old empire, and the only viable economic and political alternative the founding fathers of the republic saw was an Anschluss: a unification of German-Austria with a democratic Germany. As Germans, the representatives of German-Austria saw an Anschluss with a democratic Germany as a perfectly legitimate expression of Austrian national self-determination, and the proclamation of the republic included an Anschluss declaration: German-Austria was to be part of Germany.

At the St. Germain peace conference, however, the name of German-

Austria was not only unilaterally abbreviated to Austria; the Entente Powers also forbade an *Anschluss* because it would enlarge the territory of Germany and surround Czech Bohemia and Moravia with Germans. It also would give Germany, one malcontent, a common border with Hungary (which, as we will see, had every reason for being another malcontent) and would create German national frontiers with Italy and Yugoslavia. Consequently, Austria became an independent state against its own will, a "state no one wanted."[16]

Based on previous Entente commitments and strategic considerations, Italy was granted the Brenner Pass frontier and a Tyrolean minority of 220,000 at the expense of Austria. Troops from the Kingdom of Slovenes, Croats, and Serbs, which had been proclaimed on December 1, 1918, invaded parts of southern Austria inhabited by Slovene minorities in an attempt to claim territory by force, but they met the resistance of a hastily organized "national guard." This border conflict eventually was arbitrated with Entente intervention. (Yugoslavia did not become the official name of the country until 1929 when an authoritarian coup dispensed with the constitutional monarchy proclaimed in 1920. For the sake of convenience, we will call it the kingdom of Yugoslavia.)

More than 3 million German-Austrians lived along the southern, western, and northern frontiers of Czech Bohemia and Moravia. They were German-Austrians, not Germans, as they had been inhabitants of the Austrian empire since 1526 when the Habsburgs first assumed the Bohemian crown. Although the Austrian officials themselves recognized that they would have to abandon the German-Austrians in western Bohemia and northern Bohemia and Moravia (who had expressed their desire to be incorporated as Germans into Germany), Austria used an ethnic argument to acquire those regions along its northern frontier, which were almost exclusively German speaking but historically Bohemia. However, the Czechoslovak Republic claimed and was granted the historical borders of the kingdom of Bohemia, along with its large German minority. The frontier of the historical kingdom of Bohemia also ran along the rim of the Bohemian Basin and mountainous border areas, which also gave Czechoslovakia a natural, and hence defendable, frontier.

Given these various concerns, the Czechs viewed the German minority as the least of all potential evils, and during the peace negotiations one old solution to the problem of multinational empires resurfaced under the new circumstances of smaller, multiethnic, democratic states. Beneš spoke of "accepting as a basis of national rights the principles applied in the constitution of the Swiss Republic, that is, to make the Czecho-Slovak Republic a sort of Switzerland, taking into consideration, of course, the special conditions of Bohemia."[17] Although the Germans in Bohemia and Moravia were perhaps the best-treated minority in Central Europe during the interwar period, the Czechoslovak Republic did not succeed in becoming "a sort of Switzerland," and the status of Germans in Czechoslovakia became a primary point of domestic and foreign policy contention for the new state.

Using the ethnic argument once again, Austria demanded territories in western Hungary because they had German-speaking majorities; however,

Hungary did not feel constrained to cede them to Austria because they historically were part of the kingdom of Hungary. The contested area between Austria and Hungary also had relatively small Slovak and Croat minorities of 3 and 10 percent, respectively, and at the peace conference, Czechoslovak representatives proposed granting the area to neither Austria nor Hungary but suggested creating a "Slavic corridor" between the Czechoslovak Republic and the kingdom of Yugoslavia that would separate the feuding parties. This proposal would have had the dual benefit of giving both Slavic states a territorial bridge or avenue of secure passage between their traditional enemies and would compensate the western and southern Slavs for the fact that protoimperialistic Germans and Magyars had separated these Slavic nations from each other in the Middle Ages.[18] However, this plan was dropped, and Allied mediation came up with a compromise that more or less solved the problem to the dissatisfaction of both Austria and Hungary. The parts of western Hungary that Austria incorporated became a new Austrian province, Burgenland, but Hungary did not cede to Austria all the territories earmarked for Austrian acquisition.

The kingdom of Hungary wanted to use its historical frontiers as an argument for maintaining them after the war. However, immediately after the war Hungary slid into a state of domestic chaos that made it unable to assert or defend its national interests. The democratic republic proclaimed in November 1918 folded in March 1919 when Béla Kun, an admirer and protégé of Lenin, proclaimed a "Soviet Republic" which ruled radically for 133 days. The counterrevolution and reactionary politics that followed led to the establishment of a new kingdom of Hungary, which did not have a king but elected a "regent," the last commander in chief of the Austro-Hungarian imperial navy, Admiral Miklós Horthy, to manage the affairs of state until a king was elected. (Hungary incidentally remained a kingdom without a king until 1945, although Horthy developed regal pretensions.)

All of Hungary's neighbors had border claims, and they used the general postwar chaos to realize them. The application of the ethnic principle of national self-determination literally dismembered the historical kingdom of Hungary, which lost two-thirds of its territories and shrank in population from a multinational 18.2 million to a relatively homogeneous 7.6 million. After the Treaty of Trianon, roughly 3.3 million, or one-third, of the Magyars from the historical kingdom of Hungary ended up as "new minorities" outside the frontiers of Hungary.

The Entente Powers had promised Romania large territorial gains in the eastern and southern parts of the kingdom—Transylvania, eastern Hungary, and the Banat—and they honored their commitments to a considerable extent at the conference table. More than 2 million Magyars became Romanian citizens in the process. In addition, as a component part of the kingdom of Yugoslavia, Croatia claimed the historical borders of the medieval kingdom of Croatia, and the Yugoslavs also annexed the western Banat region: a province whose population was predominantly Serbian but included a Hungarian minority of around 500,000. Then the Yugoslavs exchanged blows with Romania over the adjoining eastern half of the Banat until the Entente intervened. The Czechoslovak Republic, which had argued for the establishment of the historical frontiers of Bohemia and Moravia against Austria's ethnic claims, used ethnic and strategic arguments against Hungary to define its Slovak frontier. It not only demanded the areas inhabited by Slovaks and the Carpathian Ukraine,[19] but also pressed for a frontier along the Danube River as a "natural border" with Hungary. Czechoslovakia was granted both, and it acquired the fertile lowlands south of ethnic Slovakia and a minority of nearly 1 million Magyars in the process.

The kingdom of Hungary had formed a cohesive political unit for more than one thousand years, and for Hungarians, the loss of 60 percent of its inhabitants along with two-thirds of its territory represented the destruction of an organic whole. Furthermore, Hungarian nationalists viewed the frontiers of the kingdom of St. Stephen as a divine entitlement. From the Hungarian national perspective, the violation of the territorial integrity of the kingdom of Hungary was nothing less than sacrilegious. During the interwar period every Hungarian schoolchild was raised with the slogan "Hungary truncated is not a country; Hungary intact is the Divine Will." A popular prayer composed after the Treaty of Trianon was the so-called National Credo: "I believe in one God, one Fatherland, and the Resurrection of Hungary."[20]

Austria and Hungary were the only two states created by the Versailles settlements that could claim that they were "national states" in the ethnic sense of the word because they had, compared with other states in the region, small minority populations. Karl Renner, an Austro-Marxist theoretician of the nationalities problem, the first chancellor of the provisional Republic of German-Austria, and the president of the Austrian peace delegation at St. Germain, summed up his criticism of the peace settlements in Central Europe:

> The former [Habsburg] Empire never pretended to be a national state, but the new succession states were falsely proclaimed as such, and a large part of the domestic difficulties which beset them is due to this pretense. The peace treaties did not solve the problem of multi-national states but transferred it from each of the big powers to several small states.[21]

The peace settlements not only subdivided the old imperial nationalities problems but also inverted them. Former imperial "lords"—Germans and Magyars—became national minorities in the new national states ruled by their previous "subjects."

The creation of new minorities was just one of the problems facing the new states of Central Europe. There also was a wide structural disparity between "Western and Eastern" regions in many of these states, and the frontiers of these structural regions frequently corresponded to ethnic and former imperial frontiers. "Special problems were created in provinces which had been ruled by 'Western' methods and, owing to the territorial settlement of 1918, came under 'Eastern' administration, or vice versa. Czechoslovakia, Yugoslavia, Romania, and Poland were states of mixed 'Western' and 'Eastern' provinces."[22] The general levels of literacy and education, economic development and urbanization, and the quality and institutions of public administration were higher in "Western regions" that had been part of Germany, Austria, or Hungary. The structurally "Western" regions of the (formerly Hungarian) Banat or Croatia and (formerly Austrian) Slovenia became parts of Yugoslavia, and (Hungarian) Transylvania and (Austrian) Bukovina were incorporated into Romania. Yugoslavia and Romania were not only structurally "Eastern" but also were dominated by Eastern Orthodox ethnic majorities. Poland fell into three West–East zones: "a Western, semi-Western, and a completely Eastern area" inhabited predominantly by Belarussians and Ukrainians. In Czechoslovakia the "Western Czechs" in (formerly Austrian) Bohemia and Moravia dominated the "Eastern Slovaks" in (formerly Hungarian) Slovakia. The structural differences between these regions exacerbated cultural and ethnic conflicts in these states in the future.

Last of all, national self-determination created two forms of irredentism in Central Europe. The smaller of the two was Hungarian. The Magyar tradition of "historical imperialism"[23] made the revision of Hungary's Trianon frontiers an issue that led to poor relations with all its new neighbors and destabilized the entire region during the interwar period. Although Hungarian irredentism was loud, it never really became menacing. The larger form of irredentism was German. After 1918, there were 7 million Germans in Austria (or German-Austrians who wanted to be German citizens), more than 3 million Germans in Czechoslovakia, and more than 1 million Germans in Poland, not to mention the hundreds of thousands of Germans in the "linguistic islands" scattered throughout Romania and northern Yugoslavia. German irredentism was much more dangerous because it relied on a belated application of the very principle that the Entente Powers had used to establish Central European frontiers in the first place.

The accusation that the Versailles settlements did not take into account the German people's right to national self-determination appealed to political principle, and it addressed a precept that the representatives of Western democracy could hardly disavow. A revision of the Treaty of Versailles was a constant goal of German foreign policy from the establishment of the Weimar Republic until the beginning of World War II. Adolf Hitler inherited this objective from the Weimar Republic, and it proved to be an enormous domestic political asset for him, because his democratic opponents could not credibly renounce the primary goal of Nazi foreign policy because it previously had been their own.

❊ 10 ❊

Spheres of Influence I

Germany and the Soviet Union

The states that were carved out of the Russian, German, and Austro-Hungarian empires after World War I—Finland, Estonia, Latvia, Lithuania, Poland, Czechoslovakia, Austria, Hungary, and Yugoslavia—initially were conceived as modern democratic nation-states. Along with Romania, they were to have the dual function of collectively containing the expansion of Germany and preventing the spread to the West of the Soviet Union's breed of Communism. The idea of a *cordon sanitaire* that stretched from the Arctic Circle to the Adriatic Sea or the Black Sea was inspired by the Western powers' experience with German *Weltpolitik* and reinforced by the Communist threat of "world revolution."

This idea correlated with a new Central European conception of Central Europe. For example, when Thomas Masaryk returned to Prague in December 1918, he spoke of the "victory of small nations" and the necessity of "close friendship with our neighbors to the East and Southeast." Masaryk envisioned regional cooperation—"an amicable group of states from the Baltic to the Adriatic"—as the alternative to a "Pan-German *Mitteleuropa*."[1] Masaryk's vision and the victorious allies' idea of a *cordon sanitaire* were based upon the assumption that these smaller democracies would be *collectively* strong enough to prevent future German or Soviet imperial transgressions. (As former allies of Germany, Austria, Hungary, and Bulgaria were initially regarded as weak links in this democratic chain.) However, neither democracy at home nor cooperation abroad was an enduring characteristic of the domestic and foreign policies pursued by the states in this region during the interwar period.

Between the Arctic and the Adriatic, Europe added eleven new states to its prewar community of twenty-six, and each had new currencies and customs barriers. National economies had to be created where none had existed previously, and none of the countries east of Germany's frontiers had economies that could be called modern in terms of their commercial and industrial structures. Czech Bohemia and a few urban-industrial regions in Austria, Hungary, and Poland were exceptions to the predominantly agrarian structures prevailing in the region. After a period of postwar disorientation and consolidation, Central Europe's fledgling democracies had only a few brief years of stable economic growth before the Great Depression hit. The subsequent economic and political crises went hand in hand. The liberal dream for this region—free people prospering in democratic states—gradually turned into a nightmare.

One of the characteristics of these states' domestic political development was a curious alliance between traditional agricultural and modern industrial or capitalistic interests, which frequently hindered the kind of land reform that many peasants anticipated and simultaneously prevented the type of social reform that the socialist- or Communist-inspired working classes envisioned. Conflicts between urban and rural economic elites—or the bourgeoisie and the large landowners—often were secondary to their common interest in maintaining the status quo. The ruling elites throughout Central Europe demonstrated an increasingly strong inclination to protect their interests by dispensing with the inconvenient institutions of parliamentary democracy and to replace them with authoritarian rule in some form.

A significant feature of the Central European political spectrum was the weakness of a liberal democratic "middle" that could balance or mediate among various national-conservative, clerical, and agrarian interests and ideologies on the right and the socialist or Communist movements on the left. The shortage of Western European–style liberals in Central Europe reflected the fact that the kind of middle class traditionally associated with the promotion of liberalism was historically underdeveloped in the region. The weakness of the liberal "middle" in many parts of Central Europe—and the farther east and southeast one went, the more pronounced this attribute became—was a social reflection of the structural legacy of economic "backwardness," the West–East gradient in terms of modern economic development.

Moreover, "Bolshevik" and "fascist" became terms that the respective parties on the right and the left generously applied to their opponents. Given the kind of political polarization typical of Central Europe in the interwar period, parties on the right viewed the enlightened, secular, tolerant, and traditionally anticlerical precepts of liberalism as encouraging the propagation of "Bolshevism," whereas the socialist and Communist left saw liberals as the agents of capitalism and the handmaidens of fascism. Although Communist parties were not especially strong in Central Europe—with the notable exception of Germany—the "Bolshevik threat" was often employed as a pretext by conservatives to combat socialist movements and by the proponents of authoritarian rule to undermine democratic institutions. In

Hungary, for example, conservatives maintained that the liberal government established under Mihály Károlyi after World War I had paved the way for Béla Kun's Bolshevik uprising in 1919.

Antisocialist and anti-Communist propaganda relied heavily on traditional associations and historical precedents. For example, the Bolsheviks were a reincarnation of the eastern hordes of the bloodthirsty and godless barbarians who down through the ages had threatened the Christian West. In terms of the (nineteenth-century) antimodernism and reactionary Romanticism that were part of many (twentieth century) authoritarian ideologics, socialists and Communists were also the perverted offspring of the Enlightenment and the French Revolution: atheists, materialists, and Jacobin revolutionaries. Liberals were perceived as a bit less dangerous, but they were just atheists and materialists of a different breed. The secularism, capitalism, and "cosmopolitanism" associated with liberalism threatened to undermine traditional Christian and national values, institutions, and ways of life just as much as Bolshevism did, but by different means.

Last of all, this authoritarian concoction of anti-Bolshevism and antiliberalism had a peculiar anti-Semitic twist. Assimilated Jews frequently were advocates of those enlightened and secular political doctrines that had facilitated Jewish assimilation. Therefore, many leading liberals and capitalists, as well as prominent socialists and Communists, had Jewish backgrounds. From the perspective of anti-Semitic nationalism, this fact merely illustrated that both liberalism and Bolshevism were Jewish: two different faces of one "international conspiracy" aimed at destroying Christian and national cultures.

Certainly the kinds of problems and conflicts mentioned here varied from state to state.[2] But it is clear that the preconditions for a tranquil domestic political and economic development simply did not exist in Central Europe after World War I; by the end of 1934 Czechoslovakia was its only functioning democracy. After the proclamation of a Hungarian republic in 1918 and the brief revolutionary interlude of Béla Kun's "Soviet republic," Horthy established a nationalistic–authoritarian regime in Hungary in 1920. Piłsudski led a "coup" that turned Poland's fledgling democracy into an authoritarian regime in 1926. Many historians have defended Piłsudski because his motives for curtailing parliamentary democracy were to prevent the rise of right-wing radical, antidemocratic Polish nationalists to power, and he introduced a relatively insipid authoritarian system that derived its legitimacy from his reputation as a national hero but was notorious for its practice of an old-boys' system: placing in public positions veteran officers from the Polish army.

In 1929 and 1930, the constitutional monarchies of Yugoslavia and Romania transformed themselves into regal dictatorships that ruled with varying degrees of rigor. Hitler came to power legally in Germany in 1933, and he then used his position as chancellor systematically to erode German democracy. In February 1934, a one-party authoritarian regime of clerical conservatives and Austro-fascists was established in Austria after a brief but bloody confrontation with Austrian Social Democrats, and the so-called

Christian Corporate State they formed then defended itself against the representatives of the more radical right: a putsch attempt by Austria's indigenous National Socialist movement in July.

The idea of a *cordon sanitaire* was based on the assumption that there would be some kind of regional cooperation among the various states in the region that would ensure their collective security. However, diplomatic relations among the various states in the region were not congenial. The dominant ethnic groups in the newly created states treated the ethnic minorities that lived in the new "national" states with varying degrees of discrimination and abuse. Hungary was on almost uniformly bad terms with all of its neighbors because the reestablishment of its historical frontiers was one of the primary points on its national political agenda. Immediately after the war, Czechoslovakia, Romania, and Yugoslavia formed the "Little Entente" by signing mutual assistance treaties aimed at containing Hungary's irredentist ambitions, a gesture that France supported as part of maintaining the order established at Versailles. France also attempted to create some kind of regional presence by signing military treaties with Czechoslovakia and Poland. However, these arrangements failed to fill the vacuum created by the collapse of the old empires and ultimately failed to replace the old Franco-Russian axis.

Mussolini's rise to power in Italy between 1922 and 1926 added another dimension to Central European instability because his vision of an Italian empire included dominating the Adriatic Sea at the expense of Yugoslavia, and so Yugoslavia's disgruntled neighbors became his good friends. Mussolini attempted to extend his influence into Central Europe by actively supporting right-wing groups in Austria and Hungary whose anti-Yugoslav sentiments and predilection for the Italian version of fascist ideology not only strengthened his foreign policy position but also advanced the processes of domestic polarization in both countries.[3]

Democratic Czechoslovakia had superb relations with Western democracies like Britain and France but cool relations with all its immediate neighbors. Its sizable German and Magyar minorities were points of contention, and Poland never seemed to digest a relatively minor issue: how and when Czechoslovakia acquired part of the duchy of Teschen in 1920. Poland was in the most precarious position of all because, aside from its chilly relations with Czechoslovakia, neither Germany nor the Soviet Union were satisfied with the way in which their frontiers with Poland had been established.

In addition to the network of contentious relationships among the newly founded states of Central Europe, there was no consensus among them concerning their common enemies or friends. There also was no single European power that, as an ally, could have promoted cooperation or, as a threat, would have helped forge a community of interests among them. Poland, Czechoslovakia, Romania, and Yugoslavia viewed distant France, the most powerful state in Continental Europe immediately after World War I, as the guarantor of freedom, whereas Austria and Hungary cultivated increasingly amiable relations with fascist Italy.

Before World War II, traditional national and modern ideological terms often were used interchangeably, and the states of Central Europe identified their respective friends and foes—or whichever foe represented the lesser of two evils—in light of their previous historical experiences with them. In other words, the distinctions between nations and ideologies—"German" and "Nazi" or "Russian" and "Soviet"—were sometimes negligible, and contemporaries living in the countries between Germany and the Soviet Union often viewed both modern ideologies in the historical context of their respective national experiences with Germany and Russia. Communism and National Socialism were often perceived as twentieth-century manifestations of traditional forms of Greater Russian or German imperialism. Furthermore, by the mid-1930s, national independence, not democratic freedom, was the primary issue for the states in the region because they themselves (with the exception of Czechoslovakia) already had dispensed with democratic institutions, to varying degrees.

In Poland anti-German (or anti-Nazi) and anti-Russian (or anti-Soviet) sentiments were equally distributed. Pro-German and anti-Russian sentiments were stronger among the non-Slavic states of Austria, Hungary, and Romania, whereas anti-German sentiments prevailed in Czechoslovakia and Yugoslavia, where many people entertained the sentimental and idealistic Pan-Slavic notion that the Soviet Union somehow had inherited the venerable Russian function of patronizing and protecting smaller Slavic nations. Czechoslovakia provides perhaps the best example of how ambivalent these national and ideological allegiances were. As a Slavic state, Czechoslovakia looked to the Soviet Union as a reincarnation of Russia for support, but as a democracy it looked to France.

German–Soviet Cooperation: The Spirit of Rapallo, 1922–1933

The fact that imperial Germany and czarist Russia were adversaries in World War I and the magnitude and ruthlessness of the tooth-and-nail conflict between Nazi Germany and the Soviet Union during World War II help create the impression that Germans and Russians were "natural enemies." However, if one is prepared to adopt a longer historical perspective, these conflicts can be seen as anomalies in the history of German–Russian relations. Prussia and Russia had relatively amiable relations with each other since their respective "Greats," Frederick and Catherine, masterminded the partitions of Poland at the end of the eighteenth century. The achievements of German science and culture were a consistent source of inspiration and emulation for Russian intellectuals, and the czars always admired the achievements of "German efficiency," ranging from public administration to military organization. The idea of Prussian-German, Austrian, and Russian imperial cooperation—Metternich's Holy Alliance after 1815 or Bismarck's Dreikaiserbund after 1871—was an essential feature of nineteenth-century Europe's continental balance of power. The breakup of the traditionally cordial German-Russian relationship in 1890 violated the logic of series of historical precedents and contributed to the demise of both empires.

Immediately after World War I, Germany and Russia were isolated. The Western powers effectively put a diplomatic quarantine on Germany. France, in particular, had a bellicose and vindictive relationship with Germany, and the "humiliation of Versailles"—combined with an inadequate reintegration of Germany into the European order—merely fueled German national resentment. The Soviet Union lived in a more or less self-imposed state of isolation. Bolshevik Russia's relationships with the West deteriorated after revolutionary Russia abandoned the Entente by signing a separate peace with the Central Powers at Brest-Litovsk in 1918, and the expeditionary forces that the Entente later sent to Russia on punitive missions did not improve them. Furthermore, the Bolshevik Revolution failed to spark the "world revolution" that so many revolutionaries had envisioned. Therefore, the Soviet Union attempted to build "socialism in one country" —incidentally the title of a book Joseph Stalin wrote in 1925—by isolating itself from decadent, capitalistic, Western influences and pursuing a policy of economic autarky.

Germany and the Soviet Union were solitary and chronically disgruntled powers, and although the reasons for their isolation and discontent were different, the prospects of cooperation gave each of them an opportunity to break out of the exclusion they shared. Since neither Germany nor the Soviet Union was bound by sympathies or commitments to the victorious Western powers, the possibility of German–Soviet cooperation was a worst-case scenario.

Although the German right and the Russian left held diametrically opposed positions on central ideological issues, they cultivated relatively amiable relations with each other until Hitler's rise to power in 1933. German–Soviet cooperation officially began in 1922 when the British prime minister, Lloyd George, masterminded the organization of an international conference in Genoa—the first convocation of all European states since the Berlin Congress of 1878 and the only Pan-European diplomatic meeting in the twentieth century until 1971—in an attempt to resolve some of the problems created by the postwar order.

Lloyd George's grand scheme, which he basically kept to himself and thought he could engineer without the customary diplomatic preparations, was based on a two-step strategy. First, he wanted to lessen the tensions between France and Germany in order to draw Germany back into the Western community of nations, and he believed he could talk France into reducing the reparations it was extracting from Germany, a proposition that did not interest France in the least. Based on some kind of Franco-German reconciliation, he then envisioned a joint effort by the leading Western European industrial nations to help reconstruct war-torn Soviet Russia. Ultimately Western aid could gradually undermine the achievements of the Bolshevik Revolution from without and within, but the Soviets viewed this project as the creation of a capitalistic anti-Soviet bloc. Furthermore, the German delegation in Genoa was treated with enough aloofness to feel that it was being kept in the dark. Therefore, it anticipated the rejuvenation of an anti-German coalition along the lines of the old Entente: Britain, France, and Russia.

Although the Conference of Genoa raised great expectations, Lloyd George did not have a chance in light of French inflexibility, Russian suspicions, German apprehensions, and his own surreptitiousness. The delegations of Germany and the Soviet Union each thought that they were going to be isolated by a coalition of all other major European powers directed against their respective vital interests, and mutual anxiety literally drove them into each other's arms.

On short notice, the Soviet delegation, which was housed in Rapallo, a spa outside Genoa, invited the German delegation to consultations, and within twenty-four hours the two countries had drafted, signed, and sealed a treaty. It normalized German–Soviet relations by formally ending the state of war that had existed between the two countries since the annulment of the Treaty of Brest-Litovsk in November 1918. (This passage was merely the *de jure* recognition of a *de facto* state of peace.) It also provided for the exchange of diplomatic and consular representatives, included clauses recognizing each state's respective frontiers and mutually repudiating reparation claims, and contained vague provisions for future economic cooperation and diplomatic consultation. It had neither secret nor military clauses, and it was not an extraordinary document overall. But the circumstances under which it was drafted and the impression it made on contemporaries were nothing less than sensational. The Congress of Genoa was convened to facilitate the integration of Germany and the Soviet Union back into the European system of powers. Instead, its only tangible result was the rapprochement of Germany and the Soviet Union.

From 1922 until Hitler's rise to power in 1933, the Treaty of Rapallo provided the basis for relatively amiable relations between the Weimar Republic and the Soviet Union. Ideologically speaking, these two countries were an odd couple, but mutual advantage and national interests provided a sound basis for intercourse between the democratic Weimar Republic and the Communist Soviet Union. Both countries wanted a revision of the postwar peace settlements imposed on them, and they sought diplomatic support from each other. Furthermore, neither Germany nor the Soviet Union viewed as unalterable their respective frontiers with Poland. German capitalists also had no scruples about doing business with the Soviet Union, which was engaged in the ambitious revolutionary project of dispensing with private property and all other institutions related to the capitalistic way of life. Soviet revolutionaries had no doubts about the advantages of access to German capital and technology and the role they would play in "building socialism."

High-ranking members of the Germany military establishment, in particular the old guard of aristocratic Prussian generals who were one of the most reactionary elites in the Weimar Republic, also had good relations with the Red Army. A series of secret agreements with the Soviets allowed the German high command to bypass the military restrictions imposed by the Treaty of Versailles. The Soviet Union let the German armed forces build and test weapons in the Soviet Union and clandestinely train German military personnel to use them. The Germans, in turn, invited Soviet officers to participate in training and exercises.

After German-Soviet relations cooled to a chill in the mid-1930s, Stalin frequently used the associations that leading officers in the Red Army had had with their German comrades, to accuse them of "espionage" or "treason," and many Soviet officers were liquidated in Stalin's great purges. It is one of those paradoxes of history that the Soviets allowed the Germans to train the men and develop the weapons in the Soviet Union that Nazi Germany then used in its attempt to annihilate the Soviet Union. The Germans also shared the fruits of their secret military development with the Soviets and instructed officers of the Red Army who eventually would lead the Soviet Union to victory over the German aggressors.[4]

The highest circles of the German military establishment not only secretly initiated German–Soviet military cooperation, but they also concealed to a great extent its nature and dimensions from the civilian governments of the Weimar Republic. Although the Treaty of Rapallo had no secret military clauses, "Rapallo" subsequently became a synonym for describing the most undesirable forms of German–Soviet cooperation. But it would be erroneous to draw a direct line from Rapallo in 1922 to the Hitler–Stalin Non-Aggression Pact of 1939, because German–Soviet relations deteriorated after Hitler came to power in 1933. Nevertheless, the Hitler–Stalin pact embodied the spirit and the specter of Rapallo, and some people still are apprehensive when the prospect of German–Russian cooperation arises. For example, some commentators referred to the grand reconciliation of the Federal Republic of Germany and the Soviet Union in of the summer of 1990—the Soviet consent to a unified Germany and the German guarantees of extensive aid to the Soviet Union—as a "Super-Rapallo."

Hitler's Foreign Policy: From the Revision of Versailles to the Nonaggression Pact with Stalin, 1933–1939

There are two extremes between which Germans have attempted to explain Adolf Hitler's rise to power. Were Hitler, Nazi Germany, and the multitude of crimes committed in the name of the German people and the Third Reich between 1933 and 1945 ultimately the culmination of a series of German traditions, or were they phenomena exceptional in German history? Historians of different generations and political persuasions disagree on which date should be used to mark the decisive turning point in twentieth-century German history, and this disagreement reflects different interpretations of the origins of National Socialism.

Immediately after World War II, for example, German historians viewed the period of National Socialism from 1933 to 1945 as a massive aberration or German historical anomaly. In this context, the establishment of the Weimar Republic after 1918 was seen not only as a radical break with the autocratic past of imperial Germany but also as a fulfillment of the democratic hopes and liberal aspirations manifested in the German revolutions of 1848. The "zero hour" of 1945 represented a return to normalcy, and the establishment of the Federal Republic of Germany in 1949 was seen as a restoration of the democratic political traditions of the Weimar Republic. Consequently, Hitler's rise to power in 1933 was viewed as both the turning point in German history and the beginning of a twelve-year deviation, and several attempts were made to explain why Hitler had succeeded in converting democratic Germany to a totalitarian state and how he could have so diabolically misguided the German people in the process.

One of the focal points of interest was the investigation of the "Hitler phenomenon," which described the methods of totalitarian rule and delved into the demonic nature of Hitler's personality. This approach frequently was coupled with the assumption that the Führer actually had as much power—and hence posthumous responsibility for National Socialism—as Nazi propagandists previously maintained he had. According to this view, Hitler and the Third Reich were not representative of German traditions but ultimately were perversions of them. Traditionalists, for example, pointed out that members of one of Germany's most conservative national elites—aristocratic Prussian officers—were responsible for conspiring against Hitler and almost succeeded in assassinating him on July 20, 1944.

The assumption that 1933 was the most dramatic turning point in German history and that Nazism was a national historical aberration were premises that a younger generation of German historians started questioning in the 1960s. They were dissatisfied with how the older generation of historians had dealt with National Socialism, and their reinterpretation of German history was fueled by all the methodological and generational issues that went along with the student revolutions of 1968. Instead of looking at the Weimar Republic as a substantial break with the imperial German past and Hitler's rise to power as a radical departure from democratic German traditions in a manner which emphasized two discontinuities—one in 1918 and the other in 1933—they began to look for the continuities between the respective periods to relativize the amplitude and success of Germany's transition to democracy after World War I.

This younger generation of historians claimed that National Socialism represented the culmination of a number of German traditions. According to their interpretation, which was the source of an unending controversy, German history from the establishment of the Kaiserreich in 1871 until the demise of the Third Reich in 1945 had to be seen as "one period" because the Weimar Republic did not represent the radical departure from Germany's imperial past to the extent that many of its defenders or admirers thought it did. It was possible to trace the origins of the Third Reich back to the flaws of the Weimar Republic and to the bad national habits (or structural deficiencies) it had inherited from the Kaiserreich. Therefore, Hitler's rise to power in 1933 was not an aberration from historical traditions as much as it was a consummation of them, and not 1918 or 1933 but, rather, the demise of Nazi Germany in 1945 had to be seen as the decisive turning point in contemporary German history.[5]

Historians discovered ominous continuities in German history: the terminology and objectives of imperial foreign policy from Bismarck to Hitler; the survival more or less intact of old imperial national-conservative elites as decision makers in the Weimar Republic, such as high-ranking officers and bureaucrats, large landowners, industrialists, and the well educated bourgeoisie; aspirations to revise the European order established at Versailles; plans for reestablishing of German economic hegemony on the Continent; and the weakness of liberal and democratic traditions in public life. In other words, contingent on the methodological instruments they used, the representatives of the "continuity school" of modern German history found peculiarities and deficiencies ranging from the development of Germany's social and economic structures to the idiosyncracies of the German national psyche with its propensities for romanticism, antimodernism, and authoritarianism.

The implications of this new interpretation were not just academic. At that time, the student revolutions of 1968 and the ideological fervor of many young Germans led them to accuse their parents of having been Nazis instead of misguided democrats. They wanted to know why the older generation had so seldom talked about the war and National Socialism, as well as what they had done during the war and why.

The idea of a radical discontinuity in German history (the demonic Führer and misguided good Germans) apologetically delegated as much responsibility as possible to Adolf Hitler and the institutions of totalitarianism, whereas the other extreme, total continuity ("the evil Germans"), fell into the trap of making all Germans from Charlemagne or Luther to Bismarck somehow responsible for National Socialism. (There is a peculiar affinity between the Nazi interpretation of German history from the 1930s, which represented the Third Reich as the culmination of German history, and the leftist, "antifascist" interpretation of the late 1960s and thereafter, which used different methodological tools but came to basically the same conclusion: Nazis, Nazis everywhere.)

Extreme or monocausal interpretations are not very credible, and historians have tried to draw a more balanced picture based on both the continuity of German traditions and the discontinuity of National Socialist innovations. Historical research has unearthed innumerable facts about National Socialism, and as far as the chronology, documentation, or historical narrative of National Socialism is concerned, a great deal of work has been done. However, despite five decades of research, historians have failed to reach a consensus on many of the fundamental issues related to the explanation and interpretation of National Socialism.[6]

One of the many major controversies pertains to the relationship of Hitler's stated intentions to the real domestic and foreign policy objectives of the Third Reich. The issue at stake here is essentially whether or not, or to what extent, there was a disparity between the radical formulations of Nazi ideology and the realistically achievable objectives of Nazi policy. This situation is complicated by the fact that Hitler was an exceptionally rare politician insofar as he outlined his political program at length long before coming to power—the two volumes of *Mein Kampf* were written between 1924 and 1927—and then proceeded to execute it step by step. Blessed with the advantage of hindsight, historians are repeatedly amazed that Hitler's contemporaries and adversaries, both domestic and foreign, did not recognize the import of Hitler's autobiographical outline of Nazi ideology or his theories of race, space, and a new European order.

For example, Hitler made it clear in *Mein Kampf* that he considered the "elimination" of Jews from Europe to be a political and racial–hygienic necessity (together with the persecution of the Gypsies and the so-called euthanasia programs directed against the mentally and physically handicapped). Although there is no denying the explicit nature of Nazi anti-Semitism, there are two broad schools of thought regarding the Nazis' conception and implementation of the "final solution."

One group of historians explains the Holocaust as part of a larger, coherent, and long-term National Socialist strategy that can be seen as the culmination of a European tradition of anti-Semitism that can be traced as far back as early Christianity. In this context, Hitler was the unavoidable consequence of previous German historical development, and the Holocaust analogously can be regarded as the inevitable outcome of almost 1,500 years of European Christian anti-Semitism.

Another school of interpretation places the Holocaust in the narrower context of the dynamics of the Nazi war effort. The impending failure of the German invasion of the Soviet Union after 1941 excluded the emigration or expatriation of European Jews from territories controlled by the Reich as possible "final solutions to the Jewish question" and therefore led to genocide as the only alternative the Nazis perceived as having for a radical "elimination" of Jews from Europe.[7]

Although the Holocaust is a phenomenon that consistently defies comprehension, the interpretation of the Third Reich's foreign policy objectives, which also were based on Hitler's strategies of race and space, is an issue that is comparatively less prone to controversy and in some respects easier to understand. Nevertheless, historians disagree on the projected magnitude of the Third Reich. Some "Eurocentric" interpretations view the German domination of Europe from the Atlantic to the Urals as the goal of National Socialist foreign policy, whereas others take literally the concept of global domination or a Nazi version of *Weltpolitik*. Regardless of whether one is a proponent of the European or global versions of the Third Reich's plans for dominion, Hitler made it clear in *Mein Kampf* that his objective of revising the Treaty of Versailles—reestablishing the old imperial borders of Germany—was not enough. The German people needed *Lebensraum*. This "living space" was in the east, and it was to be acquired in a war with the mortal enemy of the German people: Bolshevik–Jewish Russia. (The anti-Semitic twist to Nazi anti-Communism and the anti-Communist twist to Nazi anti-Semitism enabled the interchangeable use of racial and ideological categories.)

In addition, Hitler identified in *Mein Kampf* two potential allies of Germany: Italy and England. He rejected the idea of the coexistence of "two continental powers in Europe" along with the possibility of German alliances with either France or Russia, and he identified "Russian Bolshevism" as "the attempt undertaken by the Jews in the twentieth century to achieve world domination."[8] Hitler's decision to terminate German–Soviet cooperation after he came to power in 1933 was ideologically inspired and ignored the benefits of cooperation. The German–Soviet rapprochement of August 1939 appeared illogical to those contemporaries who took at face value Nazi anti-Soviet and Soviet anti-fascist propaganda, but it fit coherently into Hitler's long-term plans.

Hitler saw the revision of the Treaty of Versailles and the establishment of German hegemony in Central Europe merely as preliminary steps to a war with the Soviet Union, the acquisition of *Lebensraum*, and the achievement of a position of European dominance, and he was initially very successful in disguising his intentions. Although he had stated his objectives in *Mein Kampf*, many of his contemporaries dismissed the book as juvenile demagoguery. Many conservatives throughout Europe viewed Hitler's vitriolic anti-Marxism and anti-Bolshevism, which turned Nazi Germany into a bulwark of Western European culture, with a certain sympathy, and they generally accepted at face value Hitler's assertion that revising the Treaty of Versailles, a programmatic goal he had inherited from the Weimar Republic, was the main objective of his foreign policy. Hitler did a consummate job of creating the impression among Western politicians that the satisfaction of his demands was the best means of ensuring peace in Europe in the future. Furthermore, Western European politicians and diplomats belatedly recognized the Versailles settlement with Germany as having been too severe, and the "policy of appeasement" they pursued with Nazi Germany was based to a considerable extent on the insight that it was necessary to readmit Germany to the club of major European powers, even if this meant accepting unilateral German violations of the restrictions imposed by the Treaty of Versailles.

Although Hitler constantly preached peace, the step-by-step suspension of the various limitations placed at Versailles by the victorious powers on Germany's military potential was part of his strategy of preparing for war. If "revision of Versailles" was one maxim of his foreign policy, then "national self-determination" was the other. Hitler successfully appealed to political principle by pointing out that the German right to national self-determination had been violated by the Versailles arrangements, and he intended to bring as many Germans as possible *Heim ins Reich*, "back home into the Reich": 7 million Austrians, 3 million Germans in Czechoslovakia, and 1 million Germans in Poland. Hitler pursued these aims one by one, and the first step he took was to temporarily to reconcile Germany with Poland, nominally Nazi Germany's "last objective," by signing a ten-year German–Polish nonaggression agreement in 1934.

The Nazi occupation and annexation of Austria, the *Anschluss* of March 1938 that was carried out by the Germany army without firing a shot, marked the beginning of the Third Reich's expansion. The fact that Austria's authoritarian regime neither resisted nor received international support was

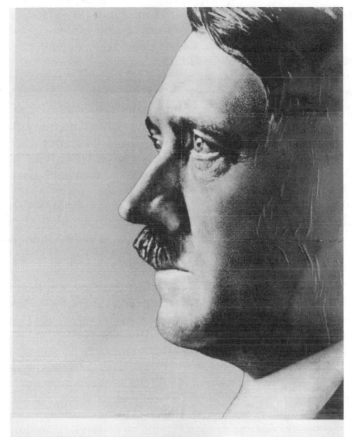

Ein Volk - ein Reich - ein Führer!

The glorification of Hitler as a visionary and a leader was a component feature of the Führer cult promoted by Nazi propaganda. A National Socialist poster from March 1938, after the occupation of Austria, with a simple but comprehensive slogan: *Ein Volk* (national unity), *ein Reich* (the reestablishment of the German empire and a revision of the Treaty of Versailles), *ein Führer* (one leader). (Wiener Stadt- und Landesarchiv, Plakatensammlung)

merely indicative of its low degree of domestic and foreign support.[9] According to Nazi propaganda, the victorious powers had frustrated German national self-determination by forbidding an Austro-German Anschluss in the treaties of Versailles and St. Germain in 1919, and Hitler "rectified" this "injustice" with a gigantic homecoming in Vienna in March 1938 at which he proclaimed the "Greater German Reich." The Nazis summarized their entire program in a simple slogan: *ein Volk, ein Reich, ein Führer*, "one people, one empire, one leader." After the Anschluss of Austria, Hitler turned his attention to the allegedly oppressed German minority in Czechoslovakia.

Nazi propagandists did a good job of portraying the satisfaction of German demands for national self-determination as a prerequisite for maintaining peace in Europe, an assumption that the leaders of Britain and France apparently shared. Given the fact that Czechoslovakia's best friends were willing to accept the logic of Czechoslovakia's mortal enemy, all attempts to maintain the territorial integrity and political sovereignty of the Czechoslovak Republic established after World War I were in vain. At the end of September 1938, the prime ministers of Britain and France, Neville Chamberlain and Edouard Daladier, met with Hitler and Mussolini in Munich (and without representatives of Czechoslovakia) to renegotiate Czechoslovakia's frontiers, and they decided to cede to Nazi Germany the territories inhabited by Germans along the Czech frontiers, the so-called Sudetenland with its German minority of 3 million.

On the eve of departing for the Munich conference on September 27, 1938, the British prime minister, Chamberlain, gave a famous radio speech symptomatic of the policy of appeasement. It contained a humiliating formulation that Czechs have never forgotten: "How horrible, fantastic, incredible it is that we should be digging trenches and trying on gas masks here because of a quarrel in a far away country between people of whom we know nothing."[10] When Chamberlain returned from Munich a few days later, he coined a phrase that is memorable for its inaccuracy. He said that the Munich agreement had secured "peace in our time."

Within a week after the Munich agreement had been signed, Germany occupied and annexed the territories it had been promised. The agreement also contained an addendum stipulating that Czechoslovakia would have to settle its other border disputes with Poland and Hungary. Poland took advantage of the situation by delivering an ultimatum to Prague demanding that Czechoslovakia cede to Poland the duchy of Teschen, an old bone of contention in Polish–Czechoslovak relations. Isolated and demoralized, the Czechoslovak government acquiesced. Germany and Italy then pressured Czechoslovakia into awarding the sections of southern Slovakia inhabited by Magyars to Hungary, which cultivated increasingly amiable relations with the Third Reich, and the Slovaks claimed autonomy for themselves based on the argument that if one national minority in Czechoslovakia—like the Germans—was entitled to national self-determination, then Slovaks also deserved to throw off the yoke of "Czech centralism." Eduard Beneš, the Czechoslovak president, resigned and went into exile, and Hitler issued secret directives to prepare for the elimination of the "remnants of Czechoslovakia," an operation executed with the help of Slovak nationalists and separatists.

After the Munich agreement, Slovak separatists negotiated with Nazi authorities in Berlin behind the back of Prague, and the declaration of an independent Slovak state on March 14, 1939, preceded the German occupation of Prague the following day. The Nazis converted Bohemia and Moravia into a "Protectorate of the Reich." An independent Slovakia with its own homegrown form of authoritarian rule—a concoction of clericalism, fascism, nationalism, corporatism, and anti-Semitism embodied by its leader, Jozef Tiso, a Catholic priest—became a client state of the Third Reich.[11] Finally, Nazi Germany appealed to Hungarian irredentism by inviting Hungary to occupy the easternmost part of the Czechoslovak Republic, the Carpatho-Ukraine, which also had been part of the historic kingdom of Hungary. The dismemberment of Czechoslovakia was truly an international affair, and it merely demonstrated to what extent Hitler managed to exploit to his advantage Western European reticence and post–World War I Central European antipathies.

Immediately after the success of the Munich agreement at the end of September 1938, Nazi diplomats began applying diplomatic pressure on Poland. They demanded the cession of Danzig which, because of conflicting Polish and German claims after World War I, had not been incorporated into the territory of either state but had been granted the status of a "free city." They also wanted Polish permission to build an extraterritorial Autobahn and rail line from Germany across the Danzig corridor to East Prussia. Poland was not prepared to concede on either of these points. The Nazi occupation and dismemberment of Czechoslovakia in mid-March 1939 also had clearly demonstrated to Britain and France that Hitler's aspirations went far beyond satisfying demands for "national self-determination." Therefore, Britain and France each issued guarantees explicitly supporting the Polish position.

Poland played a key role in the next phase of Nazi foreign policy. Hitler's major objectives were to destroy France as a Continental power and to convert Russia into German *Lebensraum*, and he had to achieve each of these goals in a way that which would avoid creating a worst-case military scenario: a war on two fronts. "To attack France, he needed Poland's neutrality. To attack Russia, he needed Poland's cooperation."[12] However, Poland saw France (or the prospect of a two-front war that Franco-Polish cooperation would create for Nazi Germany) as the guarantor of Polish independence. Although Nazi diplomats made secret advances explicitly suggesting Polish–German cooperation in a war against the Soviet Union and promised considerable territorial gains for Poland in the east, Poland refused to be enticed by these offers because it was clear that the Nazi version of German–Polish cooperation would entail a fate for Poland similar to that of the Czechoslovak Republic, in which concessions had led to occupation.

Polish intransigence, characterized by a lack of preparedness to compromise on "smaller" issues like Danzig or to cooperate on big ones like an anti-Soviet alliance, caused a shift in Nazi foreign policy during the spring of 1939. In order to attack the Soviet Union, Nazi Germany needed a Polish ally or a common border with the Soviet Union, and in order to attack France in the west, Nazi Germany needed a neutral state that would not open a second front in the rear in the east. Since Poland was not willing to play either role, it became the main obstacle in the achievement of Hitler's higher objectives. Poland, at first viewed by Nazi Germany as part of the solution to the Russian problem, thus became part of the Russian problem. On May 23, 1939, Hitler called together his leading military advisers and told them: "We cannot expect another repetition of the Czech affair. There will be war. . . . Danzig is not the subject of dispute at all. It is a question of expanding our *Lebensraum* in the East. . . . The answer, therefore, lies in Poland."[13]

By the summer of 1939, it was relatively clear to the leaders of Europe that Nazi Germany would start a war sooner or later. The potential alignment of the Soviet Union in a German–Polish conflict was a decisive issue, and during the summer Britain and France started low-level negotiations with the Soviet Union, aimed at securing anti-German cooperation. However, the Western envoys—neither ministers nor their deputies but third-ranking diplomats—did not come with concrete offers. They wanted to talk and sound out the Soviets.

Stalin saw a war coming, and he knew that the best thing he could do was to stay out of the conflict as long as possible in order to give the Soviet Union time to prepare for the inevitable showdown between Russian Communism and German capitalism—fascism being a stage in the development of capitalism, according to orthodox Marxist theory.

The Soviet Union had nothing to gain from a military alliance with Poland if it would inevitably embroil the Soviet Union in a direct and premature conflict with Germany, and the chronically strained Polish–Soviet relations precluded this option for the Poles. Furthermore, Stalin did not trust Britain or France, two bourgeois imperialistic powers, nor given their own state of military unpreparedness, did they have much to offer the Soviet Union at the time. He also assumed that the capitalistic West would be more than happy to see Nazi Germany and Communist Russia destroy each other in a conflict in the east or that a Nazi invasion of Poland might continue into the Soviet Union with the tacit support of the West. Therefore the Soviet Union had nothing to gain from an alliance with Poland or the West, especially if it meant that the Soviet Union would become the first or the primary theater of war.

Despite the stridency of the propaganda on both sides, Soviet foreign policy makers never lost interest in reviving the "spirit of Rapallo." Although the German decision to invade Poland had been made in May 1939, the free-floating status of a nonaligned Soviet Union was a source of German apprehension. Hitler was in a hurry and needed Soviet neutrality, whereas Stalin could afford to wait, which raised the price of Soviet neutrality. Under the cover of trade negotiations in late July, German and Soviet diplomats started negotiating a nonaggression pact, and the world was shocked to hear on August 23, 1939, that Nazi Germany and Soviet Union, ideological archenemies, had indeed concluded an agreement.

A secret protocol—whose existence the Soviet authorities denied until 1990—was appended to the document outlining the future German and Soviet territorial division of Poland as well as their respective spheres of influence in East Central Europe and on the Balkan Peninsula. Nazi Germany got Soviet neutrality and most of ethnic Poland; the Soviet Union obtained the eastern part of Poland inhabited by Belorussian and Ukrainian minorities; a free hand to get those territories back which had fallen away from imperial Russia after World War I: parts of Finland, the Baltic states, and Bessarabia (contemporary Moldova, which Romania had acquired after

World War I); and vague promises of influence over the Balkan Peninsula as far as the Dardanelles Straits. Hitler could afford to be generous because he had every intention of getting back everything he had given the Soviet Union in the not so distant future.

Nazi Germany invaded Poland on September 1, 1939. Much to the dismay of Hitler, who was hoping for another coup, England and France declared war on Germany two days later. While the Germans unleashed a blitzkrieg in Poland, French divisions sat behind the fortifications of the Maginot Line and fought a *Sitzkrieg:* a "sitting war." (Given Germany's military superiority in technology and troops, the Polish military estimated that they could resist for two weeks, long enough to give France time to prepare an offensive and attack in the West.)

On September 17, Soviet troops crossed the Polish frontier, ostensibly to "liberate" Belarussian and Ukrainian minorities and to prevent a further advance of German troops, and on September 28, the day after Poland capitulated, Nazi Germany and the Soviet Union signed a friendship treaty spelling out their respective spheres of influence, dividing up the territorial spoils, and regulating bilateral trade relations for the immediate future. The Soviet Union also took into custody 15,000 Polish officers, who disappeared until a mass grave was discovered by the Germans in the Katyn Forest, near Smolensk in Belarussia, in March 1943. (The consequences of the Katyn massacre will be addressed in the next chapter.)

In one of the most cynical episodes of this phase of Soviet–German cooperation, the Soviet secret police (NKVD) turned over many German Communists and left-wing Socialists, who had been living in exile in the Soviet Union, to Nazi authorities, who sardonically referred to them as "repatriates" (*Heimkehrer*). Nazi Germany provided the Soviet Union with the technology and machines it needed to modernize its armament industries, and the Soviet Union furnished Nazi Germany with the raw materials it needed to invade Western Europe. Hitler was free to wage war in the West, and Stalin was free to do as he chose in the East. The Soviet Union started a war with Finland in order to extend its frontier (and created a future ally of Nazi Germany in the process). It also occupied the Baltic states and annexed Bessarabia from Romania. Above all, Stalin bought time to prepare for the inevitable conflict with Nazi Germany. Twenty-two valuable months transpired between the Hitler–Stalin nonaggression pact in August 1939 and the Nazi invasion of the Soviet Union in June 1941.

Space, Race, and Nazi Germany's New European Order, 1939–1945

The defeat of Poland marked the beginning of a series of astounding military successes for Nazi Germany. During the spring of 1940, German forces occupied Denmark and Norway, and by the end of June they had overwhelmed the Benelux countries and France. At the beginning of April 1941, Nazi Germany and Fascist Italy invaded Yugoslavia and Greece.

Guided by a combination of opportunism, circumspection, and an absence of other viable foreign policy alternatives and impressed by Nazi Germany's initial military success, Hungary, Bulgaria, and Romania became allies of the Axis powers. On the one hand, they wanted to partake of the spoils of the Nazi reorganization of southeastern Europe, and on the other, voluntary association with the Third Reich was a means for these countries to maintain independence. Collaboration also contributed to preventing or postponing, in some respects, the full implementation of Nazi policies in these states. The establishment of the Reich's protectorate of Bohemia and Moravia, the creation of independent Slovak and Croat client states, and a greatly enlarged Hungary each illustrate to what extent Hitler used historical precedents and national antipathies to establish a new Central European order.

Bohemia and Moravia became a "Protectorate of the Reich" in March 1939. In the Nazi hierarchy of non-Aryan nations, the Czechs enjoyed a relatively privileged position compared with that of the other Slavic nations. Part of the historical logic of incorporating Bohemia and Moravia into the Third Reich was that they had been part of the First Reich. Furthermore, the Czechs had been exposed to and had assimilated German culture for centuries, and from this perspective, the Nazis regarded them as being "more civilized" or as having a higher level of "cultural participation" than other Slavic nations. The Nazi alternatives for the treatment of the Czechs included Czech autonomy within the Reich's protectorate, the expatriation or "transfer" (*Aussiedlung*) of the Czech population, and their "Germanization" (*Germanisierung* or *Eindeutschung)* or "assimilation," with the exception of those who were racially or politically "suspicious." Since the first alternative was politically unfeasible and the second one would be too disruptive and time-consuming, Hitler opted for the third. Nazi authorities assumed that approximately half the Czechs would qualify for assimilation, whereas the other half—including, in particular, "the racially mongoloid elements and the majority of the intellectual strata"—would have to be "deprived of power, eliminated, or expelled from the country."[14] Furthermore, Czech labor, which was either recruited or deported to the Reich, was one of the foreign reservoirs used to fill the gaps that military conscription had created in the German labor force. In addition, Czech industry, which had fallen more or less intact into Nazi Germany's hands in 1939, played an important role in the Nazi war effort.

Massive Nazi investment in Bohemian and Moravian industry and the relatively little damage during the war helped lay the economic foundations for Czechoslovakia's success as a Communist state after World War II. Nazi policy also contributed substantially to the modernization of industrial facilities in eastern Germany and Austria. Industrial development in eastern Germany was partly inspired by the Nazis' desire to move production facilities out of the range of Allied bombers operating from England, and despite the dismantling of factories by the Soviet Union in their eastern German zone of occupation after World War II, it provided part of the groundwork for the industrial economy of the German Democratic Republic. During the war Nazi Germany also poured extensive resources into Austria's petro-

NAZI GERMANY AND
CENTRAL EUROPE, 1938–1942

N

ESTONIA

SWEDEN

LATVIA
● Riga

DENMARK

North Sea

Baltic Sea

LITHUANIA
Vilnius●

NL

● Minsk

East Prussia

Danzig
West Prussia

● Berlin

SOVIET UNION

B

GERMANY

● Warsaw

Warteland

● Kiev

L

GENERAL
GOUVERNEMENT

FRANCE

Bohemia-Moravia

SLOVAKIA

Vienna

● Budapest

SWITZERLAND

Ostmark

HUNGARY

Zagreb

ROMANIA

CROATIA

Belgrade

Bucharest●

ITALY

Adriatic Sea

SERBIA

● Rome

MONTENEGRO

Sofia
●

BULGARIA

Black Sea

ALBANIA

Mediterrenean Sea

GREECE

TURKEY

Based on Paul Robert Magocsi, *Historical Atlas of Central Europe* (Seattle: University of Washington Press, 1993)

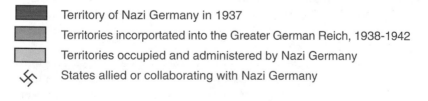

Territory of Nazi Germany in 1937

Territories incorportated into the Greater German Reich, 1938-1942

Territories occupied and administered by Nazi Germany

States allied or collaborating with Nazi Germany

Annexations

by Hungary

by Bulgaria

by Romania

Neutral states

chemical, mining, and steel industries and helped modernize them. One of the results of the Nazis' investment was to widen the structural gaps between the "western" industrialized part of Central Europe (East Germany, Bohemia and Moravia, and Austria) and the less developed eastern part of Central Europe (Poland, Slovakia, and Hungary).

Nazi conquests also produced two client states: Slovakia and Croatia. Slovakia was an accomplice and a by-product of the "elimination of the remnants of Czechoslovakia" in March 1939, and an independent Croatia was the result of the Italian–German dismemberment of Yugoslavia after April 1941. Shortly after the invasion of Yugoslavia, Serbia was converted to a Yugoslav rump state and placed directly under German military administration. (The civilian populations of Serbia, Poland, and the Soviet Union suffered most during the war because unlike the situation in Western Europe or Slovakia, Hungary, and Croatia, national governmental authorities were not invited to collaborate with the German occupational forces. As reprehensible as collaboration might have been elsewhere, it also served in some cases as a "buffer" that prevented, mitigated, or postponed the unrestrained execution of Nazi policies.)

During the interwar period, Croats had been chronically discontent with a Serbian-dominated Yugoslav state, and the Axis powers took ample advantage of this dissatisfaction. Mussolini had one of his political protégés, Ante Pavelić, a Croat fascist and the leader of the so-called Ustaša movement, appointed as the head of government of an independent Croatia, a state that was considerably larger than its historical predecessor but that nonetheless regarded itself as the resurrection of the early medieval kingdom of Croatia. This client state was sovereign in name only and was divided into spheres of influence by the Italians in the west and the Germans in the east. The Axis powers never had enough troops, however, to occupy Croatia and therefore left Pavelić with a relatively free hand in "domestic affairs."

Pavelić was a proponent of a clerical–fascist and Greater Croatian national ideology that enabled the country's exemplary cooperation with Nazi authorities when it came to the deportation of Croatian Jews, but his principal domestic enemy was independent Croatia's large Orthodox Serb minority of 1.9 million, in a state of 6.5 million. Pavelic's recipe for rectifying Croatia's denominational and ethnic borders was based on a relatively straightforward formula: He intended to convert one-third of the Serbs, expel another third, and murder the rest, and his policies led directly to the organization of Serbian resistance which later became an Italian and German problem that the Croats were called on to help solve.

A colonel in the Yugoslav army, Draža Mihailović was the leading figure in the organization of a Serbian nationalistic and royalist resistance movement, the Chetniks, which was closely associated with the Yugoslav government in exile in London. This resistance movement was not only anti-German and anti-Italian but also anti-Croat and anti-Communist. Another partisan movement organized by the general secretary of the Yugoslav Communist Party and future leader of Communist Yugoslavia, Josip Broz Tito, was based on the idea of a popular front calling for all political and national parties to unify in order to expel Yugoslavia's fascist enemies—Germans, Italians, and Croatian separatists. However, these two different movements never managed to reconcile their ideological differences and increasingly devoted their energies to combating each other. The occupation and segmentation of Yugoslavia produced a variety of national and ideological movements that entered into a virtual free-for-all guerrilla war, civil war, and war between partisans and occupants, which was notorious for its shifting fronts and the ruthlessness of all parties involved.

For example, Mihailović's anti-Communist partisans collaborated with Axis authorities against Tito's Communist partisans. The Allies eventually stopped supporting them for this reason and entered an uneasy alliance with Tito, whose partisans did a better job of tying up German troops that otherwise would have been deployed elsewhere. A German directive of September 1941 dictated that 100 civilian hostages be executed for each German killed and 50 for each wounded, and in the following month this directive was liberally applied in the Serbian city of Kragujevac, where 7,000 inhabitants, including schoolchildren, were executed in reprisal for 36 German casualties: 10 dead and 26 wounded.[15]

In relative terms, Yugoslav Jews and Muslims suffered the greatest losses during the war: 45,000 and 32,000, respectively. An estimated 350,000 Serbs and 40,000 Slovenes were killed during the war. In the case of the Serbs, the perpetrators were not only German—and, to a much lesser extent, Italian—occupational forces but also Croats, and the Ustaša regime established a Nazi-style concentration camp in Jasenovac for Serbs. Partisan tactics on all sides included murdering civilians suspected of having "collaborated with the enemy." During and after the end of the war, Tito's partisans massacred somewhere between 40,000 and 100,000 Croats: supporters of the Ustaša regime and Croatian civilians who had fled to Austria seeking asylum but were returned to Yugoslavia by British occupational authorities.[16]

If Slovakia and Croatia were "satellites *par excellence*" of the Third Reich that willingly cooperated with Nazi authorities, Hungary, Romania, and Bulgaria were "opportunistic satellites."[17] They attempted to profit as much as possible from Nazi Germany's success but then contributed as little as possible once Nazi Germany's fortunes turned. Nazi foreign policy appealed to Hungarian irredentism—the hope of restoring the historical frontiers of the kingdom of St. Stephen—and Hungary made substantial territorial acquisitions under the auspices of the German brokerage and patronage. It regained part of Slovakia after the Munich conference in 1938, the Carpatho-Ukraine in the course of Germany's "elimination of the remnants of Czechoslovakia" in 1939, northern Transylvania from Romania thanks to German leverage in 1940, and a piece of Yugoslavia as a result of the German invasion in 1941.

The affinities between Hungary's homegrown Horthy authoritarianism and German National Socialism were not as close as one might assume, but the merits of collaboration—the restoration of territories lost as part of the Versailles settlements—were something most Hungarian nationalists could not disavow. The Horthy regime was by no means enthusiastic about its military engagement on the eastern front, and it attempted to keep Hungarian commitments to a plausible minimum. The Second Hungarian Army— 200,000 soldiers and 60,000 forced Jewish laborers—was almost completely destroyed in a Soviet offensive in the winter of 1942/1943. Hungary's lack of commitment to the war effort and the diplomatic maneuvering to extricate Hungary from the conflict eventually led to a German occupation of the country in March 1944, an act marking the beginning of the destruction of the last intact national Jewish community in Europe.

The Hungarian situation illustrates the type of moral dilemmas and political paradoxes the war produced in Central Europe. On the one hand, the collaboration of the Horthy regime with Nazi Germany helped protect Hungarian Jews as Hungarian citizens until March 1944, postponed the beginning of the "final solution" in Hungary, and ultimately contributed to the survival of approximately 40 percent of Hungary's 825,000 Jews. On the other hand, the Allies were fully aware of the deportation of Hungarian Jews after March 1944 and by June 1944 finally had an accurate picture of what was happening in Auschwitz-Birkenau. Nonetheless, the Allies never acted on proposals to bomb the rail lines between Hungary and Auschwitz or the gas chambers themselves in order to prevent the deportation and murder of Hungarian Jews.[18]

The political reorganization of the "southeast" was not necessarily representative of the "new order" that National Socialist planners envisioned, partly because the national governments of Nazi Germany's allies were administrative obstacles for the execution of Nazi policy. The *Lebensraum* of the east held the greatest fascination for National Socialist planners, and the conquest of Poland and the Soviet Union gave them nearly unrestricted fields of action. The Nazis had no intention of relying on historical precedents in those areas directly under German administration and control. On the contrary, they were resolved to "innovate" on a megalomanic scale.

The Holocaust is the best-known and most nefarious example of the National Socialist conception of a "new order" in Europe. It was an unprecedented and unique event in history in a number of respects. After 1941, genocide became an intentional and premeditated state policy directed at the total extermination of the Jews in Europe. The Nazis' final solution was substantially different from previous episodes of anti-Jewish violence inspired by religiously motivated anti-Semitism. It was Pan-European, systematic, and based on a biological–racial definition of Jews. The murder of Jews was not a means to an end, such as the acquisition of territory by aggression or the destruction of opponents in a war or civil war, but an end in itself. This genocide was conceived on an unprecedented scale, and the principles of modern bureaucratic and industrial administration were applied to execute it in the most efficient manner possible: rational planning, cost control, the development of industrial technologies needed to "process" millions of people—such as poisonous gas, gas chambers, and ovens—and the commercial "utilization" of corpses as by-products of genocide. The perpetrators of the final solution saw it as an unparalleled "accomplishment" in terms of world history.[19]

Polish Jews were the first victims of the final solution in its industrially organized form. Because of the size and density of Poland's Jewish population, it was logical for the Nazis to establish death camps on Polish territory, and the absence of a Polish government made it easy for them to do so. The Nazis did not have to rely on the compliance of a national government in Poland, as they did elsewhere, in order to execute their policies. Contrary to some assumptions, Poland's indigenous traditions of anti-Semitism did not play a significant role in the Nazis' plans. The Nazis did not have the remotest intention of consulting the Poles, who, as an "inferior race," were never invited to collaborate with the Reich, and the Nazis operated virtually unbridled in Poland. Nazi planners also recognized the logistical benefits of locating death camps in Poland; their central location was convenient for deportations from all over Europe.

Poland provides one of the best national examples for dimensions in which the Nazis thought and acted. The long-term objective of Nazi policy in Poland was to eradicate it from the map. Poland was the first country in which the Nazis employed what they called "radical measures" against Jews and the civilian population at large. Shortly after the defeat of Poland in 1939, Hitler gave a speech in which he addressed the necessity of a "reorganization of ethnographic relationships" in Poland and the need there for "restorative work" (*Sanierungsarbeit*).[20] Heinrich Himmler, the *Reichsführer* of the SS, was more explicit: "The removal of foreign races from the eastern territories incorporated into the Reich is one of the most essential goals to be accomplished in the German East."[21]

The Nazi–Soviet occupation of Poland was based on a new tripartition of the country. About one-fifth of prewar Poland—the Danzig corridor and the territory between eastern Prussia in the northeast and Silesia in the southwest—was directly incorporated into the Reich. This annexation moved the Reich's eastern frontiers almost as far as a line running diagonally from Warsaw to Kraków. It increased the population of the Reich by approximately 1 million Germans and 8 million Poles and created the problem of the "Germanization" of this region. The Soviet Union absorbed nearly two-fifths of Poland in the east—the regions inhabited predominantly by Belarussian and Ukrainian minorities, which had been a point of contention and conflict after World War I, as well as a large number of Jews—and the Nazis established the so-called General Gouvernement in the remaining area in south central Poland. This territory was not a Polish client or a rump successor state but directly administered by the Reich. It was explicitly excluded from the policy of Germanization, and its rulers had no obligation to comply with the civilized norms they considered characteristic for the "German organization (*Gestaltung*) of life." In 1940, Hans Frank, the governor of the General Gouvernement, stated: "What we have here is just a gigantic work camp, where everything . . . is in German hands."[22]

Confronted with 8 million Poles inside the frontiers of the Reich, 12 million Poles in the General Gouvernement, and Poland's substantial Jewish minority, the Nazis developed two different strategies for dealing with these respective "inferior races." The treatment of Poland's 3 million Jews followed the established administrative pattern of the final solution: racial–biological and legal definition, expropriation, concentration in ghettos as a preparatory step for "relocation," and, after 1941, systematic destruction.[23]

The Nazis' racial theory and administrative practices for the treatment of the Jews provided a model for the treatment of Poles to a certain extent, but there was one crucial difference. After racial definition and expropriation, the Jews were destined for destruction. For Poles, however, "elimination" was just one of the administrative measures in the Nazis' repertoire of racial and administrative measures, which included the systematic eradication of Polish intelligentsia; plans for the selective assimilation of a minority of approximately 1 million Poles who, according to Nazi racial and genealogical criteria, could qualify for "Germanization";[24] forced labor; and the methodological relocation, reduction, and dispersion of the Polish population. The treatment of Jews was based on the rigid application of racial ideology, whereas settlement, resettlement, and economic strategies were employed in the treatment of Poles who were "racially undesirable" but economically useful as a "slave race" (*Sklavenvolk*).

The Nazis were confronted with two different problems in occupied Poland. First, the areas that had been incorporated into the Reich had to be "settled"—or, as the Nazis claimed, "resettled"—by Germans as soon as possible. This measure was part of the National Socialist *Lebensraum* strategy. Immediately after the conquest of Poland, the Third Reich negotiated treaties with the Soviet Union and Romania that facilitated the "reemigration" of some 750,000 *Volksdeutsche* who had lived outside the Reich for centuries. These "reemigrants," along with Germans from South Tyrol in Italy and Slovenia, were to provide the "human material" for the settlement of the Polish territories annexed by the Reich.

Second, the indigenous Polish population in these areas was to be either "transferred" as laborers into the Reich or relocated in the General Gouvernement. But the expulsion of approximately 1 million Poles from the territories that had been incorporated into the Reich and the relocation there of hundreds of thousands of *Volksdeutsche* was a poorly organized and chaotic operation. By 1944, 2.8 million Poles, prisoners of war and civilian "foreign workers," had been pressed into the Reich's labor force. In terms of the absolute percentage of Poland's inhabitants, this figure—8 percent of the total population or around 15 percent of the adult population[25]—was not surpassed in any other occupied country. (A total of about 2 million prisoners of war and 5.7 million civilian "foreign workers" from all over Europe were deployed in the Reich, and they provided one-quarter the industrial labor force and approximately one-half the agricultural labor force.)

Furthermore, German settlement in occupied Poland had to be accompanied by the reorganization of the "Polish economy," a pejorative term that Germans used to describe the backwardness of Poland's rural and agrarian structures. This modernization strategy entailed creating larger, more effective agricultural production units and also lowering the population density of the regions in question. The rural population density of vast stretches of Poland (and later the Soviet Union) was a source of concern for Nazi planners, because "overpopulation" detracted from the optimal use of man-power and agricultural resources. Therefore, the dislocation of the indigenous population and the reduction of the population density were measures which went hand in hand.[26] Expropriation, deportation, planned starvation, and mass executions were not measures exclusively inspired by racial ideology; they were "rational" policy instruments of Nazi settlement strategies and economic planning in the east.

In many respects, Poland was the most extreme example of an unrestrained application of Nazi policy. Nazi authorities operated there literally unchecked for almost six years, and in relative terms Poland lost more of its population in World War II than did any other European country: around 20 percent, or 6 million. Ten percent of Poland's prewar citizenry died as a result of military operations, and the rest of those who perished were killed in executions, relocations, so-called pacification campaigns, and, above all, in concentration camps. Expressed in ethnic terms, just as many Polish Poles lost their lives during the war as did Polish Jews—approximately 3 million in each case—and Polish Jews accounted for well over half the estimated 5 million to 6 million victims of the Holocaust.[27]

Since the end of World War II, the Holocaust has overshadowed Polish–Jewish relations. Many Poles feel that Jews do not appreciate the dimension of Polish losses, and many Jews feel that Poles do not understand the significance of the Holocaust. These divergent perspectives have led, in extreme cases, to Poles accusing Jews of being anti-Polish and Jews censuring Poles for being anti-Semitic and anti-Zionist.

Jews and Poles have periodically quarreled about the status of the concentration camp in Auschwitz-Birkenau as a memorial site because it is a symbol of Nazi Germany's crimes against Jews (for Jews) and Poles (for Poles), and the commemoration in late January 1995 of the fiftieth anniversary of the liberation of the camp by the Red Army was overshadowed by misunderstandings, accusations, and self-righteousness. Norman Davies has made the following observation about the Polish–Jewish problem of interpretation: "Jewish investigators tend to count Jewish victims. Polish investigators tend to count Polish victims. Neither side wishes to stress the fact that the largest category of victims was both Polish and Jewish."[28]

The quantification of suffering—history as a body count—inevitably leads to misunderstandings and controversies. For example, Stalin was responsible for the deaths of an estimated 20 million Soviet citizens, and the Soviet *gulag* predated the Nazi concentration camps. These facts can be interpreted in any number of ways. Is it an explicit or implicit attempt to relativize the Holocaust? Does placing the Holocaust in a historical context lessen its political and moral implications or entail questioning its singularity? What is the significance or intention of comparing the number of victims here and there? Does it make any sense to ask and answer questions like "Was Stalin a bigger criminal than Hitler?"

Interpreting the Holocaust is extremely difficult. The victims of the Holocaust are long dead, and the generation of survivors, perpetrators, accomplices, and bystanders is slowly dying. The inevitable expiration of eye-witnesses will contribute to making the Holocaust a historical event: perhaps one of the best-documented historical events in history, but a historical event nonetheless. This will not in the least diminish the relevance or the gravity of the admonition "Never forget!" If there are two lessons the Holocaust taught, they are remembrance and vigilance. People do disagree, nonetheless, on which form of remembrance is most appropriate and which form of vigilance is necessary or legitimate, and they most likely will continue to disagree long into the future.

⌬ 11 ⌬

Spheres of Influence II

East and West, or "Yalta Europe"

"Yalta Europe" has two relatively distinct sets of meaning. Among many East Central European intellectuals and dissidents, it is a pejorative reference to a summit meeting of the "Big Three"—Winston Churchill, Franklin Delano Roosevelt, and Joseph Stalin—held at Yalta, a resort in the Crimea on the Black Sea, on February 4 to 11, 1945. During one week of negotiations, as this version of the story goes, the two most important leaders of the Western democratic world abandoned more than 100 million people to an expanded Soviet version of the east, or the "Soviet empire." Ever since then, the word "Yalta" has evoked feelings of contempt for the sheer stupidity of the West in its dealings with Stalin as well as sentiments ranging from moral indignation to betrayal.

In a more dispassionate vein, "Yalta Europe" refers to the complicated process of multilateral negotiations among the Allies during and after World War II, on the one hand, and the gradual division of Europe into two ideologically opposed military and economic blocs, on the other. In this respect, Yalta Europe began at the first major summit of the Big Three in Teheran in 1943, was more or less complete with the division of Germany in 1949, and assumed its final shape in May 1955 when the finishing touches were put on the East and West blocs. The Federal Republic of Germany joined the North Atlantic Treaty Organization (NATO); the Warsaw Pact was established; and the signature of the Austrian State Treaty ended the Allied occupation of Austria, which then declared its permanent neutrality after occupational troops evacuated the country in October.

The defeat of Nazi Germany led to the division of Europe, and any number of events can be used to mark the turning point of the war. From the

American point of view, the landing of the western Allies in Normandy in June 1944 signaled the beginning of the end of the war in Europe. The encirclement and destruction of the German Sixth Army at the Battle of Stalingrad during the winter of 1942/1943 is generally recognized as the psychological turning point of the war. From a military point of view, Operation Zitadelle, the failure of the German offensive on the central section of the eastern front in the late spring and summer of 1943 appears decisive, because the Germans exhausted their offensive capacity in a gigantic battle that involved more than 2,000 tanks and 2 million men. Even this date is relatively late, however, because by the end of 1941, members of the German high command recognized that the war against the Soviet Union on the eastern front could not be won.

The objective of the Nazi invasion of the Soviet Union on June 22, 1941, was to "annihilate" the Soviet Union with a blitzkrieg of unprecedented dimensions. Despite massive territorial gains, the German offensive stalled at the gates of Moscow and Leningrad. Some military historians maintain that Stalin pursued a simple "space for time" strategy. Territory lost was time gained, which allowed the Soviet Union to marshal its forces for defense and then for counteroffensives. But others maintain that Stalin was responsible for enormous losses on the eastern front, which almost led to the defeat of the Soviet Union, because he did not withdraw Soviet troops fast enough or prematurely ordered them to hold positions. In any event, the sheer size of the Soviet Union led to an overextension of the German army. Winter is usually called one of Russia's most important allies, and the German troops undoubtedly were ill equipped for it. Rain in the fall and the spring were equally trying for the Germans, as the instruments of blitzkrieg, tanks and other heavy motorized vehicles, literally bogged down in the soft ground and on poorly maintained Russian roads.

In late 1941, the Soviet East and the British and American West forged an alliance. The German invasion of the Soviet Union eventually provided Great Britain with a needed ally, and vice versa, and the Japanese attack on Pearl Harbor on December 7, 1941, brought the United States into the Anglo-Soviet alliance. The Soviet Union switched allies in 1941 without changing some of the policy objectives articulated in the Hitler–Stalin pact of 1939, such as the consolidation of control over the Baltic states and eastern Poland.

Although the United States' vast reservoirs of human and material resources played an indisputably important role in winning the war in Europe and ultimately expedited its outcome, the most important European theater of military conflict was the eastern front, where Nazi Germany lost its war. The German losses of men and matériel on the eastern front between 1941 and the Normandy invasion in June 1944 were enormous. An estimated 13 million Soviet citizens in the armed forces died during World War II, in addition to 7 million civilians. Soviet combat dead outnumbered those of the United States in the Atlantic theater of war approximately 75 to 1 or, including civilians, around 115 to 1.[1] Given the enormity of Soviet losses, it is easy to understand why western allies and a western European front were so important to Stalin. The fact that his Anglo-American allies promised to open a western European front in 1942 but did not deliver on a grand scale until 1944 made him both impatient and suspicious.

The evolution of Allied policy in Europe was a long and complicated process of bi- and multilateral negotiations on many levels. The common objective of defeating Nazi Germany was the basis of the "anti-Hitler coalition," and the unconditional surrender of Nazi Germany became one of the cornerstones of Allied policy in early 1943. Churchill, Stalin, and Roosevelt also recognized that the defeat of Nazi Germany would necessarily mean reorganizing Europe so as to prevent the possibility of German aggression in the future.

Allied plans also were complicated by the fact that the alliance's common denominator of anti-Nazism was not great enough to overcome the principal ideological differences between the Anglo-American democratic West and the Soviet East. However, ideological antagonisms were played down because they could weaken the alliance and the war effort, and there were fears among the Western democracies that the Soviet Union might negotiate a separate peace with Nazi Germany, and vice versa. Therefore, the priority of maintaining East–West collaboration demanded that concessions be made on issues that the Western powers considered secondary. Negotiations among the Allies also were guided by the realistic assumption that regional "spheres of influence" would exist in Europe after the defeat of Nazi Germany.

As a matter of principle, the Western democracies agreed not to recognize territorial acquisitions made by force; this was one of the principles of the Atlantic Charter formulated by Churchill and Roosevelt in August 1941. But as a matter of fact, they did. The Western Allies disapproved of the territorial gains the Soviet Union had made under the auspices of the initial "spheres of influence" agreement between the Soviet Union and Nazi Germany, Hitler's and Stalin's nonaggression pact of 1939. Stalin had every intention of reestablishing Soviet control over the Baltic republics and territories that the Soviet Union had annexed in Finland, eastern Poland, and Romania between 1939 and 1941, areas that had been lost for the time being because of the invasion of the Soviet Union by Nazi Germany and its allies, and he made this clear to his Western allies early on in the alliance. Stalin also was intent on expanding the Soviet sphere of influence beyond these frontiers to ensure Soviet national security in the future.

If Yalta is thus understood as the democratic West's subordination of political principle to the imperial interests of the Soviet Union in East Central Europe (or, in a less moralistic vein, the compromises necessary to maintain East–West cooperation), then the evolution of Allied policy toward Poland provides the best example of how the idea of Yalta Europe developed before the Yalta conference.

The Polish Problem, 1939–1945

A brief survey of the diplomatic situation in Central Europe during World War II is necessary to appreciate the exceptional role Poland played in inter-Allied negotiations. Austria had been incorporated into the Third Reich in March 1938; Finland, Hungary, Romania, and Bulgaria were allies of Nazi Germany; and Poland, Czechoslovakia, and Yugoslavia had established governments in exile in London. The status of the states that collaborated with Nazi Germany obviously was different from the status of those that had governments in exile. The former had to be defeated along with Nazi Germany, and the latter had to be liberated from Nazi Germany.[2] The importance of the Yugoslav government in exile in London decreased as the significance of Tito and his Communist partisan movement increased in Yugoslavia and Yugoslavia assumed an increasingly "eastern," or Communist, course during the war.

Eduard Beneš, the president of the Czechoslovak Republic, who had resigned after the Munich agreement in 1938, initially was an embarrassing political exile for the Western democracies, because he reminded them that they had left Czechoslovakia in the lurch with their "policy of appeasement." Beneš's experience with Western democracies eroded his confidence in the West and led to his recognition that it also would be necessary for Czechoslovakia to reach some kind of accommodation with the Soviet Union. He therefore developed a close working relationship with Stalin, and, as many Czechs in times of duress had done in the past, saw Russia as a patron of the smaller Slavic nations.

Poland, the only country of this trio that depended completely on the support of the Western democracies, was in the least advantageous position of all. Its national interests conflicted directly with those of the Soviet Union, and this bilateral confrontation threatened the harmony of the British–American–Soviet alliance.

Britain and France had entered the war in 1939 to maintain the European status quo, which required, among other things, fighting for the reestablishment of Polish independence. The Soviet Union's participation in the invasion and occupation of Poland in 1939 made it an enemy of the Polish government in exile, but the German invasion of the Soviet Union in 1941 made the Soviet Union an ally of the United Kingdom, Poland's most important ally and advocate. The United Kingdom, in turn, pressured Poland to develop an accommodating relationship with the Soviet Union, but for obvious reasons Polish–Soviet relations were characterized by mutual suspicion instead of reciprocal trust. The Soviet Union had invaded and occupied that part of Poland it wanted to keep, and it justified this acquisition by pointing out that the region was inhabited predominantly by Belarussians and Ukrainians.

The renegotiation of the Polish–Soviet frontier is a long, complicated, and sad story. At the end of 1941, Churchill had branded the Soviet acquisitions in East Central Europe as a "shameless aggression," but in 1942 he indicated to the Soviets that he was willing to make concessions on this issue. Roosevelt secretly followed suit at the Teheran conference at the end of 1943, but he wanted to avoid making any public statements on the border issue until after the U.S. presidential elections in the fall of 1944, for fear of losing the Polish American vote. Plans for compensating Poland for the territory it was to lose in the east with German territory in the west were discussed and agreed on in principle at a summit meeting in Teheran in 1943. Churchill demonstrated the idea by putting three matches on the conference table. The ones on the left and the right represented the German–Polish and Polish–Soviet frontiers in 1939, and the one in the middle, the border the Soviets demanded. Then he took the match on the right and moved it to the far left to show how Poland would be compensated for its losses in the east by gains at the expense of Germany in the west. At Teheran, Churchill and Roosevelt also gave the Soviet Union a more or less free hand to administer the territories it was "liberating" on the eastern front.

The Allies also had bigger issues on their agenda in Teheran, such as the articulation of a grand strategy for the war, which included opening up new fronts in western and southern Europe and a Soviet commitment to enter the war against Japan; the establishment of policies for the treatment of Nazi Germany's allies; and the discussion of the framework for a permanent international peacekeeping organization. Churchill was a great proponent of a Western Allied invasion on the Balkan Peninsula, which would pierce the soft underbelly of Hilter's Europe and have the concomitant benefit of bringing Western troops into the heart of the continent, but this proposal was tabled by the Americans and eventually dismissed in favor of the Allied invasion in Normandy.

The fact that Stalin had broken off diplomatic relations with the Polish government in exile in mid-1943 also damaged Poland's prospects. The immediate cause of this rupture in relations was the Polish reaction to the German discovery of a mass grave of more than 4,000 Polish officers in the Katyn Forest (near Smolensk in Belarus) in March 1943. In the process of invading and occupying eastern Poland in 1939, the Soviet Union had taken into custody 15,000 Polish officers, professional soldiers, and reservists. These Polish officers, representatives of a national elite, then disappeared without a trace until the Germans discovered the mass grave in Katyn. The Germans accused the Soviets of having massacred them, but the Soviets reversed the allegation. However, given the evidence and an international investigation, it became clear to the Poles that the Soviets had murdered the Polish prisoners in Katyn, which also indicated that the 11,000 others most likely met similar fates elsewhere. Polish indignation and concern played directly into the hands of Nazi propaganda. The Soviet Union then accused the Polish government in exile of "pro-Hitler" agitation and broke off diplomatic relations.

Soviet authorities adamantly denied responsibility for the Katyn massacre until 1989 when they finally admitted that it was one of the many atrocities committed by the NKVD, the Soviet secret police. The Hitler–Stalin nonaggression pact, the Soviet denial of its secret protocol, and the Soviets' refusal to reveal what had happened to the Polish officers who had been taken into Soviet custody in 1939 strained Polish–Soviet relations not only throughout World War II but also during the entire postwar period of Communist "fraternal cooperation" between the two countries. Katyn, which became a symbol for the crimes the Soviet Union committed against the Polish nation, was subsequently one of the most gaping "blanks" or distortions in the official Soviet and Polish Communist histories. Although the 4,000 officers murdered at Katyn were but a fraction of Poland's total losses of 6 million during World War II, they assumed a prominent place in the Polish historical memory.

The Katyn massacre also is a good example of the type of policy the Soviet Union pursued toward non-Communist political and military organizations throughout east Central Europe. The liberation of countries from Nazi Germany went hand in hand with the persecution of anti-Nazi resisters who also were anti-Communists. They were accused of being "bourgeois," "nationalist," or "reactionary." Poland provides once again a prime example for the manner in which this policy was executed.

There was a considerable military underground organization in Poland, the Home Army, which worked closely with the Polish government in exile in London. In order to establish a political presence in Poland when it was liberated by the Soviet Union, Home Army commanders were instructed to stage local uprisings immediately before the arrival of the Soviet units. They also were advised to offer their assistance to the Red Army while simultaneously declaring their allegiance to the Polish government in exile, a practice that led in some cases to their immediate arrest or execution.[3]

The situation of the Home Army in Poland was complicated by the fact that once the Red Army reached ethnic Polish territory, Polish Communists from the Soviet Union established the "Committee for National Liberation" in the Lublin, the first major city liberated in "ethnic Poland," and the so-called Lublin Committee declared that it was the provisional legal authority for all of liberated Poland. As a result, Poland had two rival governments: one officially recognized by the Western Allies in London and another recognized only by, but fully supported by, the Soviet Union in Poland. The Lublin Committee was the first Communist puppet government in East Central Europe, and its establishment also demonstrated how the Soviet Union intended to deal with anti-Communist governments in the region in the future: They were to be discredited if possible and undermined if not.

The way in which the Soviet Red Army failed to aid an uprising of the Polish Home Army in Warsaw in August and September 1944 is yet another example of the means that the Soviets were prepared to use to eliminate anti-Communist, national opposition. In the summer of 1944, the Red Army advanced rapidly toward Warsaw. The Polish government in London called for an uprising by Polish Home Army in Warsaw, with the intention of establishing a territorial base of operations for the Polish government. The government also assumed that the Red Army would come to the aid of the Polish forces and "co-liberate" the Polish capital. But then the Red Army halted on the outskirts of Warsaw, and the stalling of the Soviet advance gave the Nazis ample opportunity to put down ruthlessly the Warsaw uprising. The elite of the Polish Home Army and 200,000 civilians died in Warsaw during sixty-three days of fighting.

In military terms, the Warsaw uprising was directed against Nazi Germany. Politically, however, it was explicitly anti-Soviet, and the Soviets let the German forces do their military and political dirty work for them. The Nazis eliminated the Polish nationalists, democrats, and anti-Communists of the Home Army, and they destroyed most of Warsaw in the process. (After the Warsaw uprising, Hitler ordered that the remains of Warsaw be razed. When it finally was "liberated" by the Red Army, the city was a depopulated pile of rubble.) Soviet histories maintained that the Red Army had overextended itself and was in no position to advance, although Poles never accepted this version of the story. Before 1989, Poles used to illustrate Poland's geopolitical predicament and their bitter feelings about Germans and Russians with a caustic joke. Question: "If Poland were to be invaded again by Germany and the Soviet Union, in which direction should one shoot first?" Answer: "To the west: first business, then pleasure."

Yalta: Bungling or Betrayal?

The Yalta conference was prefaced by an Anglo-Soviet understanding in regard to southeastern Europe. In October 1944, Churchill and Stalin met in Moscow to discuss British and Soviet interests in the region, and Churchill relayed only partial results of these meetings to Roosevelt. At that time, Churchill and Stalin came up with a "percentage agreement" that was basically a Soviet recognition of British interests in the Mediterranean (Greece, in particular) and the British acknowledgment of a Soviet sphere of influence in Romania and Bulgaria. Influence in Yugoslavia and Hungary was to be shared equally.[4] This entire agreement was made rather nonchalantly at the dinner table. Churchill jotted down the following East–West percentages on a half sheet of paper: Romania 90:10; Bulgaria 75:25; Hungary and Yugoslavia, 50:50; Greece 10:90. He passed it to Stalin, who looked at it and put a large check on it with a blue pencil and then passed it back to Churchill. (There was a bit of additional dickering on the next day between the Soviet and British foreign ministers, V. M. Molotov and Anthony Eden, and the percentages for Bulgaria and Hungary were revised to 80:20 and 75:25. However, the modalities of measurement never were discussed.)

Stalin also emphasized that he wanted Poland, Czechoslovakia, and Hungary to be "anti-Nazi, pro-Russian" states, and Churchill inconclusively broached one of his favorite ideas with Stalin: the reestablishment of a federation of states along the Danube, with Vienna as its capital. Churchill thought in the terms of the classic European balance of power in this respect, and he was concerned about the expansion of Soviet influence in Central Europe. A Danube confederation could fill the vacuum that the destruction of Austria-Hungary had created in 1918, and various schemes for a multinational cooperation in the region were popular among British planners. Representatives of the Polish and Czechoslovak governments in exile also discussed confederative plans during the war as a means of cooperatively offsetting Russian and German influence. But none of these confederative schemes materialized, and the Soviets viewed them with suspicion because they merely represented Western attempts to erect a new *cordon sanitaire.*

By the time the Big Three met in Yalta at the beginning of 1945, the end

The Big Three met at Yalta in early 1945 to negotiate a new postwar order: British prime minister Winston Churchill, ailing U.S. president Franklin Delano Roosevelt, and Soviet dictator Joseph Stalin. (U.S. Army Signal Corps, National Archives, Washington, D.C.)

of the war in Europe was in sight. The Red Army had occupied almost all of Poland and had overrun Romania, Hungary, and Bulgaria. (Romania and Bulgaria switched their allegiances and became belated members of the anti-Hitler coalition.) The Soviets had taken Budapest after three months of siege, and the Western Allies had reached German soil. The big issues on the Yalta agenda were the defeat and treatment of Nazi Germany, the future status of Poland, a hastening of the end of the war with Japan, and the development of a world security organization.

It is important to recall that British–American–Soviet cooperation reached a peak at the beginning of 1945, and there were hopes that the spirit of cooperation established during the war would carry over into the postwar period. However, critics have accused Roosevelt of trusting Stalin and of having misconceptions about Soviet Communism. Roosevelt did not have as good an understanding of Communism and Central European affairs as Churchill did, who was becoming increasingly concerned about the Soviet Union's growing influence. Churchill viewed Soviet policy in East Central Europe as a European problem with global implications for the Western democracies, whereas Roosevelt subordinated East Central European or regional issues to global considerations. He banked on the idea of the United Nations and believed that Stalin and the Soviet Union were prepared to assume the role of one of the guarantors of the free world. Therefore, concessions to the Soviet Union in East Central Europe were a means of ensuring peace on a global scale. But this situation was complicated by the fact that Roosevelt was in some respects more concerned about the gains of the British Empire during the the war than those of the Soviet Union and thus was more suspicious of Churchill than of Stalin.

At Yalta, the Allies discussed principles for the treatment of Germany, such as unconditional surrender, dismemberment, denazification, demilitarization, and reparations for the Soviet Union, and they agreed on including France in the occupation and administration of Germany and Berlin, which were to be divided up into four different zones. (This model of quadripartite administration also was applied to Austria and Vienna.) However, there was no agreement on what to do with Germany after the war, no common plan or joint vision.

An important shift in the Western perception of Poland antedated the decisions regarding the borders and the future of Poland that were made at Yalta. Both Churchill and Roosevelt had come to accept the idea that Poland had to be considered in the context of the Soviet Union's national security interests. From this perspective, the purpose of Poland would be to help protect the Soviet Union from future aggression. At Yalta, the Allies agreed to revise the eastern frontier of Poland, and they discussed new northern and western frontiers that would involve the incorporation of substantial German territories into Poland—most of East Prussia in the north and areas reaching as far west as the Oder and Western Neisse Rivers (the so-called Oder–Neisse Line). These acquisitions, in turn, would necessitate the expulsion of millions of Germans. Although the Oder–Neisse frontier was not sanctioned until the last great summit meeting that the Allies held, in Potsdam in midsummer 1945, the dye was cast in Yalta. The so-called eastern territories—East Prussia, Pomerania, and Silesia—were placed under the administration of Poland, which referred to them as "recovered territories," and then were unilaterally annexed after 1947. (The Soviet Union also occupied and then annexed a portion of northern East Prussia around Königsberg.)

At Potsdam, the Allies also formally endorsed the policy of transferring not only Germans from the German territories administered by Poland but also ethnic German minorities, or *Volksdeutsche*, from Czechoslovakia and Hungary, "in a humane and orderly manner." Finally, the Allies agreed on a "reorganization" of the Communist-dominated Lublin government in Poland, which already had been recognized by Czechoslovakia and Yugoslavia, to include some representatives of the Polish government in exile, and "the holding of free and unfettered elections as soon as possible." Long before Yalta, the Western Allies had abandoned Poland's 1939 frontiers; then at Yalta, they effectively abandoned the Polish government in exile. (Although it had lost its diplomatic status, the Polish government in exile maintained an office in London until 1989.)

It is important to distinguish here between the two different planes of Soviet and Anglo-American, or East–West, relations. Democracy and Communism were incompatible on moral, political, and ideological levels, and in this respect, the Cold War started before the hot war. Nonetheless, military cooperation was indispensable, and the overriding importance of an East–West anti-Nazi alliance made Western anti-Communism a secondary issue. At Yalta, Poland was not important enough for the Western Allies to risk a rupture with the Soviet Union, and after World War II, Western anti-Communism was subordinated in many respects to the objective of maintaining peace in Europe. If one is prepared to downplay or ignore the necessity of cooperating for the pragmatic purposes of winning the war against Nazi Germany before 1945 or keeping the peace in Europe between East and West thereafter, it is easy to use moral criteria to criticize the hypocrisy or duplicity of the Western democracies' policies, and many East Central Europeans have perceived "Yalta" or "the West" in exactly these terms.

After defeating Nazi Germany with the Soviet Union, the West was neither willing nor prepared to fight a new war with the Soviet Union in order to liberate East Central Europe. The Cold War was implicit in the dynamics of the British–American–Soviet alliance. The overriding objective of defeating Nazi Germany held the alliance together, and once it had been achieved, conflicting ideological and national interests were free to emerge. Poland was the first victim of World War II in 1939: the Hitler–Stalin pact and Nazi and Soviet aggression. It also was in the ill-fated position of being the first victim of peace in 1945: the collaboration of Western democracies with the Soviet Union that led to the defeat of Nazi Germany.

Although Europe was not divided at Yalta, the process of dividing it began there. Allied policy for the treatment of postwar Germany was fragmentary. The decisions made regarding Poland were both unfortunate and far reaching, but Czechoslovakia and Hungary were barely discussed. Among the concluding documents of the Yalta conference was an Allied "Declaration on Liberated Europe" affirming the "right of all peoples to choose the form of governments under which they will live," "the restoration of sovereign rights and self-government," and "free elections." The Western allies did not envision the Soviet sphere of influence as a closed bloc, and they hoped that the Soviet Union would respect the rules of democratic fair play in East Central Europe after the war. It did not.

The Making of Eastern Europe, 1945–1948

Churchill popularized the term "Iron Curtain" shortly after the war. This vivid metaphor tends to divert attention away from the fact that the Iron Curtain did not fall into place at one theatrical moment. Although the presence of the Red Army from the Baltic to the Balkans gave the Soviet Union massive political leverage in the region, the Communists did not take power all at once. Instead, the establishment of Communist regimes in the region was a successive process that started in 1945 but was not completed until 1948. The amounts of political sympathy and antipathy for the revolutionary program the Soviet Union propagated in the countries it liberated varied from state to state, as did the tactics the Communists employed to gain power.

The political revolutions in East Central Europe went hand-in-hand with massive ethnic and demographic dislocations. Poland is the best example of the type of chaos that World War II produced in the form of armed hostilities, deportation, genocide, settlement and resettlement campaigns, liberation, repatriation, and population exchanges. After 1939, the Soviets deported Poles from eastern Poland. The Nazis expelled Poles from the parts of Poland that had been annexed by the Third Reich into the General Gouvernement, and they "exported" Poles to Germany as forced laborers. Ethnic Germans from throughout East Central Europe were brought in to "resettle" those parts of Poland that Nazi Germany had incorporated. The Holocaust virtually annihilated the Polish Jews. After the war, Poles were repatriated from the Soviet Union and Germany, and the Germans were expelled from those parts of Germany administered by Poland, which in turn had to be "resettled" by Poles.

The expulsion of the Germans from East Central Europe took a number of forms. Many Germans—as well as the members of many other national and ethnic groups that had collaborated with Nazi Germany or merely feared the Red Army—fled to avoid ending up behind the Soviet front. (In the process of honoring repatriation agreements, the Western Allies returned more than 2 million people to the Soviet Union after the war: collaborators, who as anti-Communists and nationalists had fought with the Nazis against the Soviets; prisoners of war; and laborers the Nazis had conscripted by force from occupied territories. Upon their return to the Soviet Union, these people were frequently accused of treason (either real or imagined) prosecuted, and severely punished.) On the one hand, Nazi anti-Soviet propaganda was apocalyptic and atrocious, and it encouraged evacuation or flight. On the other hand, plundering, looting, murder, and the mass rape of German women were characteristic of the conduct of the victorious Red Army. Vengeance and greed played no small role in the initial treatment of German minorities throughout East Central Europe. The first expulsions of Germans and the appropriation of their property were spontaneous and arbitrary, but these measures evolved into national policies which the Allies sanctioned after the war.

Between 1944 and 1950, more than 11 million Germans fled or were expelled from their homes, and the number who perished in the process is unknown. Estimates range from hundreds of thousands to 2 million. Theft, rape, murder, and death caused by hunger, exposure, and exhaustion were part of the "humane and orderly" transfer of the Germans. They left homes they had inhabited for hundreds of years, and they often fled on foot in large "caravans."

The great majority of those Germans who were expelled, more than 7 million, came from the territories administered by Poland east of the Oder–Neisse Line and Poland and the Soviet Union in east Prussia. Well before the end of the war, Beneš received Stalin's consent to expel Czechoslovakia's German minority of more than 3 million, the *Sudetendeutsche*. They were collectively branded as traitors and banished after the war. Almost 90 percent of the 500,000 "ethnic Germans," or *Volksdeutsche*, from Yugoslavia emigrated during the war, fled, or were killed or deported after the war. The estimated 240,000 Germans who were evacuated, deported, or expelled from Hungary reduced the country's German minority by half. Tens of thousands of the "Transylvania Saxons" also fled their 600-year-old homes in Romania.[5]

Some people explain the treatment of the Germans in terms of biblical justice: an eye for an eye, and a tooth for a tooth. The fact that the East Central European victims of Nazi German aggression committed crimes against Germans has been consistently and conveniently ignored. After World War II no one was prepared to let the Germans be the victims of anything, and German–Polish and German–Czech relations were burdened for decades by the fact that millions of Germans in the Federal Republic of Germany who had been expelled from Poland or Czechoslovakia wanted the Poles and the Czechs as well as the Communists to admit to the violence and injustice of these expulsions. An admission of this nature was not nationally feasible for Poles or Czechs, nor was it ideologically possible for Communists. It took a revolution to address this issue. After 1989, for example, Václav Havel raised the question of Czech guilt for the expulsion of the *Sudetendeutsche*, much to the consternation of many Czechs.

If a German and Jewish as well as a German-Jewish presence was one of the distinctive characteristics of Central European culture, and multicultural symbiosis was the source of its dynamism, this culture ceased to exist during and after World War II. If Central European culture was inspired or made by Jews, it either emigrated with them before the Holocaust or died with them during it. The flight or expulsion of the Germans also dramatically diminished their presence in the region.

East Central Europe, historically part of a German "linguistic and cultural space," was de-Germanized, although the Germans' absence is seldom lamented. The combined results of Nazi *and* Allied policies—genocide for the Jews and population transfers for the Germans—were an "ethnic cleansing" of states that historically had been multi-ethnic, culturally diverse, and religiously heterodox.[6] For the first time in its history, Poland was almost exclusively ethnic Polish and Roman Catholic. The population of Bohemia and Moravia became almost exclusively Czech. In comparison, Hungary still had a considerable number of Jews and Germans, but it became much more homogeneous than it had been in the past.

If the relative absence of Jews and Germans dramatically changed the complexion of Central European culture, then the massive presence of the Russians in the region represented an unprecedented political reorientation. The eastern half of Central Europe, which had historically been oriented toward the West—Catholic Rome, the Paris of the Enlightenment and the French Revolution, or London and Washington, D.C. as the capitals of the democratic world—fell under the long shadow of Moscow. "The Second World War, or rather its outcome," Piotr Wandycz remarked, "reversed the course of history of East Central Europe. Traditionally a borderland or a

EUROPE DIVIDED, 1945–1949

The Iron Curtain in 1945

Territories occupied and annexed by the Soviet Union, 1939-1941 and 1945-1947

The "eastern territories" of Germany incorporated into Poland

and the Soviet Union, 1945-1947

Soviet zones of occupation in Germany and Austria

Year Communists came into power

semi-periphery of the West, the region became a westward extension of the Soviet East."[7]

Generalizations about how the Communists came to power in East Central Europe are difficult to make. Yugoslavia was an exception because it was liberated by Tito's National Liberation Army, not the Red Army, and it installed a Communist government without Soviet assistance, or interference, in 1945. The Communists' rise to power in other countries in the region followed more or less the same pattern. During the war, Communist parties in these states were divided into "domestic" and "Muscovite" wings. The "domestics" worked in the underground at home, whereas the "Muscovites" were in Soviet exile. (The geographical segregation of the party factions also had ideological implications.) The Muscovites returned home in the wake of the Red Army to assume leading party and governmental positions, which inevitably lead to dissatisfaction among those Communists who had done the dangerous work at home.

After the first postwar elections in the region, which were relatively free in Czechoslovakia and Hungary but much less so elsewhere, the Communist parties participated in coalition governments with social democratic, "bourgeois democratic," and agrarian parties. The Communists regularly controlled the Ministry of the Interior, an office that allowed them to misuse the police for political purposes and to manipulate the electoral process. Communists also promoted the idea of the "unity" of the left: an ideological and tactical alliance between Communists, on the one hand, and socialists and social democrats, on the other. This was just a tactical ploy, however. The destruction of independent socialist parties and the creation of "socialist unity" or "socialist workers'" parties exclusively under Communist control was one of the Communists' first objectives. The Communists also promoted policies, such as the nationalization of major industries and land reform, that were not only popular with broad sections of the population but also, to a certain extent, necessary. Nationalization was a means of reconstruction, and many East Central European states had a tremendous amount of land on their hands that had to be redistributed, for example, the former German territories in Poland, the properties of the *Sudetendeutsche* in Czechoslovakia, and the assets confiscated from "fascists" and *Volksdeutsche* in Hungary.

The Communists' methods of eliminating their opponents varied. Generally Communists exploited the results of an election, which they manipulated, or a governmental crisis, which they instigated, to undermine their opponents. Their rise to power in Bulgaria, Romania, and Poland in 1946 was straightforward, heavy-handed, and ruthless. Politicians from the opposition fled or were arrested on trumped up charges of "treason," tried, and executed, and their political parties were banned.

Hungarian Communists used the more sophisticated approach of "salami tactics." They took the whole sausage, but only one thin slice at a time, with a carefully orchestrated combination of defamation, blackmail, coercion, and police terror. In 1947, they eliminated their most formidable political opponent, the agrarian national Smallholders Party which held a majority of seats in the Hungarian parliament and had received an absolute majority (53 percent) of the votes in the 1945 elections, by discovering a "conspiracy" which ended in a gigantic show trial of 220 politicians. By 1948, the Communists had consolidated their control of Hungary. (Nevertheless, it would be technically inaccurate to label the East Central European Communist states as one-party regimes. In order to create the impression of political pluralism, a few agrarian and "liberal" parties were left nominally intact but strictly subordinated to the Communist Party as "bloc parties.")

In Czechoslovakia, the Communists enjoyed a considerable amount of authentic popular support, and they emerged from the first postwar elections with 38 percent of the vote. The Communists' rise to absolute power in February and March 1948 was an ambiguous event, and historians have had trouble deciding whether it was more of a coup by the Communists or more of a capitulation by the democrats. In any event, the Communists terrorized the non-Communist parties and called their supporters into the streets, and the Czechoslovak coalition government buckled under pressure. Eduard Beneš, who had presided over the demise of Czechoslovak democracy in 1938, had the misfortune of experiencing its renewed fall in 1948 and died shortly thereafter. His death also was symbolic, as it severed the link between the first and the second Czechoslovak republics. The democratic West was shocked by the Communist takeover in Czechoslovakia, an event that reflected Stalin's strategy for the region. He wanted the Communist parties of the region to consolidate their power, even if this meant rupturing relations with the West.

The Communist seizure of power in the individual countries of East Central Europe was comparable in a number of respects. Whether the similarities are enough to assume that they had a master plan that they all followed or, on the contrary, whether they acted on a more pragmatic and *ad hoc* basis, is difficult to determine. However, the presence of the Red Army and the allegiance of the national Communist parties to Moscow made clear the region's future political orientation. By the end of 1947, the (Moscow) party line also was clear. Communists were not to cooperate with "bourgeois democrats."

Furthermore, the experience of fascist rule had radicalized many people and made them more receptive to socialist ideas, and after the war the shining Soviet vision of a new social order based on peace, justice, equality, and prosperity appealed to many members of the younger generation and to intellectuals, in particular. Traditional political elites had been largely eliminated by the Nazis in Poland and Czechoslovakia or discredited to a significant extent by collaboration in Hungary, and the Communists defamed national traditions and prewar institutions as "feudal, bourgeois, clerical, and fascist."[8]

The new Communist intelligentsia responsible for the propagation and administration of the forthcoming revolution came predominantly out of the working class and had moved up through the party rank and file or consisted of assimilated bourgeois Jewish intellectuals with upper-class backgrounds. (In East Central Europe, both Stalinization in the immediate postwar period and de-Stalinization after 1956 had peculiar national and

anti-Semitic twists. In Czechoslovakia, many of the leading party officials accused of conspiracy and executed in 1952 were Jewish. But these roles were
reversed in Poland and Hungary, where many of the most ruthless Stalinists
were Jewish. Therefore, de-Stalinization in 1956 was explicitly anti-Semitic,
as was indigenous anti-Communism thereafter.)

The Communist parties consolidated their power in two phases. Between 1945 and 1948, they purged the non-Communist or national opposition, and then they embarked on resolute programs of Stalinization, destroying democratic institutions and suspending civil rights, oppressing
churches, nationalizing commerce and industries, collectivizing agriculture,
and purging their own ranks. Yugoslavia was the only Communist country
in East Central Europe not sucked into the Soviet bloc. Tito wanted to rule
with his own iron fist, had his own ideas about the development of communism in Yugoslavia, and refused to fall into line with the other Communist
parties and states in the region. The fact that the Red Army had not liberated Yugoslavia and the West's explicit approval of Tito's nonalignment also
gave him considerable latitude. Differences between Tito and Stalin led to
a dramatic split in 1948, and this ideological falling-out raised real and imagined tensions between "nationalists" and "Stalinists" in East Central Europe.
After Tito refused to subordinate himself to Moscow, "Titoism" became a
crime synonymous with "Troskyism," "bourgeois nationalism," "revisionism," and the betrayal of "the international proletariate," all various desig-
nations for not doing things the way Moscow wanted. Throughout East Central Europe, many alleged Communist "aberrationists" were charged with
these transgressions, prosecuted at show trials, and imprisoned or executed.

The fundamental issue at stake was whether there was "one road to socialism" designed and dictated by Moscow or many individual "national
paths" leading to the same goal. As long as Stalin lived, "national aberra-
tions" were not tolerated. But after his death in 1953, there was a struggle
between Stalinists and reform Communists in many East Central European
countries that was fueled by the official beginning of de-Stalinization in the
Soviet Union in 1956. The pattern of conflict between Stalinists (or Moscow
hard-liners) and East Central European reform Communists (who frequently appealed to national sentiments and hence were called "national
Communists") was established early on and proved to be enduring. Each attempt to change the system—Hungary in 1956, Czechoslovakia in 1968,
Poland in 1980/1981, and in the Soviet Union itself in 1991—provoked a
neo-Stalinist backlash.

Dividing Germany, 1949

Despite the big summit meetings in Teheran and Yalta, regular diplomatic
consultation on a number of subordinate levels, and the establishment of
Allied joint planning commissions during the war, the Allies never managed
to agree before the end of the war on how they were going to deal with Germany. Allied planners discussed the idea of dividing Germany into smaller

states as one means of diminishing a future German threat. But they never agreed to divide Germany into the two German states that were established in 1949: the Federal Republic of Germany in the west and the German Democratic Republic in the east. The Germans also initially had nothing to say in the whole affair. After Nazi Germany capitulated on May 8, 1945, the Allies disbanded the Nazi government under the leadership of Admiral Karl Dönitz and eventually arrested its members. The *absence* of a jointly articulated Allied policy toward Germany before the end of the war and the *absence* of a German government after the end of the war created a situation that ultimately facilitated the division of the country four years later.

The last great World War II summit meeting was held in Potsdam, outside Berlin, during July and August 1945. The composition of the Big Three had changed considerably. Churchill had won the war for Britain but lost the postwar elections; Clement Attlee was now the British prime minister. Roosevelt died shortly after the Yalta conference and his vice president, Harry Truman, assumed his place. Germany was the central issue at this meeting. The Allies decided on the Oder–Neisse Line as a provisional German–Polish frontier and endorsed the expulsion of Germans east of it as well as from Czechoslovakia and Hungary. They outlawed the Nazi Party and all its suborganizations, introduced denazification programs, and decided to prosecute leading Nazis at Nuremberg for war crimes and crimes against humanity. They also finally agreed on the modalities for the occupation of Germany and Berlin, which were divided into four zones but were to be jointly administered as a whole.

In theory, a quadripartite body, the Allied Control Council, was to agree unanimously on Allied policy for all of Germany which, in turn, was to be uniformly applied in the four zones by the respective occupational powers. This top–down administration was to be complemented by a bottom–up reorganization of Germany, which involved the reestablishment of political parties, on the one hand, and the rejuvenation of political institutions on a local and provincial levels within the four zones, on the other. The political parties and the provinces (*Länder*) were to be the building blocks of a new German state. A high degree of consensus and cooperation among the Allies would have been necessary for the quadripartite administration of Germany to function as envisioned, but the ability of the Allies to agree on fundamental policy issues disintegrated rapidly after the war. The individual occupational powers were also effectively in a position to act as they saw fit in their respective zones.

The dissension among the Allies on how to administer Germany was a manifestation of deeper differences between the Soviet East and the democratic West. Whether the Allied inability to agree on Germany directly contributed to a greater estrangement between East and West or, conversely, whether ideological confrontation caused a political gridlock in Germany has been a hotly debated issue among historians of different political dispositions. This is an important issue because it raises the question of who was ultimately responsible for the division of Germany—Communists and

Russians in the East or anti-Communists and Americans in the West—or if
the division of Germany could have been avoided in the course of dividing
of Europe.

In any event, the four Allies failed to establish a central administration
for Germany. They argued about whether economic unification should pre-
cede political unification, or vice versa, and whether or not national elections should be held. It would be unfair to blame all the Allies' problems on
the Soviets. The French, initially more anti-German than anti-Soviet, acted
obstructively, too. In 1947, the American and the British occupational
regimes created a "bizone" to coordinate their economic policies, and the
French eventually joined this configuration. Meanwhile, the Soviets pursued
their own policies in their zone. In 1948, the failure of Allied cooperation
in Germany and the success of the Communists in East Central Europe motivated the Western Allies to abandon the idea of German unity for the time
being at least, and they drew up plans for the economic and political integration of western Germany into the European and transatlantic west. The
Western Allies proposed that the German political parties in the western
zones of occupation work out a provisional constitution, and they introduced a reformed West German currency, the *deutsche Mark*. The Soviets responded by withdrawing from the Allied Control Council, introducing an
East German Mark, and blockading Berlin. However, their attempt to drive
the Western Allies out of West Berlin by starving the inhabitants in the western half of the city was frustrated by a spectacular airlift.

In September 1948, representatives from the *Länder* in the western zones
convened in Bonn to draft a provisional constitution, and the adoption and
ratification of the Bonner Grundgesetz, or Bonn Basic Law, led to the establishment of the Federal Republic of Germany (FRG) in May 1949. The Western perception of West Germany and the Western German perception of
the Allied occupation changed dramatically. The Western powers lost an old
enemy and gained a new ally. From the West German perspective, the victors stopped occupying Western Germany and began defending its independence. While democracy was being established in West Germany, full-
scale Stalinization commenced in East Germany, and it followed the
established Communist patterns of coercion and collectivization. East German Communists also drafted and adopted their own version of a constitution, and the German Democratic Republic (GDR), a state of "farmers and
workers," was proclaimed in October 1949.

The unwavering allegiance of West Germany to the West and East Germany to the East was extraordinary, and some observers ironically described
the Germans' loyalty to their respective states and ideological blocs in terms
of the German national psyche: a propensity for order, discipline, and per-
fectionism under prevailing political circumstances, whatever they may be.
After the war, the Germans in the west decided to be the best democrats,
and the Germans in the east were resolved to be the best Communists. But,
this kind of observation obscures the fact that the political culture that
evolved in the FRG represented a break with undesirable German national
traditions of authoritarianism, whereas the one that developed in the GDR

did not. The GDR was one of the most successful Communist states in the eastern bloc, not because it was Communist, but because it was "German" in the negative sense of the word. Piety, Prussian organizational logic, Nazism, and Stalinism were compatible in many respects. Thus, the transition from one form of totalitarianism to another—from "brown fascism" to "red fascism"—involved a change of ideologies more than a departure from previous political structures or attitudes.

The Bonn Basic Law and the relationship between the two German states were unusual in many respects. Although the Bonn Basic Law had the legal status of a constitution in the Federal Republic of Germany, it was a provisional document designed to bridge the gap until a definitive constitution for *all* Germany could be drafted. The FRG assumed the moral and financial responsibilities that came with being the successor state of the Third Reich, whereas the GDR as a "socialist and anti-fascist state" completely dissociated itself from Nazi Germany.

Although the Federal Republic of Germany developed a pragmatic modus vivendi with the "second German state" and began to cultivate diplomatic relations with the GDR on several levels in the early 1970s, it never formally recognized the GDR. On the contrary, the FRG considered itself the only legitimate representative of the German people, and it granted FRG citizenship to any German resident of the GDR who was in a position to request it. In this respect, the Germans who were *de facto* citizens of the GDR were *de jure* citizens of the FRG, or potential West Germans. All they had to do is get to the West.[9]

Finally, the FRG not only claimed to be the sole legitimate representative of all Germans; as the only successor state of Nazi Germany, it also maintained that any peace settlement with Germany had to be based on a territorial status quo ante bellum: the German frontiers of 1937. The legal reasoning behind this argument is complicated, but it essentially meant that the FRG—as a partial, provisional, and democratic German state—could not definitively accept those changes in the prewar frontiers of Germany that the Allies had made unilaterally after the war, because the preconditions for recognizing those changes—German unification and the conclusion of a peace treaty—had not been fulfilled. In other words, the war was over, but from a legal point of view, peace had not been concluded.

As a result, the FRG did not formally recognize the postwar annexation of the "eastern regions" of prewar German territory by Poland and the Soviet Union. Although the leading politicians of the Federal Republic of Germany recognized that the "eastern regions" were irrevocably lost for Germany and were wise enough never to turn this formal issue into an actual claim, the fact that the Federal Republic of Germany was bound by a cogent legal argument to question the legitimacy of the postwar frontiers on formal grounds burdened the relations between the FRG and Poland. West German claims were a constant source of anxiety for Poles. They also gave Communist propagandists an opportunity to accuse the Federal Republic of Germany of wanting to revise the European order that World War II had established, just as Hitler did after World War I. (The German–Polish border issue was finally settled in a bilateral treaty after the unification of Germany in 1990.)

The division of Europe into East and West was at an advanced stage before the Federal Republic of Germany and the German Democratic Republic were established in 1949. Between 1945 and 1948, the Communists had consolidated their control in Yugoslavia, Albania, Bulgaria, Romania, Poland, Hungary, and Czechoslovakia. The Iron Curtain on the "German–German" frontier and, after 1961, the Berlin Wall were the most poignant symbols for the partition of Europe. Germany was not just a microcosm of the East–West split; it was the key to overcoming the division of Europe. As long as Germany was divided, Europe would stay divided.

There were two completely different best-case scenarios for German unification: "neutrality" on Soviet terms or democracy on Western terms. In 1952, the Soviets transmitted a diplomatic note to the Western Allies in which they proposed resuming quadripartite negotiations on the "German question." The so-called Stalin note envisioned the establishment of a Pan-German government in which "progressive" political forces would be (over) represented, the negotiation of a peace treaty, and the unification of Germany based on the condition that Germany would not participate in any military coalitions or alliances in the future. German neutrality or the neutralization of Germany was the price to be paid for unification. The West German government and the Western Allies viewed this Soviet offer with suspicion and eventually rejected it.

Some historians have argued that this was merely a tactical ploy by the Soviet Union to slow down the process of Western European economic and military integration and that it was aimed at preventing the "drift" of the Federal Republic of Germany into the North Atlantic Treaty Organization. Others, however, view the West's failure to respond to this Soviet initiative as a tragically missed opportunity, and they blame Western politicians of being shortsighted and intransigent. The interpretation of Stalin's 1952 offer is still a source of controversy. In any event, the best Germany that the Soviet Union could imagine was a neutral one: either not associated with the West or disassociated from the West in military and economic terms.[10] This vision also was similar in many respects to the kind of Germany that many representatives of the West German left in the 1980s wished to see: a neutral, demilitarized, and nuclear-free state.

The Soviet proposal for German unification was based on a big compromise, and one of the reasons that the West rejected it was that it wanted reunification on its own democratic terms. These terms were unrealistic, however, because they presupposed the democratic transformation of East Germany as well as the Soviet willingness to let East Germany go. In principle, West German politicians never questioned the importance of German reunification. It was and remained a long-term policy goal and constitutional obligation of the Federal Republic of Germany. However, the prospects of reunification were so dismal that very few people believed it to be a foreseeable event.

The longer the division of Germany lasted, the more acceptable it became on both sides of the Iron Curtain. For example, in the 1950s and 1960s, between 35 and 45 percent of the West Germans surveyed considered reunification to be the most important question in the Federal Republic; after the mid-1970s, however, it was never more than 1 percent.[11] The word "reunification" effectively disappeared from the operative vocabulary of West German politicians and was replaced by other terms reflecting the Western German policy options in German–German relations: *Ostpolitik*, rapprochement, détente, cooperation, normalization. Furthermore, the idea of the unification of Germany or, after 1949, reunification, was a generational issue. That is, it meant much more to the older generations of Germans than to the younger ones who had grown up in two German states and had been taught not only that the division of Germany was the price that the Germans had to pay for the Third Reich but also that it was indispensable to the maintenance of peace in Europe.

Starting the Cold War

As long as the Cold War lasted, there was an ongoing debate among historians and political scientists in the West about who started it and whether it could have been avoided or shortened, and since 1989 they have argued about who won or lost it and why. Neither the time nor the place in which the Cold War began is a source of controversy. It started as a European affair that acquired increasingly clear contours between 1946 and 1949 and assumed global dimensions thereafter. However, historians must establish a hierarchy of causes for the Cold War, and the importance of individual variables such as ideology (or political principle), economics, or national interest can be weighted and combined in various ways. Different interpretations reflect different understandings of the roles played by the Soviet Union and the United States (as well as varying assumptions about the nature of Marxism-Leninism or capitalist democracy).

Theories of the origins of the Cold War can be divided into different schools. The traditional interpretation of the Cold War is the product of an older generation of scholars, many of whom had firsthand experience with Nazism or Stalinism, whereas revisionist interpretations have been proposed by younger generations. "Idealists" and "realists" argue about the motives behind the conflict: The former emphasize the importance of political principle, and the latter underscore the role of economics and national interest. Liberals and conservatives in the United States or representatives of the political left and right in Western Europe also regularly disagree about the Cold War. In conservative terms, the issue at stake is whether or not one was "hard" or "soft" on Communism. Generally speaking, idealists and conservatives support a traditional, pro-American interpretation of the Cold War, whereas realists and representatives of the political left advance various forms of revisionism critical of the United States' role in the initiation and continuation of the conflict.

The initial interpretation of the Cold War took Soviet ideology at face value. It was based on the assumption that the Soviet Union was an expansive and aggressive totalitarian state ruled by a ruthless and unscrupulous dictator and actively pursuing the objective of world domination. The establishment of Communist regimes in Eastern Europe and the Iron Curtain was indicative of Soviet aspirations, and the Western democratic world closed ranks to protect itself and combat the spread of Communism. These issues were not open to interpretation. They were generally recognized as matters of fact.

Revisionists later questioned this version of the story and attempted to invert the logic of the beginning of the Cold War. They maintained, for example, that Soviet policy was more reactive than aggressive, and they contended that the belligerent nature of Western anti-Communism threatened the Soviet Union to such a great extent that it was forced into a defensive posture that entailed clamping down in Eastern Europe. These two schools of thought have enjoyed varying degrees of popularity among different generations of Western Sovietologists and historians.

The older generation of analysts from the 1940s and 1950s, frequently émigrés from East Central Europe or the Soviet Union, advanced a relatively straightforward theory of totalitarianism developed during World War II to describe both Nazism and Communism. This novel form of government tried to subordinate all forms of social, economic, and political organization in a single hierarchy that in turn was dominated by one party and one individual or dictator. Totalitarian ideology envisioned the radical transformation of humankind and society and sanctioned domestic terror and foreign aggression as legitimate means for achieving these ends. Furthermore, totalitarian rule was comprehensive; it penetrated all realms of society. From this perspective, the Cold War was the logical, moral, political, and military continuation of World War II. Hitler had been defeated. Stalin had not.

The younger generation of revisionists who began their careers in the late 1960s criticized this traditional interpretation of the Cold War for being too ideological, uncritical, and methodologically unsophisticated. Instead, they assumed that the Soviet Union was not as bad as the proponents of the totalitarian theory claimed, made a variety of distinctions between Nazism and Communism, and pointed out that Soviet reality was much more complex than the gross simplifications of totalitarian theory. They also believed that the Soviet system was capable of modernization and reform.

Theories about the Cold War fell into corresponding "right-wing" and "left-wing" categories. On one side, the proponents of the traditional theory criticized as totalitarian the tenets of Marxism, socialism, and communism. On the other, many revisionists showed a certain sympathy for Marxist or socialist ideals, and in some cases, they felt that the Soviet Union was basically a good idea that had been poorly executed and had massively gone astray, especially under Stalin. From this perspective, the Soviet Union appeared to be inherently capable of developing into a freer and more prosperous system, especially after Stalin's death in 1953.

Different dates can be used to mark the beginning of the American engagement in the Cold War, each illustrating different political, economic, and strategic dimensions of the conflict. On March 5, 1946, Winston

Churchill gave a speech in Fulton, Missouri, in which he popularized the metaphor of the Iron Curtain. Just over one year later, President Harry Truman told the U.S. Congress that the world was faced with a struggle between two fundamentally incompatible ways of life. One, which the Americans understood as the American way, was based on the "will of the majority" and was "distinguished by free institutions, representative government, [and] free elections," and the other, which relied on "terror and oppression," was "based upon the will of the minority forcibly imposed upon the majority." The immediate occasion for this speech was Truman's request that the United States provide economic and military aid to Greece and Turkey in order to help their respective governments combat Communist insurgents. However, he also stated that the United States was determined in principle to assist those people elsewhere whose freedom was threatened by "armed minorities or by outside pressure."[12] The Truman Doctrine was born.

For Harry Truman and most other Americans and Europeans at this time, the Cold War was a straightforward question of political principle (or political ideology). The choice to be made was between freedom, liberty, and democracy or their absence, although subsequent interpretations made this seem less clear and almost hopelessly complicated.[13] The Cold War worldview distinguished between good and evil, or "us" and "them," in a manner that was perhaps naive, simplistic, and self-righteous. It also was responsible for a number of dubious U.S. domestic and foreign policies, vigilantes like the "Commie" hunter Senator Joseph McCarthy at home, and an assortment of politically reprehensible allies and client states in the developing world whose only redeeming value was their anti-Communism. Whether the merit of the ideals to which the United States was committed can be used as an excuse for the excesses of the Cold War or, conversely, whether the excesses were indicative of the shortcomings of the ideals themselves is a point that proponents and critics of U.S. policy during the Cold War will continue to debate. Nevertheless, if the Cold War was about ideas, the fundamental choice was clear.

George F. Kennan, one of the most influential personalities in the American foreign policy establishment after the war, was responsible for the classic formulation of the strategy that the United States was to pursue in its confrontation with the Soviet Union. In an article, "The Sources of Soviet Conduct," which he published under the pseudonym "X" in the July 1947 issue of *Foreign Affairs*, he outlined the "innate antagonism between capitalism and Socialism" and asserted that "the main element of any United States policy toward the Soviet Union must be that of a long-term, patient but firm and vigilant containment of Russian expansive tendencies."[14] The Cold War was, in this respect, a confrontation between fundamentally different social, economic, and political systems, each championed by states that emerged from World War II with an unprecedented amount of power: the United States and the Soviet Union.

A "realist" school of international relations would prefer to invert the relationship of political principle to national interest in both the American and Russian cases. The realists maintain that the divergent U.S. and Soviet ideologies merely veiled the real source of conflict: clashes of national interest on a global scale between two hegemonical powers. This interpretation downplays the importance of ideas because they are just an ideological subterfuge for national economic interests. However, it would be unwise to overlook the fact that Soviet confidence in Soviet ideology—and, one might add, American faith in the American way-of-life—had reached their zeniths after World War II.

It is important not to lose sight of the psychological factors that were at work on both sides. The Cold War was a world historical conflict for the Americans and the Soviets, and each side felt threatened by the other. Whether the mutual perception of these threats ever really matched their actual dimensions or the intentions of the adversaries is a related problem. One may argue that the American fear of Communism at the beginning of the Cold War was commensurate with the Soviet faith in Communism. Certainly one of the peculiarities of the ensuing conflict was that American anti-Communists steadfastly continued to believe in the threat of Communism long after the Communists had ceased believing in Communism's promise and potential. The manner in which the Cold War ended—the Soviet Union collapsed—seems to indicate that the Soviet Union's political posture changed dramatically somewhere along the way. Nonetheless, ideas and ideologies were important at the beginning of the Cold War, and they helped heighten or, as some critics maintain, exaggerate the conflict. This is a problem that I shall discuss later.

Once the United States had announced its intention to contain Communism, it had to articulate economic and military policies to do so, and they were the Marshall Plan and the North Atlantic Treaty Organization. In a commencement speech at Harvard University on June 5, 1947, General George Marshall, the U.S. Secretary of State, announced plans for the largest foreign aid program in history, a plan that would bear his name. Historians have argued about how altruistic or imperialist the Marshall Plan, was as well as to what extent the United States needed the "European Recovery Program" as much as the Europeans did. In his speech, Marshall emphasized the idealism underlying the proposal: "Our policy is directed not against any country or doctrine but against hunger, poverty, desperation, and chaos." He also made it clear that "governments, political parties, or groups which seek to perpetuate human misery in order to profit therefrom politically or otherwise will encounter the opposition of the United States." But, he did not technically exclude any one from the start: "The program should be a joint one, agreed to by a number of, if not all, European nations."[15]

Although Poland and Czechoslovakia were sincerely interested in participating in this program, the Soviet Union dismissed as "imperialistic" the idea of the Marshall Plan for itself and its "allies" in East Central Europe. But the Western European states participated enthusiastically, and the initial $13 billion of aid helped lay the foundations for their postwar recovery and prosperity.

The political logic of the United States for providing economic aid to Europe was relatively simple: If widespread economic hardship had provided a fertile breeding ground for left- and right-wing radicalism and totalitarianism in Europe—the hardships of World War I had directly contributed to the success of the Bolsheviks in Russia and Germany's economic duress helped precipitate the Nazis' rise to power in Germany in 1933—then economic recovery, stability, and prosperity would deprive ideological radicalism of its material basis. They also would enhance the chances of democracy. America, therefore, invested in its allies.

The United States also had concrete economic interests in European reconstruction. World War II had brought the country out of the Depression and had created the most powerful economy in the world. Government analysts recognized that the U.S. economy had to find markets for its productive potential after the war, or otherwise it would experience a dramatic downturn, the consequences of which would be magnified even further by planned cutbacks in federal expenditures related to the war effort. Thus the idea of giving Western European countries grants, credits, and subsidies earmarked for the purchase of U.S. goods and services was born, and it provided a way out of an impending economic dilemma. In helping Europe, the United States helped itself. Aid created the basis for trade and secured new export markets in a postwar global economy in which the United States enjoyed a dominant position.

Furthermore, the fact that government expenditures in the United States did not recede after the war to the extent many people had anticipated they would greatly benefited the American economy. Although government expenditures dropped sharply from 1945 to 1948, they still were more than twice what they had been in 1940, and between 1948 and the end of the 1950s, they nearly doubled again. The main reason for this remarkable increase in government spending was defense. From an ideological or strategic perspective, the obvious purpose of unprecedented peacetime expenditures on defense was to contain Communism by defending the United States, its allies, and American interests throughout the world.

From a fiscal perspective, the billions and billions of dollars spent on defense during the Cold War also helped stimulate economic growth and maintain domestic prosperity in the United States. In other words, defending the American way of life also financed the American way of life for millions of Americans, not to mention the European way of life for millions of West Europeans, too. It allowed Western European governments to invest less in defense—and more on infrastructure, health, housing, education, and social welfare—than they would have been able to if they had spent more on their own defense.

The establishment of the North Atlantic Treaty Organization (NATO) in 1949 put one of the finishing touches on the institutionalization of the Cold War in its initial phase. When World War II ended, American military planners wanted to "get the boys home." The idea of maintaining a considerable and permanent military presence in Europe and the Pacific did not correspond to the United States' isolationist traditions, but the Cold War as a European and a global conflict essentially changed the United States' foreign policy demeanor. As a result of World War II, Western European states had also learned a number of lessons about collective security, and their immediate concern after the war was the German potential for aggression in the future. But the actuality of the Soviet threat in Europe quickly displaced hypothetical considerations about a German one. Western European democracies shared the United States' perception of the Soviet Union as a threat, and they wanted to maintain a U.S. presence in order to deter it.

From the American perspective, Europe was the most important immediate theater of "containment," and the defense of the United States did not start on the Atlantic coast but on the Elbe River. The purpose of NATO was relatively straightforward. The idea of a transatlantic pact for collective security was to keep the United States in, Germany down, and the Soviet Union out. The Warsaw Pact also had similar objectives in Eastern Europe, with one important exception. Its purpose was to keep the Soviet Union in, Germany down, and—as the outcome of the Hungarian revolution in 1956 and the end of the Prague Spring in 1968 demonstrated—East Central Europe down, too.

Critics of U.S. foreign policy during the Cold War maintain that the anti-Communist rhetoric of containment obscured the United States' real objectives: the "hegemonic project"[16] of containing not only its enemies but also its friends and allies. Idealists contend that political principle—"defending the Free World"—was the most important motive of U.S. policy, whereas "realists" and revisionists identify and document less noble and self-serving incentives called "the American national interest."

There is no point denying that American hegemony in Europe (and elsewhere) developed in the course of the Cold War. However, the hegemony of the "American empire" was qualitatively different from the control the Soviets exercised in their own. The distinction between hegemony "by invitation" and by imposition is an important one.[17] "Ami go home!" belonged to the political vocabulary of many Western Europeans, and the frequency of this exhortation increased in proportion to the development of freedom, prosperity, and security in Western Europe. The reason the United States did not comply with this demand was that it represented a minority opinion in functioning democracies that ultimately identified their national security interests with a continuing U.S. presence.

The consequences of dissidence in East Central Europe were different. Nevertheless, Soviet propaganda always emphasized how "friendly" and "fraternal" the Soviet Union's relationships were with its allies. Before 1989, East Central Europeans used to ask one another rhetorically whether the Soviets were their friends or their brothers. The answer to this question was telling: "They are our brothers. You can pick your friends."

⊰ 12 ⊱

The Failure of Eastern Europe

1956–1989

When the Cold War started, the concepts of East and West were more than sufficient for describing the political reality of a divided Europe, a division that appeared to be permanent. The Soviet version of Communism and the Soviet Communist version of Eastern Europe seemed to be here to stay. The idea that the Soviet Union would let its empire go was simply unrealistic, according to the experts of that now defunct discipline called Sovietology. The assumption that any attempt to change the political status quo in Eastern Europe would endanger peace not only in Europe but also on a global scale became one of the central premises of East–West relations: peaceful coexistence after the mid-1950s and détente in the 1970s. Then East–West relations deteriorated to such an extent in the early 1980s that H. W. Brands referred to this period as the "Cold War II."[1] Détente ended with the Soviet invasion of Afghanistan in 1979 which demonstrated to the West that the Soviet Union was still intent on aggressively expanding its empire. Ronald Reagan, elected to his first term as U.S. president in 1980, shocked friend and foe alike by referring to the Soviet Union as an "evil empire." The Cold War, East and West, was here to stay.

Of course, not everyone in the Soviet East abandoned the idea of Central Europe. Many members of the older generation—socialized before World War I or during the interwar period—continued to believe in the conservative (traditional, national, and Christian) or "bourgeois" (liberal and enlightened) values that were part and parcel of that Central European tradition defining the region as the easternmost part of Western European civilization. However, the Communist control of public life, the press, and education made Central Europe a "private" and a subversive idea, and it was exactly this class of "reactionaries" that the Communists wanted to destroy. They attempted to replace traditional intelligentsia with a new class of Eastern European Communist intellectuals systematically recruited from the rural or working classes. These agents of Stalin's agenda for the region were the vanguard of building socialism in Eastern Europe, and they were, in the Communist sense of the word, Eastern Europeans. The next generation of Eastern European intellectuals had a more critical relationship with Moscow. This was partially a result of the de-Stalinization in the mid-1950s that brought the reform Communists into power. They did not believe in a the slavish imitation of the Soviet model for building socialism and were interested in pursuing a variety of different "national paths" to Communism, but they were Eastern Europeans, too, because they still embraced a Communist program.

One small group of people continued to propagate the idea of Central Europe: the first wave of Central European émigrés from Soviet Eastern Europe to the West, those who left during the initial period of Stalinization in the late 1940s or early 1950s. (Subsequent waves of émigrés followed: Hungarians in 1956, Czechs and Slovaks in 1968, and Poles in 1981.) They suffered a fate common to all exiles: Very few people in the West seemed to pay attention to them or to show even a remote understanding of the issues that concerned them.

Being disappointed in the West was one of the complaints of Central European émigrés in the West as well as Central European intellectuals in the East. Western ignorance, or a combination of negligence and amnesia, was the main problem. Most people in the West did not even know that the countries that formed the western provinces of the new Soviet empire represented the eastern frontier of Western civilization, nor did they fully understand the true nature of Communism or the implications of Russian Soviet totalitarianism. The "attitude of the average person in the people's democracies" in the East toward the West, as Czesław Miłosz observed in the early 1950s in *The Captive Mind*, his analysis of the relationship of intellectuals to Communism, was "despair mixed with a residue of hope." He described the Eastern intellectual's attitude toward the West as "somewhat like disappointed love" that "often leaves a sediment of sarcasm."[2]

Given these circumstances, it should be apparent why very few people spoke about Central Europe in the decades following World War II. With the exception of a handful of émigrés and experts, no one in the West seemed to know much about the idea or the region, and many Western specialists, who were trained during the Cold War to analyze Communism, methodologically subsumed most of the region under the umbrella concept of the Soviet East. The Soviet Union and Eastern Europe (or "the bloc") were one region, not two (Central or East Central and Eastern Europe). In Eastern Europe itself, the Communists applied the same logic of ideological unity, although they used different concepts to justify it such as "the perpetual friendship of the Soviet Union," "fraternal cooperation," and the "socialist division of labor."

Under such conditions, it seemed unrealistic to talk about Europe in any

MILITARY AND ECONOMIC BLOCS, 1955–1989

N

SWEDEN

Estonia
S.S.R.

DENMARK
EC 1973

Latvia S.S.R.

North Sea

Baltic Sea

Lithuania S.S.R.

SOVIET

NL

Belarus S.S.R.

POLAND
1980/81

UNION

FEDERAL
REPUBLIC of
GERMANY

GDR

B

L NATO 1955

Ukraine S.S.R.

FRANCE

CZECHOSLOVAKIA
1968

AUSTRIA
State Treaty &
Neutrality, 1955

Moldova
S.S.R.

SWITZERLAND

HUNGARY
1956

ROMANIA

YUGOSLAVIA
Tito-Stalin Split 1948

ITALY

Adriatic Sea

BULGARIA

Black Sea

ALBANIA

GREECE

Mediterrenean Sea

NATO 1952
EC 1981

TURKEY
NATO 1952

	Member states of the North Atlantic Treaty Organization (NATO, est.1949) and the European Economic Community (EC, est.1958)
NATO 1952	Year of accession to NATO
EC 1972	Year of accession to EC
	NATO member states only
	Nonaligned neutral states
	Member states of the Council for Mutual Economic Assistance (COMECON, est. 1949) and the Warsaw Pact (est.1955)
	Nonaligned Communist states
1956	Anti-Communist revolutions in the East bloc

other terms than East and West. But in the early 1980s an increasing number of intellectuals and dissidents in Eastern Europe, a handful of émigrés, academics, journalists, and even a few politicians in the West started to use the concept of Central Europe, or East Central Europe, with greater frequency. There was no real consensus on where this region was, and there were regional and ideological variations on the idea of Central Europe which had one common denominator: Central Europe was a means of searching for alternatives to the Iron Curtain, the Cold War, and the partition of Europe. The political implications of the idea of Central Europe were so enormous that realists tended to dismiss the concept altogether.

It is easy to retrospectively ascertain that the reemergence of the idea of Central Europe paralleled the final crisis of Communism in Eastern Europe during the 1980s. If the bankruptcy of Communism in Eastern Europe was one of the prerequisites for the reemergence of the idea of Central Europe, or some of the most important versions of it, we should look at how Communism failed in Eastern Europe in order to understand the renaissance of Central Europe as an idea and a region.

Revolutions and Reforms:
1956, 1968, and 1980–1981

In light of the failure of Communism, it might seem unnecessary to ask whether Communism was a good idea that was merely poorly executed or a bad idea to start with. The distinction between methods and principles is an important one. As long as Communists believed in method—the possibility of reforming or perfecting the Communist system—it was viable. But once they recognized that the principles on which the system was based had to be changed—such as the Communist Party's monopoly on political power or the state's monopoly on the economy—it was not.

The history of Communism in the twentieth century analogously can be written from two different perspectives. It may be viewed sympathetically as a series of missed opportunities or analyzed critically in terms of its inherent defects: the systemic flaws or moral and political misconceptions that burdened it from the very start and that became clearer with time. In the first case, Stalin may be accused of ruining or perverting the fundamentally good ideas of Lenin and Marx; in the second case, Lenin and ultimately Marx are responsible for the basically bad ideas that Stalin executed all too well. Regardless of the perspective one prefers, Stalin is the central figure in the story. He was the architect of building socialism in the Soviet Union before World War II and responsible for exporting it to Eastern Europe thereafter.

De-Stalinization in 1956 was the watershed in the history of European Communism. After Stalin's death in 1953, there was a "thaw," a period of liberalization. Nikita Khrushchev eventually emerged victorious in the struggle for power in the Soviet Union, and one of his main concerns was improving the performance of the system he had inherited from Stalin. He understood that innovation, dynamism, and growth would be difficult in an "administrative-command system" based on excessive centralization, coercion, and fear, and he recognized that the habits and interests of the party bureaucrats were one of the primary obstacles he confronted. Khrushchev also realized that he could not remedy the organizational deficiencies of the Stalinistic system without criticizing the ideology behind it. Therefore, he had to dismantle Stalin's reputation in order to reorganize the system bearing his name.

At the Twentieth Party Congress in early 1956, Khrushchev gave a "secret speech" condemning Stalin. In a tirade lasting for hours, he denounced Stalin's "personality cult," the party purges of the 1930s, the secret police, the extensive network of concentration camps or *gulags*,[3] and Stalin's blundering as a military commander during World War II. He accused Stalin of negligence, incompetence, and deceit which cost millions of Soviet citizens their lives. Stalin and his regime were criminal.

Khrushchev had to mobilize those members of the Communist Party who were interested in reform, against the Stalinist hard-liners who were not, and his strategy for de-Stalinization was to undermine the legitimacy and credibility of the old guard by making them accomplices to Stalin's crimes. Although Khrushchev's program of de-Stalinization was inspired by the domestic problems of the Soviet Union, it also had profound consequences abroad. In the West, many Communists and intellectuals sympathetic to the Soviet Union were completely disillusioned. In Eastern Europe, the Stalinists in power had not been forewarned by Khrushchev about his plans. They were shocked to hear this type of talk coming from Moscow because it undermined their positions, too.

Using the criterion of reform or innovation, the post–World War II history of Communism in the Soviet Union can be divided into four general periods, each of which had far-reaching implications for the status of Communism in Eastern Europe. Stalinism, or the totalitarian period, which lasted until Stalin's death in 1953; de-Stalinization in 1956 followed by a phase of liberalization and experimentation under Nikita Khrushchev until 1964; a period of posttotalitarian retrenchment, consolidation, and stagnation under Leonid Brezhnev from 1964 until his death in 1982 (including the governments of Yuri Andropov and Konstantin Chernenko, each of whom died shortly after coming to power); and the Gorbachev era from 1985 until 1991.

De-Stalinization illustrated the extent to which a change in Communist doctrine in the Soviet Union affected the Communist regimes in Eastern Europe. On the one hand, the Soviet Communists' willingness or unwillingness to experiment with reform at home determined the Eastern European Communists' latitude to experiment with (or against) the system in their own countries. On the other hand, innovation in the Soviet Union inevitably created problems for those Communist regimes in Eastern Europe that were more conservative than the one in Moscow itself. De-Stalinization in the Soviet Union created a crisis for the reigning Stalinists of Eastern Europe in the mid-1950s (especially Poland and Hungary), just as Gorbachev's initiatives of perestroika (restructuring) and glasnost (openness) created problems for the representatives of the old Brezhnev era in Eastern Europe in the second half of the 1980s (especially the German Democratic Republic, Czechoslovakia, and Bulgaria).

Furthermore, de-Stalinization sparked a debate among those Eastern European intellectuals who had embraced the socialist vision. These so-called revisionists were philosophers who, as Marxists, criticized Stalin and argued in the name of Marx for a return to more genuine socialist values and ideals. They assumed that there had to be not only philosophical but also political alternatives to the Russian Soviet version of Communism: perhaps even a "third way" between the type of capitalist democracy that had developed in the West and the socialism that had arisen in the East during the Cold War.

The question whether there was only one true path or many paths to socialism had been at the heart of the split between Stalin and Tito in 1948. The fact that Khrushchev sought a reconciliation with Tito in 1955 was an indication that attitudes were changing in Moscow, and after 1956 Khrushchev had to de-Stalinize Soviet foreign policy as well. Khrushchev was prepared, within limits, to allow Communist regimes in Eastern Europe a certain amount of latitude to experiment with "national paths." De-Stalinization helped to intensify the conflicts in Eastern Europe between the Moscow-oriented Stalinists, who were in power, and the reform-oriented, "national Communists," many of whom had previously been accused of "Titoism." It also provided an opportunity for the peoples of Eastern Europe to express their discontent with the Stalinist system.

Infighting among the different wings of the Communist Party and the potential for popular protest created explosive situations in Poland and Hungary in 1956, with events getting out of hand in Poland first. In June, some 50,000 workers in Poznan, an industrial center west of Warsaw, rioted against increases in prices and work quotas. The protest spread across the country, and as it began gaining momentum and support, it took on an increasingly anti-Communist tone. The Stalinists in power used Stalinist methods to squelch it, by calling on the Polish army, which led to more than fifty deaths and hundreds of wounded. Confronted with the prospect of continued unrest and pressure from the nationalistic wing of the Communist Party, the Polish Stalinists desperately sought a way to prevent the situation from deteriorating further.

This desperation paved the way for the political comeback of Władysław Gomułka, a former first secretary of the Polish Communist party who himself had been a victim of the Stalinists. (He was a national Communist who had been accused of "Titoism" in 1948 and was removed from power.) Gomułka was rehabilitated and reinstated in his old position in October 1956, and he managed to defuse the explosive situation. As a nationalist and a victim of the Stalinists, he had the sympathy of the population at large, and he announced a program of Polish de-Stalinization that enhanced his popularity. The Soviet Union followed events in Poland with great apprehension, and there was a strong likelihood of a Soviet intervention. (Khrushchev was prepared to tolerate anti-Stalinist reform but not anti-Communist revolution.) But Gomułka managed to convince Khrushchev that Poland's commitment to Communism and the Soviet Union was still intact.

The political setting in Hungary in 1956 was similar to that in Poland. There had been infighting between the Stalinists and the national reform Communists in the party and considerable popular discontent with the Stalinist system, based on its poor economic performance. The dynamics of the protest and reform evolved differently, however. In Hungary, Communist intellectuals, not workers, spearheaded the antiregime protest. They were devastated by tales of terror that accompanied de-Stalinization and wanted to see Mátyás Rákosi, Hungary's premier Stalinist, ousted from office. Many intellectuals sympathized with Imre Nagy, a more liberal and popular Communist leader who had been appointed prime minister in 1953 and tried to de-Stalinize Hungary before the official advent of de-Stalinization in the Soviet Union. However, Rákosi and his cohorts maneuvered Nagy out of office in 1955 and then expelled him from the Communist Party. In an attempt to pacify the situation, the Soviets helped orchestrate a change of leadership in July and replaced Rákosi with one of his associates, Ernö Gerö. Replacing one Stalinist with another did very little to calm the situation. Antiregime protesters, mainly students, began making bolder and bolder demands, and they were encouraged by how events had transpired in Poland in October.

At a large demonstration in Budapest on October 23, 1956, the protesters demanded political liberalization, the dissolution of the secret police, and the withdrawal of Soviet troops from Hungary. It still is not clear how the shooting started, but gunfire sparked a revolution that began on the streets of Budapest and swept through the nation like wildfire. Workers and farmers swelled the ranks of the protesters, who armed themselves and clashed with the police, the Hungarian army, and Soviet units.

The days that followed were full of confusion, attempts at reconciliation, misunderstandings, and violence. Gerö stepped down, and Nagy stepped in to form a new government that included several non-Communists. He also negotiated with the Soviet Union about withdrawing Soviet troops from Hungary, and they actually began leaving Budapest. Within a week of October 23, Nagy proclaimed the restoration of a multiparty system, announced Hungary's withdrawal from the Warsaw Pact, and declared the country's neutrality. (Nagy obviously had in mind the 1955 precedent of Austrian neutrality: neither East nor West but in the middle.) He appealed to the United Nations, and many Hungarians expected help from the West, particularly the United States. The tough talk of American anti-Communists had created the impression that the United States would help anti-Communists in Eastern Europe once they started helping themselves. But this was not to be the case.

The massive intervention of the Soviet army on November 4 crushed the Hungarian revolution which, in Communist parlance, was subsequently called the "Counterrevolution." János Kádár, a Communist who had been imprisoned under the old Stalinist regime and, like Nagy, made a political comeback during the first days of the revolution by becoming the first secretary of the Communist Party, conspired with the Soviets to form a new government. The proclamation of the new Kádár government coincided with an attack by Soviet tanks on Budapest. Nagy and a number of his compatriots sought refuge in the Yugoslav embassy in Budapest. Fighting continued around the country for about another week, but the revolutionaries were hopelessly outnumbered and outgunned. More than 10,000 people died in the uprising, and almost 200,000 fled to Austria, where they received asylum.

Although Nagy and his associates were guaranteed safe-conduct by Kádár and the Yugoslav ambassador, they were kidnapped by the Soviets as soon as they left the Yugoslav embassy, taken to Romania, and then eventually returned to Hungary. They were tried and executed on June 16, 1958, and buried in unmarked graves.

Nagy had envisioned for Hungary some "third way," a combination of neutrality and socialism. But in the eyes of the Communists he had committed two "crimes": By reintroducing a multiparty system, he had abandoned one of the central precepts of Marxism-Leninism, and by withdrawing from the Warsaw Pact, he had directly threatened the Soviet Union's national security interests. The political monopoly or "leading role" of the Communist Party and the unity of the Soviet bloc were not to be questioned. (In 1989, Hungary's reform Communist regime rehabilitated Nagy by giving him a state funeral on the thirty-first anniversary of his execution on June 16. At the time, observers interpreted the reburial of Nagy as a funeral ceremony for Hungarian Communism.)

Hungarians like to compare their revolution of 1956 with the revolution of 1848. (Incidentally, after 1989, the dates on which these revolutions began—March 15, 1848 and October 23, 1956—became Hungarian national holidays.) In both cases, they fought against imperial powers for national freedom and lost because of Russian intervention. But they won the compromises that followed the defeats, by regaining a considerable amount of national autonomy.

After 1848, Hungary eventually negotiated the Compromise of 1867 with Austria. Although Kádár initially clamped down on the "counterrevolutionary elements" after 1956, under his leadership Hungary eventually became the most liberal Communist regime in the Eastern bloc. It was characterized by a willingness to experiment with economic decentralization or market elements, modest prosperity, and a relatively good human rights record. One general assumption is that the Hungarians showed the Soviets their teeth, and as a result, the Soviets were prepared to give them an exceptional amount of leeway. This is only half of the story, however. The West, always interested in encouraging independence from Moscow, was more than glad to support experimentation and rewarded Hungary for its initiative with generous financial support and favorable trade conditions.

Czechoslovakia and the German Democratic Republic weathered relatively well the initial phase of de-Stalinization without de-Stalinizing, but this just postponed the issue. In Czechoslovakia, Antonín Novotný exercised a Stalinist monopoly on power from 1948 until 1968 as first secretary of the Communist Party and president of Czechoslovakia. The belated de-Stalinization of Czechoslovakia was not inspired by popular protest or intellectuals, however. It originated within the Communist Party itself, which was concerned about the country's sluggish economic performance and general political malaise. At the beginning of 1968, a younger generation of reform-minded Communists maneuvered Novotný and the other conservative representatives of the old guard out of power, and under the leadership of a new party secretary, the dynamic and liberal Slovak Alexander Dubček, they began a series of sweeping reforms known as the "Prague Spring."

The Czechoslovak reformers avoided going as far as Imre Nagy had done in Hungary in 1956. There is no indication that they intended to abandon the doctrine of the Communist Party's monopoly on power or withdraw from the Warsaw Pact. They still regarded the Communist Party as an agent and instrument of reform but believed that it would be possible to develop a freer and more prosperous form of "Communism with a human face," and they recognized that political liberalization was the prerequisite for economic reform. The Prague Spring changed the relationship of the citizens to the Communist party-state by granting them more political freedom, which won them over to participate in reforming the system. Censorship and restrictions on travel outside of the country were lifted, and genuine criticism and individual initiative suddenly were not only permitted but even encouraged by the Communist Party itself. A new economic strategy was instituted, based on the introduction of market elements and competition into a socialist economy that still was based on the Communist idea of the collective (or state) ownership of the means of production—that is, the absence of private property in the capitalistic sense.

The Czech and Slovak response to these innovations was enthusiastic, even euphoric, and "Back to Europe" became a popular slogan. By avoiding coercion and actually sacrificing control, Dubček gained genuine popular support which ultimately enhanced his power and the legitimacy of his regime. But conservative Communists inside and outside of Czechoslovakia did not understand how it was possible to gain control by losing it, and they viewed the Czechoslovak experiment and the people's enthusiasm for it with increasing suspicion and apprehension. If the people liked it so much, something had to be wrong.

There has been a lot of speculation about what could have happened if an invasion of Warsaw Pact troops had not ended the Prague Spring on August 20, 1968. Dubček and his compatriots either went too far, or Communists less inclined to reform assumed that they would. Unlike Hungary in 1956, there was neither revolution nor armed resistance and bloodshed. But like Hungary in 1956, the reform Communists in power condemned the intervention, and conservative Communists negotiated behind their backs directly with the Soviets to install a new regime with the help of Soviet tanks. The West was shocked, but the overriding priority of détente contributed in its own way to the occupation of Czechoslovakia.

Dubček, effectively deprived of power after the invasion, was gradually eased out of office and replaced in 1969 by Gustav Husák, a conservative Communist and former victim of Czechoslovak Stalinism. Husák then proceeded to purge the Communist Party of its reformers—one-third of its membership—and to introduce a program of "normalization" that placed greater emphasis on the production of consumer goods coupled with the systematic persecution of dissent and a debilitating maintenance of the status quo. Leonid Brezhnev justified the Warsaw Pact's occupation of Czechoslovakia in terms of defending the achievements of socialism; the Brezhnev Doctrine of "limited sovereignty" made it clear that the Soviet Union would not tolerate too much experimentation in the Warsaw Pact because it threatened the Soviet Union's vital ideological and strategic interests.

The year 1968 was a turning point in East Central Europe in a number of respects. It marked the "culmination of the conflict between critical intellectuals and political power"[4] that had started with de-Stalinization in 1956. Many intellectuals who as party members, "revisionists," or Marxists had previously believed that the system could be reformed now recognized that it could not. A new generation of dissidents was born that abandoned Marxism as an intellectual program and "Communism with a human face" as a political one. In its place they adopted a political vocabulary with a striking affinity to that used in the West at the beginning of the Cold War. They were concerned about issues of principle, the moral dimension of politics, human rights, truth, and justice. But they also dismissed as cosmetic the changes made in the system since de-Stalinization and started analyzing it in terms of the continuity between what Stalin had created and Brezhnev and his comrades were maintaining. They began to talk about a "posttotalitarian system" or a "Stalinist–Brezhnevite system."

After the Prague Spring, a number of developments in the West added to the Western inability to understand the East Central European experience with Communism. The student revolutions of 1968 accompanied the rise of the "New Left," a renaissance of interest in Marxism and neo-Marxism, and protests against the United States' involvement in the Vietnam War. Many academics and intellectuals in the West considered the right-wing rhetoric of American Cold War anti-Communism to be an ideological subterfuge for "American imperialism," and this form of anti-anti-Communism was explicitly anti-American. The American empire was frequently seen as a greater threat than the Soviet empire. Some form of Marxism-Leninism appeared to be the only antidote for "American imperialism" in the developing world, and in some circles there was open admiration for the leaders of "struggles for national liberation," such as North Vietnam's Ho Chi Minh or Cuba's Che Guevara.

At the same time, the concept of totalitarianism went out of fashion among the younger generation of Western Sovietologists—the members of the older generation were veterans of World War II and the Cold War—because it was too ideological and methodologically unsophisticated for the theoretical and empirical purposes of social scientists. The Soviet Union's system obviously was different from Western systems. Nonetheless, the Soviet system was a system, and so its behavior could be explained using system theory, and its performance could be measured using quantitative analysis. After all, it had a constitutional and an institutional framework, decision-making processes, social classes, interest groups, "lobbies" that bargained for resources, patterns of distribution, and the like, and it was pursuing a program of economic and social modernization.

Furthermore, the interplay between the spirit of leftist protest in the west and the methodological innovation in the social sciences inspired by neo-Marxist approaches increased the sympathy for socialism among a new generation of academics and intellectuals. In many cases, they sympathized with the ideals of socialism and preferred them to the materialistic and money-grubbing values of consumer capitalism. Based on their data, the Soviet system seemed to be doing well, and most Western social scientists were convinced that it could be reformed in the long run.

This was one of the premises for the "convergence theory" of capitalism and communism that was popular in the West in the 1970s. Social democratic and labor parties were in power in many Western European states. These left-of-center governments adopted policies based on state intervention, tax increases, additional public spending, and comprehensive as well as redistributive social welfare schemes, and they shared the conviction that shifting the public–private mix in the economy in favor of state expenditure, ownership, and control was the most desirable path of development. At the time, the general structural trend in Western Europe appeared to be away from capitalism and toward a social welfare system: "Less free market" and "more state" were the ideas behind "capitalism with a human face."

Although the idea of "Communism with a human face" had failed dramatically in 1968, there also were attempts to reform the Communist economies of Eastern Europe: strategies for *economic* change that left intact the Communist monopoly on *political* power. For example, in 1968 Hungary introduced a "New Economic Mechanism" that decentralized the planning process, gave individual enterprises more autonomy, introduced competition among economic agents, and placed greater emphasis on the production of consumer goods. A new school of socialist reform economists devised different "plan and market" schemes to improve the system's economic performance. Along with the relatively good human rights record of the Kádár regime, this appeared to be a promising development.

Poland launched an ambitious program of economic modernization, or "second-wave industrialization." It purchased Western technology with Western credit with the intention of producing more and better commodities. Some of them were to be sold in the West to generate the hard currency to pay the debt incurred, and the remainder would flow into the domestic or East bloc market. But grafting Western technology onto an inefficiently organized Eastern European economy failed and left Poland with a massive foreign debt. (Hungary also borrowed heavily, with fundamentally the same results.) Elsewhere there were other experiments along the lines of "consumer socialism." Incremental economic liberalization appeared to be the trend in Eastern Europe.

The proponents of the convergence theory thought that the structural experimentation of the Eastern European Communist states indicated that they were gradually moving in the same direction as the Western European social welfare states, although from a completely inverted point of departure. If more state and less market was the Western European pattern of development, then less state (centralization) and more market (elements) appeared to be the Eastern European pattern. Furthermore, if both these trends continued, the structural convergence of these divergent systems at some ideal midpoint in the future could be extrapolated. Both systems would ultimately evolve into Swedish-style social welfare states, and Eastern European Communists eventually would become Western European–style Social Democrats. The entire region would become ideologically equidistant from the Soviet Union and the United States, and Central Europe would become a neutral zone. The nonconfrontational environment of détente, the aversion of many Western social scientists to Cold War terminology, and the European vision of a symmetrical withdrawal of the superpowers from Central Europe made this scenario popular at the time.

The intellectual worlds of East Central European and Western intellectuals drifted apart during the late 1960s and 1970s. The great majority of East Central European intellectuals abandoned Marxism, adopted the concept of totalitarianism to describe Communism, and rejected the idea of being able to reform the Communist system. At the same time, many Western academics and intellectuals abandoned totalitarian terminology and adopted ideas colored by Marxism or neo-Marxism. They displayed more and more sympathy for socialism and were convinced that the Communist system could be reformed. It was truly a strange situation. After 1968, leftist intellectuals in the West started using a political vocabulary similar to the one that East Central European intellectuals had definitively abandoned in 1968, and East Central European intellectuals adopted a political vocabulary that had a great affinity to the classic Cold War terminology that Western anti-Communists started using in 1948. In both cases the problem was finding a way change the status quo. East Central Europeans looked wistfully to the West, and a fair share of Western intellectuals looked hopefully to the East.

When the independent trade union movement of Solidarity emerged in Poland in 1980, the prospects for a change in East–West relations were not very promising. The strikes that began in the Gdańsk shipyard in the summer of 1980 were precipitated by increases in food prices, and they were similar in this respect to the previous waves of protest that had erupted after price hikes in Poland in 1970 and 1976, both of which had been bloodily repressed. However, the movement for independent trade unions that emerged from this discontent went far beyond the traditional union concerns.

The Polish workers' movement was flanked by the Catholic Church, on one side, and a relatively large group of peasant-farmers who owned and tilled their own land, on the other. Both these features of Polish society indicate to what extent Stalinization had failed in Poland. The Communists had failed to break the influence of the church, which was especially strong in rural areas, and they never managed to collectivize agriculture. Given the demographics of Polish industrialization and urbanization, the average Polish workers' roots were those of a Catholic peasant-farmer, which was not the stuff out of which good Communists (and, in some cases, good workers) were made.[5]

Two important "alliances" preceded the rise of Solidarity. First, after the Polish strikes in 1976, dissident intellectuals started showing concern for the interests of the working class, and a series of initiatives helped bridge the traditional gap between the intellectual dissent of relatively isolated individuals and the workers' protest with its mass potential. Second, Polish intellectuals, many of whom were anticlerical (either as representatives of traditional, enlightened European liberalism or as former Marxists), reconciled themselves to working with the Catholic Church on practical issues, instead of against it on fundamental issues. In other words, "Catholic and non-Catholic intellectuals found more and more common ground in the defence of common values, common sense and basic rights."[6] The idea of self-defense—defending the people against the violence and transgressions of the state—became one of the unifying principles of action. Last, although we should not overestimate how religious the Poles were—Communism did succeed to a great extent in creating a modern, secular society—the church was a strong and popular organization in Poland, and it always had provided the Polish nation with a haven during times of occupation and duress.

This triangular coalition of workers, intellectuals, and priests supplied the potential for mass protest with intellectual direction and moral authority. Although the poor performance of the Polish economy and the ineptitude of the Communists who managed it were the immediate sources of popular discontent, there were a number of Polish national traditions that aggravated it: anti-Russian sentiments, revolutionary romanticism, patriotism, and Roman Catholicism. All these elements seemed to coalesce when Cardinal Karol Wojtyła, the archbishop of Kraków, was elected Pope John Paul II in 1978. The election of the first non-Italian pope in centuries was not only a spectacular confirmation of Poland's Western or "Roman" orientation; it also created a feeling of national pride and acted as a catalyst in what can only be described as a spiritual or moral revolution.

The dynamics of the "Solidarity revolution" are complicated. The Poles had learned from the Hungarian revolution of 1956 and the Prague Spring of 1968. They therefore dismissed the idea of violently overthrowing Communism because they considered violence an inappropriate means of change, and they no longer believed in the Polish Communist Party's ability to reform Communism. (Nor did the Polish Communists. Their main interest was maintaining privilege and power.) What started out as a strike in Gdańsk in the summer of 1980 ended up less than eighteen months later as an independent organization of 10 million members (almost one-third of the Polish population), and Solidarity's demands on the government grew as the movement did. The idea of self-defense made way for the concept of self-management, which implied self-government. If Poland really was a "workers' state," as the Communists always had maintained, then the workers started demanding real rights from the Communist Party in their own state.

Solidarity completely undermined the legitimacy of the Polish Communist party-state, but it did not try to seize political power. Instead, its strategy was based on the insight that the party-state could not be reformed but that society could. The idea of a society that renewed and reorganized itself—a "civil society" independent of the state and whose interaction with the state was based on the rule of law and the observation of fundamental human rights—was one of the movement's guiding principles, and Solidarity was internationally recognized in the West from the far left to the far right because virtually everybody could find something in its program with which they could identify.

Solidarity pursued a strategy of "self-limiting revolution," based on nonviolence and constraint, to wring concessions from the Communist party-state and managers of the state-run economy, and it progressively increased the scope of its autonomous activities. Pragmatists and fundamentalists in the movement argued about how far Solidarity could or should push its demands. As a precautionary measure, Solidarity explicitly stated that it had no intention of pulling Poland out of the Warsaw Pact. But it was perfectly clear to the Soviets and conservative Communist regimes elsewhere that a peaceful, democratic, national, anti-Communist revolution was in progress, and they were afraid that it might be contagious.

The Solidarity movement exacerbated the economic crisis in Poland and created a political one. A vacuum developed in which the Polish Communist Party had effectively lost control, but Solidarity—for tactical reasons and as a matter of principle—was not prepared to assume it. The Solidarity experiment thus ended on December 13, 1981, when (Communist) General Wojciech Jaruzelski proclaimed a national emergency and martial law and assumed the positions of Communist party secretary and prime minister. Because there were no emergency powers provisions in the Polish constitution, which would have given him extraordinary powers, Jaruzelski had to impose martial law. (Jaruzelski's declaration of martial law prevented a Soviet intervention, the consequences of which, most Poles agree, would have been catastrophic, and as much as Poles despised him in 1981, since then he has been rehabilitated largely for this preemptive measure.)

Since Poland obviously was not at war with a foreign state, it was clear to the members of the Solidarity movement that the government had declared war on civil society. The Jaruzelski government rounded up thousands of activists and put them in internment camps and banned Solidarity and its various suborganizations. Unlike the situation in Hungary in 1956 or Czechoslovakia in 1968, however, the Jaruzelski regime did not isolate and disperse protest effectively or break the will to resist. It merely outlawed the former and contained the latter. Solidarity then went underground as a resistance movement and continued its struggle against a government that most Poles regarded as illegitimate and perceived as foreign. The international protest was loud but ineffectual, and Poles were disappointed in those Western European heads of state, such as the West German chancellor, Helmut Schmidt, who criticized Solidarity for its recklessness and considered the Jaruzelski regime's restoration of order to be "necessary."

The initial demoralization and disillusionment were great after the declaration of martial law in Poland in December 1981, and everyone was prepared for a long political winter. The repertoire of East Central European options seemed to be exhausted: Violent revolution had failed in Hungary; "Communism with a human face" had failed in Czechoslovakia; and Solidarity's peaceful, negotiated transformation of the Communist system, "self-limiting revolution," had failed, too.

In 1982, the Hungarian dissident György Konrád made the following observation:

> The three medieval kingdoms of East Central Europe—Polish, Czech, and Hungarian—seem to have been the work of peoples who had great powers of survival. In one way or another, they paid dearly for their independence. Even though the centuries-old experiment in independence has still not reached a successful conclusion, this continuing tenacity is proof that the struggle for self-determination will go on until self-determination has been achieved.

Konrád's prognosis for the chances of change in the Communist world at that time was pessimistic and long term: "Three attempts have failed; the seventh will succeed."[7] The Communist system may not have been robust, but it was intact. In a variation on the old phrase of "Communism with a human face," the Polish dissident Adam Michnik called it "Stalinism with its teeth knocked out." Under these discouraging circumstances, people started talking about Central Europe.

The Idea of Central Europe

The career of the concept of Central Europe since 1945 has been truly unusual. After World War II, for at least three decades, people stopped using the term in the present tense. No one ever wanted Germans to talk about *Mitteleuropa* again. "Central Europe" was thus a nebulous concept when it began to come back into circulation in the early 1980s, reflecting different perceptions of the East–West problem on both sides of the Iron Curtain. Although an auspicious denouement of the East–West conflict was one of the premises of the idea of Central Europe, even those people who used the term could not agree on the causes or the nature of this conflict or on the most appropriate means of ending it. The regional dynamics of the East–West conflict and the divergent attitudes toward the reform potential of the Communist system also influenced the evolution of different Central Europe ideas. Three versions of "Central Europe" emerged: in the Federal Republic of Germany in the West, in and around the frontiers of neutral Austria, and behind the Iron Curtain in Eastern Europe.

In West Germany, Central Europe was a concept adopted by the left, ranging from the ecological–pacifist, "basis democracy" Green movement to the Social Democrats. They all were interested in reviving the process and practice of détente and believed in the central premise of Social Democratic *Ostpolitik*, that "change through rapprochement" or peaceful cooperation with the Communist system was the best means of transforming it. They also were opponents of the arms race and, in some cases, of the member- ship of the Federal Republic in NATO. Troop reductions and disarmament, the creation of a nuclear-free zone in Central Europe, neutralism or neu- trality for the Federal Republic of Germany, and a symmetrical withdrawal of the superpowers from not only Germany but also the entire region were some of the key elements of this vision for Central Europe.[8] After these pre- conditions were satisfied, German reunification could be seriously ad- dressed. Assumptions about the potential benefits of actively reintroducing détente, convergence theory, the democratic potential of reform Commu- nism, and, in some cases, the possibility of a "third way" between (Soviet) Communism and (American) capitalism all were operative here.

This version of Central Europe was the most sensitive to the international and strategic dimensions of the East–West conflict. The quality of the rela- tions between the Soviet Union and the United States and their allies in East- ern and Western Europe determined the general international framework for discussing the idea of Central Europe, based on the premise that a fun- damental change in the relationship between the superpowers—and hence their conduct and presence in Central Europe—was necessary in order to change the status quo. It was difficult to envision under what circumstances either the United States or the Soviet Union might withdraw from the re- gion, but it was clear that both of them had to go. There naturally was much disagreement on which of the superpowers represented the greater threat and hence was the bigger obstacle. For example, for the West German peace movement, it was the United States and NATO.

The German–German frontier was the toughest line of European con- frontation in the East–West conflict. In terms of troops and conventional and nuclear weapons, East and West Germany were the most highly milita- rized region in world history. Parity and deterrence—a "balance of terror"— were strategic doctrines in both East and West, but it was difficult for repre- sentatives of both military establishments to agree in quantitative and qualitative terms on who had what. The complicated tactical and strategic relationships between conventional and nuclear forces, combined with mutual suspicion and the assumption that the other side never admitted to having a critical advantage that was upsetting the balance of power, made troop and arms reduction talks between the superpowers relatively futile exercises.[9]

Furthermore, Western security experts tended to agree that unilateral Western reduction was undesirable or even dangerous, because it either would upset the balance of power or could be interpreted as a sign of weak- ness and thus encourage the Soviet Union as the benefiting power to take advantage of its position of superiority. During the renewed arms race of the 1980s, unilateral reduction and withdrawal were basically what the West Ger- man left demanded (and was lavishly praised as "progressive" by Soviet pro- paganda). The idea of getting the Americans out of West Germany, getting West Germany out of NATO, and declaring German neutralism or neutral- ity had a strong affinity to what Stalin wanted to achieve with his famous of- fer in 1952. The leftist West German scenario for Central Europe was based on the assumption that if the United States were to go, then the Soviet Union would leave. Then after the Soviets left, not only Central Europe would come into its own, but reform communism or real socialism would flourish, too. This, however, was a worst-case scenario for the conservatives: a "Finlandization" of West Germany.

Finns have always been troubled by the use of the term "Finlandization." After World War II, the Finnish government concluded a treaty of mutual cooperation and assistance with the Soviet Union that took into account certain Soviet security interests. For example, Finland was obliged to cooperate with the Soviet Union in case of another war with Germany. Otherwise, Finland pursued a judicious policy of neutrality after 1945, which ensured its independence.

In reference to Western European affairs, "Finlandization" was a negative term that reflected conservative fears that the Western European left might succeed in neutralizing Western Europe. However, in the Eastern European context, after the mid-1980s until 1989, "Finlandization" or "self-Finlandization" was a best-case scenario for countries like Poland and Hungary. Dissidents and reformers speculated that the Soviet Union might let countries out of the Eastern bloc if they, like Finland after World War II, were prepared to make some concessions to the Soviet Union's national security interests and to refrain from joining Western military or economic alliances.

If the West German debate about Central Europe reflected the immediacy of the East–West conflict, then a second, different version of Central Europe evolved in and around Austria. The Iron Curtain may have been impenetrable between East and West Germany, but the contours of the East–West conflict softened along the frontiers of neutral, nonaligned Austria. It was not a member of either of Europe's military and economic blocs—NATO and the European Community or the Warsaw Pact and COMECON—and in this respect it was neither East nor West. In terms of its economic and political systems, Austria was a Western European state, but it jutted like a peninsula into Eastern Europe.

Austria's neighbors in Eastern Europe envied its neutrality, which in 1955 had allowed it to get out of the East–West conflict. As a small and neutral state, it threatened virtually no one, and some political scientists speculated that Austrian neutrality could serve as a model for other small states in the region. No one really was sure how an incremental neutralization of the blocs, one state at a time, could be achieved, but it seemed to be a good idea.

The practice of mediating between the two rival blocs, cultivating cordial relationships with its immediate neighbors despite ideological differences, and promoting regional cooperation across national frontiers were essential to Austria's foreign policy. Austria's practice of neutrality also benefited from the admittedly nostalgic but nonetheless positive associations that the memories of "old" imperial Habsburg Austria evoked throughout the region. Despite the Iron Curtain, the peoples of various states shared a history, despite their differences. In this part of the world, *Mitteleuropa* had nothing to do with Germany. Rather, it was Habsburg territory, and Vienna was the indisputable capital of this cultural empire and the historical hub of a cosmopolitan network of cities: Trieste in Italy, Ljubljana in Slovenia, Zagreb in Croatia, Cluj in Transylvanian Romania, Chernovtsy and L'viv in Ukraine, Kraków in Poland, Prague and Bratislava in Czechoslovakia, and Budapest in Hungary.

The border between neutral and nonaligned Austria and nonaligned but Communist Yugoslavia was the least problematic seam between the Communist East and the democratic West in Europe. In the late 1970s the Austrian provinces of Upper Austria, Carinthia, and Styria; the Italian provinces of Friaul, Trentino–South Tyrol, and Venice; and the Yugoslav republics of Slovenia and Croatia established a regional "working group" to discuss shared Alpine–Adriatic problems and concerns and to arrange transnational planning in the region despite the differences in political systems. There were many topics on the agenda, ranging from traffic and ecological issues to tourism, economic cooperation, and cultural exchange.

This initiative was a modest attempt to emphasize the region's common interests, not the national or ideological frontiers that separated them, and it was not only a unique experiment in transnational cooperation but also a great popular success. The idea of a common Central European past justified the logic of cooperation. The idea of being Central European also fed on the northern Italian provinces' discontent with Roman politics and the fact that Italy's wealthier and economically more advanced north was tired of financing the country's underdeveloped south. Likewise, the northern republics of Yugoslavia were more highly developed than the southern ones. Slovenes and Croats resented footing the bill for Balkan backwardness and Communist inefficiency just as much as northern Italians did for southern Mediterranean underdevelopment and Mafia corruption. In both cases, the concept of "Central Europe" was full of separatist potential. In Yugoslavia, too, it reminded Slovene and Croatian nationalists and anti-Communists that they had previously lived outside a state dominated by Orthodox Serbs (before 1918) or Serbian Communists (before 1945). In this context, Central Europe was a Roman Catholic, Western European, and Habsburg idea.

A completely different version of Central Europe evolved between Vienna and Budapest. Austrian–Hungarian relations developed so auspiciously during the 1970s that they became a model of East–West cooperation. Austria's investments in Hungary, joint ventures, and the judicious foreign policy of the Austrian federal chancellor, Bruno Kreisky, led to cooperation reminiscent of the good old days, and in the mid-1980s, the countries lifted their bilateral visa requirements. Hundreds of thousands of Hungarians went to Austria for a taste of the West, and just as many Austrians went to Hungary to shop in the East.

Austrian neutrality combined with its good-neighbor policies helped create a nonconfrontational environment that promoted liberalization in its historical hinterland behind the Iron Curtain. Extrapolated to European politics, the Austrian–Hungarian model of neutrality and social democracy in the West plus economic and political liberalization in the East seemed to have some promise for the future.

Austrian Social Democrats shied away from using the term "Central Europe," but more conservative Austrian Christian Democrats, above all the Austrian politician Erhard Busek, did not, because they were more comfortable with Roman Catholicism and the cultural traditions of the Habsburg Empire as unifying elements of the region. In the mid-1980s, Busek brought new impetus into the Central European debate by combining the idea of common cultural traditions with demands for more human rights and cooperation in the region. He considered Central Europe to be a "project" in which Austria could play an important role, and in the early 1980s he was one of the few Western European politicians who actively sought and cultivated contacts with East European intellectuals and dissidents, in Poland and Hungary in particular.

The last and ultimately most important version of the idea of Central Europe was the product of Eastern European intellectuals: dissidents at home and émigrés abroad. It was anti-Soviet and anti-Russian, on the one hand, and "remarkable for its omission of Germany and 'the German question,'"[10] on the other. The idea of a confederation of states situated between the Soviet or Russian East and the German West and stretching from the Baltic Sea in the north to the Adriatic Sea in the south played a considerable role in many of these intellectuals' versions or visions of Central Europe. The historical precedents for Central Europe were nostalgically transfigured multinational empires—the Polish–Lithuanian Commonwealth in the north and the Habsburg Empire in the south—whose parameters could be defined not only historically but also in traditional religious and enlightened philosophical terms. Central Europe was Roman Catholic and "westward-looking, cosmopolitan, secular-humanist, and rationalist."[11]

Proponents of this idea of Central Europe shared many of the sentiments of the Western European peace movements. Although they—like most intellectuals on both sides of the Iron Curtain—were critical of the American presence in Europe and the consequences of American "cultural imperialism" and consumerism, Eastern European dissidents and intellectuals recognized the Soviet Union and Communism as greater threats. Consequently they had a rather reticent relationship with the Western European peace movements, because many of the advocates of peace and disarmament in the West failed to understand how dangerous the Soviet Union and Communism really were or to understand that the absence of human rights and democracy in the East bloc were peace issues as well.[12] This version of the Central European idea identified a fundamental change in the Eastern European political system as the prerequisite for real peace in Europe, an insight that made it anti-Communist.

The Czech novelist and essayist Milan Kundera provided a classic definition of Central Europe in an article published in November 1983 in Paris (later translated into English and German). He described the "three fundamental situations" that developed in Europe after World War II as "that of Western Europe, that of Eastern Europe, and, most complicated, that of the part of Europe situated geographically in the center, culturally in the West, and politically in the East." He also was specific about where Central Europe was. It consisted of "an uncertain zone of small nations between Russia and Germany," historically coextensive with the Habsburg Empire and Poland.

The "tragedy of Central Europe," with the exception of "little Austria," was that it had been "kidnapped" by the Soviet Union after World War II. The Western European inability to distinguish between Central and Eastern Europe also was indicative of a larger and more profound crisis. Kundera accused the West of not even noticing that part of the European West had disappeared into the Soviet East and of accepting the logic of a divided Europe. His diagnosis of the fact that "Europe no longer perceives its unity as a cultural unity" was that "Europe itself is in the process of losing its own cultural identity."[13]

Kundera did not offer a concrete political program, but he did have a political claim shared by many other representatives of the Central European idea: The division of Central Europe into an East and a West after World War II was illegitimate. Advocates of the idea of Central Europe may not have agreed on where Central Europe was or which strategies should be pursued or could be used to turn the idea of Central Europe into reality, but they shared "the experience of small nations subjected to large empires" and the "unique experience of living under Soviet-type Communist systems since Yalta."[14] The histories of these small nations and their encounters with Communism provided them with different perspectives, too, but the Eastern European proponents of the idea of Central Europe shared several attitudes and convictions.

If politics meant violently wresting power from the Communists or attempting to influence the existing state or governmental policy, most dissident intellectuals were "antipolitical." One of the problems of the totalitarian or posttotalitarian systems in the Eastern bloc was the omnipresence of politics—the state, the party, the police. Therefore, the idea was not to take the power from "them" but, rather, to destroy the system by redefining the relationship of the state to society. The idea of a "civil society" that was independent of the institutions of the centrally administered and bureaucratic party state and whose relationship to it was regulated by certain principles and game rules was shared by many proponents of the idea of Central Europe. They believed in the tenets of political liberalism but not necessarily economic liberalism,[15] and this made human rights and the rule of law into core Central European issues. It was society's task to control the state, not vice versa.

Many dissidents and intellectuals resorted to fundamental philosophical issues and moral discourse. It really did not make much difference whether their critiques of Communism were based on the terminology of modern existentialism, traditional Catholic moral theology, or common sense. For example, Václav Havel's famous samizdat essay "Living in the Truth" was inspired by the work of the Czech philosopher and fellow dissident Jan Patočka, one of the cofounders of Charta '77 who, in turn, had been influenced by German phenomenology and existentialism.

Pope John Paul II stood firmly in the tradition of Roman Catholic moral theology and social doctrine. Many advocates of the idea of Central Europe did not hesitate to talk about the differences between good and evil, truth and lies, or human dignity and moral depravity. Many dissidents believed that certain ideas were worth suffering for, and the absence of basic rights and freedoms gave them an appreciation for those things often taken for granted in functioning democracies in the West, like habeus corpus and due process or the freedoms of speech, the press, and assembly. Individual existential rectitude and the ethics of solidarity coalesced into one conviction: "our" truth versus "their" lies.

Generalizations about the dimensions and the consequences of dissidence in the region are dangerous. Both ideas and popular protest were important in the revolutions of 1989, but we should not assume that the majority of people were inspired by the dissidents' ideas for a long time before 1989 or that the Communist regimes in the region had uniformly become soft. For example, the Czechoslovak dissidents in Charta '77, were relatively isolated from the population at large and were systematically persecuted, regularly imprisoned, or forced to do menial labor. Therefore, they had a different experience with protest than did their Polish counterparts in Solidarity, who were not ostracized from society to the same extent and could rely on social support systems typical of a "civil society."

Furthermore, at a time when Czechoslovak and Polish dissidents were going in and out of jail in the early and mid-1980s, some Hungarian dissidents started to enjoy the fruits of the Kádár regime's liberality and began traveling between Eastern Europe and the West. Some Yugoslav intellectuals enjoyed similar freedoms, but there was virtually no organized dissident in East Germany. Although the regime spectacularly expelled a few prominent protesters, West Germany paid ransom for all the others. Between 1963 and 1989, the Federal Republic of Germany "bought free" around 34,000 political prisoners from the German Democratic Republic. After the late 1970s, the going rate or ransom for a political prisoner was DM 95,847 per head, around $40,000.[16] Under these circumstances, it was odd that after 1989 some West Germans had the audacity to criticize East Germany for the absence of dissidents.

The Gorbachev Factor

Virtually no one anticipated the revolutions of 1989 in the early 1980s, not to mention the collapse of the Soviet Union in 1991. It will take political scientists, economists, and historians a generation to sort out why the revolutions of 1989 happened when they did, how they were related to the ultimate collapse of Communism in the Soviet Union in 1991, and what role the Cold War played in both these dramas. Retrospectively, it is truly amazing to what extent experts on Communism and the Soviet Union failed to see what was coming.[17] Billions of dollars were spent on studing Communism, and some of the West's best minds were engaged in this enterprise. The precision instruments of Western Sovietology did not have much predictive power, nor for that matter, did the crystal balls of East Central European dissidents and intellectuals. The winners of the revolutions of 1989 (in

East Central Europe) and the Cold War (in the West) were just as surprised at their victories as the Communist losers were at their defeats in 1989 (in East Central Europe) and in the Soviet Union in 1991.

There are different schools of thought regarding the most important causes of the events of 1989 as well as their relationship to the dynamics of the Cold War as a superpower conflict. Changes in Central Europe were determined by the complex interaction of different fields of forces operating on international, regional, and national levels. The development of a qualitatively new relationship between the superpowers after Mikhail Gorbachev's rise to power in the mid-1980s, the Soviet Union's dramatic change of policy in its own sphere of influence thereafter, and the dynamics of protest throughout East Central Europe each played indisputably important roles. These issues will be addressed in terms of the possible answers to three questions: Did the West (or the United States or Ronald Reagan) win the Cold War? Did Gorbachev's attempts to reform Communism end it in a manner that created new perspectives for Central Europe, or did East Central Europeans liberate themselves?

Which strategy contributed most to the demise of Communism? Idealists and realists, people "hard" and "soft" on Communism, and advocates of deterrence and détente all want credit for making the greatest contribution to ending the Cold War. All of them certainly contributed to its demise. There was no unified Western strategy but, rather, a number of different policies that shifted from one governmental administration to the next, from "hard" to "soft," and from country to country. This in itself kept a fundamentally rigid Communist system off balance and contributed to its demise.[18] For the sake of argument, one can identify two extreme positions: the get-tough policies of the Reagan administration in the early 1980s versus the détente policies or the German Social Democratic version of *Ostpolitik* until the early 1980s.

Proponents of the arms race and rearmament maintain that the West, particularly the United States, recognized that they could be used to change the Communist system. This strategy was based on the fact that the American economy was more efficient than the Soviet economy. Therefore, increases in defense expenditures ultimately cost the Soviet Union much more than they did the United States. The arms race drew a disproportionate amount of resources in the Soviet Union and the Eastern bloc away from other economic sectors, which prevented investments in other spheres such as modernization, infrastructure, or consumer goods.

In other words, the United States' strategy for the arms race was to exploit the inherent deficiencies of Soviet-style planned economies and to drive them to the brink of economic disaster. For many years, American policymakers assumed that the Soviet Union spent about twice as much of its gross domestic product on defense as the United States did: 12 percent to the United States' 6 percent. (In the 1970s and 1980s, the figures on Soviet defense spending were revised upward to 16 or even 20 percent.) Making the Soviets compete in a race not exclusively based on arms but, rather, on the overall allocation of economic resources drove the Soviet economy into a structural crisis that forced them to reform.

One of the simplest versions of this story is that Ronald Reagan won the Cold War. The Strategic Defense Initiative (SDI) was not the straw but the two-by-four that broke the proverbial camel's back. The Soviets *reacted* to American policy by putting Mikhail Gorbachev into power. Therefore, the billions of dollars spent on defense paid off in the long run and demonstrated the systemic superiority of market economies over planned economies in terms of efficient resource allocation. The system that could produce both guns and butter—both strategic and consumer goods—won over the one that had to make a structural choice between guns or butter. Cruise missiles and Coca Cola could not be beat.

The various representatives of the German Social Democratic *Ostpolitik*, the protagonists of détente, and the left in general have a difficult time making a case for their contributions to ending the Cold War. Many believed that the Communist system somehow could be reformed. The strategy of this kind of détente was to cooperate with those in power in Moscow, East Berlin, Warsaw, and elsewhere in a manner that would contribute to the system's liberalization and thus improve the conditions of those who had the misfortune of living under it. The objective was to work with the powers that be in order to make Communism more tolerable for all the parties involved, not to win the Cold War.

According to this view, dissidents actually obstructed the process of systemic transformation via rapprochement. Therefore they did not really fit into the strategy of détente but were, on the contrary, sometimes a wrench in the works because their demands were unrealistic. From the European détente or Social Democratic perspective of *Ostpolitik*, tougher anti-Communists always used Eastern European dissidence as leverage on the Communists in order to prevent further reform. Since 1989, the representatives of the tough-on-Communism stance conversely have accused the proponents of détente of directly helping maintain the Communist system by working with it. For example, the DM 3.5 billion that West Germany paid to East Germany for humanitarian purposes between 1963 and 1989—for the release of political prisoners and the reunification of separated families—certainly did not contribute to the demise of the Communist system and was but a fraction of the monies, credits, and goods that East Germany received from West Germany over the years.

Proponents of détente have developed their own version of the story based on the same deficiencies of the Communist system, and they attempt to explain how détente, not deterrence, led to its demise. Détente always attempted to promote more openness within the Communist system itself. The Helsinki Final Act of 1975 and the beginning of the Conference on Security and Cooperation in Europe (CSCE) process, especially with its emphasis on human rights, multilateral diplomacy, and confidence-building measures, was a turning point in East–West relations.[19]

Because the Communist system collapsed *after* a new phase of East–West détente in the mid-1980s, one may argue that détente, not deterrence, was the key to the end of the Communist system. According to this view, the *external* pressure of vitriolic Western anti-Communism helped sustain a system that was terminally ill. Furthermore, it contributed to keeping in power conservative, anti-reform-minded Communists who helped maintain the system. The denouement of East–West tensions after Gorbachev's rise to power in the mid-1980s, which created an atmosphere in which the Soviet Union felt it could address domestic reform, therefore is comparable to removing the buttresses from a dilapidated building which, in this case, collapsed once it was no longer being held up by external means. The central premise of this theory is that Soviet Communism would have failed *sooner* had Western, and in particular American, anti-Communism not exerted the external pressures necessary to hold it together.

The fact that both the proponents of détente and deterrence have cogent arguments for being responsible for the end of the Cold War is a good indication that both these approaches may overestimate the consequences of Western European and American policies on the development of Soviet foreign and domestic policies. Anyone naive enough to maintain that Western policies "brought Gorbachev into power" does not understand how the Soviet system worked.

Conjectural arguments are admittedly of questionable value; however, had Chernenko or Andropov lived longer or had a younger generation "Brezhnevist" primarily interested in maintaining the status quo assumed the leadership of the Soviet Union instead of Gorbachev, the revolutions of 1989 (and 1991) most likely would not have happened when they did and how they did. It is reasonable to assume that a more conservative and ideologically orthodox Soviet leader could have maintained the Soviet system much longer—at great cost, of course—but he could have maintained it nonetheless. It was obvious to all observers that the Soviet empire was overextended, but the assumption that the Soviet Union would follow the path of all other great empires by crumbling soon was not widespread.[20]

This raises another problematic issue: the role of "great men in history." Gorbachev undoubtedly deserves to be placed in this category, although he failed to accomplish what he wanted to–that is, reform the Communist system—but he failed grandly. He can be compared with other central figures in the history of the Communist system who also attempted to reform it and failed: Imre Nagy, Alexander Dubček, and Nikita Khrushchev.

In the comparison with Nagy and Dubček, the question to ask is how a system so thoroughly based on stability, conformity, control, loyalty, and ultimately a certain lack of ingenuity could have let some one like Gorbachev—daring, prepared to experiment, and innovative—get so far? Did all the Communist Party's filtering mechanisms fail? Was Gorbachev an accident, a fluke, or, until his rise to power, a brilliant impostor? Comparisons with Khrushchev are less speculative. Gorbachev embodied the necessity of systemic change; he personified historical powers at work. Like Khrushchev, he had to dislodge entrenched interest groups in the system in order to change the system, and this required criticizing the representatives and benefactors of his predecessor, Brezhnev. Glasnost and perestroika—"de-Brezhnevization"—was a from of de-Stalinization or even a continuation of the process that Khrushchev had begun and Brezhnev had interrupted. Some sympathetic observers even felt that Gorbachev was bringing back the Russian Revolution to a point where the historical record might be rectified by a new start. In theoretical terms, he returned to the mid-1920s, the period after Lenin but before Stalin. A gigantic "New Economic Plan"[21] might have belatedly set the Soviet experiment aright.

Gorbachev was an unusual Soviet leader in a number of respects. Given the geriatric status of the leadership of the Brezhnev era, he was a young man and not a veteran of World War II. This undoubtedly was an important element of his psychological makeup and colored his perceptions of Germany in particular and the West in general. Although he sincerely believed in the principles of the socialist system, he was not an ideologue, and as a realist he knew that propaganda regarding the alleged "superiority" of Soviet system bordered on nonsense. In order to gain the political leverage he needed to reform the Soviet system, he also violated one of the fundamental rules of Communist government. Instead of beating the people over the head with the Communist Party, he began beating the party over the head with the people. He recognized that his reforms could be successful only if the people helped initiate and carry them. All the well-worn metaphors used to describe the consequences of these measures are accurate. Gorbachev let the genie out of the bottle or opened Pandora's box.

Gorbachev also recognized either that the Soviet Union had lost the arms race or that the cost of competing was too high. In any event, he needed to end it in order to divert the tremendous economic resources the Soviet Union spent on defense from military to civilian economic sectors; otherwise he would not have the resources he needed to implement his ambitious program of restructuring the Soviet economy. It is important to emphasize here that Gorbachev made a *political* decision based on the *economics* of the Cold War. Adherents of the resource allocation theory of the arms race are correct in pointing out that it cost the Soviet Union much more than it cost the United States, a fact that brought out all the deficiencies inherent in the Soviet economy to the detriment of the system as a whole. But the economics of the Cold War did not "force" Gorbachev, as some proponents of the arms race assume, to make this decision.

In order to pursue his project of sweeping domestic reform in the Soviet Union, Gorbachev had to change Soviet policy toward the West, and the denouement of East–West tensions created a new environment in superpower relations that undoubtedly enhanced the prospects of change in East Central Europe in the late 1980s. Gorbachev not only stopped seeing the Western system of military and economic alliances as an active threat. He also began perceiving Western Europe as a potential partner. He rethought the relationship of the Soviet Union with its own empire, and he concluded that East Central Europe was not as important to the Soviet Union's national security as it once had been.

He was prepared to let the states of the Soviet bloc go their own way, which he hoped would be his way, and Gorbachev's reform program undermined the legitimacy of the old Brezhnev-style regimes in Erich Honecker's East Germany, Gustáv Husák's Czechoslovakia, Nicolae Ceaușescu's Romania, and Todor Zhivkov's Bulgaria. Maintaining the Soviet empire also was expensive, and Gorbachev wanted to reallocate some of the resources that were being expended abroad for his project of reform at home. Finally, those states that went their own way also could pay their own way in the future by, for example, purchasing Soviet oil or gas in hard currency at world prices instead of at the artificially low levels institutionalized by the "socialist division of labor" in COMECON.[22] Gorbachev's grand plan was to end the Cold War in order to carry out large-scale reform in the Soviet Union. But in the process, he created a revolutionary situation not only in East Central Europe but also in the Soviet Union itself.

Gorbachev was much more popular in the West than he ever was in the Soviet Union. His reform programs produced more confusion than progress in the Soviet Union, and the conditions of daily life for the most Soviet citizens only worsened. He also was unpopular among orthodox Communists as well as anti-Communists in East Central Europe. Gorbachev weakened the legitimacy and threatened the interests of the Communists in power, especially the old hard-liners from the Brezhnev era in Czechoslovakia and East Germany. Most dissidents and intellectuals, however, disapproved of him for completely different reasons. First, he was trying to reform a system that was not only incapable of reform but also undesirable in principle. Second, they were dismayed that Gorbachev was so popular in the West because it indicated how little people in the West understood Communism or the problems of East Central Europe.

Nonetheless, Gorbachev's conduct of Soviet foreign policy opened new perspectives for Central Europe in 1989. He retracted the Brezhnev Doctrine by stating that the Soviet Union had no intention of intervening in the domestic affairs of allied states, and he affirmed that his country was prepared to reduce its military presence in the region. The specter of East Central European revolutions ending with Soviet military intervention—as they did in Hungary in 1956 or Czechoslovakia in 1968—thus evaporated. In Poland and Hungary, this gave both the Communists in power and the dissidents room to maneuver and negotiate. Gorbachev also began to criticize the most orthodox Communist regimes in the Eastern bloc—East Germany and Czechoslovakia, in particular—for their rigidity and antireform postures, and he warned them that they were unwise not to follow his lead. Indeed, at the fortieth anniversary of the establishment of the German Democratic Republic in October 1989, Gorbachev pointed out to Erich Honecker: "Life punishes those who come too late."

Epilogue

Postrevolutionary Paradoxes

Central Europe Since 1989

During the last six months of 1989 the Communist regimes in the Eastern Bloc came down one by one: in July in Poland, in Hungary in September, in East Germany in November, and in Czechoslovakia, Romania, and Bulgaria in December. One thing all of these revolutions obviously had in common was that they displaced the old Communist order, and the coincidence of 1989 with the bicentennial celebration of the French Revolution in 1789 was an appropriate historical accident. François Furet, one of the premier French historians of the French Revolution, drew parallels between 1989 and "the ideas of 1789 or the American Revolution: human rights, the sovereignty of peoples, free elections, markets" and compared the Communist regimes with the *ancien régime* of late-eighteenth-century France: hated, immobile, and incompetent.

Furet also took this opportunity to criticize the European Left, which traditionally interpreted the Bolshevik Revolution in 1917 as a legitimate expression of French revolutionary ideals. The revolutions of 1989 represented the belated victory of "old ideas"—the moderate, late-eighteenth-century principles liberal-democratic revolutions—over the radically modern ones of early-twentieth-century "Bolshevik-Jacobinism":

> We are witnesses to revolutions, which are simultaneously counter-revolutions: uprisings by the people in the name of the establishment or reestablishment of liberal democracy; we are seeing the end of the revolutionary idea that has determined the horizons of the Left, far beyond strictly Marxist-Leninist circles, for two hundred years.

According to Furet, in 1989 the future of Communism and socialist planned economies ironically became democracy and capitalist market economies.

275

The driving forces between the revolutions of 1989 were "the contradictory but inseparably related virtues of market economics and human rights."[1]

The fact that the guiding principles of the various revolutions of 1989 were fundamentally the same and revolutionary synergy helped topple six Communist regimes in the region within the relatively short period of six months actually obscures how different each of these revolutions were. The moral and political (or human rights) dimensions of these revolutions and the role the ideas of market economics played were different in each country; the durations of their respective "pre-revolutionary" phases varied widely; and the dynamics of the interaction among different actors in these revolutionary dramas—such as Mikhail Gorbachev, the regimes in power, intellectuals and dissidents, organized opposition, and the populace at large—were dissimilar.

On November 23, 1989, the seventh day of the Czechoslovak revolution, the British historian and journalist Timothy Garton Ash met Václav Havel in Prague and commented: "In Poland it took ten years, in Hungary it took ten months, in East Germany it took ten weeks: perhaps in Czechoslovakia it will take ten days!"[2] His quip was remarkably accurate. The Czechoslovak revolution ran its course in twenty-four days. Romania's bloody revolution of December 1989 was even shorter: figuratively it took "ten hours." One of the amazing characteristics of the revolutions of 1989, with the notable exception of Romania, was the absence of violence, bloodshed, and vengeance.

Furthermore, there were at least four different revolutionary patterns in East Central Europe.[3] Poland's "negotiated transition" was carried by Solidarity, a well organized coalition of antiregime forces that enjoyed broad popular support, and it occurred from the bottom up. In Hungary, a new generation of liberal reform Communists initiated a transition from the top down by inviting oppositional dissidents and intellectuals to participate in a dialogue about restructuring the system under circumstances which were considerably different than those in Poland. There was neither widespread popular protest against the regime in Hungary nor an identification of the populace with dissidents and intellectuals, or vice versa. Furthermore, there was a unique and in some cases almost symbiotic relationship between oppositional intellectuals and the Communist Party in Hungary, which was by far the most open, liberal, democratic, and reform-minded of all Communist parties in Eastern Europe. The Hungarian revolution took place for the most part without the mass protest of "the people" in the streets.

The revolutions in the German Democratic Republic and Czechoslovakia fall into a third category. They were Gorbachev-inspired to a certain extent. However, they were not instigated by reform Communists but by numerically small groups of dissidents and sudden popular protest. Gorbachev had openly criticized the repressive regimes of Erich Honecker in the GDR and Gustav Husák in Czechoslovakia for their lack of preparedness to reform, and popular protest organized by regime critics interested in truly reforming socialism (in the case of the GDR) and by students and dissidents (in the case of Czechoslovakia) dislodged the old guard. In both cases, new

Communist leaders, who quickly endorsed a Gorbachevite agenda, could not contain the dynamics of popular protest and virtually capitulated to the "democratic forces" that had helped bring them into power.

Romania and Bulgaria represent a fourth, Southeastern European category of Gorbachev-style revolutions based on the replacement of the old party leadership by reformers, followed by constrained electoral competition, and Yugoslavia was an exceptional case of national, not necessarily democratic, revolutions. Ivo Banac called 1989–90 a period of "Yugoslav non-revolutions."[4]

A brief look at the distinguishing features of the individual Central European revolutions and how they were interrelated is necessary at this point. Looking back, social scientists have ascertained that the type of Communism that existed in the states of the region before 1989 played a substantial role not only in the dynamics of the individual revolutions but also in type of post-Communism that has developed on a case-by-case basis since then. For example, states with higher levels of economic development and stronger traditions of protest or reform, such as Poland or Hungary, were in a completely different and better position than those less prosperous ones characterized by the extended success of Communist authoritarianism, such as Romania and Bulgaria. Pre-1989 traditions have played a considerable role in the post-1989 trajectories of development.

The Poles were the first to move in 1989. Preceding the Polish elections in July, the Solidarity movement in Poland negotiated a "round table" power-sharing agreement with the Jaruzelski regime, which provided for elections to the Polish parliament, the Sejm. The electoral procedures were complicated and rigged in favor the Communists, who were willing to give Solidarity part of the power but not to compete with the opposition in a free and democratic election. Although the Communists reserved the position of president for Jaruzelski and technically "won" the elections, Solidarity emerged as the moral and political victor. Tadeusz Mazowiecki, a Catholic intellectual and Solidarity activist, was elected Poland's prime minister by an overwhelming parliamentary majority at the end of August, and this marked the beginning of Poland's transition from communism to democracy.

Poland had the first revolution, and if one wishes to explain the events of 1989 in terms of a "domino effect," it was the most important. Furthermore, Poland had the longest revolution—it started with the "Solidarity Revolution" in 1980—and the largest anti-Communist movement. It was the biggest country in the East Bloc and therefore the biggest problem in the East Bloc. Poland had the weakest tradition of collaboration of all states in the region, not only with the Nazis during World War II but also with the Communists thereafter. In addition, it had the strongest tradition of resistance, which was based partly on the spiritual and institutional strength of Poland's Roman Catholic Church, the most formidable anti-Communist institution in the Eastern Bloc.

Hungary's revolution was substantially different, and some Hungarians maintain that it was actually much longer than Poland's. It started in 1956 or during the initial liberalization of Hungary under the Kádár regime in the 1960s. By 1988, when Kádár was eased out of office, Hungary had a record of at least twenty years of political liberalization and experimentation with market economics. By June 1989, a dynamic, younger triumvirate— Imre Pozsgay, Rezsö Nyers, and Miklós Németh—had control of key party and state offices, and they revolutionized Hungarian foreign and domestic policy.

On May 2, 1989, Hungarian border guards started taking down the barbed wire along the Austrian-Hungarian frontier. In the summer of 1989, Hungarian border officials barely prevented hundreds of East Germans, who were vacationing in Hungary, from fleeing to Austria, and in September the Hungarian government stopped observing an old East Bloc agreement by allowing citizens from other Communist countries in the region to leave Hungary for Austria. Thousands of "vacationing" East Germans began leaving Hungary legally, and this hole in the Iron Curtain helped bring the Berlin Wall down in November. Hungary maintained that a United Nations convention on refugees, which it had signed as the first East Bloc state in March 1989, had abrogated their obligations to prevent GDR citizens from leaving the country.

In June 1989, the Hungarian Communist Party also started round table negotiations with oppositional groups, which by Polish standards were small, poorly organized, and to a certain extent at ideological odds with each other. Urban liberals and rural nationalists and conservatives already had good (and different) ideas about what they wanted. The strategy behind the Hungarian round table was to work out a major program of political and economic liberalization, and the initiation of these negotiations reflected the party's tradition and strategy of paternalism: power-sharing "from above." However, Hungarian opposition groups proved to be tough negotiators, and after Hungary's reform Communists saw how the Polish electorate had responded to elections that had been rigged in favor of Poland's Communists in July, they abandoned the idea of limited compromise in favor of unfettered electoral competition.

Hungary's reform Communists enjoyed a genuine amount of popular support in the summer of 1989. They assumed that they could not only compete with the opposition but also beat it at the ballot box. The reform Communists concluded a round table agreement with opposition groups in September, which provided for free and democratic elections in the spring of 1990. They officially abandoned Marxism as a party doctrine in October and changed the party's name to "Socialist." Then they suffered a devastating defeat in the 1990 elections, receiving only 9 percent of the vote. The Hungarian revolution of 1989 was relatively fluid and nonconfrontational, and Hungarians, like Poles, can claim substantial responsibility for the demise of the East bloc. They reformed Communism to death and opened up the Iron Curtain in the process.

The maverick foreign policy of Hungarian reform Communists had domestic political consequences for the German Democratic Republic, whose leaders were surprised by the sheer number of GDR citizens who wanted to flee the country. The Honecker regime increased the political pressure with-

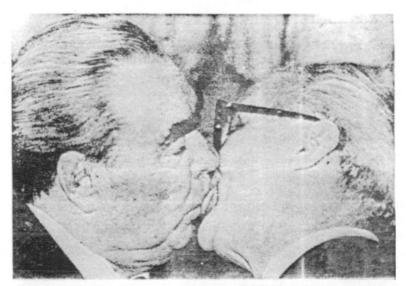

TESSÉK VÁLASZTANI

FIATAL DEMOKRATÁK SZÖVETSÉGE

Tessék Valasztani (Please Choose), a poster of the Alliance of Young Democrats (FIDESZ), a Hungarian liberal party founded by young people that inially limited its membership to people under thirty-five, from Hungary's first free election campaign in 1990. Above: Soviet leader Leonid Brezhnev (left) giving East German leader Erich Honecker a kiss that was part of the "fraternal socialist" ritual between Communist heads of state in the Eastern bloc. Below: Young Hungarians with oversized FIDESZ buttons. (Courtesy of the Alliance of Young Democrats [FIDESZ]. Bucapest).

in the GDR by quarantining East Germans with travel restrictions, and it addressed the entire issue of fleeing GDR citizens with a combination of arrogance and "socialist self-confidence," by branding those who left as morally inferior renegades whose loss was not to be lamented. The exodus of tens of thousands of East Germans and the contemptuous and restrictive conduct of the Honecker regime led churches in September 1989 to the formation a home-grown protest movement in the GDR which crystallized around intellectuals, artists, peace activists, environmentalists, and Protestant pastors and churches.

The first wave of protest in East Germany was inspired by the idea of radically reforming the GDR and creating a truly democratic socialist society, not anti-Communism or German unification. At increasingly larger demonstrations in September and October, protesters chanted Gorbachev's nickname, "Gorbi, Gorbi," "We are staying here," and "We are the people." At the beginning of October, the GDR celebrated the fortieth anniversary of its establishment with a series of pompous and pathetic events. Two weeks later Erich Honecker resigned from his offices and was replaced by a younger functionary, Egon Krenz. But there were irreconcilable tensions between the "Stayers" (*Dableiber*) in the GDR's new oppositional movements with their sense of solidarity, socialist vision, and newly felt empowerment; the "Leavers" (*Weggeher*), who wanted to get out one way or the other; and party authorities, who were confounded by the challenges both groups presented.

The Berlin Wall came down on November 9, 1989 for the same reason it went up in 1961: to keep people in the GDR. The strategy of the GDR's new leadership was that liberalizing travel restrictions would not only enhance the credibility of the new government but also keep the East Germans at home by giving them a chance to travel back and forth. It backfired. Krenz's political career lasted just seven weeks, and after his resignation a new reformer, Hans Modrow, formed a government that entered a wide-ranging dialogue with the critics of the regime. Hundreds of thousands of East Germans, especially members of the younger generation, distrusted the government, decided to "vote with their feet," and left for the Federal Republic of Germany, and the slogan "We are *one* people" began appearing at demonstrations. (This phrase also meant "We want one currency," the West German deutschmark, and "We want the West German standard of living.")

Public scrutiny of the regime by citizens' investigatory committees led to sensational revelations about the luxurious and self-aggrandizing lifestyles of party leaders, widespread corruption, and the unimaginable dimensions of the state security police's surveillance, networks of informants, and records on individuals in the country. The idea of reforming the GDR faded rapidly, and by the time the first free elections in the former Eastern Bloc were held in East Germany in March 1990, reforming the GDR was a minority proposition. German unification was on its way. On October 3, 1990, the festive proclamation of German unity simultaneously ended the existence of the GDR as an independent state and enlarged the Federal Republic of Germany by incorporating five "new *Länder*" into the "old" German federal state.[5]

Czechoslovakia's "Velvet Revolution" was prefaced by an increasing amount of popular protest on symbolic dates in the course of 1989. On August 21, 1989, the twenty-first anniversary of the Warsaw Pact intervention that ended the "Prague Spring," police broke up a peaceful demonstration of students in Prague and arrested more than 350 people. On October 28, the seventy-first anniversary of the establishment of the Czechoslovak Republic, the police forcibly dissolved the largest organized protest the country had seen in over twenty years and arrested another 350 people. On November 17, students transformed an officially sanctioned rally to commemorate the anniversary of the death of Jan Opletal, a student killed by the Nazis, into an antiregime protest, and the police and special antiterrorist squads reacted brutally with tear gas and truncheons. The escalating conflicts between students and the state and the ruthlessness with which the state dealt with its own citizens contributed to the coalescence of Czech and Slovak dissidence and broad anti-regime sentiment, which was fueled in turn by the success of protest elsewhere in East Central Europe.

Two citizen's organizations called into being by dissidents, artists, and students, the Civic Forum and the Public Against Violence, emerged almost simultaneously in Prague and Bratislava, respectively, and they organized and articulated the empowerment of a citizenry which virtually took control of the streets in regular and increasingly larger demonstrations. The children of the generation of Czechs and Slovaks, who had been inspired by the "Prague Spring" in 1968 and then so disillusioned by its failure and the process of "normalization" that followed it, played an instrumental role in this confrontation. Czechoslovakia's Velvet Revolution had elements of the Polish, Hungarian, and East German revolutions that preceded it, and it represented a distillation of their essences. Within weeks, nonviolent, mass protest led to a negotiated power-sharing arrangement with the Communist regime that culminated in its abdication. On December 29, the representatives of the Czechoslovak Socialist Republic's Federal Assembly elected Václav Havel—playwright, dissident, former political prisoner, and the mastermind of the revolution—president. This was an appropriate symbolic ending for the astonishing, exhilarating, and happy year of 1989.

The Bulgarian and Romanian revolutions of 1989 fell into a category of their own because reform minded, Gorbachev-style Communists played an important role in orchestrating them and in instrumentalizing popular protest to dislodge the Communist old guard. Furthermore, members of the old party apparatus also successfully reinvented themselves as socialists and nationalists in both of these countries, and they managed to stay in power for an extended period of time after the introduction of multi-party systems, free elections, and parliamentary rule. The Bulgarian and Romanian revolutions of 1989 were incomplete in comparison to the Polish, Hungarian, and Czechoslovak revolutions because they did not dislodge the old ruling Communist elites as completely, and this slowed down the subsequent processes of transformation in each country.

In Bulgaria, a palace revolution eased the long-term Communist strong-man Todor Zhivkov out of power in November 1989, and reformers started transforming the old Communist party into a new socialist one, the Bulgarian Socialist Party (BSF). They established roundtable discussions with oppositional groups that formed the Union of Democratic Forces (UDF) and organized free elections in the spring of 1990, which the BSF carried with a slight majority. The UDF did not mangage to dislodge the post-Communist BSF from government until the elections of April 1997.

Romania was in many respects an exceptional case because its revolution in December 1989 was so violent, and its post-revolutionary regime was so illiberal. The Ceaușescu regime was without a doubt the most oppressive in all of Eastern Europe, but a combination of popular protest and political plotting brought it down with a few weeks in December 1989. The relationship between revolutionary contagion, popular protest, and high level Communist party conspiracy against Ceaușescu in the Romanian revolution is still unclear. The regime's violent attempts to subdue popular protest and the emergence of an anti-Ceaușescu "National Salvation Front" prefaced the arrest of Nicolae and Elena Ceaușescu just before Christmas. After a kangaroo trial, the Ceaușescus were executed by a firing squad on December 25, 1989, and their deaths, captured on video, were broadcast by television stations worldwide on Christmas Day. Under the leadership of Ion Iliescu, the National Liberation Front—renamed the Democratic National Liberation Front in 1991—established a peculiar form of "post-Communist Communism" that entered an alliance with traditional Romanian nationalism. Democratic opposition parties did not manage to dislodge Iliescu's coalition of neo-Communists and ultranationalists until the elections of November 1996, but once in power they too failed to be convincing reformers. Iliescu made a political comeback in the Romanian elections of 2000 in which former Communists and ultranationalists made a strong showing. The Romanian path to democracy and a market economy has been characterized by a series of detours that are a source of continuing concern.

After the revolutions of 1989, grand plans for a cooperative or confederate reorganization of Central Europe were exceptionally popular. The pending unification of Germany was something all politicians in the region officially greeted, but it also awoke long-standing and deep-seated fears. Furthermore, the Soviet Union was still intact, and the assumption at the time that Gorbachev's experiment could fail and that he might be replaced by much more orthodox and aggressive Communist leaders also was more widespread in East Central Europe than the West. Under these circumstances, it only seemed reasonable for the countries in the region to find modes of cooperation that would offset the burgeoning influence of a united Germany in the future and the potential threat the Soviet Union still represented.

The assumption that Europe that would find new modes of regional cooperation after the disintegration of the military and economic blocs that had dictated the division of Europe as well as the scenario that Central Europe as a region would play an important role in the "new Europe" enjoyed a brief heyday after 1989. For example, at a meeting of the foreign ministers of Poland, Czechoslovakia, and Hungary held in Bratislava in April 1990, Vá- clav Havel envisioned a Baltic confederation consisting of Poland, the Baltic states, and Finland, that perhaps would include Sweden and Norway. Aus- tria, Hungary, Yugoslavia, and Italy could form a second, Danube-Adriatic confederation, and Czechoslovakia would provide the "logical nexus"[6] be- tween these two regional associations, which, in virtue of their collective sizes and geopolitical affinities, would peacefully offset the influence of large neighbors like a unified Germany and the Soviet Union. (The absence of Romania and Bulgaria here is both striking and symptomatic for Central European perceptions of Central Europe. Havel's vision for the region also had striking similarities to the one Thomas Masaryk proposed in 1918.)

Czechoslovak, Polish, and Hungarian heads of state also held a Central European summit in Visegrád in 1990. The meeting site on the Danube north of Budapest, a magnificent medieval castle of the Louis the Great, was laden with symbolism. In 1335, the kings of Bohemia, Hungary, and Poland had met there for a medieval regional summit to discuss multilateral coop- eration and regional concerns. Age-old patterns of cooperation among these states, which subsequently were labeled the "Visegrád group," were be- ing revived. The pending dissolution of COMECON and the Warsaw Pact (in January and March 1991) made it necessary to investigate new forms of cooperation. Czechoslovak, Polish, and Hungarian politicians saw great ad- vantages in terms of coordinating the region's "return to Europe." They as- sumed, for example, that they would have more political leverage if they demonstrated solidarity by acting as a group. Furthermore, they felt that they had a lot in common: "The history of these three countries under state socialism, the victory of the opposition in the first competitive elections after socialism, and the similarities of their geographical location, as well as their agendas for transformation, all worked to homogenize in effect the structure, the experiences, the interests, and the goals of the new regimes . . ."[7]

The idea of Central European cooperation was not merely something that inspired former Eastern Europeans. In May 1990 the foreign ministers of Czechoslovakia, Hungary, Austria, Yugoslavia, and Italy discussed the idea of "pentagonal" cooperation among the five states at meetings held in Vi- enna and Bratislava: a split-site agenda that symbolically demonstrated the end of East–West division of Europe and the potential of new forms of re- gional cooperation. In 1991, Poland joined the "pentagon," which then be- came the "hexagon," and after the deterioration of Yugoslavia this multilat- eral forum for regional cooperation was renamed the Central European Initiative in 1992. (The Central European Initiative floundered after the de- terioration of Yugoslavia. Slovenia, Croatia, and Bosnia-Herzegovina are its ex-Yugoslav members.)

After 1989 unrealistic expectations were an understandable part of post- revolutionary euphoria in the former Eastern Bloc, and visions about new modes of Central European and pan-European cooperation have died hard since then. Three different processes have determined the prospects and the position of Central Europe in Europe since 1989: the wars that accompanied the deterioration of Yugoslavia, the disintegration of the Soviet Union, and the economic and political integration of Western Europe.

The fall of Yugoslavia is a complicated and tragic story that testifies to the success of indigenous nationalism and the failures of international diplomacy.[8] During 1989 and 1990, an ongoing constitutional crisis in Yugoslavia created the impression that the deterioration of the old Yugoslav Communist federal state might pave the way for a series of "dual transitions"—to democracy and to independence—for the component peoples and republics of Yugoslavia, but the process of the dissolution of Yugoslavia turned into an uncontrolled and violent affair dictated by nationalism of the worst variety. The deterioration of Yugoslavia was prefaced and exacerbated by Slobodan Milošević's rise to power after the mid-1980s. He was the first representative in a new generation of Communist functionaries, who were prepared to abandon the concept of Yugoslav multinationalism for unabashed nationalism.

Milošević's combination of Serbian nationalism and Communist centralism fueled the rise of nationalism and separatism elsewhere in Yugoslavia. Slovenia, the only republic that managed to extricate itself from the Yugoslav mess without considerable losses, opted for independence in December 1990, and it unobtrusively joined the ranks of the other post-Communist states in Central Europe to become a relatively normal post-revolutionary polity. Its step toward independence was followed by Croatia in May 1991, Macedonia in September 1991, and Bosnia-Herzegovina in March 1992, and this succession of secessions left a Yugoslav rump state consisting of Serbia—along with the formerly autonomous provinces of Vojvodina and Kosovo—and Montenegro.

In June 1991, the Serb-dominated Yugoslav People's Army (JNA) made a symbolic attempt to hold Slovenia in the Yugoslav federation by fighting a series of skirmishes with Slovenian territorial defense units before withdrawing. However, the situation in Croatia was more complicated and explosive. Franjo Tudjman, a former Communist turned authoritarian nationalist, vigorously promoted the idea of Croatian independence, and he intentionally antagonized Croatia's considerable Serbian minorities in the process. During the summer of 1991, there was a dramatic increase of Croatian and Serbian paramilitary activity in Croatia, and Serbian nationalists began to establish so-called "autonomous regions" in Croatia with the explicit support of the JNA and Milošević. Paramilitary sparing unfolded into a full-fledged war and the Serbian conquest of approximately one-third of Croatia. An estimated 75,000 Croats fled or were expelled from their homes during the Serbian offensives in eastern, southern, and southwestern Croatia, which ended with an uneasy cease-fire brokered by the international community. The first of many waves of "ethnic cleansing" had taken place.

The Croatian–Serbian war of 1991 soon spilled into trinational Bosnia-

Herzegovina, where indigenous Croats and Serbs for the most part aligned
themselves with the irredentist nationalism of either Tudjman or Milošević;
Muslims aspired to maintain the territorial integrity of their multiethnic
state; and humanitarian intervention by the United Nations proved ineffectual. This triangular conflict initially was characterized by Croatian and Serbian aspirations to effectively partition Bosnia-Herzegovina and substantial
territorial gains by indigenous Serbs—vigorously assisted by the Yugoslav
Army and Serbian paramilitaries—who gained control of 70% of Bosnia-
Herzegovina's territory and engaged in a ruthless ethnic cleansing of its
Muslim populations, in particular. Confronted with aggression by a common enemy and pressured by the international community, Croatia and
Bosnia-Herzegovina eventually managed to form anti-Serb alliance.

The diplomatic initiatives of the European Community and the United
Nations did little to prevent Serbian aggression in Bosnia-Herzegovina until 1995, when a new wave of Serbian atrocities, combined with Serbian non-
compliance with a UN ultimatum, cemented the resolve of the United States
and NATO to intervene in the conflict, and NATO began punitive air strikes
against Serbian positions in May.[9] Successful offensives by the armies of
Bosnia-Herzegovina and Croatia in late summer in early fall, combined with
a new wave of NATO air strikes, drove the Serbs out of substantial portions
of western and central Bosnia and out of Croatia altogether, and these operations were accompanied by a reverse pattern of ethnic cleansing that
turned the region's Serbian populations into refugees.

In November 1995, the Dayton Peace Agreement brought an end to
hostilities; provided for the division of Bosnia-Herzegovina into two "entities"—the Bosnian-Croat Federation controlling 51% of the state's territory
and the Serbian Republic (*Republika Srpska*) with 49%—and marked the beginning of the deployment of a NATO led peace-keeping and "implementation force" (IFOR) of 60,000 that subsequently was reduced to a "stabilization force" (SFOR) of 20,000. The ambitious intentions of the Dayton
Agreements to reestablish central state authority and reverse ethnic cleansing by returning expellees to their homes have produced a stalemate status
quo, and development in the two "entities" has been uneven, partially due
to the comparative superabundance of western aid for the Bosnian-Croat
Federation.

The combined results of Serbian and Croatian nationalism and the wars
in Croatia and Bosnia-Herzegovina between 1991 and 1995 were an estimated 300,000 dead, and at the peak of the conflict, over 3 million refugees,
many of whom are still displaced at home or abroad.[10] These refugees are
mostly Bosnians but also include considerable numbers of Croats and Serbs.
Vast regions effectively were "cleansed" of their indigenous minorities: a eu-
phemism for murder, rape, expulsion, plunder, expropriation, and arson.
That this conflict emerged along the millenium-old religious fault line between the Roman Catholic West and the Orthodox East and took place
roughly along the former border lines of the military frontier between the
Habsburg and the Ottoman empires, with the Bosnian Muslims being as-

signed the historical role of "Turkish aggressors" or portrayed as "betraying Christendom," lent itself to misinterpretation. All parties involved—Catholic, Orthodox, and Muslim—generously appealed to religious mission and to History as part of their ideological subterfuge, and many western journalists unwittingly reiterated talk about "age-old ethnic enmities," where there had been little or none thereof.

As a consequence of the Yugoslav wars, Croatia did achieve full independence and managed to reestablish its territorial integrity. The West was never comfortable with Croat president Franjo Tudjman in light of his authoritarian politics, open nepotism, and nationalist rhetoric, which included an apologetic relationship to the independent Nazi client state of the Ustashe during World War II. Croatia's initial transition to independence was far from being a successful transition to democracy. However, independent Croatia officially viewed itself as a perfectly normal Central European state, and it used all of the traditional Central European points of reference to document how Central *and* Western European it was. After 900 years of foreign domination, Croatia had finally reachieved national independence. (In 1102, Croatia formally was incorporated into the Kingdom of Hungary, where it remained until becoming part of Yugoslavia in 1918. For Croatian nationalists, Yugoslavia merely was part of a Serbian imperial conspiracy to subjugate and assimilate Croats.) Croatia was a westward-looking, Roman Catholic country that historically had been one of the "bulwarks of Christendom." Croatia, like Slovenia, had been part of the Habsburg Empire. It was not part of the "Balkans": that part of Europe which western Europeans stereotypically have construed to be backward, violent, and unmanageable.[11] Furthermore, Croatia's new national ideology was definitely anti-Communist (and anti-Yugoslav and anti-Serb). Until the death of Franjo Tudjman in December 1999, western democracies preferred to keep Croatia at an arm's length. However, since the election of a new president, Stjepan Mesič, and a less nationalistic and more centerist parliament in early 2000, many observers are optimistic that Croatia is making its belated transition to democracy.

The Yugoslav problem was by no means resolved as the millenium drew to a close. In the rump state of the Federal Republic of Yugoslavia, it appeared as if Milošević was intent upon applying the policy of ethnic cleansing, which he had supported abroad, at home, too. The Serbian oppression of the Albanian inhabitants in the formerly semi-autonomous province of Kosovo—an ethnic minority that accounted for 90% of the region's inhabitants—spiraled. The increasingly excessive use of force by Serbian military and police forces contributed to a growing amount of international concern and an increase in local resistance, including the establishment of the so-called Kosovo Liberation Army (KLA) that was more than prepared to depart from the Albanian opposition's tradition of nonviolence. The KLA engaged Yugoslav security forces intermittently in 1998, and fighting escalated dramatically during the first weeks of 1999 with familiar results: atrocities, internally displaced persons, and an increasing number of refugees. The international community intervened, failed to mediate a solution for Kosovo, and issued a series of ultimatums, and Yugoslav security forces began to systematically expell tens of thousands of Albanians to neighboring Montenegro, Albania, and Macedonia.

On March 23, NATO began a 77-day bombing campaign conceived to force the Milošević regime to reason. Outflows of Albanian refugees jumped, reaching a peak of 800,000, with perhaps just as many Albanians displaced internally in Kosovo. In over 10,000 strike sorties, NATO destroyed a fair share of the infrastructure of the Federal Republic of Yugoslavia but left, surprisingly, the Milošević regime intact, which then belatedly conceded to the initial demands made.

Operating out of Albania and Macedonia, NATO forces then occupied Kosovo by agreement and dispatched another implementation and stabilization force to the region: KFOR, a contingent of over 40,000 men. Fortunately, the majority of the Kosovar Albanian refugees were eager to return home as soon as possible; unfortunately, their return was accompanied by the flight of the majority of Kosovo's ethnic minorities—Serbs and Roma (Gypsies)—to the north. Ethnic cleansing and the massive use of military force for the humanitarian purpose of ending it led to another ethnic cleansing. NATO got into the Balkans for humanitarian purposes and is occupying and administering a substantial amount of territory. The big open question remains, how and when it will get out of the Balkans?

It would be premature at this point to speculate about the extent to which the NATO bombing of Yugoslavia fueled the popular discontent that finally led Serbs to vote Slobodan Milošević out of office in October 2000. Milošević's successor, Vojislav Kostunica, has been received enthusiastically by the international community and many of the sanctions against the Federal Republic of Yugoslavia were retracted shortly after he came into power. Commentators were quick to observe that the fall of Milošević finally brought the revolutionary period that had begun in 1989 to an end. Yet it remains to be seen how Kostunica will manage Yugoslav affairs and to what extent he truly represents the beginning of a belated transition to democracy.

At the end of November 2000, the heads of government from all 15 European Union member states met in Zagreb with the heads of government from Albania, Bosnia-Herzegovina, Croatia, the Federal Republic of Yugoslavia, and the Former Yugoslav Republic of Macedonia. The symbolic importance of this meeting would be hard to exaggerate. It marked the belated "normalization" of political relations among the states of the region as well as between the EU and the states of the region. The EU heads of state attempted to provide those states of southeastern Europe, whose transitions to democracy and market economies have been thwarted by war, authoritarianism, or both, with some kind of intermediate range perspective for "returning to Europe" in the future. The simple matter of fact is that these states are far behind. The enlargement of the EU is a gigantic project without them. And they are last in line. They will have to wait.

Although the social, economic, and political structures of the Soviet Union, as well as its dynamics of protest, were considerably different from those in East Central Europe, the collapse of the USSR may be interpreted as a belated 1989 revolution. The end of the Soviet Union's "internal empire" in 1991 was a logical consequence of the demise of its "external empire" in East Central Europe in 1989, and many of the same ideas were at work, such as human rights, democracy, and national self-determination. In the spring of 1990, declarations of independence by the Soviet Union's Baltic Republics—Lithuania, Estonia, and Latvia—marked the beginning of a process that ended eighteen months later with the disintegration of the Soviet Union.

Looking back it is truly amazing to see how unprepared everyone was for the collapse of Communism in Eastern Europe and the Soviet Union itself. During the Cold War, the West, and in particular the United States, spent billions of dollars on the analysis of Communism and the study of Eastern Europe and the Soviet Union. The CIA, military intelligence, leading American universities, private foundations, and think-tanks brought decades of expertise to bear on the phenomenon of Communism. As it turned out, expert opinion on Communism in Eastern Europe turned out to be dogmatic and short-sighted. It was based on two false premises: first, that the Soviet Union would never voluntarily or unilaterally renounce its empire in Eastern Europe and second, that the Communist system was incapable of dramatic change. There were many different opinions about the prospects of the Communist system and its capacity for reform, but all of the experts seemed to agree that it was firmly intact and durable. Change would be gradual at best, if at all.[12]

Well over half of the Sovietologists in the West thought that some kind of liberalization or systematic reform was possible in the Soviet Union, and roughly one-quarter of the others assumed that the system could keep bumbling along because that is what it had done in the past. One minority group in the profession envisioned the deterioration of the system leading to collapse at some point in an undefined future, and another small group, usually dismissed for being either émigrés or alarmists, feared a worst-case scenario: the possibility of a reactionary backlash combined with a reversion to old Soviet policies.[13] The intellectuals and dissidents who were members of the first generation of leaders in the fledgling democracies of the former East Bloc shared fundamentally the same assumptions, in inverted proportions and the reverse order. Based on their experiences with Communism and the Soviet Union, they tended to view the pessimistic scenarios as more probable than the optimistic ones. No one expected the Soviet Union to collapse rapidly and completely as a result of the failure of Gorbachev's reforms and the failure of a reactionary counterreform putsch. But this is exactly what happened.

The implosion of the Soviet Union changed the relationships of the new democracies of the former Eastern bloc with the East as well as with the West. As long as a Soviet threat existed, many Poles, Czechs and Slovaks, and Hungarians assumed that the West would move quickly to fill the vacuum created by the deterioration of the Soviet empire and incorporate or "reincorporate" East Central Europe into the West where it belonged. The Visegrád states considered themselves not only historical but also logical economic, political, and strategic partners of the European Community and NATO, two organizations which were caught completely off-guard by the events of 1989.

After the collapse of the Soviet Union in 1991, the sense of urgency in the region dissipated to a certain extent, and the reform governments in East Central Europe suddenly found themselves in the strange position of competing for Western political attention as well as Western economic aid with the states and reform governments that emerged from the ruins of the Soviet Union, too. Conflicts among the newly independent states are one of the biggest problems in the former Communist East, and Russia, despite its lost of prestige and power, is still a superpower.

After the revolutions of 1989, many East Central Europeans assumed that the West would move quickly to bring the region into its economic and military fold, and they were disappointed by the lack of western initiative to do so soon. "The former East Bloc countries, convinced that integration is essential to their interests, have proposed a series of steps or trials in the direction of membership [in the European Union and NATO]," as the former Hungarian dissident and essayist, György Konrád, noted in the 1993, "but all they receive for their pains is a mysterious *mañana* ["tomorrow"]. . . . 'Now! Now! Now!' says the East. 'No! No! No!' says the West."[14] In a speech to the Sejm, the Polish Parliament, on May 8, 1995, the 50th anniversary of the end of World War II in Europe, President Lech Wałęsa critically reflected upon what this commemoration meant for most Poles, and he rhetorically asked if Poland, which had been abandoned by the democratic West to the Soviet East after the defeat of Nazi Germany, should celebrate this event as a victory. He also took this occasion to reflect upon Poland's precarious position between East and West, and he expressed his concern about the isolationistic policies of the West and the potential of a resurgent Russian empire in the East. This is Central European: reflecting upon lessons from the past as a means of orientation for the future.

Given the prevailing assumptions about the permanence of Communism, the idea of accepting members of the Warsaw Pact or COMECON into NATO or the EC seemed absurd at the beginning of 1989, but by the end of that miraculous year, the improbability of the past had become a necessity of the future. NATO and the European Community were institutions whose membership and policies had been determined by the division of Europe and the Cold War, and the denouement of East–West conflict forced them to redefine their objectives and to articulate the conditions under which they seriously would consider accepting new members. At a meeting in Copenhagen in June 1993, the members of the European Community approved the idea of enlarging the European Union in principle and established the political, economic, and institutional criteria for accepting countries from Central and Eastern Europe as members.[15] In January 1994,

NATO announced its "Partnership for Peace" program which provided all of the states of former eastern Europe with an opportunity to loosely affiliate themselves with the alliance, and in September 1995 it adopted a study on enlargement that fixed criteria for inviting countries to join the alliance.[16]

The enlargement of NATO has proceeded faster than the enlargement of the European Union. In the course of 1997, NATO held meetings with eleven Eastern European countries that were interested in joining the alliance. It soon pared the eligible candidates down to five—Poland, the Czech Republic, Hungary, Slovenia, and Romania—and then to three by taking Slovenia and Romania out of the running. On March 12, 1999, Poland, the Czech Republic, and Hungary formally became members of the Alliance, and eleven days later NATO began the largest operation in its history: the punitive bombing of the Federal Republic of Yugoslavia. The terminology and objectives of NATO have changed considerably since 1989, and it has an "open door policy" that provides for the accession of further members to the alliance in the future. One of the big open questions is how large the alliance can become or, conversely, how many members can be brought into the alliance without antagonizing Russia or threatening its own sense of security? Russia is no longer an explicit enemy of NATO, although many East Central Europeans still view it as the implicit threat in the region.

It would be difficult to overestimate the historical symbolism and the political importance of NATO membership for the East Central European newcomers to the alliance. Many Poles, Czechs, and Hungarians view their histories in the context of having been abandoned by the West to the East in the past. NATO membership not only officially documented that Poland, the Czech Republic, and Hungary have "returned" to and belong to the West. NATO provisions for collective security and mutual defense mean that Poles, Czechs, and Hungarians, who know from their own experience what it is like to have Russian tanks rolling in their streets, never again will have to worry about being reincorporated into the East.

At the fiftieth anniversary of the establishment of the alliance in Washington D.C. on April 23 1999, Hungarian Prime Minister Viktor Orbán noted that joining NATO ended "this century of suffering and uncertainty" for Hungarians. Polish President Aleksander Kwásniewski observed that "NATO membership is a symbol of the definite end of the almost 300-year-long period of misfortunes in the Polish history, . . ." and Czech President Václav Havel placed NATO membership in an even broader historical context by ascertaining: "To my country, this is one of the most important moments in its long and dramatic history."[17]

Plans for the enlargement of the European Union have moved at a slower pace, partially because the EU is a more complicated and comprehensive organization than NATO: The initial plans of the European Community to intensify Western European integration was based on the East–West division of Europe, not an *extensive* development or foreseeable enlargement of the Community. After the mid-1980s, the twelve EC member states began discussing strategies for the next phase of European integration. The creation of an economic and monetary union was the central objective, and the pursuit of this goal stimulated debates about the intermediate-range "political dimension" of European integration and the long-range dimensions of collective defense, security, and foreign policy. However, after the denouement of the East–West conflict, two new groups of states showed great interest in participating in western European integration: the prosperous, non-aligned, and neutral democracies that had been situated "between" the EC and the old East—Austria, Finland, Sweden, and Switzerland—as well as Norway, a NATO but not an EC member, on the one hand, and the "new democracies" of the former Eastern bloc on the other.

Negotiations among the twelve EC members on increasing the breadth and depth of integration, which began before 1989, led to the conclusion of the Treaty on the European Union in Maastricht in 1992, and the "Community" became the European Union at the end of 1994. Between 1989 and 1992, Austria, Finland, Sweden, Switzerland, and Norway expressed their interest in accession, and on January 1, 1995, Austria, Finland, and Sweden became full members of the European Union.[18] German unification in 1990 and the accession of these three states to the EU in 1995 increased the number of its member states from twelve to fifteen and moved its frontiers east, but there were no real aspirations to move them farther in that direction again soon.

After 1989, the European Community initiated a series of programs designed to help the countries of "Central and Eastern Europe." Official EU terminology is a bit confusing because the term "Central and Eastern Europe" not only excludes the former Soviet Union, it also officially refers to one region (despite the "and"), not two. The acronym CEEC—Central and Eastern European Countries—also has come into use. Between 1991 and 1996, the EU concluded association agreements with ten states in the region: Hungary and Poland in 1991, followed by Romania, Bulgaria, the Czech Republic, and Slovakia in 1993; Estonia, Latvia, and Lithuania in 1995; and Slovenia in 1996. Between 1994 and 1996 each of these associated countries formally submitted applications for accession to the EU, which brought the total number of accession candidates up to thirteen. (Cyprus, Malta, and Turkey all had applied for accession to the EU at earlier dates.)

The European Union initiated a "structured dialogue" with these associated countries and stated that "accession will take place as soon as an associated country is able to assume the obligations of membership by satisfying the economic and political conditions required." These conditions fall into three broad categories: the political criteria of "stability of institutions guaranteeing democracy, the rule of law, human rights, and respect for and protection of minorities;" the economic criteria of the "existence of a functioning market economy as well as the capacity to cope with competitive pressure and market forces within the Union;" and the criteria of sufficient institutional reform: "the ability to take on the obligations of membership, including adherence to the aims of political, economic and monetary union." Given the disparities between the political and economic structures of EU member states and those of the new democracies in "Central and

Eastern Europe" with their new market economies, it has been clear from the start that it will take quite some time for them to qualify for accession to the EU. Furthermore, "the Union's capacity to absorb new members, while maintaining the momentum of European integration, is also an important consideration."[19] In other words, Western European integration is obviously the EU's priority, and it will decide who gets into the EU and when on a case-by-case basis.

After the revolutions of 1989, many Eastern European states assumed that they would be in the European Union within a decade. But at the turn of the millenium they were still milling around together in the waiting room of pre-accession, and for optimists the operative horizons for the first wave of enlargement were around 2004 or 2005. After the states of "Central and Eastern Europe" applied for EU accession in the mid-1990s, the EU evaluated to what extent they fulfilled accession criteria and published a series of "opinions," which have been biannually updated since then by "reports" designed to track their progress.[20]

In 2000, all of the accession candidates received good grades on the political criteria of achieving and respecting democracy (although there were some initial reservations about Slovakia's treatment of minorities). Four to six countries seemed to be well along in terms of fulfilling the economic criteria of having established viable market economies: Poland, Hungary, the Czech Republic, and Slovenia, followed by Estonia and Slovakia. Institutional reform has been the largest obstacle for the accession candidates because it has required them to adopt the so-called Community *acquis*: roughly 80,000 pages of EU law and code. This is a gigantic job. Hungary, Poland, the Czech Republic, and Slovakia led in this field, followed by the three Baltic states and Slovenia, with Bulgaria and Romania as taillights.

The EU initially divided the ten contenders for accession from "Central and Eastern Europe" into two different groups: five "pre-accession" states that were invited to begin negotiations on accession in 1998 (the Czech Republic, Estonia, Hungary, Poland, and Slovenia) and the rest (Bulgaria, Latvia, Lithuania, Romania, and Slovakia), who were promised that they may qualify to be brought into the ranks of the "first wave" applicants. However, the EU soon recognized that this kind of grouping was demotivating for members of the second group, in particular, and adopted the "regatta principle" in the race for accession. Everyone is in the running, and may the best team win. As far as the standings go, one trio of states obviously is in the lead: the Czech Republic, Hungary, and Poland. They are being trailed closely by a second trio: Slovenia, Slovakia, and Estonia. Then there is a quartet of stragglers: Bulgaria, Romania, Latvia, and Lithuania.

The Iron Curtain went down in 1989 and, as far as many East Central Europeans are concerned, the "Golden Curtain" went up shortly thereafter. Customs and immigration officials in the Federal Republic of Germany, some of them former soldiers of the German Democratic Republic's "National People's Army" that policed the Iron Curtain, now help patrol the German–Polish border, and Austria has deployed army units along its fron-

CENTRAL EUROPE IN TRANSITION, 1989-1996

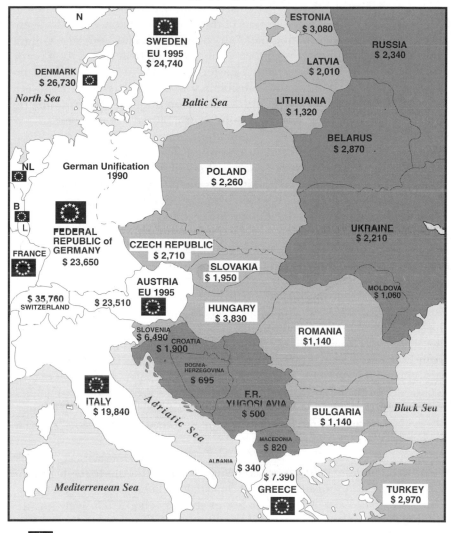

N

SWEDEN
EU 1995
$ 24,740

DENMARK
$ 26,730

North Sea

Baltic Sea

ESTONIA
$ 3,080

LATVIA
$ 2,010

RUSSIA
$ 2,340

LITHUANIA
$ 1,320

BELARUS
$ 2,870

NL

German Unification
1990

POLAND
$ 2,260

B

L

FEDERAL
REPUBLIC of
GERMANY
$ 23,650

FRANCE

CZECH REPUBLIC
$ 2,710

SLOVAKIA
$ 1,950

UKRAINE
$ 2,210

$ 35,760
SWITZERLAND

AUSTRIA
EU 1995

$ 23,510

MOLDOVA
$ 1,060

HUNGARY
$ 3,830

SLOVENIA
$ 6,490   CROATIA
$ 1,900

ROMANIA
$1,140

BOSNIA
HERZEGOVINA
$ 695

F.R.
YUGOSLAVIA
$ 500

ITALY
$ 19,840

Adriatic Sea

BULGARIA
$ 1,140

Black Sea

MACEDONIA
$ 820

ALBANIA

$ 340

$ 7,390
GREECE

Mediterrenean Sea

TURKEY
$ 2,970

Member states of the European Union, 1995

States associated with the European Union, 1991-1996, candidates for accession

Newly independent states in the former Yugoslavia and the former Soviet Union,
1991-1992 (not associated with the European Union)

$ 1,140   Per capita gross domestic product, 1993

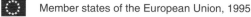

tiers to help its understaffed border personnel prevent illegal immigration. Since the implementation of the Schengen Agreement in 1998—which provides for free movement of persons between the respective Continental member states of the EU, regardless of their citizenship, once they have entered one of the participating member states—Germany and Austria have assumed responsibility for monitoring the "external frontier" of the EU (or "Schengenland") with "Central and Eastern Europe." When accession candidates join the EU, this is a responsibility that they will assume. It also is a task that will fit well into those Central European traditions that view the region in terms of its role of being a frontier or a bulwark of the West.

The initial, high, post-1989 expectations many people in the old East Bloc had in the West have been disappointed. The European Union and its member states have introduced a series of restrictive immigration and trade policies designed to keep competitive products—such as agricultural produce, textiles, and steel—and people from East Central Europe out of Western Europe while, at the same time, it is exporting more to the region than it imports from it. Many people in the region tend to feel that EU accession negotiations are not instruments for getting them into the European Union as soon as possible, as much as they are mechanisms for keeping them out as long as possible.

The pan-European ideology of the EU has required it to be inclusive since 1989; however, western European economic and political interests and the priorities of integration itself have made it an exclusive organization at the same time. Furthermore, the enlargement of the EU—theoretically from 15 to over 25 states in the future—only will be possible in conjunction with a major reform of EU institutions, subsidy structures, and modes of governance. The pace of enlargement will be determined by the "old" members of the EU in the West, many of which are adverse to the type of change that will be necessary to truly turn Europe into that "new Europe" Eastern Europeans envisioned in 1989.

The fact that the West has not come up with big solutions to the big problems of post-Communism in the East is partially related to the fact that most theories of East–West relations or Soviet studies relied exclusively on the premise that the Communist system would not change dramatically. It might stagnate, deteriorate, or be reformed, but it would not collapse. Although democrats and capitalists in the West ultimately were convinced of the superiority of the democratic and capitalist system, they never expected to see its superiority demonstrated in such a sudden and complete victory and therefore were completely unprepared to deal with its consequences. Whereas Communists wrote incessantly on the "transition from capitalism to socialism," anti-Communists wrote virtually nothing on the "transition from communism to democracy" or "the transition from socialism to capitalism." After 1989, there was a virtual absence of theories for addressing the problems of post-Communist societies. Therefore, "transformation" has been a trial-and-error process. As one Polish joke goes: "Socialism is the longest possible path from capitalism . . . to capitalism."

The guiding principles of the revolutions of 1989—national self-determination, democracy, and market economies—naturally became the objectives of gigantic transformation projects. But the perceptions of the indigenous problems each state in the region confronted varied because each country had its own particular national experience with "building socialism": a Communist heritage which ranged from the realm of individual attitudes to the sectoral structure of economies. Therefore, the project of "dismantling socialism" or "building democracy and market economies" has evolved along the lines of different national paths which in turn have been influenced by heated domestic political debates among politicians, economists, and social scientists. Experts disagree about priorities, which methods are most appropriate for achieving the objectives, and the costs and risks of individual and global transformation strategies.

Furthermore, all post-Communist countries have been confronted with the "dilemma of simultaneity"[21]—a myriad of unanticipated problems which seem to have to be addressed at the same time—and the "plurality of transitions"[22]—political, economic, and social transformations that rarely are harmonious. In Western Europe, the development of independent nation-states, capitalistic market economies, and democracy was basically a sequential process that spanned two centuries. Nation-states arose that gradually developed capitalist economies and democratic institutions. These three processes overlapped but occurred more or less in that order. In East Central Europe, however, expectations have been that these three processes should take place simultaneously in a relatively short period of time. "Sequencing" is another complicated and related issue. If everything cannot be done at once, what should be done first?

Reformers in East Central Europe could not rely on some of the best recent examples for the rapid modernization of underdeveloped economies because they were either politically undesirable or economically unfeasible. Military juntas in Greece, Spain, Portugal, and Chile did a relatively good job of modernizing the economies of these countries before they made their transitions to democracy in the 1980s. The "Asian tigers" or "newly industrialized countries," such as South Korea, Taiwan, and Singapore, are another good example of rapid economic modernization without much democracy, and their success is even more problematic because it was based on a high degree of state planning, a concept which has the status of a dirty word in East Central Europe. Many people seem to assume that capitalism and democracy go together, but there are enough counter-examples that show that "capitalism first, democracy later" is a normal pattern of development.

One of the first big post-1989 surprises in the region was a result of the achievement of national independence: the comeback of nationalism.[23] In Poland and Hungary, for example, Christian national and agrarian parties with their appeal to Roman Catholicism and traditional values emerged right of center on the political spectrum. Theoretically, they were the political compatriots of Western European Christian Democratic parties, but on occasion their rhetorical excesses and prejudices were reminiscent of interwar populism and authoritarianism. For example, they accused liberals and free-marketeers of "cosmopolitanism," an anti-Semitic slur peculiar to the political culture of the region, propagated the importance of "national values," and openly questioned the status and desirability of Roma and other minorities.

One of the major architects of Slovak independence, Vladimír Mečiar, demonstrated that Slovak nationalism was completely compatible with a conservative form of post-Communist authoritarianism, based on the maintenance of established political and economic structures. He played a major role in the Czech–Slovak confrontation which led to the "Velvet Divorce," the deterioration of the Czechoslovak Republic, in 1993. Czech nationalism played an essential role in this process, too. In Romania, the National Liberation Front propagated its own peculiar form of authoritarian post-Communist national collectivism. In former Yugoslavia, Tudjman's right-wing Croatian nationalism and Milošević's allegedly left-wing form of Serbian nationalism demonstrated how compatible nationalism was with different breeds of post-Communist authoritarianism.

The worse things are, the better the chances for nationalism seem to be. Insecurity, anxiety, and hardship have been part and parcel of the processes of transformation throughout Eastern Europe, and the psychology of nationalism in the region historically has been characterized by a sense of self-pity—related to the fact that these smaller nations have been disadvantaged, marginalized, neglected, or victimized in the past—combined with intense feelings of national pride. The xenophobic tendency to blame foreigners for the nation's predicaments or to seek scapegoats at home who are equally responsible for national misfortune is one of nationalism's illiberal reflexes: the exclusionary and aggressive distinction between "us" and "them." When it comes down to identifying enemies, ideologies are practically interchangeable in the nationalist paradigm. For example, before 1989, "the Communists" and "the Russians" were responsible for national misfortune; since 1989, "the capitalists" and "the West" are the new hegemonic powers. And Jews and Gypsies always have been good all-purpose domestic scapegoats for nationalists in the region, too.

Nationalism was an important source of anti-Communist sentiment before 1989; since then its illiberal manifestations have been a source of ongoing concern. Observers find the development of more open and liberal attitudes in East Central Europe encouraging, but at the same time feel that these young democracies might be prone to some form of authoritarian nationalism if the going gets tough. There has been much more concern about the wedding of nationalism and authoritarianism in Slovakia and on the Balkans. However, the gradual demise of national-authoritarian leaders between 1996 and 2000—Mečiar in Slovakia, Tudjman in Croatia, and Milošević in Yugoslavia—has been a source of some muted optimism, although the comeback of Iliescu in Romanian elections of 2000 also has been a source of concern.

The litmus test for the more successful democratic national states in the region will be how they deal with minorities. Hungarians in Slovakia, Romania, and the Federal Republic of Yugoslavia account for the largest "national" minority in the region, and it is worth noting in this context that mainstream Hungarian nationalism is devoid of its traditional irredentism. Roma are the fastest growing minority and the largest minority problem in the region, due to their high birth rates, low social status, historical lack of integration, and the nationalism of the host communities in which they live. Furthermore, the EU explicitly has articulated "the respect for and protection of minorities" as one of the democratic criteria it expects states seeking accession to fulfill.

Too much nationalism is bad for democracy, and excessive nationalism contributed to postponing the post-1989 transition to democracy for Slovaks and Romanians, Croats and Serbs. Other states from the region, whose transitions to democracy have been more fortuitous and more complete, also recognize that too much of the wrong kind of nationalism may contribute to preventing or postponing their accession to the EU in the future.

Democracies and markets are exceptionally complicated institutions, and although the absence of Communism obviously is a prerequisite for their emergence, the demise of Communism did not somehow naturally create democrats and capitalists, nor did it automatically decentralize state institutions or spontaneously create the framework conditions for market economies. Communist states were based on the party's control of the state and the state's control of the economy. The revolutions of 1989 in East Central Europe broke the Communist monopolies on political power, but they left monolithic state institutions and massive state involvement in the economies intact. "Less state and more market" has been a basic recipe for reform, but dismantling or "rolling back" the institutions of the post-totalitarian and paternalistic state, the privatization of state property, and the creation of market economies in the place of planned economies have been exceedingly difficult.

Some of the leaders of the movements which toppled Communism in the region initially entertained hopes that the experience of anti-Communist solidarity would somehow provide the basis for a new, specifically East Central European form of democratic political culture, and they speculated that they might even be able to engineer a new form of political and economic organization: a "third way" between the extremes of capitalism and socialism.

These fantasies faded quickly. The crumbling of Solidarity in Poland, for example, was an acrimonious affair, and the Czech Civic Forum and the Slovak Public Against Violence experienced similar fates in their respective halves of the Czechoslovak Republic in the course of its demise. The diversification of the political spectrum was one of the first signs of the "normalization" of post-revolutionary politics in East Central Europe. It led to a "remarginalization" of the dissidents and intellectuals—who had played important roles as moral authorities during the heyday of the revolutions— and a brief blossom of Western European liberal political theory and American-style free market economic theory. "Marketism" succeeded Marxism as an economic dogma, and great hopes were placed in the spontaneity and creative potential of market forces.

All this sounded fine in theory, but it was unrealistic in practice because it did not take the virtual absence of private property, private capital, capital markets, and a class of entrepreneurial capitalists as well as "capitalistic" laws governing investment, banking, property, taxes, and businesses into account. The absence of capitalistic institutions and laws also ironically slowed initial West–East flows of aids. According to a study by the New York-based Institute for East–West Studies in the mid-1990s, less than one-third of the aid committed to East Central Europe between 1990 and 1994 actually had been disbursed by 1995 because the conditions of granting (capitalistic) countries had not been fulfilled by the receiving (reform) countries.

The German Democratic Republic was not confronted with these problems because it ceased to exist as an independent state after German unification. The "old GDR" became the "five new *Länder*" of the "new" Federal Republic of Germany, and unification entailed the introduction of West German institutions and laws in East Germany. In this respect, East Germany as a region did not have to cope with many of the problems of reform and innovation that trouble the other "new democracies"—in particular, deep structural change, such as the creation of new public and private institutions and bodies of law that correspond to the demands of "market democracy"— because West Germany superimposed its legal system and structures on the region. The new Federal Republic of Germany also sent officials and experts from the "old FRG" into the "five new *Länder*" to assume leading positions in the gigantic project of *Aufbau-Ost*: "(re)building the East."

Furthermore, in comparison to the other former Communist states, there has been no shortage of investment in East Germany. Massive public funds have been transferred from the German west to the German east in various forms, ranging from infrastructure improvement programs to social security and retirement payments. In the five years following unification in 1990, the gross public expenditure of the Federal Republic of Germany in the regions of the former GDR totaled more than 800 billion deutsche marks (over 500 billion dollars), a figure that does not take private investment into account.

In this respect, the East Germans were in an enviable structural and financial position in comparison to the other peoples of the former East bloc. However, German unification has been an ambiguous affair. Due to the speed of economic and structural change, the high level of regional unemployment in the former GDR has been a great problem. A particularly violent and xenophobic form of German nationalism blossomed in East Germany after unification, and the agitation of young, alienated, right-wing skinhead extremists, who flirt with Nazi symbolism and racist ideology, is a source of ongoing concern. There also are considerable tensions between Germans in the west and the east, *Wessis* and *Ossis*, and resentment on both sides. West Germans have a variety of biases about Germans in the east and accuse them of being lazy, passive, sullen, and expensive for taxpayers. East

Germans find Germans from the west condescending, self-complacent, insensitive, and selfish.

Unlike other people in the "new democracies" after 1989, East Germans did not have an opportunity to take their collective future into their own hands. After unification, West Germany and West Germans assumed responsibility for the east to a great extent. For a fair number of East Germans, unification has been a humiliating experience, and there is a certain quiet pride among some East Germans, especially in the older generation, about being "former citizens of the GDR." Germans from the "old FRG" and the "old GDR" have problems with the fact that two fundamentally different German national cultures evolved between 1949 and 1989, and the psychology of German unification undoubtedly will continue to be a problem in the future.

The theoretical and practical aspects of the transition from Communism to capitalism are exceptionally complicated,[24] and they can best be illustrated by a joke that is popular among economists in East Central Europe. "The transition from capitalism to socialism is like taking a fish and making fish soup; the transition from socialism to capitalism is like taking fish soup and trying to make a fish." The great "achievements" of socialist-planned economies were abolition of private property for all practical purposes[25] (or its transformation into "collectively owned" state property) and the replacement of market economies with centrally planned state or command economies. One of the biggest problems the post-Communist states have confronted has been how to privatize state property, that is, how to transfer and diversify the ownership and control of assets from the state to organizations and individuals in the private sector. Privatization is related to two even messier problems: justice and economic viability. To what extent is restitution or compensation for previous expropriation feasible and fair, or, in other words, who gets what back? And to what extent does giving people private property make good structural or economic sense if it entails, for example, breaking up larger and more efficient economic units?

The so-called small privatization in the retail trade and service sector appears to have been more or less a success in East Central Europe, and the market is functioning for consumers, if the quality of food and service at restaurants or the density of electronic goods or video rental shops can be used as indicators. Prices are high by local standards, but there are no shortages of commodities, many of which are imported and contribute to negative trade balances. East Central European cities, once renowned for being monotone, drab, and dreary, make a vibrant impression on visitors today. Everything looks so much better than in the 1980s, and the proliferation of international fast-food franchises and sex shops may be used as an economic indicator. Looking back, hamburgers and pornography were among the harbingers of foreign investment and free enterprise.

There has been a variety of approaches to the privatization of large state-owned farms in different countries. In Romania, for example, collective farms have been broken up by giving back to former peasants, or to their heirs, the original small and disjointed plots of land. In Hungary, former small landholders had the opportunity to receive a corresponding amount of land back—not necessarily their original property—and in the Czech Republic authorities decided to leave the large, former collective farms intact. The Romanian solution undoubtedly was the most just, but it also made the least economic sense by creating a series of small and inefficient farms that cannot compete on the European agricultural market. The Czech solution was the least just, but it makes good economic sense.

Large scale privatization in the realms of industry and commerce—"a radical reallocation of available productive resources, a restructuring of the institutional setting in which production takes place, and the introduction of new methods of corporate governance, freed from the most noxious kinds of political interference"[26]—has been a slow and ambiguous process. After 1989, most East Central Europeans in industrial sectors continued to be employed by large state-owned companies or conglomerates. Despite the many innovative schemes for transferring titles, the introduction of holding companies, cross-ownership, "give-away" voucher schemes, and the like, this form of privatization has basically been on paper because it has not broken up the concentration of ownership or economic interest. Comrades from the old Communist networks of economic planning and management have reinvented themselves as capitalists and entrepreneurs.

It also has been difficult for the states to find buyers for their largest industries, many of which are cost-inefficient and not competitive. The shortage of domestic capital and the lack of large-scale foreign investment forced many states to hold their assets, whether they wanted to or not. Furthermore, foreign investors are interested primarily in stability, not fledgling democracy. The managers of large enterprises and the unions of the laborers employed at them also had vested interests in keeping things as they were, as well as a considerable amount of political clout. The fate of the Polish workers in the shipyards of Gdansk is particularly instructive example. In 1980, they spearheaded the Solidarity movement that ultimately toppled Communism in 1989. Then in the mid-1990s, the Polish government closed down the state-owned shipyard in the process of economic reform because it was a debt-ridden and noncompetitive operation that could not be salvaged by further subsidies or public investment. What is a state to do with unemployed heroes? ·

Privatization and economic reform has been much more difficult than initially expected and represents one of the most perplexing problems. The economies that have emerged in the region since 1989 are unprecedented hybrids: post-socialist but not yet capitalist. György Konrád described the structural peculiarities of the region after over forty years of communism and few years of freedom with a tautology: "It is neither East nor West; is both East and West."[27] Furthermore, the post-Communist understanding of capitalism seems to be based on the old Marxist interpretation of capitalism for many people. Property is theft. Capitalism is the exploitation of the weak by the strong. The rich get richer and the poor get poorer. Is this business as usual?

The post-Communist state also has had to extricate itself from the structural legacy of Communism in terms of government—or too much government. Extensive "cradle to grave" social services were part of the old Communist social contract. Socialist states provided their citizens with guaranteed employment, cheap housing, stable prices, universal medical care, and retirement benefits, and there has been a some retrospective glorification of how good the actually poor and inequitable social services were under the Communist regimes as well as some nostalgic yearning for the security of the "good old days."[28] The pressure to perform under the old system, as well as the rewards for performance were not great, and egalitarian mediocrity was one of the characteristics of the socialist societies of East Central Europe. Most people managed to get by, or, as an old East Bloc saying went: "They pretend to pay us, and we pretend to work." Social differentiation is a process that is difficult to accept for people who are accustomed to egalitarian ideology and are suddenly confronted with growing inequities.

It would be incorrect to confuse the popular rejection of socialism in East Central Europe in 1989 with a widespread affirmation or understanding of the game rules of participatory democracy or market capitalism. Participation in the electoral process throughout the region has been mediocre, and the "new democracies" have demanded considerable sacrifices from their citizens. Economic hardship—high to hyperinflation and falling real incomes—was the immediate consequence of the collapse of socialism for the majority of people. Increasing unemployment has been one of the natural and unavoidable consequences of "marketization," and cut-backs in extensive social welfare programs and the dismantling of the paternalistic socialist state have been part and parcel of stabilization and austerity programs.

Economists view the processes of transformation from a rather detached macro-economic level and recognize that "displacement" is a necessary part of structural change, and they have coined the term "transformational recession" to describe the unique state of affairs in post-Communist economies. But the recognition that things will have to get worse before they get better is seldom a source of solace for individuals confronted with microeconomic hardship, and economists, businesspeople, and politicians were surprised by the dimensions of the economic decline.

During the initial years of transformation, the gross domestic products of the countries in the region initially fell by around 20 percent and industrial production by 40 percent. Peacetime economies have not experienced such dramatic downturns in productivity since the Great Depression in the 1930s, and economic recoveries have been uneven and fragile in the region.[29] Furthermore, although economists assume that these economies in transition have bottomed out, they are unsure how dramatic comebacks in terms of real growth will be in the future. They have described their expectations for the macroeconomic development of the economies in transition in terms of a "J-curve" that drops, bottoms out, and then comes up, but they do not know how long or shallow the trough of this J might be.

According to the 1999 figures of the European Bank for Reconstruction and Development, Poland, Slovenia, and Slovakia were the only countries in all of Eastern Europe to have reachieved or surpassed their 1989 gross domestic products after ten years of democracy and capitalism, with the Czech Republic and Hungary just a few percentage points short of this goal. The numbers were poorer elsewhere in Eastern and Southeastern Europe, with shortfalls between 20 and 30 percent, and they were nothing short of catastrophic in most of the former Soviet Union. For example, in 1999, Russia's GDP was 44 percent lower than in 1989.[30]

The insight that democracy may actually contribute to hindering the transformation of the economies in the region is another post-1989 paradox. When a reform government introduces dramatic structural reform measures, the populace is bound to suffer, and when people suffer, they tend to vote for political parties that promise to alleviate the suffering. This in turn leads to a watering down of the reform process. In many countries in the region in the 1990s, the governments have moved like a pendulum from right-of-center to left-of-center and back again. Reform correspondingly started fast, slowed down, and then made a comeback.

When the former Communist party of Lithuania—rechristened as a social democratic party—won national elections in 1992, Central Europeans tended to dismiss this as an Eastern European phenomenon. However, socialist and social democratic parties (the reformed successor parties of the old Communist parties) emerged from the 1994 parliamentary elections in Poland and Hungary as the strongest single factions in their respective parliaments, partly because the Polish and Hungarian electorates were unhappy with having to bear the costs of transition.

When the reformed neo-Communist, socialist, and social democratic parties in the region won their first elections in the mid-1990s, some former anti-Communists saw a threat of "re-Communization," but with each passing year, the possibility of a reversion to the former system in some shape, manner, or form becomes more and more remote. Furthermore, many former Communists have mutated into Social Democrats with varying degrees of credibility and respectability. The Hungarian politician Gyula Horn is a good example of this kind of transformation: When the Hungarian Socialist Party won the elections in July 1994, the last Communist Foreign Minister of Hungary in 1989–90 became the first democratically elected socialist Prime Minister of Hungary.

There are many post-1989 ironies. On the one hand, former Communists have shared responsibility for introducing and managing capitalism. On the other, due to the hardships that have accompanied the processes of transformation, post-Communist socialist parties can draw on more genuine anticapitalistic sentiment in the region today than there was before 1989.

The winners and losers of the postrevolutionary period in East Central Europe can be defined in terms of generations, social groups, and regions. The older generations are among the big losers. Figuratively speaking, they spent their lives "building socialism." Now they are among the first victims of "building capitalism." Retired people living on the fixed incomes of modest state pensions were confronted with two to three figure inflation and cut-backs in social services in the 1990s, many of which have been dictated by important lending organizations, such as the International Monetary Fund or the World Bank. Many people who were over forty in 1989, and therefore in the second half of their work careers, have found the insecurity inherent in their newly gained freedoms intimidating or discouraging.

Younger generations obviously are among the big post-1989 winners, and they are enthusiastic about the prospects they have. However, some of the most talented and qualified younger people from the region have cho-sen to make their fortunes elsewhere, a "brain drain" that is a source of on-going concern. Why stay home and help "build capitalism" if you can go somewhere else and enjoy it immediately? Despite the obvious benefits and opportunities that have accompanied the demise of Communism, a UNICEF study pointed out some of the downsides for the younger genera-tion in post-Communist societies ten years after 1989: youth unemployment around 30% (a figure that was twice as high as overall adult unemployment rates); declining education rates; increasing use of legal and illegal drugs; and a dramatic increase in sexually transmitted diseases, including HIV.[31] The free world can be a dangerous place.

Those social groups least prepared to cope with the processes of politi-cal and economic transformation in East Central Europe have born a dis-proportionate amount of the related costs: the retired and the aging, women, unskilled labor, large families, rural populace, and minorities, such as the Roma. These groups are at risk in most societies, and they do not have the kind of political or economic influence necessary to improve their lot. Ironically, members of the former Communist elites in the region have been among the big winners because the material assets, such as nice homes, and social assets, such as university educations or important positions, which they or their children received in virtue of their party membership before 1989, have increased in value since 1989. In other words, the winners under the Communist system have become the big winners of democracy and mar-ketization insofar as they have succeeded in converting their old political privileges into new economic ones.[32]

There was some talk about "decommunization" immediately after 1989: the idea of legally prosecuting Communists for the crimes they committed under the auspices of the old regimes, a procedure analogous to denazifi-cation in Germany after World War II. Most countries also passed so-called "lustration" laws designed to illuminate the complicity of former Commu-nists in the machinations of the old regimes. However, "decommunization" failed to materialize, with the notable exception of East Germany. After Ger-man unification, West Germans came in and self-righteously dealt with the problem of East German Communists. The Czechoslovak, Hungarian, and Polish situations were substantially different because they had to deal with the problems of complicity themselves. Exceptionally few people can main-tain to not have collaborated with the system in some shape, manner, or form in the past, and many of the roundtable agreements that were part and parcel of the revolutions of 1989 were based on the pragmatic assumption

that Communists would not be subject to prosecution. Furthermore, qualified people, regardless of their political pedigree, are in great demand. It
would have been inexpedient to exclude former Communists from positions in public administration or industrial management, where their experience and skills were needed most, and some of them actually have turned
out to be plausible democrats and good entrepreneurial capitalists.[33]

Poland, the Czech Republic, and Hungary have been the big regional
winners of the former Eastern Bloc since 1989, and each of them can make
substantial claims to being the most successful "transformer" to date, depending upon which indicators are used. Poles refer to the best statistics in
terms of real economic growth; Czechs are proud of their privatization programs and low unemployment; and Hungarians have the highest per capita
rate of foreign investment and the most sophisticated market. This trio is
followed Slovenia, Slovakia, and Estonia.

Slovenia extricated itself from Yugoslavia in 1991 without becoming involved in the wars that squandered lives and resources in Croatia, Bosnia-
Herzegovina, and Serbia. It can in many respects compete with the other
leading transformers, although it does not receive nearly as much attention
as they do. The deterioration of the Czechoslovak Republic in 1993 benefited the more highly developed regions of Czech Bohemia and Moravia
than it did Slovakia with its lopsided industrial profile based on armament
production and traditionally underdeveloped agricultural regions. Vladimír
Mečiar, one of the dominant figures in post-1989 Slovak politics, initially
sidetracked the Slovak processes of transformation. However, Slovakia has
made a nice comeback since Mečiar was voted out of office in 1998. Estonia
also has been a big surprise. It is the only former republic of the Soviet
Union that is among the leading reform states. It has benefited tremen-
dously from Finnish advocacy and investment, and it has one of the most liberal economic regimes in the former East Bloc.

Within individual states, there also have been regional patterns of differentiation. Traditional national centers of political and economic power,
such as capital cities and major urban centers, have been among the big
winners, whereas "old" industrial regions with outdated capital bases and
technologies (steel, heavy industry, textiles) as well as traditionally underdeveloped rural and agrarian regions have been among the big losers. Furthermore, regions in the West, such as western Poland, Bohemia, and western Hungary, have benefited from their proximity to Germany and Austria.
Sharing a border with the current Austrian-German external frontier of the
EU also has other advantages. With the obvious exceptions of Ireland and
the UK, the EU currently consists of a number of contiguous member
states, and the EU most likely will want to keep it that way in the course of
enlargement.

Germany and Austria also have special historical relationships to the
states of East Central Europe, and they were the most generous providers of
initial aid and most important sources of early foreign investment for the region. For example, in 1992 Austria and Germany each committed 0.20% of
their GNPs to aid and expenditures for Central and Eastern Europe ($365

million and $3.8 billion, respectively), and this accounted for over half of the $8 billion the twenty-four leading industrial nations in the world (G-24 or OECD members) committed to the region. The United States, in comparison, committed 0.01% of its GNP or $744 million. On a psychological level, German commitments also are of belated reparation for the transgressions of the Third Reich. Austrians rely on a more pleasant and sentimental historical precedent: the Habsburgs. Central Europe, *Mitteleuropa*, is a term which German and Austrian politicians both use as an inclusive expression of solidarity with the reform states.

However, Germany and Austria have less altruistic and concrete economic interests in the region, too. Labor in the reform states is relatively well qualified, motivated, and cheap, and the ecological restrictions on production frequently are not nearly as rigorous as they are at home. Some East Central Europeans would like to see a more diversified pattern of foreign investment and regard the high profile of German investment and capital as some kind of threat to their national interests. For example, in early 1990 Rita Klímová, the newly appointed Czechoslovak ambassador to the United States, expressed concern about the possibility of a "Germanization of Central and Eastern Europe with the peaceful and laudable methods of market economics" and feared that "the German-speaking parts of Europe, including Austria, may succeed, where the Habsburgs, Bismarck, and Hitler failed."[34]

Based on their historical experience with the Germans, East Central European anxieties are understandable. But it is also necessary to ask if the contemporary Federal Republic of Germany corresponds to the Germany that unleashed two world wars in this century or if German interests and investment in the region provide sufficient grounds for assuming that Germany is going to take another run at the imperialistic version of *Mitteleuropa*. In light of its size and economic potential, Germany undoubtedly will play a large and an important role in the region in the future, just as Austria will play a smaller but still important one. Germany, however, instead of being a major part of Central Europe's problems as in the past, will be an integral part of the solutions to its problems in the future. German politicians are sensitive enough to understand their friends' and neighbors' apprehension about a renewed "Germanization" of Europe. However, at the same time, they plausibly and reassuringly assert that German participation in the processes of European integration, a "Europeanization" of Germany, is their ultimate goal.

In the early 1980s, Milan Kundera defined Central Europe as "that of the part of Europe situated geographically in the center, culturally in the West, and politically in the East." Since 1989, Central Europe could perhaps be best defined as that part of the former East that eventually will be first to make it into the political and economic haven of the West. From the mid-nineteenth century until after 1989, many people in Central Europe assumed that some kind of confederation of small states situated *between* Germany and Russia ultimately would be the solution to the region's problems, but the desire of East Central European states to become members of the

European Union, a western European confederation of states that will enlarge to the east, definitely has displaced the idea of a Central European confederation.

Poland, the Czech Republic, Hungary, Slovenia, Slovakia, and Estonia
are the prime candidates for European Union membership. If the next
phase in the enlargement of the European Union entails the membership
of this quintet or sextet of "new democracies"—and this seems most probable—the eastern frontier of the EU will, with the exceptions of Croatia,
Latvia, and Lithuania, substantially correspond to the millennium-old fault
line between western (Catholic) Europe and eastern (Orthodox) Europe.
East Central Europeans historically and culturally have identified themselves with "the West," and an enlargement of the European Union eventually will put them where they feel they always have belonged.

It is symbolically significant that the European Economic Community
was established in Rome in 1957. The Treaties of Rome laid the foundations
for European integration, and the idea of an economically and politically
unified Europe is in many respects catholic: It entails the application of certain "universal" principles. The old Roman Catholic idea of Western Europe
was based on "one, holy, Catholic, and apostolic Church"; the new catholic
idea of a unified Europe is based on economic and monetary unification—
One Market and One Currency—as the basis for political unification in the
future.

Since the end of the Cold War, Samuel Huntington has maintained
that civilizational paradigms and cultural fault lines, such as the Roman
Catholic–Orthodox one in Europe, will play a growing role in international relations and in future conflicts. If the membership of an enlarged European Union more or less corresponds to this Roman Catholic–Orthodox
fault line at some point in the future—that is, if the Catholic countries of
Central Europe are in the European Union and the Orthodox (and Islamic) ones in the Balkans and Eastern Europe are not—this may be interpreted as just a coincidence. However, the advocates of a narrow definition of
Europe and its civilization may well argue that this line actually represents
the historical and cultural frontier or the limits of Western Europe and then
use this coincidence of old and new frontiers to suggest excluding the Balkans and the rest of Eastern Europe from the processes of European integration. Central Europe was not an exclusionary ideology before 1989, and
it would be appalling, as Timothy Garton Ash has observed, to turn it into
one now.[35]

Looking back on the twentieth century, there are striking parallels between the years 1918 and 1989 in Central Europe. Both dates mark the
demise of great empires, a recession of Russian influence in the region as a
consequence of domestic revolution and turmoil, the advent of democracy
for oppressed peoples, and the beginning of national self-determination.
But post-World War I Europe failed to integrate Germany into the new European order, and the relations among the "new democracies" of the region

were full of strife. The lack of "European integration"—Germany as a free-floating malcontent in the middle of the continent—and "Central European integration"—effective cooperation among the smaller states in the region—were among the factors that ultimately led to World War II.

The post-1989 prospects for Central Europe are much better than they were in 1918. Russian imperial influence in the region has receded dramatically for a second time in this century, although the power and the unpredictability of this reclusive giant are still a source of great concern. Furthermore, Germany has been integrated thoroughly into the European Union, which, in turn, places considerable restrictions on Germany's ability to act as a completely independent player in European politics, and the European Union has explicitly stated its intention of incorporating the states of "Central and Eastern Europe" into its fold in the future. Nonetheless, being situated in the geopolitical center of Europe, Central Europeans continue to worry about the Russians and the Germans. They also continue to feel neglected by the West and threatened by the East. These are historical constants in the region.

Central Europe disappeared from the headlines and the television screens shortly after 1989, and in the 1990s disturbing news and images from former Yugoslavia dominated the coverage of that region that used to be called Eastern Europe. The scarcity of Central Europe in the news is an indication of how fortunate and successful Central European states have been. None of their problems have been commanding or violent enough to attract the attention of international news media for an extended period of time. The processes of transformation, as important as they may be, are not exciting or newsworthy; they are slow, complicated, arduous, and mundane. Democracy and a modest level of prosperity are things which people in the region slowly are beginning to take for granted. Pessimists will maintain that this confidence is premature.

The fact that Lech Wałęsa lost the Polish presidential election to the young former Communist Aleksander Kwásniewski in November 1995 was one of the first signs of normalization in the region. The sixty-two-year-old incumbent Wałęsa, one of the great heroes of the Solidarity movement, and Poland's Roman Catholic Church both attempted to portray the forty-one-year-old Kwásniewski, one of the leading figures in the social democratic party that had emerged from the Polish Communist party after 1989, as a Communist threat. Kwásniewski, a handsome, telegenic, articulate, and well-dressed younger man, as well as a sophisticated, smooth, and seasoned politician, conducted a western-style political campaign based more on images than substance, and he emphasized his commitment to reform. He also was more popular than Wałęsa with younger voters, who found Wałęsa to be a bit old-fashioned and authoritarian, and Kwásniewski won the election by a slim margin. Kwasniewski's opponents accused him of being a divisive and dangerous Communist, but he maintained that he was interested in stabilization, reconciliation, and peace. The fact that he won the election can be seen as an indication to what extent Poland is on its way to becoming a normal European democracy. Kwásniewski represented the future of Poland, and Wałęsa its past. Younger people in the region are not interested in the war stories of Communism or post-Communism. They want to lead normal, Western European lives.

Regardless of which historical agent or agents one chooses—God and the devil, fate, human error, or the blind forces of history—Central Europeans seem to have put through more than their fair share of trials, and even if this is not the case, many of them tend to believe that it is. This is one source of Central European exceptionalism, and Central Europe has been an exceptionally conflict-prone and conflict-ridden region. History does not seem to want to let Central Europeans go, or, more appropriately, Central Europeans do not show much of an inclination to want to let their histories go. Conflicts and tragedies are constituent parts of the national identities in the region, and in some cases Central Europeans are deeply attached to the idea of having suffered or that peculiar feeling of moral superiority that accompanies unjustified or inexcusable neglect. Despite the auspicious turn of events in the region since 1989, many Central Europeans prefer to view the future with caution or skepticism because history has rarely given them occasions for optimism in the past. One may only hope that the Central European obsession with the past will not become an obstacle in the future.

NOTES

The accessibility of recent works with excellent and extensive bibliographies explains the absence of one here. A nation-by-nation and a period-by-period bibliography of literature in English on Poland, Bohemia-Czechoslovakia, and Hungary, which also addresses relevant material on the Habsburg Empire, can be found in Piotr Wandycz, *The Price of Freedom: A History of East Central Europe from the Middle Ages to the Present* (London: Routledge, 1992), a book based on a lifetime of scholarship that any serious student of the region must consult. Peter F. Sugar and Donald W. Treadgold are the editors of a ten-volume series, *A History of East Central Europe*, a twenty-year project that is now approaching completion and covers the region, including the Balkans, from the fall of the Roman Empire to the present. The first volume in this series, Paul Robert Magocsi's *Historical Atlas of East Central Europe* (Seattle: University of Washington Press, 1993), is an essential resource for anyone interested in literally developing a picture of the region. The doyen of American historians of Germany, Gordan Craig, has written prolifically on German history, and his *The Germans* (New York: Meridian, 1991) is still an excellent introduction to the people and their history. It is complemented nicely by Mary Fulbrook's *A Concise History of Modern Germany* (Cambridge: Cambridge University Press, 1991), which synthesizes a tremendous material while taking into account recent scholarship and debates. Readers particularly interested in contemporary history should consult Joseph Rothschild, *Return to Diversity: A Political History of East Central Europe Since World War II*, 2nd ed. (New York: Oxford University Press, 1993).

The scope and the format of this book have dictated a sparse use of notes. Therefore, I wish to recognize a number of scholars here and, in the notes, refer readers to those works on which I have relied: Ivo Banac, Iván Berend, Daniel Chirot, Norman Davies, István Deák, Richard Evans, R.J.W. Evans, Timothy Garton Ash, Ernest Gellner, David Good, Friedrich Heer, E. J. Hobsbawm, Robert Kann, Jan Karski, György Ránki, Jaques Rupnik, Hugh Seton-Watson, Jenö Szücs, A.J.P. Taylor, Piotr Wandycz, and Z.A.B. Zeman.

Introduction

1. See Jenö Szücs's seminal article "The Three Historical Regions of Europe," *Acta Historica Academiae Scientarium Hungaricae* (Budapest) 29, nos. 2–4 (1983): 131–184.

2. Using the longitudinal coordinates of the Atlantic coast of the Iberian Peninsula in the west and the watershed of the Ural Mountains in the east as well as the latitudinal coordinates of Sicily in the south and the end of the Scandinavian landmass in the north, the indisputable spatial center of Europe is 25 degrees east of Greenwich and 53.5 degrees north of the equator: approximately 62 miles south of Vilnius and 93 miles west of Minsk, the capitals of Lithuania and Belarus. In other words, the center of Europe as a physical region is on the eastern frontier of Central Europe as a historical region.

3. See Daniel Chirot, ed., *The Origins of Backwardness in Eastern Europe: Economics & Politics from the Middle Ages to the Early Twentieth Century* (Berkeley: University of California Press, 1989).

4. See the photo in Karl-Peter Schwarz, "Präsidenten-Small-Talk im Schlachtensaal," *Die Presse* (Vienna), April 18, 1994, p. 3.

5. Piotr Wandycz discusses the terminological history and peculiarities of the concepts of Western, West Central, East Central, and Eastern Europe in the introduction to his *The Price of Freedom: A History of East Central Europe from the Middle Ages to the Present* (London: Routledge, 1992), pp. 1–11.

6. "Finlandization" was a pejorative term used by conservatives in the 1970s and 1980s to describe a scenario that anticipated a possible "alliance" between the Western European Left and the Soviet Union that could lead individual member states to abandon NATO for the sake of neutrality.

7. See Jacques Rupnik's "In Search of Central Europe," the introduction to his *The Other Europe* (London: Weidenfeld & Nicholson, 1989), pp. 3–24.

8. See Timothy Garton Ash, "Does Central Europe Exist?" *New York Review of Books*, October 9, 1986, pp. 45–52, reprinted in his *The Uses of Adversity: Essays on the Fate of Central Europe* (Cambridge: Granta Books, 1989), pp. 95–108.

9. "Yalta" has two meanings in this context. First, it broadly refers to the post–World War II division of Europe, a long process that was not completed until the Federal Republic of Germany joined NATO in 1955. Second, it insinuates that Churchill, Roosevelt, and Stalin agreed to neatly divide up Europe at the Yalta Conference in 1945.

10. For this "classic" definition of Central Europe in the early 1980s, see Milan Kundera, "The Tragedy of Central Europe," *New York Review of Books*, April 26, 1984, pp. 33–38.

11. See Václav Havel, "The Power of the Powerless," in *The Power of the Powerless: Citizens Against the State in Central Eastern Europe*, ed. John Keane (London: Hutchinson, 1985), pp. 22–96.

12. Croatia is an exception because it understands itself as a Central European state, but based on the economic indicators that Western experts use to define the region and gauge performance, it has an "Eastern European" economy. This, in turn, is one of the consequences of the wars in the former Yugoslavia.

Chapter 1

1. A Roman Catholic initiative to mend the East–West schism in the sixteenth century led to a further split within the Orthodox world and the establishment of Uniate churches that straddled the denominational border. They were Eastern in that they retained most features of the Eastern rite, but they were Western because they accepted the authority of the papacy. The Uniates, synonymous with schismatics for the Russian Orthodox, were strongly represented in Belarussian and Ukrainian territories in the Polish–Lithuanian Commonwealth and in Transylvania in the kingdom of Hungary.

2. There is an ongoing and unresolved scholarly debate about where this Moravian kingdom was. The orthodox opinion is that it was located in Moravia, Slovakia, and northern Hungary, whereas revisionists maintain that it was located farther south in contemporary Serbia.

3. Jenő Szűcs, "The Three Historical Regions of Europe," *Acta Historica Academiae Scientarium Hungaricae* (Budapest) 29, nos. 2–4 (1983): 131.

4. I would like to thank Harry E. Bergold Jr., former U.S. ambassador to Hungary and Nicaragua, for this formulation, although he himself suspects that it is not his own.

5. See Samuel P. Huntington, "The Clash of Civilizations?" *Foreign Affairs* 72 (Summer 1993):

22–49, and the series of articles in the next two issues criticizing both his position and his response to his critics.

Chapter 2

1. Cited in Jörg K. Hoenesch, *Premysl Otakar II. von Böhmen: Der Goldene König* (Graz: Verlag Styria, 1989), p. 158, an excellent study on which I have relied.
2. The famous German universities were founded after Prague (1348), Kraków (1364), and Vienna (1365): for example, Erfurt (1379) and Heidelberg (1385). Although each of these universities attracted an international faculty and student body in the medieval sense of the word, Czechs, Poles, and Austrians like to point out that their universities have longer traditions than do the famous German ones.
3. See Sarah Miekeljohn Terry, *Poland's Place in Europe: General Sikorski and the Origin of the Oder–Neisse Line* (Princeton, N.J.: Princeton University Press, 1983), pp. 66–118.
4. See Walter Schlesinger, ed., *Die Deutsche Ostbewegung des Mittelalters als Problem der europäischen Geschichte* (Sigmaringen: Jan Thorbecke Verlag, 1975).
5. In 1913, the German empire passed a law regarding citizenship based on an ethnic, national, and racial concept of *das deutsche Volk* that made *Abstammung*, "descent," the primary criterion for obtaining German citizenship. In this respect, Germans who had lived for centuries outside Germany never ceased to be Germans because of their descent. The Nazis distinguished between *Reichsdeutsche*, those Germans who lived in the Third Reich, and *Volksdeutsche*, ethnic Germans throughout Central Europe who did not but were "members of the German people." More than one-third of the more than 10 million Germans who were "relocated" or "repatriated" to Germany after World War II were *Volksdeutsche* who had lived for centuries outside Germany's prewar frontiers. The Federal Republic of Germany also employed the principle of *Abstammung* to pursue a policy of "repatriating" *Volksdeutsche* from East Central Europe. Coming from a German-speaking family in Romania, for example, has been a ticket to immigration for many "Transylvanian Saxons" whose families initially settled there five or six centuries ago.
6. There is, however, a Russian tradition of national exceptionalism that has an inverted or East–West theory of the "cultural gradient" that uses different religious and ethnic criteria—the superiority of Eastern Orthodox and Slavic cultures over "Latin" (Western Christian) and non-Slavic ones—and interprets Western European influences as fundamentally negative phenomena.
7. The fact that German crusaders, missionaries, colonists, and merchants drew the eastern Baltic coast into the sphere of the Christian West is one of the reasons that Estonians, Latvians, and Lithuanians consider themselves Central Europeans. Because of their Western Christian, Baltic, or "Hanseatic" orientation, they maintain that the most important formative cultural impulses historically came from the West, not the Russian East.
8. Norman Davies, *God's Playground: A History of Poland* (Oxford: Oxford University Press, 1981), vol. 1, pp. 120–125.

Chapter 3

1. Jenő Szűcs, "The Three Historical Regions of Europe," *Acta Historica Academiae Scientarium Hungaricae* (Budapest) 29, nos. 2–4 (1983): 154–155.
2. An East–West cultural watershed runs through the Ukraine. The eastern Ukraine was dominated by Orthodox Russia, whereas the western Ukraine was Roman Catholic and Uniate as well as part of the Polish–Lithuanian Commonwealth until the partitions of Poland at the end of the eighteenth century. Thereafter, parts of western Ukraine was incorporated into the Habsburg Empire. The inhabitants of L'viv in western Ukraine look back on traditions different from those of Kiev in the east, and this is a source of tension in Ukraine today.
3. For a more extensive treatment of the Polish–Lithuanian relationship, see Norman Davies, *God's Playground: A History of Poland* (Oxford: Oxford University Press, 1981), vol. 1, pp. 115–159.

4. From the Romanian national perspective, János Hunyadi (or Ioan de Hunedoara) and his son Matthias (Matei) were Romanians. Transylvania, historically a component of the kingdom of Hungary, was annexed by Romania after World War I.

5. Péter Hanák, ed., *One Thousand Years: A Concise History of Hungary* (Budapest: Corvina, 1988), p. 36.

6. I wish to thank Géza Kállay for pointing this out and translating this text.

7. For an overview of the consolidation of the Habsburgs' holdings, see Charles Ingrao, *The Habsburg Monarchy, 1618–1815* (Cambridge: Cambridge University Press, 1994), pp. 1–22.

Chapter 4

1. This formulation comes from the Nicene Creed named after the Council of Nicaea (325) which formulated a credo directed against the schismatic tendencies in the early Christian church.

2. See Friederich Heer, *Der Kampf um die österreichische Identität* (Graz: Böhlau, 1981), pp. 41–44.

3. For Max Weber's investigation, the consequences of Calvinism were much more profound than those of Lutheranism. See his *Protestant Ethic and the Spirit of Capitalism*, trans. Talcott Parsons (New York: Scribner, 1958), pp. 47–128.

4. See Andreas Dorpalen, *German History in Marxist Perspective: The East German Approach* (London: Tauris, 1985), pp. 99–123.

5. See Martin Bernal's treatment of the rise of the "Aryan model" in his *Black Athena: The Afroasiatic Roots of Classical Civilization* (New Brunswick, N.J.: Rutgers University Press, 1987), vol. 1, pp. 281–337.

6. For a collection of primary sources, see the section on theology in Léon Poliakov and Joseph Wulf, eds., *Das Dritte Reich und seine Denker* (Wiesbaden: Fourier, 1989), pp. 165–262.

7. For a detailed description of events leading up to the Battle of Nicopolis and its consequences, see Barbara Tuchman, *A Distant Mirror: The Calamitous 14th Century* (New York: Knopf, 1979), pp. 538–563.

8. See Kristian Gerner, *The Soviet Union and Central Europe in the Post-War Era: A Study in Precarious Security*, Research Report no. 10 (Stockholm: Swedish Institute of International Affairs, 1984), pp. 95–107.

9. See the introduction to Iván Berend and György Ránki, *Economic Development in East-Central Europe in the 19th and 20th Centuries* (New York: Columbia University Press, 1974), pp. 1–11; or Iván Berend, *The Crisis Zone of Europe: An Interpretation of East-Central European History in the First Half of the Twentieth Century*, trans. Adrienne Makkay-Chambers (Cambridge: Cambridge University Press, 1986), pp. 1–21.

10. See John Lampe, "Imperial Borderlands or Capitalist Periphery? Redefining Balkan Backwardness, 1520–1914," in *The Origins of Backwardness in Eastern Europe: Economics & Politics from the Middle Ages to the Early Twentieth Century*, ed. Daniel Chirot (Berkeley: University of California Press, 1989), pp. 177–210.

11. Cited in Hugo Hantsch, *Die Geschichte Österreichs* (Graz: Styria, 1959), vol. 1, p. 231.

Chapter 5

1. For a detailed study, see R.J.W. Evans, *The Making of the Habsburg Empire, 1550–1770: An Interpretation* (Oxford: Oxford University Press, 1979).

2. Iván Berend and György Ránki, *Economic Development in East-Central Europe in the 19th and 20th Centuries* (New York: Columbia University Press, 1974), p. 7.

3. E. J. Hobsbawm, *The Age of Revolutions: 1789–1848* (London: Weidenfeld & Nicholson, 1962), pp. 17–20.

4. There are, of course, a number of simplifications here. For an introduction to the complexity of the economic history of this region, see David Good, introduction to *The Economic Rise of the Habsburg Empire, 1750–1914* (Berkeley: University of California Press, 1984). Good identifies at least seven distinct economic regions in the Habsburg Empire.

5. During the 1980s, a time when the Poles were locked in struggle with the Jaruzelski regime

after Solidarity had been banned and the Czechs continued to live with the "normaliza-tion" that followed the end of the Prague Spring in 1968, a joke Poles loved to tell to illus-trate this point was about a Czech dog and a Polish dog that met each other on the border. The Czech dog—fat, well groomed, and well fed—asked the scruffy and obviously under-nourished Polish dog, "When was the last time your owner gave you something to eat?" The Polish dog replied: "What owner? And when was the last time you barked?"

6. Jacques Rupnik, *The Other Europe* (London: Weidenfeld & Nicholson, 1989), p. 16.
7. Milan Šimečka, cited in Ernest Gellner, "The Captive Hamlet of Europe," in his *Culture, Identity, and Politics* (Cambridge: Cambridge University Press, 1987), p. 126.
8. Jaroslav Hasek, *The Good Soldier Svejk and His Fortunes in the World War*, introduction and translation by Cecil Parrott (London: Penguin Books, 1980).
9. See Robert A. Kann and Zdenek V. David, *The Peoples of the Eastern Habsburg Lands, 1526–1918*, vol. 6 of *A History of East Central Europe*, ed. Peter Sugar and Donald Treadgold (Seattle: University of Washington Press, 1984), pp. 105–122.
10. Cited in Norman Davies, *God's Playground: A History of Poland* (Oxford: Oxford University Press, 1981), vol. 1, pp. 484–485.
11. Péter Hanák, ed., *One Thousand Years: A Concise History of Hungary* (Budapest: Corvina, 1988), p. 82.

Chapter 6

1. The three Polish kings were Michael Korbut Wísniowecki (1669–1673), whose reign was characterized by its brevity and his mediocrity; the famous Jan Sobieski (1673–1696), "the savior of the West"; and the hapless Stanislaw-August Poniatowski (1764–1795), who presided over the three partitions of Poland which ended with his abdication. The lineage of the other seven kings elected merely illustrates to what extent the Polish throne figured into the plans of foreign powers. Polish kings included a Frenchman from the Valois line; a Hungarian prince of Transylvania; three members of Sweden's Vasa dynasty (whose con-version from Lutheranism to Roman Catholicism and technical claims to the Swedish throne were additional sources of Polish–Swedish conflict in the seventeenth century); and two Germans from Saxony's dynastic ducal line, the Wettins.
2. For an analysis of the constitutional development of the Polish–Lithuanian Common-wealth, see Norman Davies, *God's Playground: A History of Poland* (Oxford: Oxford Univer-sity Press, 1981), vol. 1, pp. 321–372, as well as Andrezej Walicki, "The Three Traditions of Polish Patriotism," in *Polish Paradoxes*, ed. Stanislaw Gomulka and Antony Polonsky (Lon-don: Routledge, 1990), pp. 21–39.
3. Alexander and Margarete Mitscherlich, *Die Unfähigkeit zu Trauern: Grundlagen kollektiven Verhaltens* (Munich: Piper, 1977), p. 55. Also see pp. 142–165 on the "psychology of preju-dice."
4. See Richard Evans, "In Pursuit of the *Untertanengeist*: Crime, Law, and Social Order in Ger-man History," in his *Rethinking German History: Nineteenth Century Germany and the Origins of the Third Reich* (London: Unwin Hyman, 1987), pp. 156–191.
5. Max Weber, "Economics and Society," in *Weber: Selections in Translation*, ed. W. G. Runciman and trans. Eric Matthews (Cambridge: Cambridge University Press, 1978), p. 38.
6. Adolf Hitler, *Mein Kampf*, trans. Ralph Manheim (London: Hutchinson, 1969), p. 114.
7. See James H. Billington, *The Icon and the Axe: An Interpretive History of Russian Culture* (New York: Random House, 1970), pp. 163–268.
8. See Jenö Szücs, "The Three Historical Regions of Europe," *Acta Historica Academiae Scien-tarium Hungaricae* (Budapest) 29, nos. 2–4 (1983): 163–164.
9. R.J.W. Evans, *The Making of the Habsburg Monarchy: 1550–1700: An Interpretation* (Oxford: Oxford University Press, 1979), p. 449.
10. For an overview, see Charles Ingrao, *The Habsburg Monarchy, 1618–1815* (Cambridge: Cam-bridge University Press, 1994), pp. 178–219.
11. See Robert A. Kann, *Kanzel und Katheder: Studien zur österreichischen Geistesgeschichte vom Spät-barock zur Frühromantik* (Vienna: Herder, 1962), pp. 146–148.
12. Immanuel Kant, "What Is Enlightenment?" in *Kant: On History*, ed. Lewis White Beck and

trans. Lewis White Beck, Robert E. Anchor, and Emil L. Fackenheim (Indianapolis: Bobbs-Merrill, 1963), p. 3.

Chapter 7

1. The last Habsburg Holy Roman Emperor, Francis II, saw the demise of the empire coming and followed the example of Napoleon (who had proclaimed himself emperor of France in 1804), by inventing a new imperial title, emperor of Austria, for himself and his dynasty. Then he disbanded the Holy Roman Empire in 1806 to save himself the embarrassment of having Napoleon do it for him. Subsequently, Francis II, the last Holy Roman Emperor, became Francis I, the first emperor of Austria.

2. J.E.E.D. Acton, "Nationality," *Home and Foreign Review* 1 (July 1862), reprinted in Acton's *Essays on Freedom and Power*, with a new introduction by Gertrude Himmelfarb (New York: Meridian Books, 1984), pp. 146–147. Lord Acton believed that institutions for the establishment and preservation of liberty, such as those of the United Kingdom, not nations or nationalism, provided the only sound basis for a state. He explained that "those states are substantially the most perfect which, like the British and Austrian Empires, include various distinct nationalities without oppressing them" (p. 168). It is questionable whether the various nationalities in the British and Austrian empires shared his opinion.

3. Given the step-by-step liberalization of the Habsburgs' imperial policies in Galicia, the southern portion of occupied Poland gradually became a center of Polish culture in the nineteenth century, and some historians have compared this "reemergence" of Poland with the Hungarians' achievement of more autonomy, the Compromise of 1867, in the Habsburg Empire. However, the Poles achieved cultural autonomy in only part of Poland, whereas the Hungarians realized a considerable amount of political autonomy in all of Hungary.

4. Norman Davies, *God's Playground: A History of Poland* (Oxford: Oxford University Press, 1981), vol. 1, p. 525.

5. Herder and his contemporaries used a number of different but related terms such as "national spirit," "spirit or soul of the people," "the spirit or genius of the nation," and "national character": *Nationalgeist, Geist des Volkes, Seele des Volkes, Geist der Nation, Genius der Nation, Nationalcharakter.*

6. Isaiah Berlin, *Vico and Herder: Two Studies in the History of Ideas* (New York: Viking Press, 1976), p. 176.

7. Cited in ibid., p. 157.

8. This and the following quotations from Herder are from the sixteenth book of Herder's *Ideas for the History of Mankind* (1784–1791), a portion of which is translated and reprinted in *Nationalism: Its Meaning and History*, ed. Hans Kohn (New York: Van Nostrand Reinhold, 1965), pp. 104–108.

9. For the influence of Herder and liberalism on Czech historiography, see Richard G. Plaschka, "The Political Significance of František Palacký," in *Nationalismus, Staatsgewalt, Widerstand*, ed. Horst Haselsteiner et al. (Vienna: Verlag für Geschichte und Politik, 1985), pp. 163–179.

10. See Liah Greenfeld, *Nationalism: Five Roads to Modernity* (Cambridge, Mass.: Harvard University Press, 1992), as well as the works of E. J. Hobsbawm, Ernest Gellner, and Benedikt Anderson, cited in the following notes. In particular, Hobsbawm and Gellner address the distinctiveness of the Central European situation.

11. Ernest Gellner, *Nations and Nationalism* (Oxford: Blackwell, 1988), p. 1.

12. Croatia formed a union with the kingdom of Hungary in 1102, yet from the constitutional point of view, it was a separate political entity in the kingdom of Hungary, with special historical rights and privileges. The Croats then used their "historical rights" to bicker with the Hungarians about their status in the kingdom of Hungary, just as the Hungarians used their "historical rights" to argue with the Habsburgs about the status of the kingdom of Hungary in the Habsburg Empire.

13. In this context, "nationality" does not refer to citizenship but, rather, the legal status of national minorities in the empire and their relationship to its predominant political "historical nations": German-Austrians and Hungarians.

14. E. J. Hobsbawn, *Nations and Nationalism Since 1780: Programme, Myth, Reality* (Cambridge: Cambridge University Press, 1990), p. 12. Hobsbawm refers to Miroslav Hroch's three-phase periodization in his *Social Preconditions of National Revival in Europe* (Cambridge: Cambridge University Press, 1985).

15. Hobsbawm, *Nations and Nationalism Since 1780*, p. 10.

16. See the excellent study by Benedict Anderson, *Imagined Communities: Reflections on the Origin and Spread of Nationalism* (London: Verso, 1983).

17. France is frequently cited as the prime example of the nation-state. But often the fact is overlooked that the homogenization of France and the creation of a more uniform national culture were a long and complicated process, which Eugen Weber analyzed in his study *Peasants into Frenchmen: The Modernization of Rural France, 1870–1914* (Stanford, Calif.: Stanford University Press, 1974). To Weber, mandatory public education, military conscription, and railroads were the most important instruments and institutions of nation-building.

18. "L'erreur historique, sont un facteur essentiel de la formation d'une nation" (Ernest Renan, *Qu'est que c'est une nation?* [Paris, 1882], pp. 7–8, cited in Ernest Gellner, *Culture, Identity, and Politics* [Cambridge: Cambridge University Press, 1987], p. 6).

19. See Hobsbawm, *Nations and Nationalism Since 1780*, p. 37–38. Hobsbawm also mentions a third criterion which, with the exception of Germany, is hardly applicable to Central Europe: "a proven capacity for conquest."

20. The kingdom of Bohemia, with its admixture of Czech and German nobles, had been part of the Holy Roman Empire of the German Nation without, of course, being German. However, in the nineteenth century, Czech nationalists started to interpret the history of the kingdom of Bohemia in Czech national terms.

21. Although the Habsburgs spoke German, they never pursued "Germanization" policies. Rather, their main interest was in consolidating and increasing their dynastic power.

22. Although there was a distinguished Hungarian literary tradition, Magyar lacked modern administrative, technical, and scientific terms. For example, the Hungarian word for "state," *álladalom* (today, *állam*), was invented in this period. The development of modern Magyar relied heavily on borrowing from German or imitating German constructions such as compound words.

23. See Gábor Pajkossy, "Problems of the Language of State in a Multinational Country: Debates at the Hungarian Diets of the 1840s," in *Ethnicity and Society in Hungary*, ed. Ferenc Glatz (Budapest: Institute of History of the Hungarian Academy of Sciences, 1990), vol. 2, pp. 97–110.

24. Barbara Jelavich, *History of the Balkans: Eighteenth and Nineteenth Centuries* (Cambridge: Cambridge University Press, 1983), vol. 1, p. 306.

25. The standardization of Serbo-Croatian was asymmetrical in that it relied to a somewhat greater extent on Serbian usage. However, vernacular Croatian maintained its indigenous vocabulary despite standardization. Since the deterioration of Yugoslavia and the proclamation of Croatian independence in 1991, the gap between the two languages has increased because Croatian nationalists have promoted the use of "authentic" Croatian.

26. Cited in Plaschka, "Political Significance of František Palacký," p. 171.

27. On the demographic development of Central European Jews in the Habsburg Empire, see William O. McCagg Jr., *A History of Habsburg Jews, 1670–1918* (Bloomington: Indiana University Press, 1989), pp. 146–48, 190–191. The westward migration of Jews from the region was not merely continental. For many reasons, millions of Jews from Galicia and Russia emigrated at the end of the nineteenth century to the United States. They sought economic opportunity, wished to avoid being conscripted into the army, and were fleeing pogroms.

28. See Steve Beller, *Vienna and the Jews, 1967–1938: A Cultural History* (Cambridge: Cambridge University Press, 1989), pp. 122–188.

29. This is the conclusion that McCagg reaches in his comprehensive study, *History of Habsburg Jews*, pp. 224–226.

30. Milan Kundera, "The Tragedy of Central Europe," *New York Review of Books*, April 26, 1984, p. 35.

Chapter 8

1. Henry A. Kissinger, *A World Restored: The Politics of Conservatism in a Revolutionary Age* (New York: Grosset & Dunlap, 1964), pp. 1–3.
2. Timothy Garton Ash, "Eastern Europe: The Year of Truth," *New York Review of Books*, February 15, 1990, p. 17.
3. Norman Davies, *God's Playground: A History of Poland* (Oxford: Oxford University Press, 1981), vol. 2, p. 340.
4. Cited in Richard G. Plaschka, "The Political Significance of František Palacký," in *Nationalismus, Staatsgewalt, Widerstand,* ed. Horst Haselsteiner et al. (Vienna: Verlag für Geschichte und Politik, 1985), p. 173.
5. In November 1918, after the end of the World War I, German-speaking Austrians wanted an *Anschluss* with Germany, but the victorious powers forbade it. In March 1938, Nazi Germany executed the *Anschluss*: the occupation of Austria and its integration into the Third Reich. Thereafter, the German Reich was called the Greater German (*Grossdeutsches*) Reich. After 1989, that minority of East Germans who wanted to maintain the German Democratic Republic as an independent state pejoratively called the irreversible process of unification with the Federal Republic of Germany an *Anschluss*.
6. Cited in Plaschka, "Political Significance of František Palacký," p. 174.
7. A.J.P. Taylor, *The Habsburg Monarchy: 1908–1918* (London: Penguin Books, 1981), p. 74.
8. See István Deák, *The Lawful Revolution: Louis Kossuth and the Hungarians, 1848–1849* (New York: Columbia University Press, 1979).
9. An old imperial statue of Jelačić stood on the central square of Zagreb, the capital of Croatia, until the Yugoslav Communists removed it after World War II. In October 1990, Croat nationalists ceremoniously returned it to its original place. The reinstatement of this Croat national hero, who fought the Hungarians, was an anti-Serb gesture.
10. Cited in Richard Evans, "The Myth of Germany's Missing Revolution," in his *Rethinking German History: Nineteenth Century Germany and the Origins of the Third Reich* (London: Unwin Hyman, 1987), p. 96.
11. Friedrich Heer, *Der Kampf um die österreichische Identität* (Graz: Böhlau, 1981), p. 123.
12. W. N. Medlicott and Dorthy K. Coveny, eds., *Bismarck and Europe* (Edinburgh: Edward Arnold, 1971), p. 31.
13. The special note of irony in this defeat was that the inventor of this weapon system offered it to the Austrians before the Prussians, because they had a larger army. But Austrian imperial officials rejected it in part because they thought it would result in a wasteful use of ammunition.
14. Golo Mann, *The History of Germany Since 1789* (London: Chatto & Windus, 1968), p. 185.
15. See Evans, "From Hitler to Bismarck: The Third Reich and Kaiserreich in Recent Historiography," in his *Rethinking German History*, pp. 55–92.
16. It was important enough to be translated shortly thereafter into English. See Friedrich Naumann, *Central Europe*, trans. Christabel M. Meredith and with an introduction by W. J. Ashley (London: King, 1916). Meredith translated *Mitteleuropa* as "Mid-Europe."
17. See Woodruff D. Smith, *The Ideological Origins of Nazi Imperialism* (Oxford: Oxford University Press, 1986).
18. Cited in ibid., p. 53.
19. For example, they emphasized the medieval conflicts between the Stauffer dynasty and the papacy between the tenth and the thirteenth centuries, the implication being that the genuine German imperial tradition of resisting papal, "Roman," and foreign intervention was quintessentially "Protestant."

Chapter 9

1. *Pijemont* (Piedmont) was the programmatic title of a periodical published by the radical Greater Serbian terror organization, the "Black Hand," which organized the assassination of Archduke Francis Ferdinand.
2. Aurel Popovici, *Die Vereinigten Staaten von Groß-Österreich. Politische Studie zur Lösung der na-*

tionalen Fragen und staatstrechtlichen Krisen in Österreich-Ungarn (Leipzig: B. Elischer Nach-folger, 1906).

3. See ibid., pp. 308–309. These states were (1) "German-Austria," coextensive with contemporary Austria and including those parts of southern Bohemia and Moravia inhabited by German speakers until 1945 and German-speaking South Tyrol; (2) "German Bohemia" for the Germans inhabiting western and northern Bohemia; (3) "German Moravia-Silesia," the so-called Sudetenland that the Nazis annexed in 1938 from Czechoslovakia, along with "German Bohemia"; (4) Hungary, roughly in its post–World War I borders; (5) the Hungarian enclave in Transylvania; (6) Romanian Transylvania; (7) Bohemia approximately coextensive with ethnic Bohemia and Moravia, or the "Reich's Protectorate of Bohemia" that the Nazis established in 1939; (8) Slovakia, also roughly coextensive with the Nazi client "republic" of Slovakia from 1939 to 1945, or the current Republic of Slovakia; (9) Croatia with Dalmatia and Croatian Istria, roughly coextensive with contemporary Croatia; (10) Carniola, coextensive with contemporary Slovenia; (11) Vojvodina, the section of the kingdom of Hungary inhabited predominantly by Serbs; (12) west Galicia, the Austrian portion of partitioned Poland inhabited by Poles, which went to Poland in 1918; (13) east Galicia, the Austrian portion of partitioned Poland inhabited by Ukrainians, which went to Poland in 1918 and to the Soviet Union in 1939; (14) Italian-speaking Trento; and (15) Trieste with Italian Istria.

4. Hugo von Hofmannsthal, *Reden und Aufsätze II: 1914–1924* (Frankfurt: Fischer, 1979), pp. 454–458.

5. See Karl Stadler, *Austria* (London: Ernest Benn, 1971), pp. 71–82.

6. Neither Lenin nor Stalin thought much of these Austro-Marxist plans. At the end of 1912, Stalin visited Lenin, who was living in Kraków in exile, and then went on to Vienna at the beginning of 1913 to study the nationalities question. Shortly thereafter Stalin wrote his classic Marxist–Leninist tract, *Marxism and the National Question*, and during the Russian Revolution Lenin appointed Stalin the commissar for nationality affairs. According to Stalin, the Austro-Marxist idea of preserving or promoting the national attributes of peoples was "bourgcois." It had to be subordinated to organizing the masses for class struggle or replaced by the spirit of proletarian internationalism.

7. The national composition of the imperial army was 25 percent German-Austrian; 22.5 percent Magyar; 13 percent Czech; 7–9 percent Croat, Serb, Polish, Ukrainian, and Romanian; 3 percent Slovene and Slovak; and 1.3 percent Italian, with the remaining fraction distributed among other ethnic groups. In theory, if more than 20 percent of the soldiers in a given regiment spoke a foreign language, the officers and noncommissioned officers were expected to know it. In addition to the 142 monolingual regiments—and only 31 of them were German speaking—there were 162 bilingual and 24 trilingual regiments in the imperial army. See István Deák, *Beyond Nationalism: A Social and Political History of the Habsburg Officer Corps, 1848–1918* (Oxford: Oxford University Press, 1992), pp. 99, 178–180.

8. This hyphenated spelling may seem a bit strange, but this was how the movement spelled its name at the time. Slovak nationalists regard the subsequent abandonment of the hyphen, which orthographically transformed Czecho-Slovak to Czechoslovak, as part of a Czech device to belittle or ignore the existence of an independent Slovak nation.

9. See Deák, *Beyond Nationalism*, pp. 197–204.

10. This concept was popularized during World War I by exile politicians from Austria-Hungary. Austrian and Hungarian historians argue among themselves about which half of the Dual Monarchy had a worse record in dealing with its minorities and hence is responsible for the bad reputation of both halves. The first manifestations of a nostalgic rehabilitation of the Austria-Hungary, a phenomenon that Claudio Magris labeled the "Habsburg myth" in his *Der habsburgische Mythos in der österreichischen Literatur*, trans. Madeleine von Pésztory (Salzbürg: Müller, 1996), can be found among Austrian authors in the interwar period, who transformed "the prison of nations" into one, big, happy, multinational family with a benevolent old father, Emperor Francis Joseph. Hungarian literature, however, contain practically no comparable literary nostalgia.

11. Robert E. Tucker, ed., *The Lenin Anthology* (New York: Norton, 1975), p. 180. For a survey

of Lenin's national self-determination in practice, see E. H. Carr, *The Bolshevik Revolution: 1917–1923* (London: Penguin Books, 1975), vol. 1, pp. 292–382.

12. In his famous "Peace Without Victory" address on January 17, 1917.

13. For a description of the vacillations of the Entente policy toward Poland, see Jan Karski, *The Great Powers and Poland: 1919–1945* (Lanham, Md.: University Press of America, 1985), pp. 3–30.

14. Both Western diplomats and Bolshevik leaders accused Piłsudski of being an "imperialist." See ibid., pp. 57–62; and Hugh Seton-Watson's discussion of Polish "small power imperialism" in *Eastern Europe Between the Wars: 1918–1941* (New York: Harper & Row, 1967), pp. 320–341.

15. The Czechs claimed the 880-square-mile duchy of Teschen, which was rich in coal and had an important rail connection, because it historically belonged to the lands of the Bohemian crown. Poland demanded Teschen using the ethnic argument that the majority of its some 400,000 inhabitants were Poles. The Entente's Supreme Council decided to cede 490 square miles of the duchy (and 140,000 Poles) to Czechoslovakia. Overlooking the fact that it was an Entente decision, Poles consequently regarded the Czechoslovak acquisition of Teschen as a perfidious exploitation of Poland's predicament.

16. This is the title of a book by the Austrian historian and journalist Helmut Andics: *Der Staat, den keiner wollte* (Munich: Goldmann, 1984). The Allies already had forbidden an *Anschluss* in the Treaty of Versailles with Germany. But the Austrian delegation at St. Germain had hoped that the Entente Powers could be convinced that it was an absolute national necessity.

17. This formulation was in a Czech note of May 20, 1919, cited in Elizabeth Wiskemann, *Czechs and Germans: A Study of the Struggle in the Historic Provinces of Bohemia and Moravia* (London: Macmillan, 1967), p. 92.

18. Masaryk formulated this idea as early as 1915. See Zybnek Zeman, *The Masaryks: The Making of Czechoslovakia* (London: Tauris, 1976), pp. 71–73. In a note the Czechs submitted at the peace conference, they maintained that the Germans and the Magyars had deliberately occupied the area in question during the thirteenth and fourteenth centuries in order to separate the western and southern Slavs. See Stadler, *Austria*, pp. 100–101.

19. The Czechoslovak Republic acquired part of the Carpathian Ukraine inhabited predominantly by Rusyns, a small group of Slavic people consisting primarily of peasants who lived in the highlands. This was arranged not because Czechs or Slovaks had any historical aspirations to this area, which had been part of the historical kingdom of Hungary, but because it appeared to be the only place for it to go. After World War II, the Soviet Union annexed this region and incorporated it into the Soviet Socialist Republic of the Ukraine, which had the strategic advantage of creating a common border with Hungary.

20. I would like to thank Géza Kállay for giving me and translating these examples.

21. Karl Renner, *Die Nation: Mythos und Wirklichkeit*, cited in Stadler, *Austria*, p. 77.

22. See Seton-Watson, *Eastern Europe Between the Wars*, pp. 150–156.

23. Seton-Watson uses this term in ibid., p. 345. He includes Hungary in his discussion of "small power imperialism" not because Hungary was successful in realizing its aims, as Poland or Serbia was, but because it tried to do so.

Chapter 10

1. Cited in George J. Kovtun, ed., *The Spirit of Thomas G. Masaryk, 1850–1937: An Anthology* (New York: St. Martin's Press, 1990), pp. 197–198.

2. For a state-by-state analysis, see Hugh Seton-Watson, *Eastern Europe Between the Wars, 1918–1941* (New York: Harper & Row, 1967), pp. 157–267.

3. Because of the historical magnitude of Hitler and Nazi Germany, one tends to forget that until the mid-1930s Mussolini was Europe's premier fascist. After Mussolini and Hitler began to cooperate in 1936, Mussolini abandoned Austria and Hungary to Nazi Germany's sphere of influence and devoted more attention to expanding Italy's "Adriatic empire" at the expense of Yugoslavia, Albania, and Greece.

4. See Sebastian Haffner, *Der Teufelspakt: Die deutsch–russischen Beziehungen vom Ersten zum Zweiten Weltkrieg* (Zurich: Manesse Verlag, 1989), pp. 114–133.

5. For an overview of the "turning point debate," see Carola Stern and Heinrich A. Winkler, *Wendepunkte deutscher Geschichte: 1848–1945* (Frankfurt: Fischer, 1979).

6. See Ian Kershaw, *The Nazi Dictatorship: Problems and Perspectives of Interpretation*, 3rd rev. ed. (London: Edward Arnold, 1993).

7. The first volume of Steven T. Katz, *The Holocaust in Historical Context* (Oxford: Oxford University Press, 1994), provides an excellent overview of the problems of interpretation. Also see Kershaw, *Nazi Dictatorship*, chap. 5; and Saul Friedländer, "Die Endlösung: Über das Unbehagen in der Geschichtsschreibung," in *Der historische Ort des Nationalsozialismus*, ed. Walter H. Pehle (Frankfurt: Fischer, 1990), pp. 81–93.

8. Adolf Hitler, *Mein Kampf*, trans. Ralph Mannheim (London: Hutchinson, 1969), pp. 604–607.

9. The Austrian federal chancellor, Kurt von Schuschnigg, closed his last speech with the appeal: "God protect Austria!" Mexico was the only country immediately to protest the Nazi occupation of Austria.

10. Cited in Zybnek Zeman, *The Masaryks: The Making of Czechoslovakia* (London: Tauris, 1976), p. 164. In regard to English remarks on the alleged obscurity of Bohemia, Czechs are more amused by a few references in Shakespeare's *A Winter's Tale*: "Bohemia. A desert country near the sea" (a stage direction from act 3, scene 3) and Leontes' question "Where is Bohemia? Speak!" (act 5, scene 2).

11. The fact that the Slovaks' only precedent in their history for an independent state is the clerical–authoritarian republic of Slovakia does not seem to disturb those Slovak nationalists who view Tiso not as an accomplice of National Socialism but, rather, as a national hero. When Václav Havel, the Czechoslovak president, visited Bratislava, the capital of Slovakia, on March 14, 1991, the anniversary of the proclamation of the Slovak Republic in 1939, a group of Slovak nationalists scandalously harassed him. It was difficult not only for Czechs in general but also for the majority of democratic Slovaks to accept that a certain breed of Slovak nationalists commemorated March 14, 1939, as a Slovak "national holiday," because the following day the Nazis occupied Bohemia and Moravia.

12. Jan Karski, *The Great Powers and Poland, 1919–1945* (Lanham, Md.: University Press of America, 1985), p. 301.

13. Cited in Ibid., p. 279.

14. Cited in Léon Poliakov and Joseph Wulf, eds., *Das Dritte Reich und seine Denker* (Wiesbaden: Jourier, 1989), pp. 492–94.

15. Retaliation did more to promote resistance than prevent it. The Czechs also have a comparable, but smaller, example of Nazi brutality in their history. After the Czech resistance movement assassinated Reinhard Heydrich, the deputy protector of Bohemia Moravia, in 1942, the Nazis shot the 200 male inhabitants of the Czech village of Lidice, deported some 180 women to concentration camps, placed 90 children in the custody of German families, and razed the village to the ground.

16. See Barbara Jelavich, *History of the Balkans: Twentieth Century* (Cambridge: Cambridge University Press, 1983), vol. 2, pp. 263–273. The total number of war losses in Yugoslavia and their distribution among various national groups are still controversial. See Ljubo Boban, "Jasenovac and the Manipulation of History," in *East European Politics and Societies* 4 (Fall 1990): 580–593.

17. Raul Hilberg makes this distinction in his *The Destruction of European Jews* (Chicago: Quadrangle Books, 1961), p. 473, in reference to the manner in which states treated their Jews. It is applicable in other spheres as well.

18. See Martin Gilbert, *Auschwitz and the Allies* (London: Michael Joseph, 1981), pp. 231 ff.

19. On the singularity of the Holocaust, see Katz, *Holocaust in Historical Context*. The catalog written by Michael Berenbaum for the United States Holocaust Memorial Museum also is a sound and well-illustrated introduction to this subject: *The World Must Know* (Boston: Little, Brown, 1993).

20. Hitler's speech to the Reichstag on October 6, 1939, cited in Martin Brozat, *Nationalsozialistische Polenpolitik, 1939–1945* (Frankfurt: Fischer, 1965), p. 23.

21. Cited in Norman Davies, *God's Playground: A History of Poland* (Oxford: Oxford University Press, 1981), vol. 2, p. 445.
22. Cited in Poliakov and Wulf, *Das Dritte Reich und seine Denker*, p. 504. ·
23. Hilberg describes these four phases in *Destruction of European Jews*, pp. 43–177.
24. In the occupied territories, Nazis distinguished among "Germans," people "of German descent," people with the capacity of being "Germanized" (*Eindeutschungsfähig*), and "foreign peoples." Genealogy—to what extent individual Poles had German ancestors and how remote they were—was important. The records the Nazi authorities produced were used by the authorities of the Federal Republic of Germany to help ascertain the legal status of immigrants from east Central Europe: whether or not they qualified for the status of "repatriated Germans" (*Umsiedler*) or had the less advantageous status of foreigners interested in immigration or asylum.
25. Waclaw Długoborski, "Die deutsche Besatzungspolitik gegenüber Polen," in *National-sozialistische Diktatur, 1933–1945: Eine Bilanz*, ed. Karl Dietrich Bracher, Manfred Funke, and Hans-Adolf Jacobsen (Düsseldorf: Droste Verlag, 1983), pp. 583–584.
26. On how economic considerations played a role in the articulation of Nazi "population policies" in the occupied territories of Poland and the Soviet Union, see Götz Aly and Susanne Heim, *Vordenker der Vernichtung: Auschwitz und die deutschen Pläne für eine neue europäische Ordnung* (Hamburg: Hoffmann und Campe, 1991), pp. 102–124.
27. Six million is the figure cited at the Nuremberg trials. Expert opinion on both the number of Jews in Europe and the number killed in the Holocaust varies, although there is general agreement that the number of Polish Jews was around 3 million. According to Raul Hilberg, 4.7 million of the 5.1 million Jews killed in the Holocaust were from East Central and Eastern Europe. Evyatar Friesel maintains that more than 5.4 million Jews were killed in East Central and Eastern Europe. See Paul Robert Magosci, *A Historical Atlas of East Central Europe* (Seattle: University of Washington Press, 1993), p. 164.
28. Davies, *God's Playground*, vol. 2, p. 463.

Chapter 11

1. The United States sustained around 750,000 casualties, including 177,100 dead, in the Atlantic theater of combat in World War II. The Soviet Union received materials valued at $9.5 billion from the United States under the auspices of the Lend-Lease program, 20 percent of the total aid the United States provided for its allies. These deliveries included not only tens of thousands of planes, jeeps, and trucks but also 15 million pairs of boots.
2. Austria was in an unusual position. In terms of international law, the Republic of Austria did not participate in World War II because it had been occupied and annexed by Nazi Germany. However, during the war, 1.2 million Austrians served in the German armed forces as Germans, and 600,000 Austrians were members of the Nazi Party. Until 1943, the U.S. and British governments recognized Austria as part of the Third Reich. But in November 1943, they issued a joint declaration with the Soviet Union in Moscow that called Austria the first victim of Hitler's aggression and formulated the reestablishment of a free and independent Austria as an Allied war objective. This was part of the Allied plans for reducing the territory of the Third Reich as well as a measure of psychological warfare. Consequently, Austria was "liberated" in 1945, not defeated. See Robert H. Keyerlingk, *Austria in World War II: An Anglo-American Dilemma* (Montreal: McGill-Queen's University Press, 1988).
3. Jan Karski, *The Great Powers and Poland, 1919–1945* (Lanham, Md.: University Press of America, 1985), p. 489.
4. Winston Churchill, *The Second World War* (Boston: Houghton Mifflin, 1951), vol. 5, pp. 198, 210.
5. See Z.A.B. Zeman, *Pursued by a Bear: The Making of Eastern Europe* (London: Chatto & Windus, 1989), pp. 196–210, for an overview of "the great migration of peoples" during and after World War II, and Paul Robert Magosci, *A Historical Atlas of East Central Europe* (Seattle: University of Washington Press, 1993), pp. 164–168.

6. The parallels to the situation in the former Yugoslavia are obvious. The instruments that nationalists of all parties use to achieve ethnic homogeneity in multi-ethnic regions are war, terror, murder, and population transfers.

7. Piotr Wandycz, *The Price of Freedom: A History of East Central Europe from the Middle Ages to the Present* (London: Routledge, 1992), p. 236.

8. Ibid., p. 237.

9. Between 1949 and 1961, approximately 2.5 million East Germans moved to the West. (There also was some ideologically inspired West–East emigration, but it was negligible in comparison.) The GDR successively clamped down on the "German–German" border after 1949 and made "fleeing the republic" a crime. Nonetheless, East Germans could still emigrate to the West via Berlin which, despite the establishment of the two German states, remained under quadripartite administration. The East German motives for erecting the Berlin Wall in 1961 were thus both ideological and demographic. That is, the GDR could not "build socialism" if it lost its labor force.

10. One of the most notable exceptions in East–West relations during the Cold War, the negotiation of the Austrian State Treaty of May 15, 1955, was based on a similar diplomatic scenario. The Allies' willingness to sign the State Treaty was based on the explicit understanding that Austria would "voluntarily" proclaim its neutrality after the East and the West had withdrawn their occupational forces. Austrian independence was a political gain for the West, which assumed that it had a "secret ally," and it was a strategic gain for the East. Austria and Switzerland were "neutral wedges" that separated the Federal Republic of Germany from Italy, the northern and southern tiers of NATO.

11. Timothy Garton Ash, *In Europe's Name: Germany and the Divided Europe* (London: Jonathan Cape, 1993), pp. 133–134.

12. Cited in H. W. Brands, *The Devil We Knew: Americans and the Cold War* (Oxford: Oxford University Press, 1993), p. 21.

13. See the excellent analysis by John Lewis Gaddis, "The Tragedy of Cold War History: Reflections on Revisionism," *Foreign Affairs* 73 (January–February 1994): 142–154, as well as his *The United States and the End of the Cold War: Implications, Reconsiderations, Provocations* (New York: Oxford University Press, 1992).

14. X [George F. Kennan], "The Sources of Soviet Conduct," reprinted in *Foreign Affairs* 65 (July 1987): 858, 861.

15. Cited in Brands, *Devil We Knew*, pp. 16–17.

16. Bruce Cummings, "The Wicked Witch of the West Is Dead. Long Live the Wicked Witch of the East," in *The End of the Cold War: Its Meanings and Implications*, ed. Michael J. Hogan (Cambridge: Cambridge University Press, 1992), p. 89.

17. See Gier Lundestad, *The American "Empire"* (New York: Oxford University Press, 1990), p. 32.

Chapter 12

1. H. W. Brands, *The Devil We Knew: Americans and the Cold War* (Oxford: Oxford University Press, 1993), p. 163.

2. Czeslaw Miłosz, *The Captive Mind* (London: Penguin Books, 1985), pp. 25, 52. Miłosz, a Polish poet and essayist, was born in 1911 in the Polish partition of czarist Russia to partly Polish and partly Lithuanian parents and was brought up in Vilnius, which became part of Poland after World War I. He was initially sympathetic to the idea of radical social change, but he later left a diplomatic position in 1951 in Paris to settle in the West. He subsequently taught Slavic languages and literature at the University of California at Berkeley, wrote extensively on Central Europe as a lost or forgotten world, and received the Nobel Prize for literature in 1980. His career illustrates to what extent "Central Europe" was a literary and, in both the institutional and the speculative sense of the word, an academic topic.

3. De-Stalinization facilitated the publication of *One Day in the Life of Ivan Denisovich*, the first major work by Alexander Solzhenitsyn, the Russian recipient of the Nobel Prize for literature in 1970, in which he described life in a *gulag*. Solzhenitsyn's monumental *Gulag Arch-*

ipelago was published in 1973 under different political circumstances, and his criticism of the Soviet system led to his expulsion from the Soviet Union. He lived in American exile until 1994.

4. Jacques Rupnik, *The Other Europe* (London: Weidenfeld & Nicholson, 1989), p. 216.

5. Peasants frequently did not have the skills required for industrial production, nor were they accustomed to industrial discipline. The initially poor performance of agricultural labor in an industrial setting is a problem that all modernizing economies face. One of the peculiarities of the Soviet method of modernization was that it turned peasants into "proletarians" without giving them incentives to work.

6. Timothy Garton Ash, *The Polish Revolution: Solidarity* (New York: Vintage Books, 1985), p. 21.

7. George Konrád, *Antipolitics: An Essay*, trans. Richard E. Allen (New York: Harcourt Brace Jovanovich, 1984), pp. 150, 147.

8. See, for example, Jochen Löscher and Ulrike Schilling, *Neutralität für Mitteleuropa: Das Ende der Blöcke* (Munich: Bertelsmann, 1984).

9. The MBFR (Mutual and Bilateral Force Reduction) negotiations started in Vienna in 1974 but produced negligible results in fifteen years. In the 1970s, the SALT I and II agreements (Strategic Arms Limitations Talks), the second of which was never ratified by the U.S. Congress, merely sought to establish future ceilings for nuclear armaments. The idea of START (Strategic Arms Reduction Talks) did not make progress until the mid-1980s.

10. Timothy Garton Ash, "Mitteleuropa?" *Daedalus* (Winter 1990), "Eastern Europe . . . Central Europe . . . Europe," issued as vol. 119, no. 1, of the *Proceedings of the American Academy of Arts and Sciences*, p. 2.

11. Timothy Garton Ash, "Does Central Europe Exist?" *New York Review of Books*, October 9, 1986, p. 51, reprinted in his *The Uses of Adversity: Essays on the Fate of Central Europe* (Cambridge: Granta, 1989), pp. 161–191.

12. See Václav Havel, *The Anatomy of a Reticence: Eastern European Dissidents and the Peace Movement in the West*, trans. E. Kohák (Stockholm: Charta '77 Foundation, 1985).

13. Milan Kundera, "The Tragedy of Central Europe," *New York Review of Books*, April 26, 1984, pp. 33, 36, 38.

14. Garton Ash, "Does Central Europe Exist?" p. 47.

15. The distinction between classical political liberalism before 1989 and contemporary economic liberalism thereafter is important. The political idea of "more (civil) society and less (Communist) state" before 1989 should not be confused with the post-1989 debates among economists and policymakers ("more market, less state") about the most desirable degree of public–private mix for East Central European economies in transition.

16. See Timothy Garton Ash, *In Europe's Name: Germany and the Divided Continent* (London: Jonathan Cape, 1993), p. 146.

17. See Peter Rutland, "Sovietology: Notes for a Post-Mortem" *National Interest*, no. 31 (Spring 1993): 109–123; and Theodore Draper, "Who Killed Soviet Communism?" *New York Review of Books*, June 11, 1992, pp. 7–14.

18. See Stephan Sestanovich, "Did the West Undo the East?" *National Interest*, no. 31 (Spring 1993): 26–34.

19. The Final Act of the Conference on Security and Cooperation in Europe consisted of three "baskets" for security, cooperation, and humanitarian issues. One of the main diplomatic trade-offs made in negotiating the Final Act was the West's recognition of the "inviolatibility of frontiers" in Eastern Europe in exchange for the Soviet Union's recognition of "human rights and fundamental freedoms." With its emphasis on cooperation, the CSCE process was an instrument for promoting détente and maintaining the status quo. But its human rights dimension also made it an instrument for challenging the status quo in the East bloc.

20. See Paul Kennedy, *The Rise and Fall of Great Powers: Economic Change and Military Conflict from 1500 to 2000* (New York: Random House, 1988), pp. 631–665.

21. The period of "War Communism," which was based on expropriation and coercion, ended with the introduction of the "New Economic Policy" in 1922, which was characterized by a "return" to certain capitalist modes of production and exchange as well as political

pragmatism and a certain amount of pluralism within the Communist Party. Until Stalin's rise to power, his promotion of the forced collectivization of agriculture, and the introduction of the First Five-Year Plan in 1928, the Soviet Union had a mixed economy based on nationalized industry but private agriculture and service sectors.

22. There is an unresolved debate among former Eastern Europeans and former Soviets about who profited most from the Soviet bloc. The East Central European position is that the Soviets extracted more from the bloc than they invested, but Russians maintain that they put much more into the bloc than they ever got out. The standard of living was much lower in the former Soviet Union than in Eastern Europe. Soviet visitors to Budapest or Warsaw considered them Western European cities.

Epilogue

1. See François Furet, "1789–1917, Rückfahrkarte" in *Transit. Europäische Revue*, Heft 1 (Fall 1990): 60–61, and Daniel Chirot, "What Happened in Eastern Europe in 1989," in *The Crisis of Leninism and the Decline of the Left: The Revolutions of 1989*, ed. Daniel Chirot (Seattle & London: University of Washington Press, 1990), pp. 3–32, who emphasizes that although "understanding economic problems is fundamental, it is nevertheless the changing moral and political climate of Eastern Europe that really destroyed communism there" (p. 9).

2. Timothy Garton Ash, *We the People: The Revolutions of '89 Witnessed in Warsaw, Budapest, Berlin & Prague* (London: Granta Books, 1990), p. 78.

3. See Ivo Banac, ed., *Eastern Europe in Revolution* (Ithaca, N.Y.: Cornell University Press, 1992), particularly the typological analysis of the revolutions of 1989 by László Bruszt and David Stark, "Remaking the Political Field in Hungary: From the Politics of Confrontation to the Politics of Competition," pp. 13–55. For a panoramic narrative of revolutions of 1989, see Gale Stokes, *The Walls Came Tumbling Down: The Collapse of Communism in Eastern Europe* (New York & Oxford: Oxford University Press, 1993). For an important comparative study of national differences in post-revolutionary development, see David Stark and László Bruszt, *Postsocialist Pathways: Transforming Politics and Property in East Central Europe* (Cambridge: Cambridge University Press, 1998)

4. Ivo Banac, "Post-Communism as Post-Yugoslavism: The Yugoslav Non-Revolutions of 1989–1990," in *Eastern Europe in Revolution*, ed. Ivo Banac, p. 168. Since 1991, Slovenia has succeeded to a great extent in establishing a democratic system; Croatia's transition to democracy was a precarious and incomplete enterprise until the death of President Franjo Tudjman in December 1999; and Slobodan Milošević's Serbian national and authoritarian regime could not be called post-Communist.

5. For an excellent history of the demise of the GDR, see Charles S. Maier, *Dissolution: The Crisis of Communism and the End of East Germany* (Princeton, N.J.: Princeton University Press, 1997).

6. Cited in Hubert Margl, "Globale Visionen, nationale Spannungen," *Die Presse* (Vienna), April 11, 1990, p. 4.

7. See Valerie Bunce, "The Visegrad Group: Regional Cooperation and European Integration in Post-Communist Europe," in Peter J. Katzenstein, ed., *Mitteleuropa: Between Europe and Germany* (Oxford & Providence: Berghahn Books, 1997), p. 258.

8. See John Lampe, *Yugoslavia as History: Twice There Was a Country* (Cambridge: Cambridge University Press, 1996) for a longer perspective or Misha Glenny, *The Fall of Yugoslavia*, rev. ed. (London: Penguin, 1996) for the best on-site narrative.

9. For NATO documentation consult <http://www.nato.int>

10. For updated statistics, consult the website of the United Nation's High Commission for Refugees: <http://www.unhcr.ch/world/euro/seo/main.htm>.

11. For the history of western bias on the Balkans, consult Maria Todorova, *Imagining the Balkans* (New York & Oxford: Oxford University Press, 1997). For an ingenious historical overview that shows to what extent the great powers regularly have contributed to making the Balkans a violent and allegedly unmanageable place, see Misha Glenny, *The Balkans, 1804–1999: Nationalism, War, and the Great Powers* (London: Granta, 1999).

12. For a conservative overview of the failures of Sovietology and the dynamics of the collapse

of Communism, see Lee Edwards, ed., *The Collapse of Communism* (Stanford: Hoover Institution Press, 1999).

13. See Peter Rutland, "Sovietology: Notes for a Post-Mortem," *The National Interest*, no. 31 (Spring 1993): pp. 120–121.

14. George Konrád, "Central Europe Redivivus," in *The Yale Review* 83, no. 2 (April 1995): 38; reprinted in George Konrád, *The Melancholy of Rebirth: Essays from Post-Communist Central Europe, 1989–1994*, translated by Michael Henry Heim, (New York: Harcourt Brace, 1995).

15. For relevant background materials on EU policy on enlargement, consult <http://europa.eu.int/comm/enlargement/>.

16. For the text of the "Study on NATO Enlargement" consult <http://www. nato.int/docu/basictxt/enl-9501.htm>.

17. For official transcripts of the speeches held at the NATO Commemoration of its fiftieth anniversary consult: <http://www.nato.int/docu/comm/1999/9904-wsh/9904-wsh. htm#3>.

18. The electorates of Switzerland and Norway decided in referenda not to participate in the process of European integration. The end of the Cold War turned European neutrality from a foreign policy asset into a deficit for Austria, Finland, and Sweden. There no longer was anyone to be "neutral against," and these states quickly recognized that adhering to a traditional interpretation of neutrality would prevent their accession to the EU.

19. Commission of the European Communities, "The Europe Agreements and Beyond: A Strategy to Prepare the Countries of Central and Eastern Europe for Accession," COM(94) 320 final, Brussels, July 7, 1994, p. 1.

20. For an overview of the shifting sands of EU policy, see Alan Mayhew, *Recreating Europe: The European Union's Policy Toward Central and Eastern Europe* (Cambridge: Cambridge University Press, 1998). Full texts of "Commission opinions concerning the applications for membership to the European Union presented by the candidate countries" and "Reports on progress towards accession by each of the candidate countries" are archived at the EU website cited in note 15.

21. See Claus Offe, "Capitalism by Democratic Design? Democratic Theory Facing the Triple Transition in East Central Europe," *Social Research* 58, no. 4 (Winter 1991): 872–873, for an early take on this problem, and Jon Elster, Claus Offe, and Ulrich K. Preuss, *Institutional Design in Post-Communist Societies: Rebuilding the Ship at Sea* (Cambridge: Cambridge University Press, 1998) for a more detailed later analysis.

22. For a comparative analysis of the problems related to the parallel introduction of democracy and capitalism, see David Stark and László Bruszt, *Postsocialist Pathways: Transforming Politics and Property in East Central Europe*.

23. See Vladimir Tismaneanu, *Fantasies of Salvation: Democracy, Nationalism, and Myth in Post-Communist Europe* (Princeton, N.J.: Princeton University Press, 1998) for an excellent overview of the psychology and the problems of post-1989 Eastern Europe.

24. In addition to the literature cited in notes 20–23 above, see the collection of articles in *Daedalus*, Spring 1992, "The Exit from Communism," issued as vol. 121, no. 2, of the *Proceedings of the American Academy of Arts and Sciences*; the series of symposium essays "The Great Transformation? Social Change in Eastern Europe," in *Contemporary Sociology* 21, no. 3 (May 1992) and János Mátyás Kovács, ed., *Transition to Capitalism? The Communist Legacy in Eastern Europe* (Brunswick, N.J.: Transaction, 1994). For an on-going on-line discussion of the problems of transition, consult "Transitions On-Line": <http:www.tol.cz/> or the "Central European Review": <http://www.ce-review.org/>

25. Polish and Yugoslav agriculture were exceptional cases of failed collectivization, albeit for different reasons

26. Roman Frydman and Andrzej Rapaczynski, "Is Privatization Working?" in *Open Society News*, Summer 1994, p. 9. For a lively overview of the relative success and failure of privatization in the region, see Kenneth Murphy, Andrzej Rapaczynski, and Roman Frydman, *Capitalism with a Comrade's Face* (Budapest: Central European University Press, 1998)

27. Konrad, "Central Europe Redivivus," p. 35.

28. For example, medical coverage was universal. However, for good and quick treatment "tipping" physicians generously was a common practice.

29. See Robert Holzmann, János Gács, and Georg Winkler, eds., *Output Decline in Eastern Eu-*

rope—Unavoidable, External Influence or Homemade? (Dortrecht: Kluwer Academic Publishers, 1995).

30. For figures on the growth in real GDP in central and eastern Europe, the Baltic states and the CIS since 1989, consult the European Bank for Recovery and Development's *Annual Report 1999* (London: Ventura Litho Limited), p. 13. This report also can be accessed on-line: <http://www.ebrd.com>.

31. See UNICEF's Regional Monitoring Report No. 7, 2000, *Young People in Changing Societies* (Florence: UNICEF Innocenti Research Centre), which is also available on-line: <http://www.unicef-icdc.org/>

32. See Zsuzsa Ferge, "Winners and Losers After the Collapse of State Socialism" in *Social Policy Review*, no. 5 (1993): 270–286.

33. See Steven Holmes, "The End of Decommunization" in *Eastern European Constitutional Review* 3, no. 3 (Summer 1994): 33–36, and "The Myth of Decommunization and the Quest for Political Justice" in Vladimir Tismaneanu, *Fantatsies of Salvation: Democracy, Nationalism, and Myth in Post-Communist Europe*, pp. 111–140.

34. Cited in [Associated Press, Deutsche Presse Agentur] "USA helfen Prag. 'Germanisierung' soll verhindert werden," in *Die Presse* (Vienna), February 22, 1990, p. 1.

35. For the Roman Catholic–Orthodox fault line, see the map on page 19 of this book, "The 'Roman West' and Central Europe," or the map "The Eastern Boundary of Western Civilization" on page 159 of Samuel P. Huntington's *The Clash of Civilizations: Remaking the World Order* (New York: Touchstone, 1997), where Huntington also ruminates about the limits of Europe. For Timothy Garton Ash's reflections on what he calls "Vulgar Huntingtonism" and the exclusive potential of the concept of Central Europe see "Where is Central Europe Now?" [February 1999] in his *History of the Present: Essays, Sketches and Despatches from Europe in the 1990s* (London: Penguin, 1999), pp. 383–397

INDEX

absolutism, 51, 87, 91, 103–5. *See also*
    enlightened absolutism; neoabso-
    lutism
Acton, Lord J.E.E.D., 127
Adler, Viktor, 148
Adriatic Sea, 14, 29, 35, 54, 58, 100,
    140, 173, 176, 197, 200, 266, 267,
    283
Afghanistan, 9, 249
Africa, 131, 167
agricultur(e)al. *See also* peasants; serf-
    dom
    "backwardness" of, in East Central
        Europe, 91, 198, 200
    collectivization of, 118, 188, 240, 273,
        299
    colonization and *Lebensraum*, 170
    failed collectivization of, in Poland,
        323n.13
    labor in Third Reich, 220
    periphery and industrial core of *Mit-
        teleuropa*, 165–66
    political parties and interests, 198,
        236, 237
    produce and European Union, 294
    regions of, in East Central
        Europe since 1989, 304

revolution in early Middle Ages, 5,
    38
Akindshi, 83
Albania, 82, 242, 286–87, 318n.3
Albrecht of Austria, 47, 54, 55, 57
Allied policy, evolution of. *See* Cold
    War; Potsdam Conference;
    Teheran Conference; Yalta Con-
    ference.
Allied powers, 7, 31, 155, 217–18, 224,
    227, 223–25, 227–28, 230–33,
    238–42. *See also* World War II.
    and occupation of Germany, 232,
        234, 238–40
    and occupation of Austria, 234
Alpine–Adriatic cooperation, 266
Alps, 14, 39, 58, 82, 87, 125, 140, 176
Alsace, 164, 171
ancient freedoms, 49, 50, 133
ancient rights, 28, 47, 56, 100
Anderson, Benedikt, 136
Andrew II, 28
Andrew III, 36
Andropov, Yuri, 253, 272
Angevin dynasty, 49, 76. *See also* Charles
    Robert of Anjou; Louis I of Anjou
Anna (Habsburg), 61